Social psychology at work

Social psychology has much to offer real world problems, especially in industrial and organizational settings. In *Social Psychology at Work* leading researchers in their respective fields discuss recent findings and their implications for the commercial world of work.

All the contributors have been greatly influenced by Michael Argyle, to whom this book is dedicated. They examine aspects of the workplace from the perspectives of personality and individual difference, social psychology and organizational psychology. Subjects covered include the effects of age on work, leadership, productivity, how we are socialized for work, stress and anxiety, and the effect of the physical environment on working behaviour.

Social Psychology at Work is a rich source book of up-to-date ideas, research findings and reviews at the interface of pure and applied psychology. It will be important and rewarding reading for all those such as students, consultants and managers and trainers who are interested in psychology at work.

Peter Collett is a Research Psychologist at the University of Oxford, and **Adrian Furnham** is Professor of Psychology at University College London.

Also available from Routledge

The Social Psychology of Everyday Life
Michael Argyle

Cooperation: the basis of sociability
Michael Argyle

The Psychology of Happiness
Michael Argyle

Bodily Communication
Michael Argyle

Psychology and Social Class
Michael Argyle

Social Skills and Health
Edited by Michael Argyle

Social psychology at work

Essays in honour of Michael Argyle

Edited by
Peter Collett and Adrian Furnham

London and New York

First published 1995
by Routledge
11 New Fetter Lane, London EC4P 4EE

Simultaneously published in the USA and Canada
by Routledge
29 West 35th Street, New York, NY 10001

© 1995 Selection and editorial matter, Peter Collett
and Adrian Furnham; individual chapters, the contributors.

Typeset in Times by Datix International Limited, Bungay, Suffolk

Printed and bound in Great Britain by
Biddles Ltd, Guildford and King's Lynn

British Library Cataloguing in Publication Data
A catalogue record for this book is available from the British Library

Library of Congress Cataloging in Publication Data
A catalog record for this book has been requested

ISBN 0–415–09754–1

Contents

Figures and tables

FIGURES

TABLES

Contributors

Robert A. Baron, Department of Managerial Policy and Organization, Rensselaer Polytechnic Institute, Troy, New York 12180-3590, USA

Leonard Berkowitz, Department of Psychology, University of Wisconsin, Madison, Madison 53706, USA

Donald Broadbent (Executors), Department of Psychology, South Parks Road, Oxford OX1 3UD

David D. Clarke, Department of Psychology, University of Nottingham, University Park, Nottingham NG7 2RD

Peter Collett, Department of Experimental Psychology, South Parks Road, Oxford OX1 3UD

Mark Cook, Department of Psychology, University College of Swansea, Singleton Park, Swansea SA2 8PP

Nicholas Emler, Department of Experimental Psychology, South Parks Road, Oxford OX1 3UD

Colin Fraser, Department of Social and Political Sciences, Free School Lane, Cambridge CB2 3RQ

Adrian Furnham, Department of Psychology, University College London, Gower Street, London WC1E 6BT

Edwin P. Hollander, Baruch College, Psychology, Box 512, The City University of New York, 17 Lexington Avenue, New York, NY 10010, USA

Henk T. van der Molen, Department of Social Sciences, Dutch Open University, Heerlen, Postbus 2960, 6401 DL Heerlen, The Netherlands

Katharine R. Parkes, Department of Psychology, South Parks Road, Oxford OX1 3UD

David Pendleton, Opus Consultancy, 11 Beaconsfield Road, Bristol

Peter Robinson, Department of Psychology, University of Bristol, Bristol BS8 1TN

Peter Trower, School of Psychology, University of Birmingham, Edgbaston, Birmingham B15 2TT

Peter Warr, Department of Psychology, University of Sheffield, Sheffield S10 2TN

Editorial introduction

Britain has produced many famous social psychologists, but none has made such an important contribution to so many areas of the discipline as Michael Argyle. When Michael retired at the end of 1992, it was decided that a Festschrift should be produced to mark the occasion. With most Festschrifts the editor turns out to be the person who wasn't quick enough to think of an excuse, and the contributors are either bullied or press-ganged into producing a chapter. This Festschrift was very different, because several of Michael's colleagues volunteered to act as editor, and even more asked if they could write a chapter for the volume. In choosing contributors we had to disappoint a lot of people, but there was no way we could include everyone without expanding the Festschrift to several volumes. The fact that so many people wanted to be involved is a sign of the enormous respect and affection in which Michael is held by those who have been fortunate to work with him or study under him.

The enormous breadth of Michael's interests made it rather difficult to choose a theme for the Festschrift. With most Festschrifts there is no choice at all, because the person who is being honoured has spent his or her entire academic career working on the same old issue, and flogging it to death in the process. In Michael's case we were faced with an encyclopaedic range of topics on which to base a collection of papers. These extended from his early research on non-verbal behaviour to his recent writings on leisure, and they include topics like social skills, long-term relationships, happiness, religion, co-operation and work. Most psychologists would be proud to have mastered one of these subjects. Michael, on the other hand, has made a lasting contribution to all of them, and in many cases he remains the recognized authority on the subject.

Michael was educated at Nottingham High School, and after a period of wartime service in the RAF, he went up to Emmanuel College, Cambridge, where he obtained a first class honours degree in experimental psychology. It was there that he met his future wife, Sonia. In 1952 he moved to Oxford where he took up the post of University Lecturer in Social Psychology. He became a fellow of Wolfson College in 1965, and University Reader in Social Psychology in 1969. He was the acting Head of the Department of

Experimental Psychology from 1978 to 1980, and the Viceregent of Wolfson College from 1989 to 1991. On his retirement he became Emeritus Reader at Oxford University, and he was elected as the first Emeritus Professor at Oxford Brookes University. Michael has also been visiting professor at many universities and his lecture tours have taken him all round the world.

For most people retirement provides a chance to put their feet up and take things easy. Someone obviously forgot to tell Michael this, because since he retired there has been no reduction in his activities or his output. Over the past two years Michael has continued to produce articles and conference papers at the same frenzied pace as before, and he has even managed to produce three books – one on everyday life, another on social class and a third on the psychology of leisure. As if this wasn't enough to keep him busy, he has also updated his book on *The Social Psychology of Religion* and completed the fifth edition of *The Psychology of Interpersonal Behaviour*.

Of all his books, *The Psychology of Interpersonal Behaviour* is the one for which Michael is best known. It was the first time that the research on face-to-face behaviour had been brought together properly and made accessible to psychologist and layperson alike. But what made the book so famous was the idea that social behaviour could be understood as a skill. The 'Social Skills Model', as it became known, focused attention on the relationship between the cognitive aspects of behaviour and their outward expression, as well as the way that one person's behaviour can influence the responses and actions of others.

The book also offered the rather radical suggestion that many of the chronic problems that people experience in their relationships can be explained as a failure of social skills, rather than as some form of psychopathology. Michael pointed out that these failures could be remedied by teaching people how to behave appropriately in different social situations, thereby providing them with a way of eliciting positive responses from others. Michael was able to put these ideas into practice when, together with Peter Trower and Bridget Bryant, he devised a 'Social Skills Training' package for patients referred by the Littlemore Hospital. The project provided convincing support for the Social Skills Model, showing that it was possible to train people to behave in a socially appropriate fashion, and to alleviate their social and psychological problems in the process. In fact, there were even some cases where medical problems were eliminated by the training, and where it proved to be as good as, if not better than, psychotherapy.

Since this research project was conducted, Social Skills Training has been applied to a wide range of professions and problems. The idea that deficiencies in social behaviour can be quickly corrected by teaching people how to behave differently now enjoys widespread acceptance within psychology. The notion that social behaviour is like a skill is also widely accepted outside the discipline, largely because 'social skills', the term that Michael coined, has become part of our everyday vocabulary about behaviour.

Michael's theoretical originality has been matched by a host of empirical studies. At the last count he had published twenty books, and well over 200 articles – a feat which very few psychologists have managed to achieve. His enormous output, coupled with an ability to write clearly and attractively, has ensured an enormous audience for Michael's ideas in academic as well as lay circles. The paper that Michael published with Janet Dean in 1965 on 'Eye-contact, distance and affiliation' is one of the most frequently cited papers in psychology, and it is rightly regarded as a 'citation classic'. But Michael's influence on his colleagues has been much more pervasive. In 1975, for example, he occupied third position in the citation index of British psychologists, just behind Hans Eysenck and Jerome Bruner, while in 1985 he was in fifth position. Michael has been in the 'top ten' ever since, and he seems likely to remain there for a long time to come.

There are several things that distinguish Michael's approach to social psychology. One is his enormous enthusiasm for the subject, coupled with the belief that it has a crucial role to play in helping to solve everyday social problems. The first book that he published, *The Scientific Study of Social Behaviour* (1957), advanced the idea that social behaviour could be studied with the methods of science, and that social psychology could help to improve people's lives. This pragmatic optimism was also evident in *Psychology and Social Problems* (1964). It has remained with him ever since, and it continues to be reflected in his attraction to important and 'uplifting' topics like religion, happiness and co-operation.

Michael's commitment to social psychology has shown itself in several ways. He has played an important role in the British Psychology Society, helping to establish the *British Journal of Social and Clinical Psychology*, which he later edited. He was also the Chair of the Social Psychology Section of the British Psychology Society from 1964 to 1967. His contribution to psychology, and social psychology in particular, has been acknowledged by the Universities of Adelaide and Brussels, which awarded him honorary doctorates. In 1990 he was awarded a 'Distinguished Career Contribution Award' by the International Society for the Study of Personal Relationships.

Less tangible, but much more important than all these public accolades, is the enduring effect that Michael has had on his students. Michael has now supervised over fifty doctoral dissertations. When he reached his first quarter-century his ex-students presented him with a collection of essays entitled *The Psychology of Playing the Goat*. This was a spoof Festschrift, and it took its title from Michael's admission, in one of his books, that his favourite pastimes were 'Scottish dancing, utopian speculation, and playing the goat'. While Michael has tended to keep his utopian speculations and his Scottish dancing to himself, he has never shied away from an opportunity to play the goat with his students. This has certainly contributed to the warm relationship that he has enjoyed with his students, but the main reason for their affection is that Michael has always shown enormous tolerance. His students always found him available, supportive and encouraging. He insisted on seeing all his graduate students weekly, which was another reason why so many of them managed to complete their dissertations.

In most departments graduate students end up working on the topic of their supervisor, not because they want to, but because it helps to further the supervisor's career. This never happened with Michael. He has always been open to new ideas, and he frequently took on students who had a different approach or who wanted to work on topics very different from his own. The result of this was that Michael ended up presiding over a group of psychologists with a wide range of interests and opinions. Normally this sort of divergence leads to fragmentation of the group. But under Michael's leadership it led to intellectual ferment and an outbreak of new ideas. During the 1980s the social psychology group in Oxford earned a reputation for its theoretical and methodological innovations. A great deal of the credit for this has to go to Michael and the intellectual climate that he created around him.

We come, at last, to the theme of this book and the reasons why it was chosen. The first reason is that work has always featured very prominently in Michael's academic interests. He produced *The Social Psychology of Work* in 1972, and a revised edition in 1989, and over the years he has published numerous papers on the subject. It is only fitting that a collection of papers in his honour should reflect one of his main interests, and work certainly fits the bill. The second reason for choosing work is that it is very important to Michael's own life. Although he has a number of hobbies, like gardening and Scottish dancing, work remains extremely important to him personally. It is what structures his life, satisfies his curiosity and defines his relationships with other people. The final reason for choosing work is that everything else revolves around it. As Michael himself points out, 'Work is one of the central activities of life, and social behaviour at work is one of the most important and interesting forms of social behaviour.' What better reason to choose it as the theme for the book?

ACKNOWLEDGEMENTS

We would like to thank Ann MacKendry, Mansur Lalljee and Roger Lamb for their help and suggestions.

REFERENCES

Argyle, M. (1957) *The Scientific Study of Social Behaviour*. London: Methuen.
Argyle, M. (1964) *Psychology and Social Problems*. London: Methuen.

Argyle, M. (1967) *The Psychology of Interpersonal Behaviour*. London: Penguin, 1972, 1978, 1983, 1994.

Argyle, M. (1972) *The Social Psychology of Work*. London: Allen Lane, 1989.

Argyle, M. (1987) *The Psychology of Happiness*. London: Methuen.

Argyle, M. (1991) *Cooperation: The Basis of Sociability*. London: Routledge.

Argyle, M. (1992) *The Social Psychology of Everyday Life*. London: Routledge.

Argyle, M. *The Social Psychology of Leisure*. Forthcoming.

Argyle, M. and Dean, J. (1965) Eye-contact, distance and affiliation. *Sociometry*, *28*, 289–304.

Argyle, M., Beit-Hallahmi, B. and Brown, L. (1975) *The Social Psychology of Religion*. London: Routledge & Kegan Paul; Routledge, 1994.

MacKendry, A. (ed.) (1987) *The Psychology of Playing the Goat*. Oxford: Capra Press.

1 Socialization for work

Nicholas Emler

INTRODUCTION

We are in the habit of regarding the sphere of work as belonging to adult life, contrasting this with a childhood which revolves around learning, education and play. The purpose of this chapter is not to make a point about the cultural and historical relativity of this contrast, though relative it is (cf. Aries, 1962), but rather to consider how childhood prepares individuals for adult work roles. For not only is the association of work with adulthood a contemporary, Western peculiarity, the structuring of adult roles and motivations within the economic life of society are similarly cultural phenomena. If human societies can be regarded as 'open systems' (cf. Katz and Kahn, 1978) the survival of which require the input of energy, or 'work', on the part of their members, there are none the less many different ways in which those inputs can be arranged. The collectivist economies of hunter-gatherers, the feudal systems of medieval Europe and pre-revolutionary China, and the slave economies of ancient Rome and the Ante-Bellum Confederacy are among some of the very different arrangements which have each proved viable.

The organization of work which characterizes contemporary Britain and many other societies has a number of distinctive features. Foremost among these is a sharp division between two systems of labour. On the one hand, work is provided for a financial reward, primarily in the context of employment relations. On the other hand, there is voluntary work, the most but not the only significant form of which is domestic labour. An interesting feature of this division is that these two systems are distinguished only by the motivations which sustain them, and not in terms of any intrinsic differences in the content or objectives of the work or the people involved.

Another distinctive feature of contemporary ways of organizing work is the degree to which work roles are specialized. In Britain at present more than 20,000 distinct kinds of job are recognized in employment statistics. In the domestic system, by contrast, the trend has, if anything, been the reverse so that there are now seldom more than two distinct roles and occasionally only a minimal specialization by person.

Related to the high levels of specialization prevailing in the employment system is the formalization of work roles and relationships, a feature which can be seen to be in part a consequence of the need to co-ordinate and integrate highly specialized activities. Historically also there has been a transition from a task to a time emphasis in work (Thompson, 1967), timetables and schedules assuming greater importance.

I have suggested that there is nothing in any way natural or inevitable about these particular ways of organizing labour. It is worth recalling, for instance, that when the basic principle of modern employment relations – selling one's labour for a wage – was first introduced on a large scale as part of the factory system of manufacturing, it was considered so unnatural that only criminals and paupers could be induced to accept it (Hearn, 1978). And this was a mere 200 years ago. Today, perhaps 85 per cent of those who earn an income from their labour do so in the context of employment relations. Similarly in an African household, 4- and 5-year-olds may well have extensive responsibilities for tasks which many British adults are inclined to regard as the natural province of parents – doing household shopping, looking after and even tutoring younger family members.

So how are the systems of labour with which we are so familiar, and which we are perhaps so inclined to take for granted, reproduced and sustained across the generations? The aim of this chapter is to draw attention to some of the parameters of what must be one part of the answer, namely the economic socialization of the child. The starting point for this exercise is the observation that young people arrive at the verge of adulthood, not only apparently accepting these labour arrangements as entirely normal, but also prepared in many ways for their peculiar requirements.

The relevant preparation is both intellectual and moral, both motivational and technical, both general and specific. It is intellectual in that children are equipped with the various cognitive requirements for adult economic roles, notable among which are the skills of numeracy and literacy. Intellectual preparation shades into the moral in children's understanding of the principles underpinning role relationships in the different systems. Thus, with respect to employment relations children may learn that level of pay varies as a function of job content but also that these contingencies are in some way right and just. The motivational preparation is well documented, for example in terms of the connection between the operation of a free-market economy and the socialization of an appropriate 'work ethic' (cf. Weber, 1930; McClelland, 1961; Furnham, 1990). But what is the motivational preparation for the domestic system? As we shall see, the motivational dynamics are less well understood here. Finally, socialization also has differentiating effects, preparing different children for different economic roles in both systems.

In the remainder of this chapter I will consider some of ways in which children are prepared for adult economic roles. I shall look first at the distinction between the employment and domestic/voluntary systems, then at domestic socialization and finally at employment socialization.

PAID AND UNPAID WORK

When and how do children learn that some work is paid work and some is not? How do they learn to distinguish the two? Partly, it is a matter of intellectual development. The study of children's understanding of the means of production and the relationship between work and money has revealed a fairly stable developmental sequence between 4 and 11 years (Danziger, 1958; Jahoda, 1979; Furth, 1980; Berti and Bombi, 1988). The youngest children usually fail to draw a connection between employment and wages. They may realize that many adults go to work and that money is required to buy food and other goods but think that work is a voluntary activity and that money comes from change in shops or banks or even God.

By 6 or 7 years they recognize that money is obtained by working and often make a dramatic distinction between the working 'rich' and unemployed 'poor'. Their understanding of the process of production, however, is still very naive. For example, they do not connect the sale of goods with income for the producers. They may think that factory owners are given money by the government or banks to pay the workers or even that the factory owner has to earn money elsewhere, in another job. They may imagine that teachers' wages come directly from pupils' parents, that bus drivers' wages are the fares they receive or that bosses earn less than workers because 'nobody pays them' (Dickinson, 1986; Berti and Bombi, 1988).

At 8 to 9 years they begin to understand that there is an exchange relationship between the boss and the worker and to assume a simple relationship between the amount of money earned and the amount of work done. The next two or three years see a growing awareness that the relationship between the amount of work and the amount of money is less straightforward and that different types of jobs receive different pay.

Insight into the relationship between employment and money entails some degree of co-ordination between knowledge of three different aspects of work: production of goods, selling of goods and exchange of labour for wages. Furth (1980), Jahoda (1984) and Berti and Bombi (1988) have all argued that the development of insight into economic relations is dependent upon cognitive growth and that the ability to make connections between different aspects of production is restricted by the child's ability to make inferences and integrate pieces of knowledge.

This makes for similarities in the sequence of development, at least across cultures with money-based economies, but the rate of progress can be affected by experience and the availability of information. For example, children whose fathers run small businesses show accelerated development of the understanding of the exchange of goods for money (Jahoda, 1983; Berti and Bombi, 1988) while children further removed from work often retain early misconceptions. Jahoda (1979) found that the children of unemployed parents were likely to think everyone's income came from social security. Berti and Bombi (1988) found that Italian middle-class children thought all money was handed out by the bank or council, whereas working-class children, whose fathers worked in the local Fiat factory, attributed a similar omnipotent role to Fiat. The rate of development can also vary between economic spheres. Berti, Bombi and Lis (1982) found that the children of factory workers understood much more about factory production than agricultural production.

Duveen and Shields (1985) found that pre-schoolers did make a clear distinction between domestic work and employment; at this age this is more likely to be a distinction between domestic and public spheres of work than an understanding of the distinction between paid and unpaid work. Goodnow and Warton (1991) suggest children learn the distinction as part of learning about social relationships: unpaid work is an appropriate expression of a particular kind of personal relationship.

THE DOMESTIC SYSTEM

One of the most salient features of the household economic system in contemporary society is the gender-based division of responsibilities. Despite much interest in the emergence of 'egalitarian' marriages with undifferentiated responsibilities, it remains the norm for adult males and females to contribute very different kinds of labour to their domestic partnerships. Moreover, the characteristic division of labour is established very rapidly. Atkinson and Huston (1984) found that a sample of young American couples, surveyed within a few months of marriage, already had an established gender-based pattern: male partners were more likely to undertake repairs and renovations to the house, the females were more likely to take on the routine tasks of household shopping, preparing meals and cleaning. It is also clear from this and other research that husbands and wives contribute labour which differs quantitatively as well as qualitatively: wives contribute far more.

It is tempting to view this pattern in terms of a more general gender division of economic roles: the assumption by wives of primary responsibility for the domestic sphere complements their husbands' assumption of primary responsibility for income generation on behalf of the family, a responsibility discharged by the latter's participation in the employment system. However, it would be a mistake to conclude that participation in the two systems is simply balanced out in this way or that the domestic division could be generated and sustained by the straightforward internalization of such a definition of gender roles. There is, it turns out, little evidence for any direct balancing of roles: many married women also participate in the employment system, many do so on a full-time basis, and women are also sometimes the principal income generators in the family. Moreover, none of these tendencies is associated with a gender reversal of domestic responsibilities (e.g. Witherspoon, 1985).

Atkinson and Huston (1984) suggest two ways in which the observed gender division might be generated so rapidly in marriage. Partners come to the marriage with established beliefs about appropriate sex roles in the family, and they also divide responsibilities according to perceived skill differences. However, there are reasons to doubt that this provides a completely satisfactory explanation. First, it begs questions both about origins of perceptions of skill differences and about the origins and reality of the differences to which these perceptions relate. Second, perceptions of one's own and one's partner's skills accounted for very little of the variance that Atkinson and Huston observed in the distribution of domestic work. The same was true of sex-role beliefs.

We have explored the development of sex-role beliefs in late adolescence and their ability to predict contributions to household labour (Emler and Abrams, 1989; Emler and Hall, in press). Our data indicate that such beliefs can predict some of the variance in the level of such contributions, but only among males and only while they remain in their parents' homes. In effect, 16–20-year-old males are more likely to contribute to traditionally female areas of household labour if they develop egalitarian beliefs about sex roles generally. In contrast, whatever beliefs females develop about gender roles have no consequences for the level or extent of their contributions in these areas.

Perhaps the most important preparation that childhood provides for adult economic roles in the domestic system is not assimilation of sex-role ideologies or even the opportunity for observational learning in which their parents provide role models, but rather direct practice in these roles and the explicit teaching which accompanies this (Warton and Goodnow, 1991). From relatively early in life, children are contributors to the household economic system and by late adolescence their contributions are often quite extensive, including money as well as labour. But even at this level the participation is not a simple rehearsal of different roles for males and females, in which the former primarily contribute money and the latter labour; in fact, adolescent females are likely to contribute proportionately more of any earned income than are their male counterparts (Emler and Hall, in press).

Initially, children contribute self-care labour which might, for example, take the form of tidying their own rooms. But progressively they become more involved in doing work for the family (Goodnow, 1988). This latter kind of work is also gender-differentiated: almost from the beginning girls and boys are expected to perform different kinds of work around the house. Thus, by 8 years children already have a well-developed sense of the 'ownership' (cf. Warton and Goodnow, 1991) of various domestic responsibilities. Additionally, boys are more likely than girls to be paid for jobs around the home, perhaps in the process learning to regard their own labour as a commodity to be sold. Certainly for males household work appears to belong more to the category of 'voluntary' contributions and is more strongly associated with the generally 'altruistic' inclinations of the individual (Emler and Hall, in press). The contributions of females are more directly governed by the immediate expectations of others (Emler, 1993).

SOCIALIZATION FOR EMPLOYMENT RELATIONS

What does a modern economy, and particularly one based extensively on employment relations, require of economic socialization? The answer is probably 'rather a lot'. Here I focus on just four areas: cognitive skills, distributive justice, legal-rational authority and occupational selection.

Specific cognitive skills

The most conspicuous cognitive skill among adults in an employment culture is literacy. When Max Weber (1947) argued that the dominant organizational form in the modern world would be the bureaucracy, he meant that organization would be centred on the bureau or office as a place where the instruments of organizational control are decisions recorded in writing. He thus assumed that this kind of organization would depend on staff capable of making and referring to written records. He did not specify what proportion of the staff would require this ability but research on industrialization gives us some clues.

Industrialization, mass urbanization and bureacratization of economic institutions have been correlated trends. In a survey of seventy-three countries, Lerner (1958) was able to show that these processes are in turn closely related to levels of literacy within a population. Thus, once urbanization has reached about 10 per cent, literacy becomes closely correlated with urbanization. It is as if such forms of social organization cannot function unless a large proportion of the population can read and write. Postman and Weingartner (1969) note that the recreational reading of most adults is limited to the tabloid press and the occasional comic, only a small percentage regularly read books and an even more minute percentage write novels or poems, even unpublished ones. More relevant, Postman and Weingartner say, is the capacity literacy skills give people to read timetables, signs, directions, instructions and operating manuals, and to complete census and tax returns. It takes many years to become proficient in reading and writing skills – reading-level norms are specified in modern education systems at least up to 12 years. Presumably these skills are sufficiently vital to a modern economy to defer eligibility for employment relations until they are acquired by most children. And without formal schooling only a few would acquire them.

Distributive justice

The remunerations for employment vary enormously. In Britain there is currently no legal minimum wage and it is not uncommon for people to be paid less than £2.00 per hour. At the other end of the scale, some corporation CEOs receive financial compensation in excess of half a million pounds a year. Of course there are disagreements about the justice of these differentials; most people would like more, whatever their current income, and most probably think they deserve more. What is far more remarkable is that there is not a great deal more dissatisfaction and discord about income differences. In effect, people have notions about what their own and other occupations deserve which are quite close to what they actually receive, and their estimates of what is fair are by no means indexed to any absolute or objective criteria. So, again, it seems that most adults have been prepared in childhood to accept some very detailed and differentiated standards of just deserts for work. How does this happen?

To understand wage relations children need to develop conceptions of the principles which underlie payment. Piaget's (1932) work on distributive justice suggested that early beliefs about the desirability of parity in the distribution of rewards are displaced by the principle of equity. That is, children begin to believe that people should be rewarded in accordance with their relative contributions. Research on children's allocation decisions (Hook and Cook, 1979) has confirmed that beyond 6–7 years children are increasingly likely to allocate rewards on the basis of relative effort, time worked or amount of work completed.

A similar developmental change has been observed in children's beliefs about the desirability of wage differentials. Connell (1977) asked children aged 5–16 years whether it was fair that some people were rich and some poor. The youngest children thought it unfair, but with increasing age more children thought the differences were fair and justified by differential efforts expended to acquire wealth. Siegal (1981) also found an increase between 6 and 13 years in the attitude that inequality in wages was fair, while Emler and Dickinson (1985) found a similar age pattern in the rejection of equality as an appropriate basis for earnings.

It is worth noting that, although children rapidly come to support inequality in wages, their perceptions of the degree of inequality are extremely imprecise. Studies in which children have been asked to estimate wages have revealed that young children perceive very little inequality between jobs and systematically underestimate incomes (Emler and Dickinson, 1985; Emler, Ohana and Dickinson, 1990). The estimates and the perceived differentials increase with age, but still fall short of accuracy even in adulthood (Dickinson, 1986). In other words, people will say wage differentials are fair even though they are ignorant of the scale of these differentials.

Emler and Dickinson (1985) found that, although both working- and middle-class children believed that income differences were fair, middle-class children, and adolescents (Dickinson, 1990), expressed greater support for wage differentials than did their working-class peers. Interestingly, the middle-class children also perceived significantly larger differences in income than did the working-class children. This finding has been replicated in both America and France, though somewhat less clearly in the latter case (Emler, Ohana and Dickinson, 1990). These findings are consistent with other studies showing that middle-class children are more conscious of occupational status (Simmons and Rosenberg, 1971; Dickinson, 1986).

One implication of this class difference is that middle- and working-class children embark upon a critical stage of their educational careers with quite different assumptions about the economic consequences of their efforts. If working-class children really believe there is very little difference between the pay of a professional and that of a manual worker they may feel there is little reason to invest in educational qualifications. Middle-class children, recognizing that there is a substantial difference, might be expected to act rather differently.

To summarize, it appears that children acquire a range of justifications for inequality, but not that they apply some version of the contributions rule or equity principle to decide what the relations between incomes should be. Rather, their culture confronts them with a particular pattern of distribution which is extensively defended by 'equity-like' arguments. The child's capacity to understand and reproduce these arguments will undoubtedly be limited by cognitive capacity. However, the precise nature and application of arguments for equity, and indeed the priority accorded to such arguments, will all derive from their currency in the individual's social environment. Children in more collectivist cultures like Japan, for example, give less weight to equity than to parity (Mann, Radford and Kanagawa, 1985).

By the time they enter the labour market young people are equipped with the argumentative terms of employment relations. They are already discussing the cash value of jobs in terms of skill, responsibility, effort and qualifications, and therefore prepared for a particular way of defining a fair day's pay.

Authority relations

Weber regarded as a defining characteristic of bureaucracy the quality of the authority exercised within it, what he referred to as legal-rational authority. Katz and Kahn (1978), discussing the conditions for obedience to authority in the bureaucratized workplace, note that it has little to do with the capacity of an organization to coerce compliance from its members.

Instead, it depends substantially on their willingness to obey someone simply because he or she is formally entitled to exercise authority and is doing so within legitimate limits. This willingness, Katz and Kahn conclude, must be in part a consequence of socialization.

Respect for authority certainly has its origins in the family, but legal-rational authority is rather different from the kind commonly exercised by parents. To the extent that parents successfully wield authority over their children, this success is likely to derive from the personal ties between these individuals (Hoffman, 1977). It is characteristic of legal-rational authority that it does not depend on personal ties, whether of affection, respect, fear or anything else, between people. Instead, it is based on recognition that 'obedience is owed to the legally established impersonal order. It extends to the persons exercising the authority of office under it only by virtue of the formal legality of their commands and only within the scope of authority of the office' (Weber, 1947, p. 328). Bureaucracy in effect formalizes roles and role relationships. The rights and obligations of office holders, to whom they are answerable, what they are responsible for, and who and what they have authority over, are formally set down, at least in theory. This is 'in theory' because, as Weber emphasized, this is an idealization of employment relations; in practice much is left unspecified and there remains considerable scope for negotiation, interpretation and discretion. But the basic point remains: employment relations are in principle governed by formalized and impersonal requirements.

Research by Adelson (1971), Furth (1980) and Kohlberg (1984) suggests that children do not recognize the formal and impersonal elements in role relations until they reach adolescence. They are not initially able to recognize that relations between people could be regulated by anything beyond personal inclinations or preferences. 'Societal decisions are thought to emanate from the free will of a particular person' (Furth, 1978, p. 251). In other words, the distinction between the formal and the personal is a cognitively complex notion which appears relatively late in development.

Several studies have revealed, however, that even quite young children, 7- and sometimes even 5-year-olds, perceive authority to have limits (Damon, 1977; Laupa and Turiel, 1986). Furthermore, there are grounds for regarding experience of school as the single most important socializing experience here. Formal schooling is the child's first extended introduction to a bureaucracy, one which bears marked similarities to employing organizations. The school is clearly separated off from domestic life. Activities within it are organized according to a timetable. Within the institution, and between the hours formally laid down, individuals relate to one another in terms of their respective formally defined roles. Performances are appraised according to universalistic criteria. Authority is exercised impersonally and in accordance with written procedures.

It seems sensible therefore to ask how children represent social relations in this context. Emler, Ohana and Moscovici (1987) examined Scottish and

French children's representations of the teacher as an organizational role. They found that by 11 years almost all children recognized that there is a hierarchy of authority in the school and that teachers are in their turn subject to the authority of office holders, such as headteachers, who are above them in this hierarchy. By this age almost all children recognized that teachers did not have the power to alter or ignore any rule, and most also believed it was wrong for teachers to allow their personal preferences to influence decisions about which pupils they would and would not help. In these cases the middle-class children were more likely to show these insights than the working-class, and the French children were more sophisticated about these bureaucratic features than the Scottish. In general, the data suggest that children progressively assimilate culturally dominant interpretations rather than developing a single objective understanding of a factual reality (Emler, 1992).

Selection for work roles

Despite the prevalence of the Western democratic myth of equal opportunity, research by Simmons and Rosenberg (1971) has shown that American children and adolescents do not actually believe that everyone has the same chance to achieve economic success, and they are aware of socio-economic and racial disadvantage. However, this awareness does not prevent them from being optimistic about their own personal chances. Of Simmons and Rosenberg's sample of 9- to 18-year-olds, 97 per cent believed they had 'as good or better a chance to rise in the world than most'.

Jencks (1972) regarded career choice as dictated by the opportunity structures to which individuals are exposed, first in education and subsequently in employment. It seems, he suggested, 'that many (perhaps most) young people have very little idea what they want to do, change their aspirations easily and often, and follow the course of least resistance into whatever slots the economy makes available' (Jencks, 1972, p. 185).

From the point of view of society and its continued cohesion, the problem of occupational choice, as Durkheim (1964) saw it, was persuading its members to accept limited, finite and specific aspirations in a context of almost limitless options. The problem is solved principally in two ways, by self-selection and by social selection. The first ensures that individuals put themselves forward only for certain opportunities. The second entails more overt and direct constraints on decisions. Though in practice these two processes are interdependent, the distinction has the advantage of directing our attention to the internal and psychological as well as immediate external forces operating on choice. A simple illustration of this point must suffice. People cannot train as vets without certain academic credentials normally obtained in secondary school. But many young people never seek these credentials in the first place; they never embark upon the relevant courses of study or present themselves for the necessary examinations. As Bourdieu and Passeron (1977) have observed, more people eliminate themselves before exams than are ever eliminated by the exams themselves. These actions and decisions are programmed in all kinds of ways, in complex interactions between individuals and their social environments beginning very early in life.

Attempts have been made to define developmental phases in the formation of career aspirations. Ginzberg *et al.* (1951) suggested that there is an initial fantasy period in occupational aspirations which lasts until approximately 11 years, when children desire romantic jobs like 'footballer', 'pop star' and 'explorer'. In early adolescence these desires are redirected towards more normal jobs, first by interests, then by increasing awareness of one's capabilities and finally by personal values. In the later teens, when occupational decisions loom closer, a compromise is sought between one's desires and the opportunities offered.

Gottfredson (1981) proposed four stages in the development of occupational preference that are related to cognitive development, to social knowledge and to occupational perceptions. In the first stage, corresponding to 3–5 years, children are aware of occupations only as adult roles. But by the next stage, at 6–8 years, gender stereotypes of adult roles and developing gender identity begin to affect occupational preferences. Sex-typed choices appear. The third stage, at 9–13 years, sees a growing awareness of social class and educational differences in relation to the prestige level of jobs, and children start to orientate themselves to jobs considered suitable to their class background. Finally, personal interests, values and competencies direct occupational choices within the boundaries laid down by gender, class and ability. At each stage in this process changes in occupational aspirations match changes in social and personal identity: instead of perceiving social structural limitations on their future careers, children see the circumscription as natural and desirable.

Let us now look at some of the factors which shape eventual occupational status, and the manner in which they might operate.

Gender

Within the first eighteen months of life most children have learned to label themselves as their parents and other adults do, namely as a boy or a girl (Money and Erhardt, 1972). They then set about learning what this label means; in effect, they learn a script for the role of male or female. There are many sources for the script, including the examples provided by their own parents, but also other adults, and of course television (in other cultures, stories, written or told, might be more important). They also begin rehearsals. These scripts outline among other things the supposed virtues and talents that are peculiar to each sex, but also and centrally the economic and occupational roles they each play. What children understand of the script, their progress in learning it, the qualities displayed in rehearsal, are all limited by intellectual development, as are their perceptions of the degree of choice involved. Thus 6-year-olds may play at doctors and nurses, not only casting themselves in these roles strictly by sex but also believing that it could not be any other way. The idea that occupations may be matters of taste and preference will only emerge later (Kohlberg and Ullman, 1974).

By then, however, tastes and preferences have also been strongly moulded. Though they are theoretically free to do so, very few girls seek careers in engineering, regarding an interest in heavy machinery as unfeminine. Nor will they study technical subjects or computing in secondary school in numbers similar to boys. Boys in their turn will rule out all kinds of careers which they have learned to regard as either unmasculine or too low in status or both. These acquired inclinations are reinforced by strong biases in the perception and evaluation of male and female performances (cf. Stein, 1971). These tendencies all contribute to the remarkable divide between the occupational choices boys and girls appear to make voluntarily at the end of compulsory schooling.

Social class and schooling

Working-class boys and girls are unlikely to occupy anything other than working-class jobs as adults. In so far as 'working-class' describes the relative status of these occupations, the single most important determinant of these statuses is amount of education (Jencks, 1972). In Britain a crucial division occurs at the end of compulsory schooling when many young people abandon full-time academic education; in the 1980s this was about half the age group (Banks *et al.*, 1992). As the research reported by Banks *et al.* shows, this decision has major and virtually irreversible repercussions for the segment of the labour market into which young people move, for prospects of full-time employment of any kind, and for subsequent earnings.

So why is it that children born into the working class end up with less education than those born into the middle class? Jencks (1972) suggested five reasons: genetic endowment; a home environment which is less likely to help them acquire the intellectual skills needed for success at school; more economic obstacles to school attendance (in the USA, for example, middle-class youth are less likely to have to work their way through college); less positive attitudes to education and less likelihood of attending academically orientated schools.

Jencks believed the most important of these factors in educational success was attitude to education and he argued that middle-class children have more positive attitudes because they have higher occupational aspirations and are under pressure from home to do well at school. The class difference in occupational aspirations also increases with age. Dickinson's (1986) study of the occupational preferences of privately and state-educated 10- to

16-year-olds in Britain revealed a number of differences. Middle-class, private-school adolescents specified professional jobs such as 'doctor', 'engineer' and 'teacher'. The working-class adolescents aspired to jobs over a much wider socio-economic range than the middle-class adolescents. Both professional jobs and skilled manual jobs were desired although few wanted semi- or unskilled jobs.

Despite the differences in occupational aspirations the reasons given for their choices were remarkably similar. Many adolescents simply described the characteristics of the job: they would like to be a teacher because they would really like to teach children, or they mentioned job satisfaction and the intrinsic interest of the job. So, for instance, middle-class boys regarded professional jobs as 'interesting' and many working-class boys regarded skilled manual jobs as 'interesting'. Few subjects referred to wages, responsibility, training or skill and few mentioned the sex or class appropriateness of the job. 'Interest' is the normal justification for occupational preference in this age group.

Aspirations also interact with perceptions of what is realistic. Rosen (1964), in an experimental study of occupational choice, found that when subjects were asked to rate jobs in order of preference before and after having been given (false) information about their chances of getting the jobs, they raised their rating of jobs for which they stood a good chance and lowered their rating of those for which they stood little chance. This must raise some doubt as to whether social class has a direct effect on career aspirations or whether these are the outcome of other variables associated with social class.

Attitudes and values

We have already seen that employment relations entail particular kinds of authority relations. There is also evidence that people differ in their attitudes to formal authority, independently of their capacity to articulate insights into its principles. Differences in these attitudes become particularly apparent in adolescence (Emler and Reicher, 1987; Reicher and Emler, 1985). Attitudes as a whole become less uniformly positive at least between 12 and 16, though it should be said they are still positive rather than negative: most 16-year-olds do express a belief in the impartiality of institutional authority and do assert that those exercising such authority should be obeyed. Girls are on average even more positive than boys (Emler and Reicher, 1987).

This research provides further evidence for the central role of formal schooling in the development of attitudes to institutional authority. Attitudes to such authority as encountered in the school are highly correlated with attitudes to institutional authority more generally (Reicher and Emler, 1985; Rigby and Rump, 1979). Most significantly, however, attitudes to formal authority are strongly associated with educational attainment. They are correlated with both qualifications obtained and amount of formal education (Emler and St James, 1990; Emler, 1990). Can we therefore confirm the suggestions of Jencks, Willis (1977) and others that the effect of social class on education is mediated by attitudes? Not entirely, because variations in attitudes to authority, and indeed some of the other attitudes which predicted educational attainment in the same study, such as attachment to locality and belief in the value of work, are only partly a function of social background.

On the other hand, this link between educational credentials and attitudes to authority is consistent with the argument (cf. Danziger, 1971; Jencks, 1972) that the former provide potential employers with a proxy measure of the inclination or capacity of potential applicants to accommodate to one of the central features of workplace organizations: the co-ordination of activities through systems of formal authority.

Parents and family

Family background has an influence on occupational aspiration and educational achievement. However, relationships with kin, most obviously parents but also other relatives, provide social capital which can be and often is traded for specific job opportunities. A boy may go to work in his father's shop or his uncle's garage. A girl may secure a position with a law firm or dental practice through family contacts (cf. Lin *et al.*, 1981). In the East London docks during the early 1970s 90 per cent of those employed there were able to name at least one relative working in the docks; direct father-to-son inheritance accounted for two-thirds of the jobs (Hill, 1976).

Area of residence

Local labour markets vary in the opportunities they provide. There is no ship-building industry in the suburbs of Paris, no coal mine in Iowa, no Ford motor company in Dundee. The point is obvious but important when young people differ in their mobility. Locales also differ in the number as well as the kind of employment opportunities. A boy may leave school with few formal qualifications in one part of the country and immediately be taken on by a local employer. In a more depressed area, leaving school with the same lack of qualifications, he may find himself almost indefinitely unemployed. Two hypotheses are relevant here. The structural hypothesis (Ashton and Maguire, 1983) assumes that low-skill jobs are disappearing from modern economies in the West. The labour market now requires a greater preponderance of qualified school leavers. The labour queue hypothesis (Main, 1985) assumes that the labour market in the late 1970s did not so much shift as contract. Employers select applicants according to their expected labour costs, starting with the least costly and moving down the queue until all the slots are filled. As the labour market contracts, only those with lower anticipated costs, typically the better qualified, will be selected. Conversely, as the labour supply contracts, employers lower the educational requirements and may even tempt into early employment young people who would otherwise have continued into higher education.

CONCLUSIONS

Many of the qualities that typify the dominant character structure in an employment culture are already strongly established before individuals actually assume economic roles in adulthood – notions of fairness, the vocabulary of equity, the cognitive orientations of literacy, numeracy and formal operations, appropriate attitudes to time, an understanding of the nature of bureaucracy and legal-rational authority. Much of the task of sorting individuals into the thousands of different employee roles has also occurred, and perhaps the priority is that this extensive pre-sorting should occur rather than that it achieve perfect matches.

If a broad principle can be discerned in all of this it is that the system selects in terms of the degree to which prototypical socialization is accomplished. The more an individual matches the prototype of the perfectly socialized member of an industrial culture – a positive attitude to institutional authority, strong commitment to the principle of equity, highly developed literacy skills, a capacity for abstract thought, etc. – the greater his or her chances of being selected into higher-status occupations.

One question for future research must concern the implications of this pattern of socialization for the future of work. Is the socialization of our children still preparing them for the economic realities of yesterday or will patterns of socialization shift to keep pace with changing economic realities?

REFERENCES

Adelson, J. (1971) The political imagination of the young adolescent. *Daedalus*, *100*, 1013–50.
Aries, P. (1962) *Centuries of Childhood*. New York: Knopf.
Ashton, D. and Maguire, M. (1983) *The Vanishing Youth Labour Market*. London: Youthaid.
Atkinson, J. and Huston, T. (1984) Sex role orientation and division of labor in early marriage. *Journal of Personality and Social Psychology*, *46*, 330–45.
Banks, M., Bates, I., Breakwell, G., Bynner, J., Emler, N., Jamieson, L. and Roberts, K. (1992) *Careers and Identities*. Milton Keynes: Open University Press.
Berti, A.E. and Bombi, A.S. (1988) *The Child's Construction of Economics*. Cambridge: Cambridge University Press.
Berti, A.E., Bombi, A.S. and Lis, A. (1982) The child's conceptions about means of production and their ownership. *European Journal of Social Psychology*, *12*, 221–39.
Bourdieu, P. and Passeron, J.C. (1977) *Reproduction in Education, Society and Culture*. London: Sage.

Connell, R.W. (1977) *Ruling Class Ruling Culture*. Cambridge: Cambridge University Press.

Damon, W. (1977) *The Social World of the Child*. San Francisco: Jossey-Bass.

Danziger, K. (1958) Children's earliest conceptions of economic relationships (Australia). *Journal of Social Psychology*, *47*, 231–40.

Danziger, K. (1971) *Socialisation*. Harmondsworth: Penguin.

Dickinson, J. (1986) *The Development of Representations of Social Inequality*. Unpublished PhD thesis, University of Dundee.

Dickinson, J. (1990) Adolescent representations of socio-economic inequality. *British Journal of Developmental Psychology*, *8*, 351–71.

Durkheim, E. (1964) *The Division of Labour in Society*. New York: Free Press.

Duveen, G. and Shields, M. (1985) Children's ideas about work, wages, and social rank. *Cahiers de Psychologie Cognitif*, *5*, 411–12.

Emler, N. (1990) *Adolescents and their Relation to Formal Authority*. Paper presented at the General Meeting of the European Association of Experimental Social Psychology, Budapest.

Emler, N. (1992) Childhood origins of beliefs about institutional authority. *New Directions for Child Development*, *56*, 65–78.

Emler, N. (1993) *Young People's Contributions to Household Labour*. Paper presented at the General Meeting of the European Association of Experimental Social Psychology, Lisbon conference.

Emler, N. and Abrams, D. (1989) The sexual distribution of benefits and burdens in the household: adolescent experiences and expectations. *Social Justice Research*, *3*, 139–56.

Emler, N. and Dickinson, J. (1985) Children's representations of economic inequalities: the effects of social class. *British Journal of Developmental Psychology*, *3*, 191–8.

Emler, N. and Hall, S. (in press) Gender inequality in the household. In M. Lerner and G. Mikula (eds) *Entitlement in Close Relationships*. New York: Plenum.

Emler, N. and Reicher, S. (1987) Orientations to institutional authority in adolescence. *Journal of Moral Education*, *16*, 108–16.

Emler, N. and St James, A. (1990) Staying on at school after sixteen: social and psychological correlates. *British Journal of Education and Work*, *3*, 61–70.

Emler, N., Ohana, J. and Dickinson, J. (1990) Children's representations of social relations. In G. Duveen and B. Lloyd (eds) *Social Representations and the Development of Knowledge*. Cambridge: Cambridge University Press, pp. 47–69.

Emler, N., Ohana, J. and Moscovici, S. (1987) Children's beliefs about institutional roles: a cross-national study of representations of the teacher's role. *British Journal of Educational Psychology*, *57*, 26–37.

Furnham, A. (1990) *The Protestant Work Ethic*. London: Routledge.

Furth, H.G. (1978) Young children's understanding of society. In H. McGurk (ed.) *Issues in Childhood Social Development*. London: Methuen.

Furth, H. (1980) *The World of Grown Ups*. New York: Elsevier.

Ginzberg, E., Ginzberg, S.W., Axelard, S. and Herma, J.L. (1951) *Occupational Choice: An Approach to a General Theory*. New York: Columbia University Press.

Goodnow, J.J. (1988) Children's household work: its nature and functions. *Psychological Bulletin*, *103*, 5–36.

Goodnow, J.J. and Delaney, S. (1989) Children's household work: differentiating types of work and styles of assignment. *Journal of Applied Developmental Psychology*, *10*, 209–26.

Goodnow, J.J. and Warton, P. (1991) The social bases of social cognition: interactions about work and their implications. *Merrill Palmer Quarterly*, *37*, 27–58.

Gottfredson, L.S. (1981) Circumscription and compromise: a developmental theory of occupational aspirations. *Journal of Counselling Psychology*, *28*, 545–79.

Hearn, F. (1978) *Domination, Legitimation and Resistance: The Incorporation of the Nineteenth Century English Working Class.* Westport, Conn.: Greenwood Press.

Hill, S. (1976) *The Dockers: Class and Tradition in London.* London: Heinemann.

Hoffman, M.L. (1977) Moral internalization: current theory and research. In L. Berkowitz (ed.) *Advances in Experimental Social Psychology*, Volume 10. New York: Academic Press.

Hook, J. and Cook, T. (1979) Equity theory and the cognitive ability of children. *Psychological Bulletin, 86*, 429–45.

Jahoda, G. (1979) The construction of economic reality by some Glaswegian children. *European Journal of Social Psychology, 9*, 115–27.

Jahoda, G. (1983) European 'lag' in the development of an economic concept: a study in Zimbabwe. *British Journal of Developmental Psychology, 1*, 113–20.

Jahoda, G. (1984) The development of thinking about socio-economic systems. In H. Tajfel (ed.) *The Social Dimension: European Developments in Social Psychology*, Volume 1. Cambridge: Cambridge University Press.

Jencks, C. (1972) *Inequality.* Harmondsworth: Penguin.

Katz, D. and Kahn, R.L. (1978) *The Social Psychology of Organisations.* New York: Wiley.

Kohlberg, L. (1984) *Essays on Moral Development*, Volume 2. *The Psychology of Moral Development.* San Francisco: Harper & Row.

Kohlberg, L. and Ullman, D. (1974) Stages in the development of psychosexual concepts and attitudes. In R.C. Friedman, R.M. Richart and R.L. Van de Wiele (eds) *Sex Differences in Behavior*. New York: Wiley.

Laupa, M. and Turiel, E. (1986) Children's conceptions of adult and peer authority. *Child Development, 57*, 405–12.

Lerner, D. (1958) *The Passing of Traditional Society.* New York: Free Press.

Lin, N., Ensel, W. and Vaughn, J. (1981) Social resources and strength of ties: structural factors in occupational status attainment. *American Sociological Review, 46*, 393–405.

McClelland, D.C. (1961) *The Achieving Society.* Princeton, NJ: Van Nostrand.

Main, D. (1985) School leaver unemployment and the youth opportunities programme in Scotland. *Oxford Economic Papers, 37*, 426–47.

Mann, L., Radford, M. and Kanagawa, C. (1985) Cross-cultural differences in children's use of decision rules: a comparison between Japan and Australia. *Journal of Personality and Social Psychology, 14*, 1557–64.

Money, J. and Erhardt, A. (1972) *Man and Woman, Boy and Girl.* Baltimore, MD: Johns Hopkins University Press.

Piaget, J. (1932) *The Moral Judgement of the Child.* London: Routledge & Kegan Paul.

Postman, N. and Weingartner, C. (1969) *Teaching as a Subversive Activity.* New York: Delacourt.

Reicher, S. and Emler, N. (1985) Delinquent behaviour and attitudes to formal authority. *British Journal of Social Psychology, 3*, 161–8.

Rigby, K. and Rump, E.E. (1979) The generality of attitude to authority. *Human Relations, 32*, 469–87.

Rosen, M. (1964) Valence, expectancy and dissonance reduction in the prediction of goal striving. In V. Vroom (ed.) *Work and Motivation*. New York: Wiley.

Siegal, M. (1981) Children's perceptions of adult economic needs. *Child Development, 52*, 379–82.

Simmons, R.G. and Rosenberg, M. (1971) Functions of children's perceptions of the stratification system. *American Sociological Review, 36*, 235–49.

Stein, A.H. (1971) The effects of sex-role standards for achievement and sex-role preference on three determinants of achievement. *Developmental Psychology, 4,* 219–31.

Thompson, E.P. (1967) Time, work discipline and industrial capitalism. *Past and Present, 38,* 56–97.

Warton, P. and Goodnow, J.J. (1991) The nature of responsibility: children's understanding of 'your job'. *Child Development, 62,* 156–65.

Weber, M. (1930) *The Protestant Ethic and the Spirit of Capitalism.* New York: Scribner.

Weber, M. (1947) *The Theory of Social and Economic Organisations,* ed. T. Parsons; trans. A.M. Henderson and T. Parsons. New York: Free Press.

Willis, P. (1977) *Learning to Labour: How Working Class Kids Get Working Class Jobs.* Farnborough: Saxon House.

Witherspoon, S. (1985) Sex roles and gender issues. In R. Jowell and S. Witherspoon (eds) *British Social Attitudes: The 1985 Report.* Aldershot: Gower.

2 Personality at work

Adrian Furnham

INTRODUCTION

Despite the fact that personality and social psychologists have often shared the same journal (e.g. *The Journal of Personality and Social Psychology, Personality and Social Psychology Bulletin, Journal of Social Behaviour and Personality*), the marriage has not always been happy. Social psychologists have preferred to focus on group, situational and contextual variables as 'determinants' of behaviour, while personality theorists choose often to look at traits or individual difference variables.

In the 1980s the two came to blows over the person–situation debate, and for a long period of time it seemed that the social psychologists were winning. Argyle played a major part in this debate, though typically he was not interested in point-scoring against personality theorists so much as describing which, how and why situational variables influenced social behaviour (Argyle, Furnham and Graham, 1981; Furnham and Argyle, 1981).

While personality and social psychologists have periodically fought about the determinants of behaviour, personality and occupational psychologists have largely ignored one another. In Britain many occupational psychologists, organizational behaviour theorists and management scientists have neglected to examine individual differences in any systematic way, so personality theorists have failed to take occupational behaviour seriously as a correlate of individual differences. A cursory glance at the many textbooks from these two sub-disciplines clearly shows their ignorance of one another. While textbooks on occupational/organizational behaviour may even have a chapter (or part of a chapter) labelled personality, it is frequently dealt with in a cursory and tangential manner. The latter's interest is faddish, eccentric and capricious. Some personality dimensions such as Machiavellianism, self-monitoring or A-type behaviour frequently excite temporary interest, but are soon forgotten. Major debates in personality theory – for example, the person–situation debate, the issue of the basic super-factors describing personality or the biological/genetic determinants of behaviour – are often not considered worthy of attention. Though occupational and organizational theorists may occasionally admit the importance of individual differences they seem unable to deal with the subject appropriately. On the other hand, there are those with a more sociological training who tend to underplay individual differences for various politico-philosophical reasons, and who believe that individual differences play a very small role, in comparison with socio-structural and organizational factors, in determining behaviour at work.

However, the paucity of literature at the interface between personality and occupational psychology/organizational behaviour cannot all be blamed on the ignorance of one party. Surprisingly, while personality theorists have been eager to examine clinical, educational, medical and social correlates of individual differences/personality dimensions, they have consistently ignored occupational and organizational correlates. Hence, one finds the journals examining the links between personality and social behaviour, personality and clinical behaviour, but none dedicated to personality at work. Where personality researchers have examined occupational/organizational correlates, it has nearly always been to test their theories rather than actually to examine the latter in depth. It should be pointed out, however, that this is not true of the East European literature – the Russians and Poles have always stressed the relationship between personality dimensions (particularly those derived from the Pavlovian model) and work-related behaviours (Strelau, 1981). It is not clear why Western personality theorists are so unconcerned with occupational/organizational correlates of personality, except perhaps that many of them are originally trained as either clinical or social psychologists and naturally examine abnormal behaviours and beliefs as the primary dependent variable.

Whereas personality theorists have usually conceived of personality as the independent variable and work behaviour as the dependent variable, occupational/organizational psychologists have done the precise opposite. On the one hand, it could be argued that it does not fundamentally matter which is the dependent and which the independent variable as any relationship will be manifest in the results. But it is critical to scientific method and the notion of causality which is cause and which effect. It does seem that researchers are frequently more skilled and knowledgeable about independent variables, compared to the dependent variable. That is, their knowledge of the dependent variable is less comprehensive because it is often seen as only a way of checking the validity of the theory about the independent variable.

SIX APPROACHES TO PERSONALITY AT WORK

An examination of the highly diverse, dispersed and divergent literature concerning personality at work has highlighted six rather different approaches to the topic.

Classic personality theory

This approach starts with a theory of personality and relates empirically assessed measures (as the independent variable) to various work-related behaviours. The personality variable chosen may vary on a number of dimensions:

- Single or multiple traits are measured. A single trait might be considered, e.g. self-monitoring (Snyder, 1974) or locus of control (Rotter, 1966), or alternatively a trait system, bound up in an elaborate theory like that of Eysenck (1967) or Cattell (1971). It is frequently the case that multiple traits are used, as single-trait theories are usually not as rich a source of hypotheses.
- Cognitive or biologically based traits are measured. For instance, some 'traits' or personality dimensions are quite clearly conceived of in cognitive terms, e.g. belief systems such as conservatism (Wilson, 1973) or attributional styles (Brewin, 1988). These cognitive traits refer to the way people perceive the world, or attribute the cause of their own or others' behaviour. On the other hand, some traits, e.g. extraversion (Eysenck, 1967) or sensation-seeking (Zuckerman, 1979), are conceived of in biological terms such that the person's behaviour is a function of biological differences. Both approaches seem equally popular.
- 'Normal' and 'abnormal' traits can be measured. For instance, some traits, like depression, psychopathy or hypochondriasis, are clearly conceived of in terms of abnormal behaviour. These traits measure some aspect of 'abnormal' behaviour which, though valid and indeed at times quite relevant to work-related behaviours, seems less useful than 'normal' traits, because many working people do not exhibit these traits to any degree. This is, however, not true of neuroticism or anxiety or stress which are very common.
- Dynamic vs. stylistic traits. This is the distinction made between Freudian/neo-Freudian ideas (such as the oral or anal personality which supposedly measures deep-seated, possibly unconscious, needs and fears) and stylistic traits which do not presume the same aetiology or processes. To date, however, very few Freudian personality tests have been applied to the workplace, save perhaps for Kline's (1978) work on the oral and anal personality.

The basic tenet of this 'classic personality theory' approach is to measure personality as the independent variable and see how it correlates with some (often rather arbitrarily chosen) work-related behaviour. In criticism of this approach, it should be pointed out that, so far, the approach has been piecemeal and there is very little evidence of a concerted, systematic and programmatic research effort, which is perhaps not that unusual. Sometimes this research has been laboratory-based, and hence it frequently has poor ecological validity. Furthermore, the selection of work-related variables is somewhat random and based on convenience because researchers are either unable to get better measures, or, indeed, not sure what to look for.

Compared to the extensive research on the relationship between personality and, say, learning, mental health or social behaviour, the extant research from classic personality theory on occupational and organizational variables has been disappointing.

Classic occupational psychology/organizational behaviour

This approach starts with some work-related variable, be it conceived at the individual, group or organizational level, and examines its personality correlates. Again the independent variables may be conceived of, or measured, quite differently.

- Self-report vs. behavioural. Some variables are measured by questionnaire ratings or interviews, while others are measured by actual behaviour such as absenteeism, productivity, sales or number of promotions. Both self-report and behavioural measures are subject to different forms of systematic error.
- Single vs. aggregate measures. The work-related behaviour may be a single, one-off assessment or an aggregate measure made up either from different sources (e.g. combining superior, subordinate, self and colleague assessments) or measurements conducted over time. Clearly, in terms of reliability and representativeness, aggregate measures are preferable.
- Within vs. between organizations. Sometimes variables are examined only within an organization while others are compared between organizations. The clear advantage of the latter approach is that one can control for organizational variables which are quite likely to have major effects.

Researchers in this tradition are usually interested in examining personality correlates of specific work behaviours which might help personnel and human resource professionals select, appraise, promote or train individuals. But this research has a number of limitations. First, the choice of personality variables has not been based on sound theory or good psychometrics. Some personality tests have been favoured mainly because they have been commercially exploited rather than because they are reliable and valid. Some outdated tests, largely forgotten and condemned by psychometricians, remain popular.

Similarly, statistical analyses have been simple and naive. As a rule, simple correlations have been computed rather than partial correlations or, even more to be preferred, multivariate statistics to prevent type II errors (finding more significant differences than actually occur). Given that both independent and dependent variables are multi-factorial, it is essential that sufficiently robust and sensitive multivariate statistics are used to analyse results. Third, studies in this area are frequently exploratory and are a-theoretical rather than based on a sound theory or programmatic research endeavour. As a result, interesting results are rarely followed up and the theoretical implications rarely exploited. Finally, researchers ignore possible organizational and societal factors that either directly or indirectly affect the dependent variable. That is, work-related behaviours are rarely under the control of the individual and may be moderated by powerful organizational factors which need to be taken into account.

The occupational psychology and organizational behaviour literature is diverse, often poor but sometimes very good. Alas, the good research and theorizing is difficult to find and limited in both quantity and scope.

The development of a work-specific individual difference measure

A third approach is to develop a personality measure aimed at predicting exclusively a specific work-related behaviour (like absenteeism) and to use this measure to predict that behaviour. This is not necessarily tautological though at first it may seem so. A fairly large number of these measures already exist. But they are highly varied and may be:

- Narrow vs. wide in conceptualization. For instance, the personality measures might attempt to predict a specific (narrow) form of occupational behaviour, such as absenteeism, or a much wider range of occupational behaviours such as satisfaction or productivity. It is probably true that the former is a much more common approach than the latter (Cook *et al.*, 1981; Furnham, 1990).
- Single vs. multiple traits. That is, the measure (usually a questionnaire) could be multi-dimensional, supposedly measuring many different behaviours/beliefs at work, or a single trait measure that measures only one dimension.
- Self-report vs. behaviour. There is no reason why the individual-difference measure need necessarily be self-report based. It could just as well be biographical, behavioural or physiological and, indeed, all of these have been used at one time or another to try to predict work-related behaviour.
- Attitudinal vs. attributional. Most of these measures are of the self-report kind but some are attitudinal, systematically examining work-related attitudes and beliefs (Buchholz, 1976), while others are quite specifically concerned with attributional styles.

The approach of developing a work-specific individual difference measure has been taken by those from both personality and occupational psychology traditions. However, there are a number of self-evident drawbacks. Rarely, if ever, do researchers pay much attention to the aetiology of the trait or dimension being measured. This could be an important feature in understanding developmental features associated with the trait. Second, almost by definition the measures have limited applicability, as they are designed specifically for the workplace and are therefore presumably restricted to it in terms of predictability. Third, the background theoretical work on the processes, mechanisms and phenomena associated with the trait (which explains how and why the trait determines behaviour) is not done sufficiently or sufficiently well, no doubt because the task is seen primarily as an applied one. Finally, there is frequently a confounding or overlap between the independent and dependent variable leading to spurious results.

The current literature shows sporadic rather than sustained effort and some evidence of faddishness regarding the choice of both independent and dependent variable. Nevertheless, there is considerable evidence that this approach may prove very fruitful, e.g. the work on occupationally salient attributional style (Furnham, Sadka and Brewin, 1991).

The concept of 'fit' and 'misfit' at work

Probably because of its intuitive appeal this approach has a fairly long history (Pervin, 1967). The idea is quite simple: based on personality predispositions, some jobs are more suitable for the individual than others. Based on a comparable analysis of both the person and the job it may be possible accurately to measure the degree of fit (which is desirable) or misfit (undesirable). The work of Holland is most relevant here. Variations on this theme include:

- Whether the analysis is based more on jobs or individuals. Clearly, to obtain a measure of fit, both people and jobs need to be analysed and measured; however, the measurement of the one is nearly always based on the concepts/language developed by the other. In most cases, and for obvious reasons, the conceptual language of fit is based on personality or individual differences rather than jobs.
- Impressionistic vs. 'geometric'. A second crucial feature is whether the concept of 'fit' is simply subjectively impressionistic or, rather, is objective, measurable and 'geometric'. Few would argue that the former approach is the more desirable but there are certain difficulties associated with the latter approach, notably the complexity of the multi-dimensional geometric model.
- Similarity vs. complementarity. There is extensive, if somewhat equivocal literature on similarity and attraction between individuals, which offers three hypotheses: similar people are attracted; the attraction of opposites; and the concept of complementarity. Though there is no evidence for the attraction of opposites concept (which in the context of Pervin's work becomes the misfit hypothesis), it remains uncertain whether the similarity or complementarity hypothesis is to be supported.

This approach, like the others, is not without its problems, especially the issue of whether one is looking for a pattern and formulae. One approach to this area is to devise a limited number of types (of people and/or jobs) and show their relationships in some mosaic or pattern. This allows for some nice geometric (Euclidean) calculations. On the other hand, it may be possible to write a formula that expresses fit in the form of simultaneous equations.

'Fit' studies are by definition correlational and not causal; hence it is not possible to infer directionality, such as the idea that misfit *leads to* absenteeism. Indeed, it is quite possible and feasible to derive hypotheses and explanations with fit as the dependent, not the independent variable. Finally, everything in this approach is based on the veridical nature, sensitivity, comprehensiveness and clarity of conceptualization of the variables that make up the fit. Where these are (for instance) conceived too vaguely or widely, the resultant fit measures are practically worthless.

Because of its predictive power, this remains one of the most promising areas of research. Predictably, the concept of fit has been popular in such research areas as vocational choice and 'problems' at work, for instance stress and health. However, the real promise of the fit–misfit approach lies in predicting motivation and satisfaction at work, an area still currently neglected.

Longitudinal studies of people in work

It is almost universally recognized that longitudinal research is invaluable in examining how a multitude of variables (personality, psychographic, demographic) change over time, relate to one another at different periods and *predict* behaviour. That is to say, the concept of cause is best examined longitudinally. However, it is also widely recognized that longitudinal research is fiendishly difficult, expensive and problematic. Nevertheless, some studies have examined personality at work over time.

Again, studies come in many different forms:

- Short vs. long time spans. It is not always clear what comprises a 'longitudinal' time span – a year, five years, ten years? Studies of less than a couple of years cannot reveal substantial differences which operate over longer periods such as decades. On the other hand, studies carried out over very long periods (twenty years or more) have difficulties in accounting for drop-outs, etc.
- Within or between organizations. Some organizations have sponsored or allowed research to be conducted within their organization. Within-organization studies, by definition, seriously restrict the range and type of variables that can be examined. On the other hand, between-organizational longitudinal studies (following individuals over time) frequently do not allow for sufficient comparisons.
- Retrospective vs. prospective. Some longitudinal studies are done by archival research, where past records are compared to current data. Where these records exist, the studies are usually robust, useful and

sensitive. Alternatively, one can begin a study now and plan it into the future. The latter approach is clearly preferable because one has more control over what is measured, how and when.

Longitudinal research has problems only if it is done badly or, of course, if it is discontinued for one reason or another. Scarcity of resources frequently means that good research is not done. A major problem is too few subjects, or not knowing whether 'drop-outs' occur for systematic reasons. Tracing people's behaviour at work over lengthy periods is difficult, but restricting numbers because of costs only limits the generalizability of the research. A second problem is poor measurement of the variables. Either because one is limited to the organization's own records (such as application and assessment forms) or because measurement techniques have substantially improved over the years, early measures may be psycho-metrically unsound, thus threatening the quality of the results. Finally, there is the issue of restricted range of variables. Studies done on particular individuals (e.g. a class of students), or of employees from a particular organization, are by definition restricted and thus may not be reliable. In addition, between-organization variables cannot be considered. Clearly, this is only important if these unmeasured variables are significant, but one can know this only if they are examined.

Biographical or case-history research

This approach, akin to the 'great-man' theory of history, examines in detail the life of one individual to see what clues it provides as to which biographi-cal factors predict job success. There are not many examples of this approach but those that do exist differ on various criteria:

- Individuals vs. groups. Some approaches consider only the lives of particular individuals, while others consider a whole family (a dynasty) or people who have attended a particular institution and done well later in life.
- Monetary vs. 'other' success criteria. It is rather difficult to decide which criteria of success (or failure) are appropriate to use in order to select the 'successful' people to examine.
- Impressionistic vs. scholarly. Some studies on successful entrepreneurs are in the 'best seller' tradition where the 'readability' of the story is more important than obtaining or understanding the facts. On the other hand, scholarly biographies rarely interpret how, when and why biographical factors predict occupational success.

The biographical approach is intuitively appealing, and often most inter-esting to the general public, but it is very uncertain to what extent it can and does inform the issue of personality determinants of work success. Major problems include the fact that only highly successful people are considered. Thus there is a very serious sampling problem because there appears to be no theoretical reason why particular people are chosen for analysis. This means that the data used are highly unrepresentative. Second, there is almost never a control group. That is, there is no comparison person or group to compare to those studied in detail. It is therefore impossible to understand precisely which factors do or do not relate to occupational success. Finally, a-theoretical research means no systematic testing of hypotheses. Rarely, if ever, do biographers attempt to seek out particular facts to test hypotheses.

A RESEARCH MODEL

Much of the research literature in the field of personality and behaviour at work is theoretically naive and methodologically weak. How, then, might one conceive of a useful model to derive theoretically based hypotheses which may be tested empirically? A major problem at present appears to be that practitioners (and some researchers) hope to find personality correlates of occupational behaviour without understanding the reason for this relationship.

The research model set out below attempts to describe some of the major factors that affect the relationship between personality and occupational variables. Figure 2.1 shows a simple model which may help to demonstrate some of the variables that explain the relationship between personality variables and work-related behaviour.

1 The primary interest of practitioners such as personnel and human resource professionals is the simple relationship between personality and work-related behaviour. Two features need to be mentioned which can be seen from Figure 2.1. The first is that the line between personality characteristics and occupational variables is discontinuous, emphasizing the important point that this relationship is moderated by a whole range of other, significantly important variables. The second feature is that the relationship between the two variables is bi-directional. That is, personality factors influence work-related behaviours (the predispositional model), while organizational and occupational variables shape and selectively reward personality functioning (the socialization model). Thus, the relationship between personality and work-related outcomes is *neither* direct *nor* uni-causal.

2 The second 'path' in this model is the traditional occupational/industrial psychology model that is well informed about personality theory. Nearly all reputable theories describe some phenomenon, mechanism or process which causes the trait. Indeed, if they did not, the theories would be merely descriptive. Different theories offer very different accounts of the 'workings' of the trait. For instance, Eysenck's (1967) theory of *extraversion* is based on the concept of arousal which leads to many predictions

Organizational behaviour

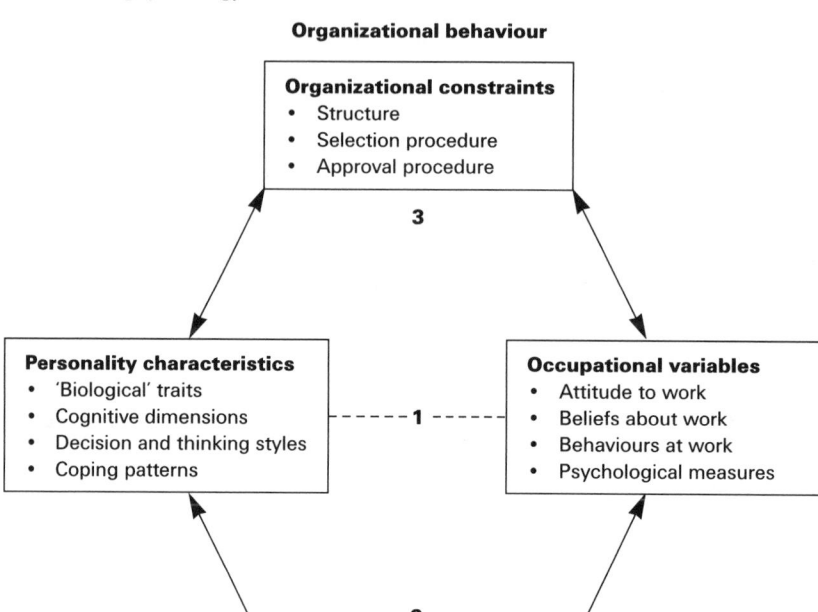

Figure 2.1 A research model for examining the relationship between personality and work

about the choice, avoidance and performance in specific situations. Some of the phenomena or processes associated with a trait or personality system are subtle and complex, while others are highly simplistic. Clearly the number, type and precision of hypotheses derived from the personality theory as they relate to occupational variables depends on a thorough understanding of the personality mechanisms and processes involved.

3 The third 'path' is of organizational or structural (and procedural) factors that mediate between an individual and the organization in which he/she works. Organizations all have a formal (and informal) structure which can be described on an organizational chart. Such a chart indicates who reports to whom. It shows how multi-layered or flat the organization is, and the paths of communication up, down and sideways in the organization. Organizations also very quickly develop norms of working as well as specific procedures which may endure over very long periods of time. These formal procedures and informal work norms can have a very powerful effect on an individual's work-related behaviour, so moderating

the natural effects of their personality. Indeed it is from this 'path' that one gets the concept of *person-job fit* which has so influenced vocational and occupational psychology (see Chapter 3). Organizational factors may promote and facilitate a person's behaviour at work or constrain it.

ELEMENTS IN THE MODEL

One of the features that frustrates any reviewer in this area is the loose use of terminology. Hence it becomes difficult to specify the basic factors in the model and how they are related to each other. Figure 2.2 shows five basic factors and how they relate to occupational behaviour.

- *Ability*: this refers to the extent to which a person can *efficiently* carry out multiple processes in co-ordination to achieve a specified goal. They range from relatively simple dextrous, hand–eye co-ordination tasks to complex intellectual decision-making processes, and are thus related to intelligence but distinguished from it.
- *Demographic factors*: this refers to background factors such as sex, age, class, education. Demographic factors usually relate to biographic factors in the life of a particular person – e.g. birth order, occupation of parents, type of school attended – and are distinguishable from psychographic factors which refer to beliefs and values.
- *Intelligence*: this refers to the individual's capacity for abstract and critical thinking. A large number of controversies surround this concept, for instance whether it is uni- or multi-dimensional; to what extent it is inherited or learnt; and how it should be measured. Despite all the concerns of investigators, few doubt the effect of intelligence on organizational behaviour.
- *Motivation*: this, like intelligence, is a multi-dimensional, abstract concept that refers to the tendency to attend to some stimuli rather than others, with accompanying emotion, and the drive to cause some actions rather than others. Hence one talks of the strength of particular motivations, such as a weak need for achievement (low nAch).
- *Personality*: this refers to all those fundamental traits or characteristics of the person (or of people generally) that endure over time and that account for consistent patterns of responses to everyday situations. Personality traits supposedly account for the what, why and how of social behaviour

The model presented in Figure 2.2 is important for four reasons. First, it separates the five features distinguished above. Second, the bi-directionality of the arrows suggests that all these factors are reciprocally influential. Third, the concept of personality is placed at the centre of the model to suggest its precedence in explanatory terms over the others. Finally, it is suggested that *each* of these factors reciprocally influences occupational behaviour both on its own and in combination with others.

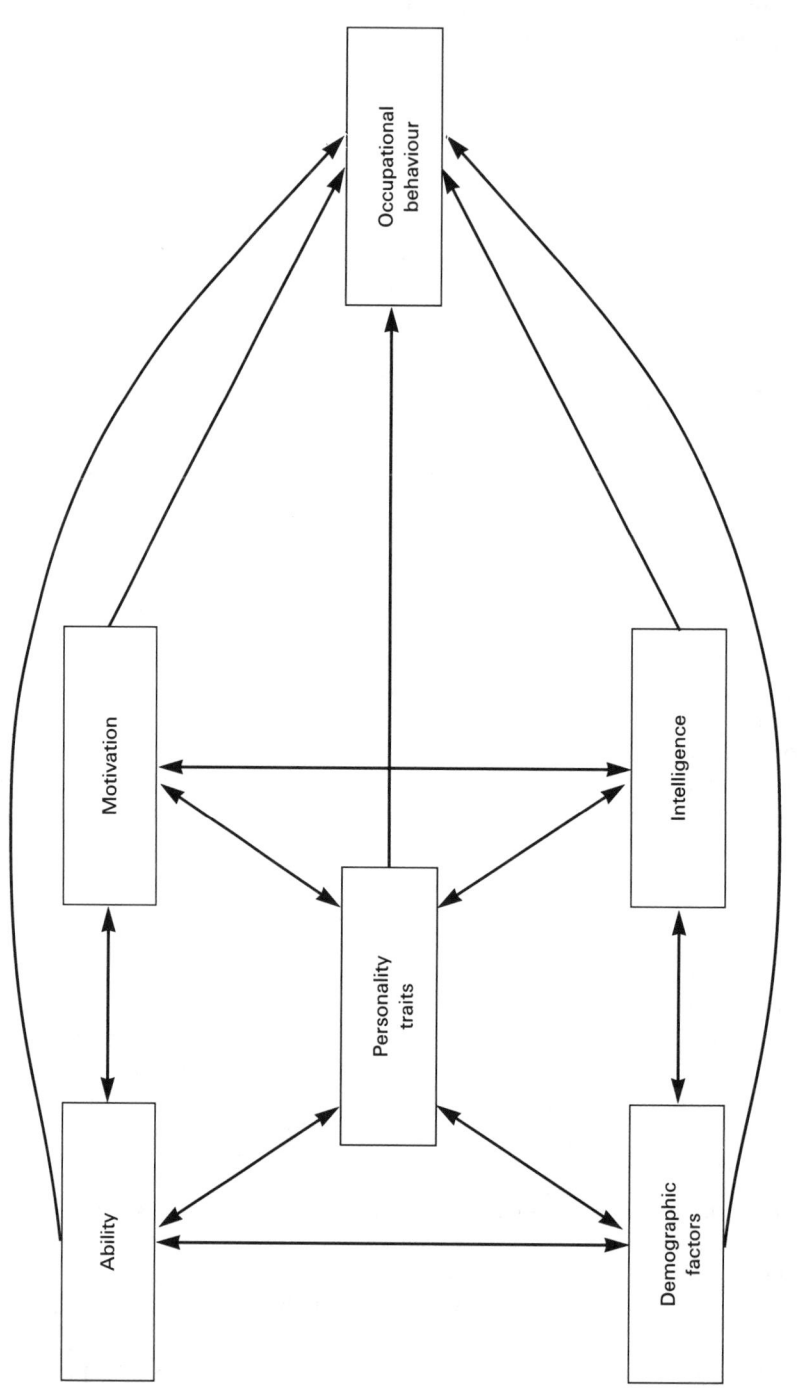

Figure 2.2 Some of the main factors predicting occupational behaviour

THE TRAIT MODEL

The trait approach to the prediction of social behaviour is fairly straight-forward. For the layperson (committing the fundamental attribution error) it is a completely self-evident truism that work-related behaviours such as absenteeism, motivation, productivity and trainability are primarily a function of personality and individual differences. Many will argue, with passion born out of 'personal experience', that various personality types are either ideal (most suitable) while others are completely inappropriate (least suit-able) for various jobs. They may cite various cases they know of or point out that successful people in similar jobs appear to share similar characteris-tics. Thus, many entrepreneurs appear to be extraverted, self-confident, non-risk-averse, while 'boffin' research scientists are nearly always intro-verted, conservative and obsessive.

Currently the term *trait* appears to have been replaced, at least in the jargon of human resource professionals and management consultants, by the term *competency*. Is this concept of corporate competency a useful clarification or just another popular myth?

Managers at all levels are encouraged to list the corporate/organization competencies that any employee in the company needs to operate success-fully. These competencies are then used in selection, promotion, appraisal, counselling and vocational guidance. These lists, which, managers are encouraged to believe, are quite specific in their organization (or part of it), are derived in a variety of ways. Sometimes an autocratic CEO simply sketches them on the back of a share certificate; at other times all the directors undergo a 'focused' interview and the results are collated. Still other methods include group discussions, the use of repertory grids, biodata analysis or, more simply, 'tweaking' other lists to suit the current circumstances.

Having obtained their 'unique and comprehensive' list of competencies, organizations set out to devise ways of measuring them so that applicants and employees can be 'compared and contrasted'. How well and accurately this is done is another question.

- But before that is considered, it is important to ask what exactly are these 'competencies'? Are they just a new name for traits and abilities? Or are they like skills? The former imply cross-situational stability and cross-temporal reliability: i.e. they are relatively permanent. Furthermore, there is a wealth of studies attempting to specify the basic traits and abilities which are common across all people, irrespective of the organiza-tion where they work. There is a body of research on this topic which could be most fruitfully tapped. On the other hand, if competencies are not stable, how, when and why do they change? Do they decay if not used? Likewise, do they improve with practice?
- How are the competencies related to one another? A list of competencies is nearly always just that – a list. But human abilities are clearly related.

Depending on intelligence, thinking styles (i.e. convergent vs. divergent) and temperament, certain human factors are clearly related. For instance, extraverts tend to be more socially skilled; more likely to be 'evening people'; more likely to excel in brief 'timed' tests; more likely to be involved in accidents, etc., than introverts. Inevitably some competencies will be related and some unrelated to each other, but which? What, in short, is the structure of competencies?

- Are competencies primarily learned or inherited (or both)? Clearly there are important implications of the question – if they are primarily learned (e.g. interpersonal skills) they can be taught; if inherited (general intelligence) they have to be selected. This leads on to the thorny ground of the heredity vs. environment debate and, despite caution, the question remains both important and valid. For instance, if they are learned, are they best taught at a particular age (say adolescence or younger) and in a particular way? Do some people learn the competencies more effectively and efficiently than others?

- Are they likely to be found in some groups more than others? It is quite possible that competencies are found among certain demographic (young men), linguistic (Francophone), religious (Protestant), etc., groups more than others. Certainly some groups of people excel at sport; others at science; so it might not be unreasonable to assume that organizational competencies are found more in some groups than others. But which? And how does one square the selection of these people with equal opportunity and other non-discriminatory legislation?

- Are competencies dimensional or categorial? Is it the case that competencies have a mutually exclusive equality about them and that people can and should be categorized into types, or is it the case that competencies are dimensional and people fall along a continuum, from being highly, through fairly, moderate or average, poor and low competence? If the latter (i.e. dimensional) what are the anchors of that dimension and what the intervening markers?

- What is the universe of competencies from which specific organizational lists were derived? Is there a finite, exhaustive, comprehensive, universal list of competencies from which to devise a subset? Indeed, where does one find this list? Or are competencies so numerous, so subtle, so variable that no such list could ever be derived? What strikes a reviewer of numerous organization-specific competencies is how similar they are, both in the number of competencies specified and in the fact that what is suggested is a relatively simple list. If competencies are organization-specific, then by definition organizations cannot be compared. Yet such specificity is highly unlikely.

- Are all competencies equally reliably measurable? The whole point of specifying competencies is so that people can be measured, compared, tracked over time, rated before and after training courses, etc. But how are they measured? What sort of technique should be used – behavioural observation? questionnaires? ratings? of the subject, his subordinates, or both?, etc. Each assessment method has problems associated with it leading to systematic bias and error. Furthermore, not all competencies are likely to be equally reliably measured. It is easier to measure certain traits (extraversion) than others (intelligence). Many proven psycho-metrically valid tests exist to measure certain abilities, traits and beliefs but others, e.g. 'forward planning', 'coping with change', are very difficult to measure. Comparing people on unreliable measures is of course highly problematic. Indeed, how does one measure common sense or ability to motivate others?

- Are the competencies the sole or even the major determinant of behaviour in the organization? This is similar to the old question of whether personality traits determine social behaviour. Presumably the competen-cies are chosen because they represent the fundamental abilities/capacities needed to do the job well. But does having a competency mean that it will be used? And what other factors prevent competent people from performing? For instance, people might have less desirable personality traits which prevent them doing the job well, irrespective of their competency. Anxiety, obsessionality, phobias, or poor personal coping strategies for everyday stress may mean that competencies are never allowed to manifest themselves in competent behaviour. Equally, various organizational procedures and rules may prevent competent behaviour.
- Can one compensate for not having a particular competency? It is possible that people can function quite well in an organization without having a particular competency or indeed set of competencies. They might do this through hard work, delegation, redefinition of their job, etc. People with specific physical handicaps have been shown to triumph over considerable difficulties, so is it possible that absence of some competencies can be overcome?
- What does it mean to lack a particular competency? Is the opposite of competence incompetence or no competence? What kinds of performance will be impaired if that competency does not exist, or exists in insufficient amount? There is quite a difference between knowing how to do a job, doing it badly (incompetence) and not knowing how to do it (no competence). Indeed, what is the cause of incompetence?
- Are 'people-related' competencies different from 'object-related' competencies? Some people are attracted to computers, accounting systems, etc., because they are logical, predictable and rational, while others shun these and prefer to deal with people so that intuitions, sensitivities, etc., can be used. Managerial jobs usually demand both competencies, but is it possible to find each equally?
- Do organizational competencies change over time? All organizations live in a dynamic environment which demands adaptation and innovation. Does selecting a clearly homogeneous workforce (in terms of salient and non-salient competencies) render an organization less able to deal with

change? From this point of view perhaps the most salient, overriding competency to seek out is ability to deal with change (or indeed seeker-after-change) and the most important to reject are rigidity, conservatism and resistance to change.

Psychological questions are neither trivial nor simple, nor should they be dismissed as of academic interest only. The answer to them is of crucial importance for any organization in search of the competencies of their executives and employees.

THE IDENTIFICATION OF AN OCCUPATIONAL TRAIT

Which personality traits predict occupational success? There are, to the outsider to personality theory, a perplexing list from which to choose. More importantly, how are traits identified? How do they come to be part of the canon of literature?

The number of single-trait studies are legion and include such dimensions as authoritarianism, achievement motivation, A/B-type behaviour, field dependence–independence, conservatism, locus of control, just-world beliefs, assertiveness, Protestant work ethic beliefs, self-monitoring, etc. Three points need to be made about this list, which may extend to nearly eighty traits or more. First, although the factors on the list are usually described as traits or dimensions, some researchers resist the term trait and prefer the terms type, style or need, because, while they believe the dimension that they have isolated is stable over time and across situations and highly predictive of certain types of behaviour, the term trait can have certain implications which are not necessarily inherent to their approach. For instance, in some contexts, the term trait suggests a biological rather than a learning aetiology, or may imply a continuous variable where in fact the dimension is discontinuous. Hence some authors who describe single-dimension personality or individual difference variables reinforce the ascription of the term trait.

Second, the origin of these traits is highly varied. Some have arisen from cognitive, social and clinical psychology, and some even from research on perception. Some, such as the trait of authoritarianism, might have first been articulated within a psychoanalytic framework, while others such as locus of control originated firmly within a behaviourist tradition. Hence there are very wide differences in how these traits are measured and the terminology employed in their use. Despite this, all single-trait theories share some major assumptions.

Third, it is rare that any single-trait measure is entirely unique in terms of the way it is conceived, described or measured. Although there are exceptions, it is frequently the case that researchers, after extensive reading, notice a consistent pattern in previous studies which makes sense of their results and which could be explained in terms of a 'new' trait. Frequently then, the origin of a trait term can be ascribed to a particular source or research team, but the ideas that are articulated can be traced back to many other authors including those who were not psychologists or who never actively conducted research.

Despite the enormous number of 'single-trait' theories in psychology with variously different origins, terminologies and measurement techniques, they frequently share similar histories. That is, the developmental history from the first published study on a new trait to world-wide research efforts often follows a standard pattern.

The development of single-trait theories appears to go through most of the following stages. There are, of course, many problems associated with any stage-wise theory – how long each stage lasts; what determines movement from the one stage to the next; whether one can skip a stage or not; whether one might return to an earlier stage; and whether all phenomena pass through all stages (Furnham and Bochner, 1986). Despite these obvious and important shortcomings, seven stages of development can be identified.

Identification of the phenomenon

This may occur as a result of laboratory experimentation or observation in a clinic, at work or through critical reading. It may occur when a researcher operationalizes that which is well known in literature into a psychological measure such as was the case with the Protestant work ethic (Furnham, 1990). But what is more normally the case is that a researcher observes a psychological phenomenon to which he or she gives a name. Examples are legion: Seligman (1975) noticed learned helplessness, the behaviour in dogs which later became translated into an attribution-style questionnaire to identify the same behaviour in humans. Lerner (1980) observed that people tended to blame victims of misfortune for their own fate and this observation was developed into self-report measures of the Just World. Rosenman *et al.*'s (1975) studies on coronary-prone behaviour led to the development of the original Type A behaviour description. A number of points need to be made about this first stage. First, the person or persons who originally make the observations need not necessarily be the ones who develop the single-trait theory or the self-report measure. Second, the phenomenon is often new only in the sense that it has not been recorded before in quite the same way. Third, this stage often occurs in the laboratory as a by-product of observational studies, or occasionally from the systematic recordings of clinicians who note consistent relationships in the behaviour of their patients. Very rarely, if ever, are the researchers intentionally engaged in developing a trait measure of theory.

Replication of the effect

The second stage is characterized by replications and considerably more experimental work on the nature of the effect observed. An excellent illustration of this can be found in Lerner's (1980) book on Just World beliefs which reports on numerous experiments using the concept. The idea of this phase is to test the robustness of the findings, often by subtle yet simple means: a case of data gathering in an attempt to find support for observations made, while other series of studies attempt to test the various hypotheses that make up the nascent theory. These studies are usually reported in the first paper or book to describe the behaviour pattern/phenomenon.

The development of a self-report measure

Despite the fact that the original researchers may not be personality, clinical or social psychologists, and may in fact have little faith in self-report measures, the next stage does involve the development of a self-report measure. The questionnaires used may be of highly variable psychometric quality and the research that goes into establishing them somewhat inadequate. Reliability, validity and normative statistics may be fairly minimal to begin with, and it is unlikely that the first versions to be published are validated in a manner acceptable to psychometricians. Indeed, it is precisely because the originators of the concept are not psychometricians (being clinicians or experimentalists) that they do not always know the minimum criteria required of a good self-report measure. Frequently the self-report measure is developed some years after the concept/behaviour pattern has been described in the literature. In this case, what might occur is that, over the space of a few years, a number of similar (but not highly correlated) measures will be developed. For instance over a ten-year period at least half a dozen assertiveness inventories were developed by different researchers in the social skills literature (Furnham and Henderson, 1981, 1983). Similarly, there are about the same number of tests all attempting to measure the Type A behaviour pattern (Linden, 1987). More popular concepts, such as locus of control, might have at least a dozen self-report questionnaires all supposedly providing a reliable and valid measure of the concept (Furnham, 1986).

Validation of the measure

The fourth phase may continue for some time and involves numerous experimental and correlational studies of various sorts, all aiming to validate the measure and its underlying concepts. Studies are often of the kind that make up a PhD and include a programmatic series aimed to test corollaries of the theory. What links the studies is the uni-dimensional trait measure used to assess the independent variable. A large number of these studies are essentially attempts to establish the concurrent, construct and predictive validity of the self-report scale by correlating it with other well-known measures or behaviours. The danger of this sort of approach, as Kline (1983) has pointed out, is that correlating a new measure with an established but itself poorly psychometrized measure does not provide good evidence of the validity of the theory or research. Some studies provide nice evidence of the construct validity of the measure, but, possibly because of the difficulty and expense associated with longitudinal work, a glance at the citation index of any well-known self-report measure shows the extent to which, though some may be by the original author and his/her acolytes, validation studies are commonly done by researchers from different laboratories. Paradoxically, it is not lack of validity that prevents research into a measure or concept, but more likely the extent to which the measure taps the *Zeitgeist* of (North American) psychology.

Factor analysis work and multi-dimensionality

Although researchers may identify what they believe to be a single, albeit complex, dimension or phenomenon, and hence develop a uni-dimensional scale, subsequent multivariate statistics (cluster analysis, factor analysis, multi-dimensional scaling) nearly always show the measure to be multi-dimensional with specific interpretable primary factors which may be orthogonal or oblique. Assertiveness questionnaires, for instance, have been shown to tap four quite different types of assertiveness depending on whether the behaviour is positive or negative, initiating or responsive (Furnham and Henderson, 1984).

Similarly, many distinctions have been made in the A-type literature, such as healthy/adaptive–unhealthy/unadaptive A and B behaviours, but factor analysis of the widely used Jenkins Activity survey (Jenkins *et al.*, 1979) revealed the following four factors: the original Type A; speed and impatience; job involvement; hard-driving and competitive. Considerable debate still surrounds the psychometric properties of these scales (Boyd and Begley, 1987). Locus of control scales have also proved to be multi-dimensional though there is predictably some debate as to the number of dimensions, their relationship and how they should be labelled (Collins, 1974).

Factor analytic work usually poses problems for the original author because the theory upon which the measure is founded usually assumes a uni-dimensional concept. At least three responses are common. One is to maintain that the concept, measure and trait are unified at a higher order (i.e. super factors) and that, although it may have various components, these are second-order (secondary) distinctions/factors which do not threaten the theory. A second approach is to revise the scale, either by attempting to eradicate items that load on irrelevant factors or by building a truly multi-dimensional instrument. An example of the former is Snyder's

(1974) attempt to revise the self-monitoring scale after its multi-dimensional nature had been clearly established (Furnham and Capon, 1983). A third approach is to do a meta-analysis of factor-analytic studies, decide on the factor structure and accept the original scale as multi-dimensional. This phase may last many years but may help resolve equivocal findings when they can be attributed to the multi-dimensional structure of the trait measure.

Multiple, multi-dimensional measures

The malaise following repeated psychometric investigations into an established uni-trait measure often leads scholars to despair because, as has been noted, it is uncertain at which level analysis should proceed. A common response however is for a team of psychometrically oriented researchers to develop a new, better scale or self-report device. These new 'improved' measures often have various specific features. First, they are nearly always multi-dimensional in the sense that they provide subscale scores which may or may not be combined into a single score depending on the needs of the researchers. Hence, Levensohn (1974) developed a three-dimensional locus of control scale (internal, chance and powerful others). Second, many researchers develop sphere-specific scales to measure the trait, belief or behaviour system within a very restricted range of behaviours, as this has been shown to improve the predictive validity considerably. Thus there are measures of *health* locus of control (Lau and Ware, 1981), *weight* locus of control (Saltzer, 1982), *mental health* locus of control (Calhoun, Pierce and Dawes, 1978), *dental health* locus of control (Ludenia and Denham, 1983), *political* locus of control (Davis, 1983) and *economic* locus of control (Furnham, 1986). There are, of course, problems with this proliferation of measures because studies using different measures are not strictly comparable. Second, it is possible that a person may score highly on one measure (internal economic locus of control), but low on a related measure (external mental health locus of control). Some authors have attempted to produce not so much a multi-dimensional measure as sphere-specific measures which set out to measure the same beliefs (i.e. locus of control or just world) in different contexts (intra-, interpersonal, socio-political) (Furnham and Procter, 1989).

Doubts about the original concept

It is not infrequent that, after a decade or so of intensive psychometric work on a measure/concept, authors begin to have doubts about its conceptual and psychometric status. Researchers concerned with the measurement of assertion construct now believe it is outmoded and should be relinquished. 'The construction has proven to be vague, difficult to define and laden with assumptions reflecting traditional rather than more contemporary views of personality and behaviour change. In the future, we need to concentrate more on response- and situation-specific behaviour falling under the rubric of social skills–social competence and retire the assertiveness (assertion) construct' (Galassi, Galassi and Vedder, 1981, p. 330). 'The Type A coronary-prone behaviour pattern, when seen as a global construct has lost its usefulness. Recent empirical evidence is reviewed to justify this claim. It is clear that much initial promise of the Type A construct has not been borne out, and it is argued that only the hostility component of the Type A construct continues to possess predictive and concurrent validity and therefore, usefulness' (Linden, 1987, p. 177).

In other words, the complexity of measurement and the equivocal nature of the findings leads reviewers to conclude that the original concept/ phenomenon/behaviour pattern, and all questionnaires that attempt to measure it, should be abandoned, either in favour of a new concept, usually a subscale of the former, or else totally in that the original behaviour pattern is too unstable to be considered as a trait. This stage is characterized, not like the last two by increased empirical work, but by theoretical reconceptualization. Naturally, the commitment of researchers to a particular concept or scale means that they are loath to relinquish it, but happy to make further attempts to refine it.

Acceptance and 'text-bookization'

Having gone through the above seven stages and having survived the last one, the concept and its measures are usually accepted into the canon of individual differences measures. A sure sign of this process is inclusion in the numerous, benevolent, eclectic textbooks on personality. By this stage, there is probably a sizeable literature on the concept and the measure, as shown by citation counts. However, one should not assume that, because a test (and concept) has won through the above baptismal and confirmatory process, it is therefore necessarily a psychometrically valid, theoretically important or diagnostically useful measure. Small bands of zealots wedded to the original ideas in the scale can propel a measure of dubious theoretical and psychometrical validity into the textbooks and research consciousness. Equally, extremely good measures based on sound theory and careful psychometric work can get 'lost' and never make it to the laboratories of the world.

Like all stage-wise theories the above sequence has its limitations and unanswered questions. Do theories/measures have to go through all the stages sequentially? Can some stages be skipped? Does development have to be linear or can it be cyclical? What prompts movement from one stage to another?

Despite these unresolved questions, it may be useful to adapt the above stage-wise model to evaluate the progress of a trait measure, or indeed to predict further developments. Thus, for instance, one might predict that recent work showing that the Kirton (1976) adaptor–innovator measure is multi-dimensional (with three clear interpretable factors) would mean that it has reached the sixth stage, and that a multi-dimensional measure will soon be developed. Similarly, despite doubts about the validity of both measures, it is probable that sphere-specific measures (i.e. work-related, non-work-related) of both assertiveness and A type are constructed.

It should not be assumed that a robust, valid and pretty universally accepted measure undergoes no further development or refinement. Through exhaustive and extensive work on its factor structure, construct validity and theoretical parsimony, Eysenck and Eysenck (1985) have revised the EPQ-R in order to make the measure as psychometrically sound as possible.

PERSONALITY AND ORGANIZATIONAL BEHAVIOUR

Although laypeople view individual differences and personality as the most central, crucial, salient and interesting of psychologists' many missions, academic psychologists, particularly industrial/organizational psychologists, tend to take the opposite view. Despite the fact that I/O psychologists usually proclaim that personality testing is useful in neither selection nor the prediction of productivity, many human resources personnel as well as negotiators and economic columnists stress the importance of understanding individual differences. Of course the word 'personality' is used differently: laypeople usually mean public reputation, while psychologists usually mean structure and dynamic inner processes which are private. 'Personality' refers to stylistic consistencies in social behaviour which are a reflection of an inner structure and process.

Most laypeople are type rather than trait theorists. Types are categories, syndromes, trait summaries. They are the oldest and simplest way to classify people, hence their abiding popularity, but they still find a role in modern psychology. Traits refer to single dimensions made up of related components. Thus the trait of neuroticism, isolated by many researchers as a fundamental and unique trait, includes behaviours and cognitions associated with guilt, low self-esteem, depression, phobia, anxiety and psychosomatic illnesses. Both trait and type theories provide useful heuristics with which to describe people. However, laypeople shy away from using 'negative' traits like neuroticism, preferring more 'positive' traits such as insightful. While laypeople prefer to look for positive correlates of occupational success, many psychologists are interested in (equally predictive) negative correlates of success. It seems as if the layperson infers failure from success while psychologists infer success variables, processes, structures and criteria from failure.

CONCLUSION

This chapter focused on the role of personality and other individual differences in the world of work. It seems that there are six rather different approaches to studying individual differences as they relate to occupational behaviour. Each method has its strengths and weaknesses, and through each tradition it may be possible to build up a picture of which, how and when individual differences affect work-related behaviour. A research model was proposed which looked at some of the moderating variables and constraints which affect the relationship between personality and work variables. The trait model was considered, as was the concept of competencies, which is currently much used but little understood. To some extent traits may be seen as akin to the concept of skill. Quite how occupationally relevant traits are identified was also considered rather sceptically, as it was suggested that some researchers in this field might sacrifice veridical findings for popular acclaim.

REFERENCES

Argyle, M., Furnham, A. and Graham, J. (1981) *Social Situations*. Cambridge: Cambridge University Press.

Boyd, D. and Begley, T. (1987) Assessing the type A behaviour pattern with the Jenkins Activity Survey. *British Journal of Medical Psychology*, 60, 155–61.

Brewin, C. (1988) *Cognitive Foundations of Clinical Psychology*. London: Erlbaum.

Buchholz, R. (1976) Measurement of beliefs. *Human Relations*, 29, 1177–88.

Calhoun, A., Pierce, J. and Dawes, A. (1978) Attributions theory concepts and outpatients' perceptions of the causal locus of their psychological problems. *Journal of Community Psychology*, 1, 52–8.

Cattell, R. (1971) *The Scientific Analysis of Personality*. Baltimore: Penguin.

Collins, B. (1974) Four components of the Rotter internal external scale. *Journal of Personality and Social Psychology*, 29, 381–91.

Cook, J., Hepworth, D., Wall, T. and Warr, P. (1981) *The Experience of Work*. London: Academic Press.

Davis, J. (1983) Does authority generalize? *Political Psychology*, 4, 101–20.

Eysenck, H. (1967) *The Biological Basis of Personality*. Springfield, IL: Thomas.

Eysenck, H. and Eysenck, M. (1985) *Personality and Individual Differences: A Natural Science Approach*. London: Plenum.

Furnham, A. (1986) Economic locus of control. *Human Relations*, 39, 29–43.

Furnham, A. (1990) *The Protestant Work Ethic*. London: Routledge.

Furnham, A. and Argyle, M. (eds) (1981) *The Psychology of Social Situations*. Oxford: Pergamon.

Furnham, A. and Bochner, S. (1986) *Culture Shock*. London: Methuen.

Furnham, A. and Capon, M. (1983) Social skills and self monitoring processes. *Personality and Individual Differences*, 4, 171–8.

Furnham, A. and Henderson, M. (1981) Sex differences in self-reported assertiveness in Britain. *British Journal of Clinical Psychology*, 20, 50–62.

Furnham, A. and Henderson, M. (1983) The mote in thy brother's eye and the beam in thy own. *British Journal of Psychology*, 74, 381–9.

Furnham, A. and Henderson, M. (1984) Assessing assertiveness. *Behavioural Assessment*, 6, 79–88.

Furnham, A. and Procter, E. (1989) Belief in a just world. *British Journal of Social Psychology, 28*, 365–84.

Furnham, A., Sadka, V. and Brewin, C. (1991) The development of an occupational attribution style questionnaire. *Journal of Occupational Psychology, 13*, 27–39.

Galassi, J., Galassi, J. and Vedder, M. (1981) Perspectives on assertion as a social skills model. In J. Wine and H. Smye (eds) *Social Competence*. New York: Guilford Press.

Jenkins, C., Zyzanski, S. and Rosenman, R. (1979) *Jenkins Activity Survey Manual.* New York: Psychological Corporation.

Kirton, M. (1976) Adaptors and innovators: a description and measure. *Journal of Applied Psychology, 61*, 622–9.

Kline, P. (1978) *OOQ and OQP Personality Tests.* Windsor: NFER.

Kline, P. (1983) *Personality Measurement and Theory.* London: Hutchinson.

Lau, R. and Ware, J. (1981) Refinements in the measurements of health specific locus of control beliefs. *Medical Care, 19*, 1147–58.

Lerner, M. (1980) *The Belief in a Just World.* New York: Plenum.

Levensohn, M. (1974) Activism and powerful others. *Journal of Personality Assessment, 38*, 377–83.

Linden, W. (1987) On the impending death of type A construct. *Canadian Journal of Behavioural Sciences, 19*, 178–90.

Ludenia, K. and Denham, G. (1983) Dental outpatients: health locus of control correlates. *Journal of Clinical Psychology, 39*, 854–8.

Pervin, L. (1967) *Personality: Theory and Research.* New York: Wiley.

Rosenman, R., Brand, R., Jenkins, C., Friedman, M., Strauss, R. and Wurm, M. (1975) Coronary heart disease in the Western Collaboration Group Study. *Journal of the American Medical Association, 233*, 872–7.

Rotter, J. (1966) Generalized expectancies for internal vs. external control of reinforcement. *Psychological Monographs, 80*, 601.

Saltzer, E. (1982) The weight locus of control. *Journal of Personality Assessment, 46*, 620–8.

Seligman, M. (1975) *Helplessness: On Depression, Development and Death.* San Francisco: Freeman.

Snyder, M. (1974) Self-monitoring of expressive behaviour. *Journal of Personality and Social Psychology, 30*, 526–37.

Strelau, J. (1981) *Temperament, Personality, Activity.* London: Academic Press.

Wilson, G. (1973) *The Psychology of Conservatism.* London: Academic Press.

Zuckerman, M. (1979) *Sensation Seeking: Beyond the Optimal Level of Arousal.* London: Wiley.

3 Personality and productivity

Mark Cook

Psychologists and employers alike have always thought personality and productivity at work were closely linked. One of the earliest books of selection, Laird's (1925) *Psychology of Selecting Men*, has chapters on 'reading character' and 'measuring personality traits'. Some 'character reading' systems relied on approaches psychology has long since discredited, such as phrenology. Physiognomy still retained some credibility in the 1920s, and offered detailed interpretations of 'character'. It provided a basis, for example, for a conclusion about the guilt of Loeb and Leopold, two famous murderers of the time. Their combined width of mouth, it was said, was small in relation to their size of head, indicating 'petty character', while their slightly bulging eyes indicated 'uncanny memories'. Laird quotes advertisements claiming that hair colour is an infallible guide to personality and productivity, blondes being 'active, aggressive, variety loving', hence ideal salesmen, whereas dark-haired men are 'the plodders, the planners'.

Laird didn't mention personality questionnaires, or inventories, whose day was still to come. During the war years, and for twenty years after, American psychologists developed personality tests, and used them to try to select productive workers. Serious doubts about their value did not start to surface until the mid-1960s. Mischel (1968) reviewed evidence, much of it ancient even twenty-five years ago, that seemed to show that behaviour wasn't consistent enough to make general statements about personality meaningful. Hartshorne and May's Character Education Inquiry, in the late 1920s, found measures of honesty virtually uncorrelated, implying that it is meaningless to describe someone as 'honest' unless one specifies when, where, with what, with whom. Mischel reviews similar evidence for other traits often listed in job descriptions: extraversion, punctuality, curiosity, persistence, attitude to authority. Personality theorists argue that Hartshorne and May's tests of honesty, while very ingenious, were single-item tests, hence inherently unreliable, and unlikely to predict anything.

Recently Blinkhorn (1989) has dismissed personality tests as 'a crutch used by a blind assessor as an excuse for turning a deaf ear to a dumb candidate'. Blinkhorn's most damaging criticisms are *lack of validity* and *failure to replicate.* Personality inventories cannot break the '0.30 barrier': they cannot achieve correlations with work performance greater than 0.30, which accounts for less than 10 per cent of the variance. When an inventory score breaks the '0.30 barrier', it usually turns out to be fluke, because the finding cannot be replicated.

OVERVIEW

The basic selection paradigm correlates a predictor with a criterion. Predictors, or measures of personality, include questionnaires, projective tests, letters of reference, assessment centres and 'weird and wonderful' tests, such as graphology. Ideally, two or more different types of predictor should be used – *multi-trait, multi-method measurement* – because of *method variance* – the tendency for questionnaire (or rating) measures of different traits to correlate very highly.

Criteria used in selection research divide into objective, such as units produced or items sold, and subjective, usually ratings. Subjective criteria are more popular, being used in 60 per cent to 80 per cent of validation studies (Lent *et al.*, 1971; Guion, 1965). In North America annual performance appraisals are standard practice in virtually all large organizations, and supply the personnel researcher with a 'ready-made' criterion. Objective and subjective criteria are however *not* interchangeable: Heneman (1986) reports an overall correlation between subjective and objective criteria of only 0.26, even making every allowance for error of measurement. Subjective criteria moreover can create serious problems of interpretation when comparing personality and productivity.

The selection paradigm asks three main questions about personality and productivity:

1 has he/she got the right personality for the job?
2 will he/she be good at the job?
3 is there anything wrong with him/her?

PERSONALITY QUESTIONNAIRES

Some research with inventories addresses *Question 1: Does he/she have the right personality for the job?* Miller (1976) comments that many employers seem to want a book of perfect personality profiles for manager, salesman, engineer, computer programmer, etc. Manuals for some tests meet this demand: 16PF and CPI manuals both give norms for different occupations. The *perfect profile* approach has several major limitations.

1 The perfect profile is an average, about which scores vary a lot.
2 Most perfect profiles derive from people doing the job, taking no account of how well they do it, nor how happy they are.

3 The perfect profile may show how well the person has adapted to the job's demands, not how well people with that profile will fit the job.

A larger body of inventory research addresses *Question 2: Will he/she be successful?* Conventional 'narrative' reviews of personality and productivity (Guion and Gottier, 1965; Lent *et al.*, 1971) generally make depressing reading, low correlations and insignificant differences being the usual outcome. However, two recent developments change this gloomy picture. The first is *meta-analysis/validity generalization analysis* (*VGA*); the second is the mapping of a multi-dimensional *criterion space* by Project A research in the US military.

Meta-analysis

Research on inventory validity, like most selection research, creates a lot of 'little' studies, with smaller sample sizes than ideal. Correlations calculated on small sample sizes fluctuate widely, giving the impression of inconsistency. *Meta-analysis* pools data from different studies, to generate a single overall estimate of validity. For example, Ghiselli (1973) calculated pooled validities across eight broad classes of job, for training and proficiency criteria; validity averaged at or below 0.20 for most jobs, but reached 0.30 for executives and sales staff. Dunnette (1972) meta-analysed 134 validity coefficients for the American petroleum industry. Interest and personality inventories both achieved near zero median validity, although the best 25 per cent of coefficients for personality tests exceeded 0.37.

Validity generalization analysis (VGA)

Selection research has two other limitations, besides sample size: *unreliability of criterion* and *restricted range*. Research on supervisor ratings (Rothstein, 1990) shows that the best reliability they achieve, after twenty years' acquaintance with the person rated, does not exceed 0.60. Other criteria – sales, output, etc. – are also unreliable (Cook, 1993). Unreliable criteria limit the correlation obtainable between inventory and work performance. VGA corrects correlations for criterion unreliability. Restricted range means validation studies include only successful candidates, who may vary less in personality than applicants. Restricted range limits the correlation obtainable; VGA corrects correlations to allow for this limitation as well. Correlations corrected for both criterion reliability and restricted range estimate a test's 'true' validity, which is often much higher than its observed or raw validity.

Four meta-analytic reviews of personality and productivity have been calculated, three of them also using VGA (Hough, 1988, 1992; Barrick and Mount, 1991; Tett *et al.*, 1991; Ones *et al.*, 1993). Two reviews use the 'big five' model of personality (Table 3.1), while a third (Hough, 1992) uses an extended form of it. The fourth review (Ones *et al.*) analyses 'integrity' tests, which measure one of the 'big five' – honesty. Three reviews show that a general *job proficiency* criterion is poorly predicted by personality tests (Table 3.1); even making every possible allowance, for restricted range, unreliability, etc., personality inventories mostly could not even reach the 0.30 barrier, let alone break it. The fourth analysis reports that 'integrity' tests achieve good *true validity* (0.41) against a supervisor rating criterion.

Barrick and Mount's average validities are lower than Tett *et al.*'s, because Tett *et al.* ignored sign when averaging correlations, whereas Barrick and Mount's analysis averaged − 0.20 and + 0.20 to give 0.00, which clearly tends to depress average validity. (While the correlation between intelligence and productivity is always positive, the relationship between personality and performance isn't necessarily; extraversion might be an asset in some jobs, e.g. selling, but a liability in others, e.g. lighthouse keeper.) Tett *et al.*'s average validities are higher, because they include only studies that stated a hypothesis about personality and productivity. Neither difference however explains why Tett *et al.* find *openness* and *agreeableness* achieve higher validities, whereas Barrick and Mount find *conscientiousness* achieves the highest validity. Ones *et al.* (1993) note that Tett *et al.* include only published studies, which may be biased towards 'more positive' results; they also argue that Tett *et al.*'s meta-analysis contains errors of interpretation.

Tett *et al.*'s VGA identifies several moderators of personality test validity. Validity is higher when the experimenter is testing a hypothesis about personality and work performance, rather than firing a shotgun full of scales. Ones *et al.* argue however that many researchers 'find' hypotheses after they have found significant correlations. Tett *et al.* report validity is higher still (0.38) when job analysis is used to select the tests, almost justifying the 0.40 estimate for inventory validity optimistically quoted in some quarters. Barrick and Mount found one occupational difference: extraversion predicts success in sales and management but not in other occupations. Tett *et al.* found no occupational differences.

Hough's meta-analysis reaches several important conclusions:

1 Hough started with the 'big five', but found it useful to split extraversion into *ascendancy* and *affiliation*. She also found that some personality traits that did not fit into the 'big five' had much higher validity, leading her to conclude the 'big five' is an unhelpful over-simplification.
2 Hough's (1988) analysis distinguishes six other criteria besides *job proficiency*, including *training success, commendable behaviour, non-delinquency* and *non-substance abuse*. *Commendable behaviour* is defined by 'letters of recommendation, letters of reprimand, disciplinary actions, demotions, involuntary terminations, ratings of effort, hard work'. *Delinquency* means actual theft, conviction or imprisonment; *substance abuse* means drink and drugs. While inventories generally failed to predict the *job proficiency* criterion, they could predict *commendable behaviour* and *non-*

Table 3.1 Four meta-analyses of personality test validity, using the 'big five' categorization of personality (the outcome predicted is job proficiency)

	Corrected validity			Raw validity		
	B&M	Tett	Ones	B&M	Tett	Hough
Big five						
extraversion	10	16		06	10	
ascendancy						10
sociability						00
adjustment	07	22		04	15	09
agreeableness	06	33		04	22	05
conscientiousness	23	18	41	13	12	08
openness	− 03	27		− 02	18	01
Hough's three extra scales						
achievement						15
locus control						11
masculinity						08

Notes
B&M – Barrick and Mount (1991), data from Table 2, values based on between 82 and 124 correlations, and total pooled sample of between 14,236 and 19,511; correlations are corrected for restricted range, criterion reliability *and test reliability*.

Ones – Ones *et al.* (1993), data from Table 8, value based on 23 correlations and 7,550 subjects; correlations are corrected for restricted range and criterion reliability.

Tett – Tett *et al.* (1991), data from Table 5, based on between 4 and 15 correlations, and between 280 and 2,302 subjects. 'Corrected' validity corrected for criterion reliability *and test reliability*, but not restricted range.

Hough – Hough (1992), data from Table 3, based on between 15 and 274 correlations, and between 2,811 and 65,876 subjects. Correlations are not corrected for unreliability of test or criterion, nor for restricted range.

substance abuse moderately well (0.20 to 0.39), and *non-delinquency* very well (up to 0.52).

Ones *et al.* confirm this, finding a *true validity* of 0.32 for honesty tests predicting *counter-productive behaviours*, defined as breaking rules, being disciplined, being dismissed for theft, or being rated as disruptive by supervisor.

3 Hough (1988) compared thirty-seven different inventories, and concluded some predicted productivity much better than others. The 'best all-round inventory' was the California Psychological Inventory, which achieved *uncorrected* correlations as high as 0.64 with *non-delinquency* (Table 3.2). The CPI also predicted *commendable behaviours* and drink and drug problems in the workplace very well. The 16PF, widely used in Britain to predict productivity, achieved noticeably poorer results (Table 3.3).

Table 3.2 Meta-analysis of the validity of scales of the California Psychological Inventory, against five criteria (Hough, 1988)

	JOB	*TRN*	*COM*	*NDL*	*NSA*
dominance	–	–	30	38	–
capacity status	–	–	–	39	–
sociability	–	–	–	25	–
social presence	–	–	–	29	–
self-acceptance	–	–	–	20	–
well being	–	–	–	35	–
responsibility	–	–	44	56	32
socialization	–	–	32*	64*	41
self-control	–	–	–	20	24
tolerance	–	–	–	48	–
good impression	–	–	–	–	–
communality	–	–	–	–	–
achievement via conformance	–	–	–	43	26
achievement via independence	–	21	33	42	– 27
intellectual efficiency	–	–	–	46	– 23
psychological mindedness	–	–	–	–	–
flexibility	–	–	–	–	–
femininity/masculinity	–	–	–	–	–
N correlations/N subjects		9/1160	2/4144	2/5918	2/148
			*4/4318	*7/15851	

Notes

JOB: overall job proficiency; technical proficiency, advancement.

TRN: training grades and ratings.

COM: commendable behaviours: reprimands, disciplinary, dismissals, demotions.

NDL: non-delinquency: theft, offences, imprisonment.

NSA: non-substance abuse: drugs, alcohol consumed, addiction.

Assessment of background and life experiences (ABLE)

ABLE is one of the few major new questionnaires to appear in recent times. ABLE was written for the US armed forces as part of Project A. ABLE has 205 items, and measures six temperament constructs: surgency (defined as happy-go-lucky, uninhibited and enthusiastic), adjustment, agreeableness, dependability, intellectance, affiliation. ABLE also has four control scales: random responding, social desirability, poor impression and self-knowledge (Hough *et al.*, 1990). ABLE has been validated against five criteria, in very large samples of seven or eight thousand soldiers (Hough *et al.*, 1990; McHenry *et al.*, 1990). ABLE scales predict three composite criteria: *effort*

Table 3.3 Meta-analysis of the validity of scales of the 16PF, against five criteria (Hough, 1988)

		JOB	*TRN*	*COM*	*NDL*	*NSA*
A	outgoing	–	–	–	–	–
B	intelligent	–	–	–	–	–
C	emotionally stable	–	–	–	–	03
E	assertive	– 08	–	–	–	–
F	happy-go-lucky	– 03	–	–	–	–
G	conscientious	–	–	–	–	33
H	venturesome	– 03	–	–	–	–
I	tender-minded	–	–	–	–	–
L	suspicious	07	–	–	–	24
M	imaginative	–	–	–	–	–
N	shrewd	–	–	–	–	–
O	apprehensive	–	–	–	–	– 05
Q1	experimenting	–	–	–	–	– 18
Q2	self-sufficient	–	–	–	–	–
Q3	controlled	–	–	–	–	12
Q4	tense	–	–	–	–	– 01
N correlations/N subjects			2/820			2/632

and leadership, personal discipline, physical fitness and military bearing, but not the other two: *technical proficiency* or *general soldiering proficiency*; the correlations are modest – 0.10s and 0.20s – but have not been corrected for criterion reliability or restricted range. Furthermore, ABLE contributes *incremental validity*, predicting aspects of soldiers' performance that weren't predicted by intelligence tests. The sample size was large enough to permit internal analyses that showed that faking good, malingering or lack of self-knowledge did not reduce correlations between ABLE scores and the five criteria. Only careless responding lowered ABLE's validity.

Screening by inventory

Another large body of research addresses *Question 3: Is there anything wrong with him/her?* Honesty testing is used on a very large scale in the USA. Employees are also screened for (mal)adjustment. Anderson's (1929) survey of staff at Macy's department store found 20 per cent employees fell into the 'problem' category – can't learn, suffer chronic ill-health, in constant trouble with fellow-employees, can't adjust satisfactorily to their work. Culpin and Smith's (1930) survey of 1,000 British postal workers found 20 to 30 per cent suffering some measurable level of neurosis. In the USA, many police forces screen applicants to identify those who are emotionally or psychologically unfit for police work; MMPI is the favourite test, with CPI and 16PF the runners up. Hargrave and Hiatt (1989) compared CPI profiles of forty-five 'problem' police officers and forty-five matched controls; the problem group showed greater impulsivity, risk-taking, intolerance and willingness to break the rules.

Very large numbers of US servicemen were screened during World War II (Ellis and Conrad, 1948). Some studies reported very high correlations between inventory scores and adjustment – as high as 0.80; other studies reported cutting points that distinguished problem from well-adjusted recruits with amazing efficiency. Some military screening results *were* too good to be true. Many studies suffered *criterion contamination*, which means the psychiatrist making the diagnosis knew the man's test score. Other researches suffered an unusual statistical problem – *excessive* (as opposed to *restricted*) *range*. Military testing reached men other test programmes never saw: 'unemployables, tramps, loafers, "bums", alcoholics, frank neurotics'. It is useful to know how a test performs on a complete cross-section of American men, but not that relevant to civilian employers who aren't interested in screening out people who'd never apply anyway, or wouldn't get past reception if they did.

Honesty testing

Questionnaires measuring honesty are widely used in the USA (Sackett and Harris, 1984; Ones *et al.*, 1994), and have gained greater popularity since the Employee Polygraph Protection Act of 1988 restricted use of the polygraph. Ones *et al.* were able to find 665 validity coefficients, across 576,460 subjects, for their VGA. Honesty tests use indirect questions that assume dishonest people see crime as more frequent, or see crime as easier, or use questions that present dishonesty as meriting less punishment, or as more easily justified (by low wages, etc.). Honesty tests have been validated against supervisor rating or externally measured behaviour; the VGA concludes honesty tests predict both general *job proficiency* and *counter-productive behaviours* very well.

Employee *(un)reliability* is a broader concept than honesty; Hogan and Hogan (1989) define it as 'counterproductive acts such as: theft, drug and alcohol abuse, lying, insubordination, vandalism, sabotage, absenteeism and assaultive actions'. Hogan and Hogan describe an inventory, based on *homogeneous item composites*, and report thirteen concurrent validation studies against very varied organizational delinquency criteria: injuries, rated attitude, and sales figures.

All screening tests create false positives – persons identified by the test as *dis*honest or *mal*adjusted, who are really honest or well adjusted. Some critics think the existence of *false positives* a strong argument for not using honesty tests. Martin and Terris (1991) argue the false positive issue is irrelevant; if the test has any validity, then using it will benefit the organization by excluding some dishonest persons. Guastello and Rieke (1991) disagree with Martin and Terris: a *false positive* on an honesty test means labelling someone dishonest when he/she is not and abridging that person's civil rights by implicitly accusing them of theft but denying them any opportunity to answer. Screening tests also create *false negatives*, meaning people who prove dishonest, although the test characterized them as honest. *False negatives* do not create any moral problems for the test's user, but do have the important practical implication that dishonest persons are admitted to the workforce – the very outcome the test was designed to prevent.

PROJECTIVE TESTS

Projective tests assume everything a person does, says, writes, thinks, paints or even dreams reflects his/her personality. If people don't know they are revealing their personalities, they can't censor themselves and 'fake good'. Kinslinger (1966) reviewed several projective tests widely used in personnel research.

Rorschach Rorschach scores are very poor at differentiating physical scientists, technicians, biologists, anthropologists, psychologists and artists. Early researchers, listed in Dorcus and Jones (1950), thought TAT and Rorschach the ideal way to predict turnover or accident proneness in tram drivers in Southern California, but were mistaken: neither test predicted anything. Kelly and Fiske's (1951) study found Rorschach scores unable to predict success in clinical psychology. Other studies reviewed by Kinslinger similarly failed to find Rorschach scores reliably predicted any aspect of productivity.

Thematic Apperception Test (TAT) Rodger (1959) found 'route' sales-men, tested by Rorschach and TAT, showed 'markedly rigid personality structures and personality impoverishment'; the salesmen had no strongly held opinions of their own, but were skilled at taking the lead from what others thought; they were materially oriented, to the point of being 'less inhibited by concepts of right and wrong'; their relations with others were superficial, to the point of 'conceal[ing] distrust behind a facade of congeniality'.

Tomkins–Horn Picture Arrangement Test (PAT) Miner (1971) used PAT to describe the successful management consultant as: drawn to authority figures, not wanting to be alone when away from work, preferring physically close relationships and moving towards supportive relationships. Consult-ants can act independently, want to be with more powerful people and don't want to be with peers. The results make sense, given that management consultants spend a lot of time with bosses of large companies.

Worthington Personal History Blank (WPHB) A specially designed four-page application form that gives the applicant the fullest scope for revealing his/her personality. For example, the space for name is just that – a space, with no indication whether to put surname first, use full initials, titles or whatever. An applicant who wrote 'Jonathan Jasper Jones Jnr' stood out because men usually use initials; exceptions tend to be 'young men who haven't yet made their way in the world' (Spencer and Worthing-

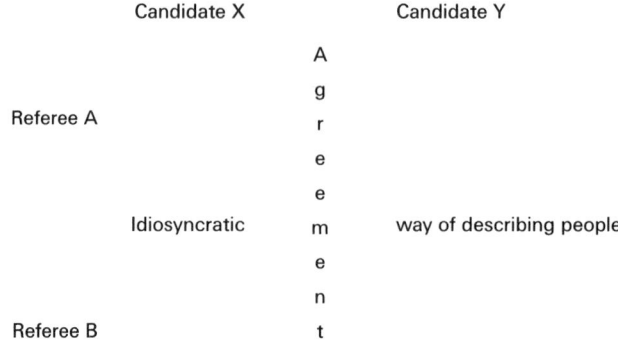

Figure 3.1 Schematic representation of the study by Baxter *et al.* (1981) of letters of
    reference

ton, 1952). Worthington's own research suggested the WPHB was very
promising; research by Clark and Owens (1954), by contrast, found the
WPHB of little value.

REFERENCES

In theory, 'references' should give useful, accurate information about personality and productivity. The writer knows the subject well, can report how
he/she *typically* behaves in the workplace, with colleagues, etc. A reference
written by a disinterested third person should tell the truth, unlike a
questionnaire completed by the person who wants the job on offer. However, the reference doesn't live up to its promise. Research finds references
generally fail to break the '0.30 barrier' (Mosel and Goheen, 1958). Summarizing all available US data, Reilly and Chao (1982) conclude that reference
checks give poor predictions of supervisor ratings (0.18) and turnover
(0.08). Correcting for criterion reliability, Hunter and Hunter (1984) calculated mean validities of 0.26, against supervisor ratings, and 0.16 for
promotion. Only one study, of references for candidates for Royal Naval
officer college by their school headteachers, achieves better results. College
ratings of leadership were best predicted by headteacher's rating of *sporting
and extra-curricular activities*, while exam mark was best predicted by
rating of *application to studies* (Jones and Harrison, 1982). Jones and
Harrison note overall (corrected) validity of headteacher's report equals
that reported for psychological tests predicting training grades (Ghiselli,
1966). Jones and Harrison find the prediction of leadership and conduct
'particularly encouraging', given how difficult these are to measure by any
other test. Jones and Harrison do not expect such good results every time;
headteachers are more likely (than former employers) to write careful,
critical references, because they know they will be writing Naval College
references for future pupils, and because their own credibility is at stake.

References fail to link personality to productivity because their authors are too idiosyncratic and because their authors are typically reluctant to say anything negative. Baxter *et al.* (1981) searched medical school files to find twenty cases where the same two referees had written references for the same two applicants (Figure 3.1). If references are useful, what referee A says about applicant X ought to resemble what referee B says about applicant X. Analysis of the qualities listed in the letters – intelligent, reserved, unimaginative, etc. – revealed a completely different pattern. What referee A said about applicant X didn't resemble what referee B said about applicant X, but did resemble what referee A said about applicant Y. Baxter's study shows the reference tells you more about its author than about its subject.

A very early (1923) survey, described by Moore (1942), found most reference writers said (a) they always gave the employee the benefit of the doubt, (b) they said only good things about him/her and (c) they didn't point out his/her failings. In fact, in some circles it is considered bad form to write an unfavourable reference. Mosel and Goheen found reference ratings highly skewed, with 'outstanding' or 'good' opinions greatly outnumbering 'satisfactory' or 'poor' opinions. Employees were hardly ever rated 'poor'. If referees are reluctant to say anything unkind, references will clearly prove a poor source of information and personality and productivity.

ASSESSMENT CENTRES

Assessment centres are planned around the principle of *multi-trait, multi-method* assessment. Any single assessment method may give misleading results: some people 'interview well', while others are 'good at tests'. The *key* feature of the true AC is the *dimension × assessment method matrix* (Figure 3.2). Having decided what *dimensions* of work performance are to be assessed, the AC planners select or devise *at least two, qualitatively different methods of assessing* each dimension. In Figure 3.2, *ability to influence* is assessed by group exercise *and* personality inventory. An assessment centre that doesn't have a matrix plan isn't a real AC, just a superstitious imitation of one. Unfortunately, one all too often encounters people whose idea of an AC is any old collection of begged, borrowed or stolen tests and exercises.

ACs achieve impressively good predictive validity, which accounts for their popularity and justifies their cost. AT&T's Management Progress Study assessed new college hires and non-graduate first-level managers. On follow-up, eight years later, the AC had identified 82 per cent of the college group and 75 per cent of the non-graduates who had reached middle management (Bray and Grant, 1966). The AC identified unsuccessful managers equally accurately. Reviews of AC validity (Cohen *et al.*, 1974; Schmitt *et al.*, 1984; Gaugler *et al.*, 1987) distinguish between different criteria of success: performance ratings, promotion, rated potential for further promo-

COMPONENTS	DIMENSIONS			
	Influence	Numerical abilty	Strategic vision	etc.
Group exercise 'Future'				
Group exercise 'Manufacture'				
Mental ability (numerical)				
Personality inventory				
etc.				

Figure 3.2 The dimension × component matrix underlying every assessment centre (the dimension influence is assessed by group exercise 'Future' and the personality inventory)

Table 3.4 Summary of four analyses of assessment centre validity (data from Cohen *et al.*, 1974; Hunter and Hunter, 1984; Schmitt *et al.*, 1984; Gaugler *et al.*, 1987)

	Reviewer			
	Cohen	*Hunter*	*Schmitt*	*Gaugler*
Criterion				
Performance	0.33	0.43	0.43	0.37
Promotion	0.40		0.41	0.36
'Potential'	0.63			0.53
Achievement			0.31	
Wages			0.24	
Training				0.35

tion, achievement/grades, status change, wages (Table 3.4). The third review (Gaugler *et al.*, 1987) is a *validity generalization analysis* covering fifty studies; the authors report a median raw validity of 0.29, and estimated true validity of 0.37.

There are however several qualifications that must be voiced about the AC's validity, especially as a personality measure.

Which components contribute to validity? The AC, by its very nature, contains a wide range of tests and assessments, whose contributions to the method's overall success are rarely analysed. Given that AC validity is only slightly higher than that of intelligence tests (Hunter and Hunter, 1984), and given that many ACs contain intelligence tests, it is possible that AC validity derives largely from tests of intelligence.

Discriminant/convergent validity The logic of the AC method implies assessors should rate candidates on *dimensions*; research suggests strongly however that assessors often rate them on *exercises*. Instead of rating influence, social skill, etc., as revealed in various exercises, assessors rate overall performance in group discussion, overall performance in tray exercise, etc. Ratings of *different dimensions* made after the *same exercise* correlate very highly, whereas ratings of the *same trait in different exercises* hardly correlate at all (Sackett and Dreher, 1982). This implies ACs operate as a series of work samples, and not – as they are meant to – like a long, multi-faceted personality test.

Other doubts about AC validity, discussed in the next section, suggest they work by answering the wrong question about personality and productivity.

PERSONALITY AND CRITERIA OF PRODUCTIVITY

Most research on productivity uses supervisor ratings as criterion, instead of 'actual' output. The possible problems created by supervisor rating criteria were first noted in research on assessment centres. Cohen *et al.*'s (1974) review finds AC ratings predict *actual job performance* moderately well, but predict *higher management ratings of management potential* much better. A later study by Klimoski and Strickland (1981) reported that AC ratings predicted promotion and ratings of potential, but not good performance. Klimoski and Strickland (1977) suggest ACs pick up the personal mannerisms that top management use in promotion, which may not have much to do with actual effectiveness. On this argument ACs answer the question 'does his/her face fit?' – but not the question 'does he/she do good work?' The general class of supervisor rating criterion can be viewed as answering the question: does Smith make a good impression on management? Klimoski is arguing that the AC – more than other selection tests – asks basically the same question, which makes its high 'validity' unsurprising, perhaps even trivial.

Schmitt *et al.*'s review strongly confirms Klimoski's argument that 'face fits' criteria are more popular for ACs. Twelve coefficients, based on 14,662 subjects, used status change and wages criteria, whereas only six coefficients, based on a mere 394 subjects, used performance ratings. In a sense, however, all these researches are irrelevant to Klimoski's criticism, because 'performance' criteria in AC research are still ratings, i.e. still management's opinion of the candidate. The solution lies in validating ACs against objective criteria, such as sales or output, not against different wordings ('potential'/ 'performance') of the general favourable-impression-on-management criterion. However, very few studies have used objective criteria, because ACs are mostly used to select managers, who rarely produce anything tangible or countable.

Other research has identified problem areas with subjective rating criteria, especially when they are used to demonstrate a link between personality and productivity.

Personal like/dislike Longenecker (1987) reports a content analysis of sixty 'in depth' interviews with managers who make performance ratings (PRs). Three-quarters said they allowed liking to inflate PRs and dislike to lower PRs. Experimental studies have confirmed that personal like or dislike can affect PRs (Tsui and Barry, 1986; Kingstrom and Mainstone, 1985). Longenecker *et al.* (1992) used a 'paper people' paradigm, in which performance (good/poor) and personality (extraversion/introversion) were varied. Longenecker reports a significant effect of personality, extraverts tending to get better PRs, which he interprets as mediated by managers liking extraverts more.

Organizational fads and chairman's whims Many organizations set great store by relatively trivial details, which often have little to do with effective work performance. Klimoski and Strickland (1977) argue that assessment centres may achieve their apparently high validity by picking up trivial details of this type: the right mannerism, the right buzz words, that impress senior management. Padfield (1972) reports that promotion in the Royal Navy of the 1890s went to officers with the most highly polished ships, which caused a few to behave as if they had forgotten what navies and battleships were for; some officers were said to try to avoid gunnery practice in case the powder smoke spoiled their paintwork.

An extreme case of this trend may be termed *World War I mentality*. Organizations occasionally exist in which subordinates gain credit for pushing ahead with management plans that are absurdly wrong, in pursuit of aims which are completely pointless, stifling criticism of either purpose or method with cries of 'commitment' and 'loyalty'.

Ingratiation English has a rich vocabulary to describe workplace ingratiators – often using words listed in dictionaries as 'not in polite use'. This implies the behaviour is widely recognized, but generally unpopular. Several authors have collected examples of ingratiating behaviour, or 'upwards influence style', and produced questionnaire measures of workplace ingratiation (Kipnis *et al.*, 1980; Kumar and Beyerlein, 1991). Wayne and Ferris (1990) extract three factors:

- *job-focused ingratiation* – claiming credit for things you have done, claiming credit for things you haven't done, claiming credit for what the group has done, etc.
- *supervisor-focused ingratiation* – praising supervisor, doing favours for supervisor, volunteering to help supervisor, complimenting supervisor, etc.
- *self-focused ingratiation* – presenting oneself as a friendly person, and as a polite person, etc.

Wayne and Ferris (1990) report a field study, linking ingratiation to PRs in bank clerks. Job-focused and supervisor-focused ingratiation succeeded in

Figure 3.2 The dimension x component matrix underlying every assessment centre the dimension influence is assessed by group exercise "Future" and the personality inventory

Implications of using PRs as criterion   Liking bias implies a liked person whose true performance is average may get a high PR, whereas a disliked person whose true performance is high may get an average PR. Ingratiation will sometimes achieve the same effect. Liking bias, or ingratiation, alters the rank order of subjects on the criterion, and reduces its correspondence to true performance. In Blum and Naylor's (1968) terminology, the *ultimate criterion*, or true performance, is *contaminated* by deficiencies in the *actual criterion*, in the shape of *performance rating*.

Liking and ingratiation can easily create misleading correlations between personality and 'productivity'. Longenecker's (1992) data showed most sales managers preferred extravert salespersons, and that this preference is reflected in their PRs. This may create a spurious correlation between rating criterion and personality test – spurious, because it might not be found in a comparison between personality test and an objective criterion, such as sales figures. PRs based on 'pleasing management' are especially likely to generate spurious correlations between predictors and 'productivity'. Any predictor that reflects the desire and/or ability to ingratiate will tend to correlate with the PR criterion. The desire to ingratiate is measured directly in many personality inventories, by social desirability or 'fake good' scales.

The undeserved reputation

A good reputation can be earned by good work, but many features of large organizations make it possible to earn one in other ways, which may in turn mediate apparent links between personality and productivity, when productivity is defined by subjective ratings.

The non-working day

Only part of an academic's day is spent doing core job-description activities – teaching students and conducting research. The rest of the day gets filled up by chattering, drinking coffee, tidying up, meetings, paperwork, etc. The more of the working day is filled by non-work or semi-work, the more time there is to set about making oneself well thought of, without necessarily doing any good teaching or useful research. Two surveys suggest this problem is not confined to academics. Bialek *et al.* (1977) used time sampling observation to analyse how a large number of enlisted infantry spent their time. In a typical training day the average soldier spends 25 minutes receiving instruction and 57 minutes practising the task; the rest of the day is swallowed up by being 'en route', parades, polishing boots, hanging about, etc. Campbell *et al.* (1970) report that a substantial part of the manager's day is spent doing things that cannot be unambiguously linked to the accomplishment of specific tasks.

It's who you know, not what you know

A widely voiced observation, which implies the employee's time may often be as usefully spent creating a network of allies and contacts as in doing any actual work. Research shows that members of the 'in group' get better PRs, better possibly than their true performance merits (Vecchio and Gobdel, 1984). 'Team building' or being 'a team player' are phrases often used in job advertisements or person specifications. Co-operating with one's colleagues is very important in most work – but could 'team player' sometimes also refer to individuals very good at making themselves liked, or good at appearing indispensable, but not necessarily very effective performers?

Public relations

Some individuals consciously set about building themselves a reputation, by conventional 'public relations' techniques of controlling information about themselves and their doings. Professional politicians are notoriously adept at this. In certain types of characteristically cautious organizations a good reputation is built largely by *not* doing things: not making controversial decisions, not attracting complaints, not getting bad publicity, etc. Many a politician has blighted his or her career by some trivial action or comment that has little or no bearing on their fitness for office.

Establishing a social reality

A company that manufactures gearboxes has its success defined externally, and unambiguously, by its sales figures. A university by contrast constructs its own *social reality* about success. A consensus of academics decides what issues are worth researching and teaching, and by implication whose work has merit. Research topics become fashionable, generate publications and attract research money, then 'just fade away' without achieving any lasting addition to the sum of human knowledge (Meehl, 1978).

Stature and credibility

It has been said of Parliament, that no Minister has really 'arrived' until he/she has passed an Act. Critics argue this accounts for the enactment of numerous pointless, badly drafted, unenforceable laws. Similar 'mark making' mechanisms in other spheres include opening a new department or new building (or sometimes *closing* a department or building) and reorganizations. Some job advertisements appear to be groping towards aspects of this 'mark making' mechanism with references to 'stature' (not referring to physical build) and 'credibility' (not meaning that the person hasn't been caught telling lies recently).

Implications for using PRs as criterion

Someone whose true performance is poor, but who is a good self-publicist, or good at claiming responsibility for others' successes, or successful at defining his/her achievements as useful and important, will achieve better PRs. Conversely someone whose true performance is good, but who isn't a good self-publicist, or doesn't claim responsibility for others' successes, or who fails to get his/her work defined as important, may be rated poor. Once again the PR criterion becomes *contaminated*, and less accurately reflects true performance.

Correlations between personality and PR criteria of 'productivity' may again turn out to be mediated by aspects of personality that don't necessarily contribute to true productivity: political skill, deviousness, even dishonesty. Gotz and Gotz (1979) report that successful artists score higher on Eysenck's psychoticism dimension, and suggest that psychoticism manifests itself as true creativity, but also as a ruthless determination to sell their work. Their 'success' as artists is partly genuine, but partly mediated by other, irrelevant aspects of their personality.

REFERENCES

Anderson, V.V. (1929) *Psychiatry in Industry*. New York: Holt.

Barrick, M.R. and Mount, M.K. (1991) The big five personality dimensions and job performance: a meta-analysis. *Personnel Psychology*, *44*, 1–26.

Baxter, J.C., Brock, B., Hill, P.C. and Rozelle, R.M. (1981) Letters of recommendation: a question of value. *Journal of Applied Psychology*, *66*, 296–301.

Bialek, H., Zapf, D. and McGuire, W. (1977) *Personnel Turbulence and Time Utilisation in an Infantry Division*. HumRRO FR-WD-CA.77–11. Alexandria, VA: Human Relations Research Organisation.

Blinkhorn, S. (1989) *On the Relation between Test Theory and Personality*. Paper presented at conference on Selection and Use of Psychometric Tests, London, July, 1989.

Blum, M.L. and Naylor, J.C. (1968) *Industrial Psychology*, revised edition. New York: Harper & Row.

Bray, D.W. and Grant, D.L. (1966) The assessment center in the measurement of potential for business management. *Psychological Monographs*, *80* (17, whole No. 625).

Campbell, J.P., Dunnette, M.D., Lawler, E.E. and Weick, K.E. (1970) *Managerial Behavior, Performance, and Effectiveness*. New York: McGraw-Hill.

Clark, J.G. and Owens, W.A. (1954) A validation study of the Worthington Personal History Blank. *Journal of Applied Psychology*, *38*, 85–8.

Cohen, B.M., Moses, J.L. and Byham, W.C. (1974) *The Validity of Assessment Centers: A Literature Review*. Pittsburgh: Development Dimensions Press.

Cook, M. (1993) *Personnel Selection and Productivity*, 2nd edition. Chichester: Wiley.

Culpin, M. and Smith, M. (1930) *The Nervous Temperament*. London: Medica Research Council, Industrial Health Research Board.

Dorcus, R.M. and Jones, M.H. (1950) *Handbook of Employee Selection*. New York: McGraw-Hill.

Dunnette, M.D. (1972) *Validity Study Results for Jobs Relevant to the Petroleum Refining Industry*. American Petroleum Institute.

Ellis, A. and Conrad, H.S. (1948) The validity of personality inventories in military practice. *Psychological Bulletin*, *45*, 385–426.

Gaugler, B.B., Rosenthal, D.B., Thornton, G.C. and Bentson, C. (1987) Meta-analysis of assessment center validity. *Journal of Applied Psychology*, *72*, 493–511.

Ghiselli, E.E. (1966) *The Validity of Occupational Aptitude Tests*. New York: Wiley.

Ghiselli, E.E. (1973) The validity of aptitude tests in personnel selection. *Personnel Psychology*, *26*, 461–77.

Gotz, K.O. and Gotz, K. (1979) Personality characteristics of successful artists. *Perceptual and Motor Skills*, *49*, 919–24.

Guastello, S.J. and Rieke, M.L. (1991) A review and critique of honesty testing. *Behavioral Sciences and the Law*, *9*, 501–23.

Guion, R.M. (1965) *Personnel Testing*. New York: McGraw-Hill.

Guion, R.M. and Gottier, R.F. (1965) Validity of personality measures in personnel selection. *Personnel Psychology*, *18*, 135–64.

Hargrave, G.E. and Hiatt, D. (1989) Use of the California Psychological Inventory in law enforcement officer selection. *Journal of Personality Assessment*, *53*, 267–77.

Hartshorne, H. and May, M.A. (1928) *Studies in the Nature of Character*, Volume 1. *Studies in Deceit*. New York: Macmillan.

Heneman, R.L. (1986) The relationship between supervisory ratings and results oriented measures of performance: a meta-analysis. *Personnel Psychology*, *39*, 811–26.

Hogan, J. and Hogan, R. (1989) How to measure employee reliability. *Journal of Applied Psychology*, *74*, 273–9.

Hough, L.M. (1988) *Personality Assessment for Selection and Placement Decisions*. Paper presented at Third Annual Conference of the Society for Industrial and Organisational Psychology, Dallas, TX, 21 April 1988.

Hough, L.M. (1992) The 'big five' personality variables – construct confusion: description versus prediction. *Human Performance*, in press.

Hough, L.M., Eaton, N.K., Dunnette, M.D., Kamp, J.D. and McCloy, R.A. (1990) Criterion-related validities of personality constructs and the effect of response distortion on those validities. *Journal of Applied Psychology*, *75*, 581–95.

Hunter, J.E. and Hunter, R.F. (1984) Validity and utility of alternate predictors of job performance. *Psychological Bulletin*, *96*, 72–98.

Jones, A. and Harrison, E. (1982) Prediction of performance in initial officer training using reference reports. *Journal of Occupational Psychology*, *55*, 35–42.

Kelly, E.L. and Fiske, D.W. (1951) *The Prediction of Performance in Clinical Psychology*. Ann Arbor: University of Michigan Press.

Kingstrom, P.O. and Mainstone, L.E. (1985) An investigation of the rater–ratee acquaintance and rater bias. *Academy of Management Journal*, *28*, 641–53.

Kinslinger, H.J. (1966) Application of projective techniques in personnel psychology since 1940. *Psychological Bulletin*, *66*, 134–50.

Kipnis, D., Schmidt, S.M. and Wilkinson, I. (1980) Intra-organisational influence tactics: explorations in getting one's way. *Journal of Applied Psychology*, *65*, 440–52.

Klimoski, R.J. and Strickland, W.J. (1977) Assessment centers – valid or merely prescient? *Personnel Psychology*, *30*, 353–61.

Klimoski, R.J. and Strickland, W.J. (1981) *The Comparative View of Assessment*

Centers. Unpublished manuscript, Department of Psychology, University of Ohio.

Kumar, K. and Beyerlein, M. (1991) Construction and validation of an instrument for measuring ingratiatory behaviors in organisational setting. *Journal of Applied Psychology*, 76, 619–27.

Laird, D. (1925) *The Psychology of Selecting Men*. New York: McGraw-Hill.

Lent, R.H., Aurbach, H.A. and Levin, L.S. (1971) Predictors, criteria, and significant results. *Personnel Psychology*, 24, 519–33.

Longenecker, C.O. (1987) Behind the mask: the politics of employee appraisal. *Academy of Management Executive*, 1, 183–93.

Longenecker, C.O., Jaccoud, A.J., Sims, H.P. and Gioia, D.A. (1992) Quantitative and qualitative investigations of affect in executive judgment. *Applied Psychology: An International Review*, 41, 21–41.

McHenry, J.J., Hough, L.M., Toquam, J.L., Hanson, M.A. and Ashworth, S. (1990) Project A validity results: the relationship between predictor and criterion domains. *Personnel Psychology*, 43, 335–54.

Martin, S.L. and Terris, W. (1991) Predicting infrequent behavior: clarifying the impact on false-positive rates. *Journal of Applied Psychology*, 76, 484–7.

Meehl, P.E. (1978) Theoretical risks and tabular asterisks: Sir Karl, Sir Ronald, and the slow progress of soft psychology. *Journal of Consulting and Clinical Psychology*, 46, 806–34.

Miller, K. (1976) Personality assessment. In B. Ungerson (ed.) *Recruitment Handbook*. Aldershot: Gower.

Miner, J.B. (1971) Personality tests as predictors of consulting success. *Personnel Psychology*, 24, 191–204.

Mischel, W. (1968) *Personality and Assessment*. New York: Wiley.

Moore, H. (1942) *Psychology for Business and Industry*. New York: McGraw-Hill.

Mosel, J.N. and Goheen, H.W. (1958) The validity of the Employment Recommendation Questionnaire in personnel selection. I. Skilled trades. *Personnel Psychology*, 11, 481–90.

Ones, D.S., Mount, M.K., Barrick, M.R. and Hunter, J.E. (1994) Personality and job performance: a critique of the Tett, Jackson & Rothstein (1991) meta-analysis. *Personnel Psychology*, 47, 147–56.

Ones, D.S., Viswesvaran, C. and Schmidt, F.L. (1993) Meta-analysis of integrity test validities: findings and implications for personnel selection and theories of job performance. *Journal of Applied Psychology*, 78, 679–703.

Padfield, P. (1972) *The Battleship Era*. London: Hart-Davis.

Parkinson, C.N. (1958) *Parkinson's Law*. London: John Murray.

Reilly, R.R. and Chao, G.T. (1982) Validity and fairness of some alternative employee selection procedures. *Personnel Psychology*, 35, 1–62.

Rodger, D.A. (1959) Personality of the route salesman in a basic food industry. *Journal of Applied Psychology*, 43, 235–9.

Rothstein, H.R. (1990) Interrater reliability of job performance ratings: growth to asymptote level with increasing opportunity to observe. *Journal of Applied Psychology*, 75, 322–7.

Sackett, P.R. and Dreher, G.F. (1982) Constructs and assessment center dimensions: some troubling empirical findings. *Journal of Applied Psychology*, 67, 401–10.

Sackett, P.R. and Harris, M.M. (1984) Honesty testing for personnel selection: a review and critique. *Personnel Psychology*, 37, 221–45.

Schmitt, N., Gooding, R.Z., Noe, R.A. and Kirsch, M. (1984) Metaanalyses of validity studies published between 1964 and 1982 and the investigation of study characteristics. *Personnel Psychology*, 37, 407–22.

Spencer, G.J. and Worthington, R. (1952) Validity of a projective technique in predicting sales effectiveness. *Personnel Psychology*, 5, 125–44.

Tett, R.P., Jackson, D.N. and Rothstein, M. (1991) Personality measures as predictors of job performance. *Personnel Psychology, 44*, 407–21.

Tsui, A.S. and Barry, B. (1986) Interpersonal affect and rating errors. *Academy of Management Journal, 29*, 586–99.

Vecchio, R.P. and Gobdel, B.C. (1984) The vertical dyadic linkage mode of leadership: problems and prospects. *Organisational Behavior and Human Performance, 34*, 5–20.

Wayne, S.J. and Ferris, G.R. (1990) Influence tactic affect, and exchange quality in supervisor–subordinate interactions: a laboratory and field study. *Journal of Applied Psychology, 75*, 487–99.

4 Organizational leadership and followership

The role of interpersonal relations

Edwin P. Hollander

INTRODUCTION

Leadership has traditionally been approached as a matter of leader qualities and behaviours. The leader draws attention as the major actor, and followers are largely disregarded as relatively passive and less important. However, the follower role is now increasingly recognized as holding the potential for both assessing and taking on leadership functions, beyond what Meyer (1982) called 'anachronistic models of leader–follower relationships' (p. 930). Most particularly, it is clear that leadership involves an interdependent relationship with followers, aimed at co-operative team achievements.

This chapter examines the leader–follower relationship as a centrepiece for contemporary approaches to understanding and improving essential organizational outcomes. A starting place for exploring this relationship is the evident truth that there is no leadership without followership; they are a unity (see Hollander, 1992a). But the implications of this need to be understood more fully as requiring active followership, rather than with the more usual reliance on leader-centric actions. As Reich (1987) puts it, 'We need to honor our teams more, our aggressive leaders and maverick geniuses less' (p. 78).

The way the leader and followers mutually perceive and respond to each other's personal qualities and actions is a crucial factor in this relationship. In their landmark coverage of relationships, Argyle and Henderson capture a number of these elements in stating that

> [T]he superior–subordinate relationship at work is seen by most people as full of conflict and as providing little satisfaction. On the other hand supervisors *can* have a considerable effect on health and satisfaction, if the right skills are used. Supervisors have power to reward and punish, and there is usually not a very close relationship . . . and no permanent bonds are formed . . . [T]he barriers created by differences of power and status can be reduced by the use of certain supervisory skills, and reduced even more by an attitude of concern for one another.
>
> (Argyle and Henderson, 1985, p. 262)

Several of these points, notably about power and status differences, reward and punishment, and their effects, recur here as significant issues in dealing with leader–follower relations. All are necessarily parts of the rules of conduct understood as applicable in any particular role relationship (Argyle, 1983).

BACKGROUND AND DEFINITIONS

Although the central feature of leadership is direction of activity, it embodies other important functions which can be distributed. They include decision making, goal setting, communicating, resolving conflict and maintaining the enterprise, in the classic sense of stewardship. These are not just the leader's functions, but instead may be and are dispersed through varying degrees of delegation to followers, though even more may be desirable in the direction of team effort (see e.g. Hackman, 1990; Katzenbach and Smith, 1993; Sundstrom *et al.*, 1990).

In addition to other conditions, leadership operates within the constraints and opportunities presented by followers (see Stewart, 1982). The constraints include the expectations and perceptions of followers that can influence leaders (Hollander, 1985, 1986; Lord and Maher, 1990). An early proponent of this general view was Fillmore Sanford (1950) who asserted that followers are crucial to any leadership event and deserve more attention. Mary Parker Follett (1949) expressed a comparable point in a paper delivered at the University of London in the early 1930s, emphasizing her concept of 'power with' followers.

Leadership and followership are required throughout teams and organizations, with the same individuals needing to act in both capacities, at least enough so that the distinction becomes less an impediment to action (see e.g. Barnes and Kriger, 1986; Vanderslice, 1988). The characterization of the follower role as mainly passive is therefore inappropriate when considering it as part of an active counterpart to leadership (see Kelley, 1988). Leaders do command greater attention and influence, but followers can affect leaders and the entire enterprise in important ways. Not least, followers are usually the leader's most attentive strategic audience, who experience at first hand the leader's behaviour, and can make attributions about his or her intentions and values.

Being in the follower role also holds within it the potential for taking on the leader role. Indeed, behaviours found to represent effective leadership include attributes of good followership (see Hollander and Webb, 1955; Kouzes and Posner, 1987) such as dependability, competence and honesty. Granted an imbalance of power, influence can be exerted in both roles, as part of a social exchange (Homans, 1961) and the practice of loyalty down as well as loyalty up. Effective leadership is more likely to be achieved by a process in which there is reciprocity and the potential for two-way influence and power sharing, rather than by simply relying on authority and the exercise of power over others.

In this respect, Katz and Kahn (1978) have defined organizational leadership as the influence increment over and above mechanical compliance with routine directives. That means having a personal following beyond what is demanded by one's position of authority. They say that the importance of leadership is to fulfil three main behavioural requirements of organizational functioning, which broadly are: (1) recruit and retain capable staff; (2) maintain essential functions and roles; and (3) provide a climate for making creative contributions. The achievement of these requirements depends upon positive leader–follower relations, with a sense of cohesiveness, which is basic to work teams.

Work teams are interdependent collections of individuals who share responsibility for specific outcomes for their organizations (Sundstrom *et al.*, 1990, p. 120). They are not just groups called teams by higher authority, but must cohere about a performance focus with clear goals pursued with discipline (Katzenbach and Smith, 1993, pp. 12–15). Though the success of a team depends upon so-called 'teamwork', fundamentally it pivots on leader–follower relations. This is exemplified in a study of high performance US Navy ships by Whiteside (1985). He found that the critical element that made a difference was how the young officers functioned as a cohesive followership team, especially by: supporting their leaders, but none the less raising questions and concerns, including bad news; taking initiatives when necessary, without being told; and showing personal care and responsibility. This is also exemplified in some of the best features of self-managed work teams (Manz and Sims, 1987).

In his landmark work, *The Functions of the Executive* (1938), Chester Barnard put forth his 'acceptance theory of authority', stating that the follower has a pivotal role in judging whether an order is authoritative, in so far as: he or she understands it; believes it is not inconsistent with organizational or personal goals; has the ability to comply with it; and sees more rewards than costs in complying and remaining with the organization or group (Hollander, 1978, p. 47). This conception was significant in bringing attention to the place of followership in leadership.

EARLY WORK ON INTERPERSONAL AND GROUP PROCESSES

Various studies early in this century on team and organizational leadership indicated the importance of the leader–follower relationship, including the nature of supposed leadership tasks that could be performed by followers. The pioneering work of Hugo Munsterberg (1914) and Floyd Allport (1924) on influence and social facilitation in group performance opened the way for more experimentation on such elements.

The well-known Hawthorne studies (Mayo, 1933; Roethlisberger and Dickson, 1939) were field experiments that generated interest in social facilitation effects in work groups. Though not directly focused on leadership, they spawned experiments by others such as Gunnar Westerlund

(1952) in Sweden on 'group leadership', with telephone operators allowed more contact with their supervisors, as needed. This provided followers with a greater stake in the workplace, and was illustrative of the way the so-called human relations approach would move towards a more active conception of leader–follower relations.

The Lewin, Lippitt and White (1939) experiments on the effects of autocratic, democratic and *laissez-faire* leadership styles represented another landmark in studying outcomes of leader–follower interaction. Although the subjects used were from boys' clubs, wider implications were none the less drawn.

More importantly, Kurt Lewin's (1947) group decision-making research established group dynamics on an experimental foundation and had resounding influence in generating research and theory about group processes, including the important interrelationships of communication, cohesiveness and conformity. Lewin is credited with saying that 'nothing is so practical as a good theory', but he might as readily have said it about a 'good team', given his pioneering work on applications of group dynamics (see Marrow, 1969). Industrial Japan discovered this message and took it to heart, with their *work team* thrust, before it returned repackaged through such works as *Theory Z* (Ouchi, 1981). There is more than a little irony in the fact that group dynamics and a team emphasis originated in North America and the UK though their workplace implications were evidently better received elsewhere.

THE SITUATIONAL APPROACH: ANTECEDENTS AND ACCOMPANIMENTS

With the human relations movement taking hold (see e.g. Likert, 1961; McGregor, 1960) the situational approach to leadership developed just over forty years ago. A new paradigm emerged which helped to shift the balance from traits to interpersonal relations. It implicitly considered leadership not as a thing a leader possesses so much as a process that involves followers in a particular situation. This development emphasized the context in which the leader and followers functioned, and the demands the task there made for various leader qualities. More recently, others (e.g. Kirkpatrick and Locke, 1991) have asserted a case for studying necessary leader qualities, notably in the motivation and cognition arenas (cf. Hogan *et al.*, 1994).

Ralph Stogdill's 1948 review of the early literature showed the limits of just looking at leader traits, and encouraged that shift to the situational approach. However, a significant break had occurred even earlier when follower reports of leader behaviour were given attention in the Ohio State University Leadership Studies, in which Carrol Shartle and Stogdill played such a pivotal role. The work was begun soon after World War II and represents one of the most significant research programmes done on leader behaviour as reported by followers (see Shartle, Stogdill and Campbell,

1949; Stogdill and Shartle, 1948). With their colleagues, they developed a questionnaire and administered it to members of the many, mostly US Naval, organizations who were asked to describe their leaders by the frequency with which they displayed various behaviours from 'always' to 'never'. When these ratings were analysed, they were found to represent four major factors. As is by now well known, the two chief factors accounting for the bulk of leader behaviour were consideration and initiation of structure (see Fleishman, 1973).

The emergence of the situational approach came most notably through the writings of John Hemphill (1949), Fillmore Sanford (1950) and Alvin Gouldner (1950), among others. Sanford wrote:

> There is some justification for regarding the follower as the most crucial factor in any leadership event and for arguing that research directed at the follower will eventually yield a handsome pay-off. Not only is it the follower who accepts or rejects leadership, but it is the follower who perceives both the leader and the situation and who reacts in terms of what he perceives.
>
> (Sanford, 1950, p. 4)

The subsequent upsurge in interest in situational factors had a profound effect on research and theory, eventually including 'the nature of the task or activity, its history, the availability of human and material resources, and the quality of leader–follower relations' (Hollander and Offermann, 1990, p. 180). This development also helped to open the way for contingency models of leadership (see e.g. Fiedler, 1964, 1967; House, 1971; Vroom and Yetton, 1973), as well as transactional models (see e.g. Hollander, 1958, 1964, 1978; Hollander and Julian, 1969; Homans, 1961; Graen, 1975; Dienesch and Liden, 1986).

Reflecting this relational emphasis was John Flanagan's (1954) assessment of leader behaviour by followers using his 'critical incident technique', developed first to evaluate US Air Corps pilots in World War II, with considerable success. Basically, critical incidents are reports of actual behaviours observed and evaluated by those on the scene as examples of what is particularly effective or ineffective, in this case leadership. The observer-respondent chooses the incidents to report without identifying the actor.

While on duty as a naval aviation psychologist at Pensacola in the early 1950s, together with John Bair, I obtained and content analysed critical incidents to compare naval aviation cadets who successfully completed basic flight training with those who voluntarily withdrew (Hollander and Bair, 1954). All of those respondents were asked to describe their 'best' and 'worst' flight instructors. Content analyses revealed a significant attitudinal difference in the descriptions they gave: those who *successfully completed* training more often described their 'best' and 'worst' instructors with regard to interpersonal qualities, while those who *withdrew* from flight training emphasized the dimension of instructor competence–incompetence.

These findings suggested that identification with the instructor was a factor associated with success in this programme.

Another significant approach with earlier roots was the use of sociometric procedures, pioneered by Jacob Moreno (1934). Assessing impressions of leadership qualities by this method was important in my own early studies at Pensacola and Newport (see Hollander, 1964, Part III; 1979, pp. 159–60). During this period, we developed peer nominations and ratings to assess effective and ineffective leadership in groups of US naval aviation cadets. Among other findings, this research indicated that peer nominations significantly predicted completion of the US Naval Air Training Program. We also found that leadership and followership peer nominations were highly related and largely unaffected by friendship ties, despite conventional beliefs to the contrary (Hollander and Webb, 1955). A programme of research I conducted at the US Navy OCS (Officer Candidate School) at Newport, Rhode Island, validated the impression that peer nominations tap a reservoir of interpersonal perceptions of considerable value for predicting complex, later performance (see Hollander, 1964, 1965).

More generally, this research again substantiated how basic interpersonal evaluation is in the leader–follower relationship. This point came through in a later series of experiments on leader legitimacy and authority, with respect to the leader's latitude for exerting influence and taking innovative action, which I developed as the 'idiosyncrasy credit' model of leadership (see Hollander, 1958, 1960, 1961a, 1961b, 1964; Hollander and Julian, 1970, 1978). Follower perceptions of the leader were found to affect their responsiveness to the leader and their willingness to have the leader take initiatives as well as to retain authority.

Still another development during this period was the study of emergent leadership by the 'leaderless group discussion' (LGD) technique (see Bass, 1950). Used during World War II for the selection and training of military officers and others, such as the OSS, in the United States, England and Australia, it was reportedly employed in the German military beginning in 1935 (Ansbacher, 1951). Today it is often used as a standard feature of assessment centres designed as one way to select promising managers (see Howard and Bray, 1988).

SOME ASPECTS OF POWER AND IDENTIFICATION IN THE LEADER–FOLLOWER RELATIONSHIP

A major component of the leader–follower relationship is the leader's perception of his or her self relative to followers, and how they in turn perceive the leader. This raises important ethical issues concerning how followers are involved, used or abused, especially in a relationship that is imbalanced in the direction of a leader's power over them. Such a dominance theme is antagonistic to a view of followers as team members in so far as it countenances their abuse by a superior. One expression of this pattern is from a corporate CEO saying in a *Fortune* magazine article on 'The ten toughest bosses' that 'leadership is confirmed when the ability to inflict pain is demonstrated' (Menzies, 1980). A more recent *Business Week* article entitled 'The CEO disease' (Byrne *et al.*, 1991) further examines the extent of this pattern.

Clearly, such abuse of power runs counter to the idea of mutual dependence in a shared enterprise. Further, it may also deprive a leader of honest inputs of information and judgements from subordinates who have been cowed. This only adds to the self-absorption and self-deception that are pitfalls of arbitrary power.

In his classic conception of powerholding, Kipnis (1976) identified four corrupting influences of power affecting the powerholder and those in a relationship with that individual. Briefly these 'metamorphic effects' are: (1) power becomes desired as an end in itself, to be sought at virtually any cost; (2) holding power tempts the individual to use organizational resources for self-benefit, even illegally; (3) creates the basis for false feedback from them, and an exalted sense of self-worth; (4) and a devaluation of others' worth, with a desire to avoid close contact with them. Mulder (1981) extended the last point especially in his concept of 'power distance', which he sees as heightening the differential status of leader and followers, as a function, for example, of disparities in available information or resources.

Regarding this point, Emerson (1962) said that the explicit recognition of *dependence* by a lower-power person on one of higher power can promote resentment by the former. This effect is likely to be detrimental to mutual efforts, though it has not been given as much attention as other, tangible rewards, such as economic benefits. Also, the element of trust may be undercut by a leader's self-serving activity and a lack of accountability when he or she is manifestly failing in a higher-power position.

With their traditional superordinate position, leaders also may be given to self-serving biases beyond those that exist in other social relationships. In his analysis of some key psychological processes involved, Greenwald (1985) presents an interpretation of how the leader's ego or self incorporates several distinctive cognitive biases. These include the self as focus of knowledge, 'beneffectance' as the perception of responsibility for desired, but not for undesired, outcomes, and resistance to change.

This set of tendencies is further enhanced by power over others and a sense of being different, with accompanying social distance, and potential manipulation of others as objects. A necessary corrective is for the leader to be attuned to the needs of followers, their perceptions and expectancies. However, the narcissism associated with craving the affection of followers, as in 'mirror-hungry' charismatic leaders, often deprives them of this corrective (see Post, 1986). A counterpart is seen in followers who are vulnerable to perceptual distortions as a feature of the self-serving bias and identification with the leader, which together bolster their followers' own selves (see Hollander, 1992b).

An alternative view, more in keeping with responsive participation, considers the leader–follower relationship within a mutual identification process. This includes the prospect of two-way influence, and the perception and counterperception of leader and followers (Cantril, 1958). Identification with the leader is exemplified in Freud's (1921) concept of the leader as a shared 'ego-ideal' with whom members of a group mutually identify. Fromm (1941) extended this conception in personality terms, in his contention that 'the psychology of the leader and that of his followers, are, of course, closely linked with each other' (p. 65). Erikson (1975) made an associated point about this linkage in asserting that followers 'join a leader and are joined together by him' (p. 153). They are bonded as a unit.

Inadequate and inattentive leadership was found to be responsible for the failure to maintain 'unit cohesion' in the US Army serving in Vietnam, according to military historians Gabriel and Savage. They say:

> the officer corps grew in inverse proportion to its quality . . . [and] could be described as both bloated in number and poorer in quality . . .. One result was My Lai. Even the staunchest defenders of the Army agree that in normal times a man of Lieutenant Calley's low intelligence and predispositions would never have been allowed to hold a commission . . ..
> The lowering of standards was a wound that the officer corps inflicted on itself.
>
> (Gabriel and Savage, 1978, p. 10)

They also detailed the way that the senior officer corps successfully managed to position themselves far from the action.

By contrast, the identification process is enhanced in those production firms where managers have closer contact with their workforce on the shop-floor and in the cafeteria, often wearing the same company uniform. This pattern is the opposite of distancing employees. It is usually noted in the context of observing how unique it is considered, as in the *New York Times* article (Hicks, 1992) about the CEO of US Steel, featured on the first page of the Business Section. Thomas Usher, it reported, took the unusual step of unexpectedly going to the offices of the United Steelworkers at the company's largest mill in Gary, Indiana. What he said there was not as interesting as the *fact* of his being there. In acknowledging that, Mr Usher commented that:

> Our long-term interests are exactly the same. Whether you are a manager or a member of the union, everyone wants to do a good job . . .. I think there is a growing realization that we are not going to make it without the union and the union . . . without us.
>
> (Hicks, 1992, p. D3).

The Usher view does not seem to represent a common one among corporate executives. Indeed, the founder of Total Quality Management (TQM), W. Edwards Deming (1992), contended that the enormous financial incentives that corporate executives receive have destroyed team work at many American companies.

Some leaders have become so removed from followers' perceptions and needs that they may cease to be aware of how their actions affect the 'team' they wish to foster. A pertinent example of this is seen in the issue of high compensation packages given to American CEOs (see Byrne *et al.*, 1991; Crystal, 1991) even when there are manifestly poor outcomes for their firms. *Business Week, Forbes* and *Fortune* are among the major business publications that recently featured articles on this issue.

Criticisms have centred on how these sums greatly exceed the pay of the average worker, as compared to what is found in foreign competitors.

> In Japan, the compensation of major CEOs is 17 times that of average workers; in France and Germany, 23–25 times; in Britain, 35 times; in America, between 85 and 100-plus times. In 1990, CEO pay rose 7 percent while corporate profits fell 7 percent . . .. United Airlines' CEO . . . received $18.3 million (1,200 times what a new flight attendant makes) [though] United's profits fell 71 percent.
>
> (Will, 1991)

Management performance decrements can also have calamitous effects on the organization and others, but not necessarily on the rewards given to these managers, as revealed in Crystal's (1991) book, *In Search of Excess*. Responsibility for performance is often detached from them so that rewards rise even with poor team and organizational outcomes. A recent case in point is seen in Roger Smith's tenure from 1981 to 1990 as CEO of General Motors. During that time his company lost almost 20 per cent of its US market share. But, on his retirement, his already generous pension was increased to over a million dollars a year by the GM board.

Disparities and perceived inequities such as these make leaders even more likely to be objects of disdain or contempt. Though leaders are needed, they may also be resented for holding a position of authority and having special benefits that accompany it. Least of all are leaders who are not performing productively, but are still well rewarded, able to encourage good follower-ship and team effort. Indeed, it is quite to the contrary when they violate an equity norm by failing to provide something of value, especially given loyalty and trust by followers.

On the larger issue of moral responsibility, Emler and Hogan say:

> There is no inbuilt tendency to use power responsibly. You cannot randomly allocate leadership responsibility and expect the interests of justice or society to be well served. Those in charge have a responsibility to make moral decisions greater than those they command . . . [and] those differences become more consequential the further up the hierarchy one goes.
>
> (Emler and Hogan, 1991, p. 86).

Accordingly, a reasonable question, not asked enough in selecting leaders, is: What are the costs of putting this person in a position of authority and responsibility? (Hollander, 1992b, p. 43). The followers' perceptions of the leader's actions and motives have broader ethical and performance consequences. These include obvious instances of unfairness, self-seeking at others' expense, weakness, vacillation and outright misconduct, all of which undermine the leader's standing and the vital bonds within the team.

The leader role is still seen more often as *power over* others, rather than as stewardship, or even as a *service to* others (see DePree, 1989). Not least there is the very real problem of what Drucker (1988) calls 'misleaders' who are dysfunctional. From a ten-year perspective, DeVries (1992) estimates that the base rate for executive incompetence is at least 50 per cent. Hogan, Raskin and Fazzini (1990) found that organizational climate studies from the mid-1950s onwards show 60 to 75 per cent of organizational respondents reporting their immediate supervisor as the worst or most stressful aspect of their job.

Such findings highlight the importance of followers as perceivers with expectations of and attributions about leader performance. Lord and Maher (1990) say that these perceptions are checked against prototypes held by followers and expectations of how leaders should perform. Positive or negative outcomes are more likely to be attributed to a leader's action, as seen in the concept of the 'romance of leadership' (Meindl *et al.*, 1985). Argyle and Henderson (1985) indicate that the rules for superiors include planning and assigning work efficiently, informing, advising and encouraging subordinates (p. 261).

CHARISMATIC, TRANSFORMATIONAL AND TRANSACTIONAL LEADERSHIP

Renewed interest in charisma, now associated with transformational (TF) leadership (Burns, 1978; Bass, 1985), also shows how important it is to learn about the followers' perspective in understanding such phenomena. Originally Max Weber (1946) conceived of charismatic leaders as attracting others because of their strong appeal and extraordinary determination, especially in time of crisis. But Weber also stated that if the leader was 'long unsuccessful, above all if his leadership fails to benefit followers, it is likely that his charisma will disappear' (p. 360).

There also is a need to take account of the ethical distinction Burns (1978) made between the self-serving and socially responsible kinds of transformational leaders. In the world of organizations, as well as in politics, charismatic leaders are still sought as saviours. But they also may present difficulties, such as tendencies towards narcissism (e.g. Post, 1986) and unethical behaviour. For example, Howell and Avolio (1992) cite the dubious ethical standards associated with such business leaders as Robert Campeau, John DeLorean and Michael Milkin, all of whom were acknowledged to have charisma for many of their followers. Unethical leaders are more likely to use their charisma for *power over* followers, directed towards self-serving ends, usually in a calculated manipulative way. Ethical leaders are considered to use their charisma in a socially constructive way to serve others.

Charisma and transformational leadership are frequently linked in the literature. Transactional leadership (TA) refers to a fair exchange in which the leader gives something to followers and receives esteem and latitude for action in return (Homans, 1961). Charisma may not necessarily be part of TF leadership, but it is routinely imputed to the TF leader: as, for example, in Bass's first aspect of TF and in House and Shamir's (1993) work. However, the research by Ehrlich *et al.* (1990) suggests that 'more transactionally oriented activities by a leader may also contribute to a leader's charismatic appeal' (p. 242). At its heart charisma is attributed to a leader by followers. In that respect, when the charismatic leader loses followers who had granted unquestioning trust, the charisma effectively vanishes.

TF leaders do provide rewards to followers, as Bass (1985) notes, listing personal attention and intellectual stimulation. However, the followers' reciprocation to the leader is usually unacknowledged since that would support the view that a transaction has occurred. This would breach the artificial separation of measures that is maintained by Bass (1985), through that process of labelling TA leadership in a stripped-down form rather than as originally described. Curphy (1993), for example, found that TF and TA leadership were not independent, but were highly related in ratings given by cadets to their squadron commanding officer at the US Air Force Academy.

As Ehrlich *et al.* (1990) note, 'Conceptually, the basis for either form of leadership is a relational and perceptual exchange developed between a leader and his or her subordinates' (p. 231). But the actuality of this transaction between leader and followers is usually denied in accounting for the TF phenomenon. Instead there is an insistence on a rigid dichotomy between TA and TF leadership, maintained by considering only tangible rewards and failing to acknowledge the intangible ones followers receive from TF as well as TA leaders. Yet, Chemers (1993) contends that the intrinsic reward of 'self-esteem, a sense of purpose, or salvation . . . becomes highly attractive, and supremely motivating' when followers' needs are intense enough. 'Under such circumstances charismatic or transformational leadership may be seen as a special, elevated case of the more mundane transactional exchange processes that are the basis of all, person-to-person, team leadership' (p. 312).

In sum, TF leadership can be seen as an extension of TA leadership, in which there is greater leader intensity and follower arousal. This amounts to having a large fund of credits accorded to the leader by followers, thereby granting esteem and more sway in being influential. Finally, to achieve a responsive following it is essential at the outset to establish and build upon TA leadership before expecting an adequate response to TF leadership.

RECENT RESEARCH ON RELATIONAL QUALITIES OF LEADERSHIP

Followers are the ones who experience the actuality of a leader's approach to leadership, and are uniquely able to evaluate it and its effects. A prominent example of the usefulness of this source is shown in a study on 'derailment' (McCall, Lombardo and Morrison, 1988) with 400 promising managers, seen to be on a fast track. Those who failed to reach their expected potential were more often found to lack interpersonal skills, especially in relating to subordinates, but not to be deficient in their technical skills. Also, research by Kouzes and Posner (1987), with a sample of 3,400 organizational respondents, dealt with qualities they admired in their leaders, and found the relational realm to be significant. The four qualities that more than half of these respondents said they admired most were being honest, competent, forward looking and inspiring.

Our recent research programme (Hollander and Kelly, 1990, 1992; Kelly, Julien and Hollander, 1992; Schwager *et al.*, 1993) used critical incidents to study these relationships further. These were supplemented by open-ended questions and rating scales, to study followers' perceptions of actual leader behaviour in good or bad leadership situations and followers' perceptions of ideal leader behaviour. Based on previous findings, our hypothesis was that relational qualities would be emphasized in reports and evaluations distinguishing good from bad leadership. We also predicted that characteristics reported for good leadership would closely correspond to those independently described as those of ideal leadership.

The most recent results are based on a total sample of 280 respondents, half male and half female, drawn primarily from organizationally based master's degree students enrolled in evening courses on organizational behaviour or leadership. Two-thirds held professional and/or administrative positions, and the great majority (80 per cent) were employed full-time.

Respondents were first asked to describe an incident that occurred between them and a superior where either *good* leadership, for one half of the respondents, or *bad* leadership, for the other half, was displayed. No identifying information was requested, to protect anonymity. Other follow-up questions asked respondents what they found rewarding or not from what that superior did or said as leader, what their own response was and what effect this event had on the relationship with this superior. They also rated the leader on 6-point Likert rating scales of seven leader characteristics, e.g. involvement, directiveness, as representative of major qualities of leadership reported in the literature. In addition, they evaluated the leader in the incident on ten 6-point semantic differential scales, e.g. capable–incapable, helpful–unhelpful, summed as a 'favourability index'.

Subsequent forms of the questionnaire were identical but added two items to the seven leader characteristics (observing and informing), and later substituted two others. Both had an additional open-ended question, asking what an 'ideal' leader's behaviour would be like in the event described as demonstrating either good or bad leadership, and an exercise requiring respondents to rank order the nine characteristics for an ideal leader to possess. The respondent was also provided with the opportunity to record up to three additional characteristics of the ideal leader and to show their place if included with the list of nine characteristics.

Content analyses of the first open-ended question indicated that in good leadership leaders were primarily seen to be supportive. They were also seen to have good communication skills in providing clarity and/or being good listeners, to be action/results oriented, to delegate to and/or empower subordinates and to be fair. In bad leadership, leaders were reported to be unsupportive, to show a lack of communication skills, to be uninvolving, unfair, angry or harsh, autocratic and sometimes poor managers of resources.

The content categories for the second question asked respondents to identify what they found rewarding from what the superior did or said in the leadership situation. The positive rewards of support, sensitivity to followers, fairness and trust dominated good but were absent or negative in bad leadership; this was in line with the themes emerging from the content analysis of the first open-ended question on good and bad leadership.

A further question asked about the effect the event had on the follower's relationship with this supervisor. Over three-quarters of followers in the good leadership condition indicated that the incident strengthened their working/personal relationship with their superior. Others indicated increased respect or performance/commitment. Not surprisingly, bad leadership often weakened the relationship and resulted in a loss of respect or trust in the leader; other responses included avoidance and/or job termination.

As hypothesized from our previous results, the mean ratings for the nine characteristics again showed that *good* and *bad* leaders differed significantly on the cluster of four relational items of trustworthiness, perceptiveness, involvement and rewardingness, but not on the other three of compliance, directiveness and time orientation. These four relational characteristics were also ranked as most important for the ideal leader. As expected, good and bad leaders were also found to be significantly differentiated by the degree to which they observe and inform followers.

When respondents who had described a good leadership incident were asked what the ideal leader in that same situation would have done, their most frequent response was 'the ideal leader behaviour has already been described' (54 per cent). The remaining content categories in the good leadership incident had a large degree of overlap with the categories found in question one, which asked respondents to describe an incident where good leadership was displayed. Categories mentioned again included communication, involvement, support, rewardingness, taking action and honesty.

In a further analysis, the main focus was the overlap of the content categories from respondents who had described good leadership with the content categories of *ideal* leader behaviour proposed by the separate group of respondents who had previously rated bad leadership. This ensured that there was comparability of categories for different groups of respondents, and limited any influence of previous ratings of good leadership on perceptions of the ideal leader.

When respondents *who had described bad leadership* were asked what an ideal leader would have done, communication was more often mentioned. Respondents frequently indicated that the ideal leader would have utilized followers more often in seeking input, information and ideas, and also would have provided feedback and rewards, support, a mission or goals and guidance. In a more general vein, respondents viewed an ideal leader as someone who would take action and achieve results. Finally, respondents mentioned two personal qualities that an ideal leader would possess: honesty/trustworthiness and confidence/competency that generate respect by followers.

As expected, a high degree of overlap was found between actual leader behaviour and ideal leader behaviour. These findings compellingly show that there is a strong relationship between ratings of good leadership and rankings of the importance of these same characteristics for the ideal leader. Those characteristics rated high or low when describing the actual leader were also ranked by other respondents correspondingly high or low regarding the ideal leader. Therefore, whether leadership is called transactional or transformational, the common persisting element is the significant *relational* nature of the intangible rewards provided to followers by leaders. This gets to the heart of motivations to follow, beyond sheer sustenance.

A subsequent analysis (Schwager *et al.*, 1993) compared the response of women and men in the aforementioned sample. They were found to report similarly about leadership qualities in their incidents (i.e. communication skills, action/results oriented and provided support) and comparable rewards (i.e. supportiveness and sensitivity). In the second question, regarding rewards from the incident, men were more likely to mention taking needed action and women receiving instruction and fairness. As instances of bad leadership, both women and men reported a lack of the relational qualities described in the good condition and various unrewarding or even punitive behaviours displayed by the superior. Unfairness was the only significant gender difference revealed, with women mentioning it twice as often as men, but with neither very prominent (27 to 13 per cent).

In response to the good leadership incident, both women and men increased participation or followership, expressed satisfaction, felt more comfortable or valued and talked more freely. Positive effects on the follower's relationship with the superior included 'strengthened the working and/or personal relationship' and 'increased respect'. The only significant gender difference was that women were twice as likely to increase their performance and/or commitment as a result of the good leadership incident

(25 to 12 per cent). Furthermore, the gender comparisons revealed no difference in perceptions of the 'ideal' leader, which suggests the commonality of cultural experience shared by women and men. In sum, this analysis demonstrated little variation in the perceptions of good and bad leadership by these women and men as followers. This strengthens the conclusion that such relationship elements are essential aspects of the leader–follower bond.

SUMMARY AND CONCLUSIONS

We are now in an era where a more active role for followership is clearly evident. This includes a team emphasis and the implementation of empowerment systems, through delegation and participative decision making. It represents an alternative to traditional power conceptions of leadership and followership.

Leaders and their qualities are still important, but particularly in how those qualities engage followers in productive and mutually satisfying teams. This marks a departure from the usual way of seeing leader qualities as possessions instead of interpersonal links with others involved in mutual pursuits.

ACKNOWLEDGEMENTS

The contributions of Elisa H. Schwager and Dennis R. Kelly to the preparation of this chapter are gratefully acknowledged.

REFERENCES

Allport, F.H. (1924) *Social Psychology*. Boston, Mass.: Houghton Mifflin.
Ansbacher, H.L. (1951) The history of the leaderless group discussion technique. *Psychological Bulletin, 48*, 383–90.
Argyle, M. (1983) *The Psychology of Interpersonal Behaviour*, 4th edition. Harmondsworth: Penguin.
Argyle, M. and Henderson, M. (1985) *The Anatomy of Relationships*. London: Heinemann.
Barnard, C.I. (1938) *The Functions of the Executive*. Cambridge, Mass.: Harvard University Press.
Barnes, L.B. and Kriger, M.P. (1986) The hidden side of organizational leadership. *Sloan Management Review, 28*, 15–25.
Bass, B.M. (1950) The leaderless group discussion technique. *Personnel Psychology, 3*, 17–32.
Bass, B.M. (1985) *Leadership and Performance beyond Expectations*. New York: Free Press.
Burns, J.M. (1978) *Leadership*. New York: Harper & Row.
Byrne, J.A., Symonds, W.C. and Siler, J.F. (1991) The CEO disease. *Business Week*, 1 April, pp. 52–60.
Cantril, H. (1958) Effective democratic leadership: a psychological interpretation. *Journal of Individual Psychology, 14*, 128–38.
Chemers, M.M. (1993) An integrative theory of leadership. In M.M. Chemers and

R. Ayman (eds) *Leadership Theory and Research: Perspectives and Directions.* San Diego, CA: Academic Press, pp. 293–319.

Crystal, G. (1991) *In Search of Excess: The Overcompensation of American Executives.* New York: Norton.

Curphy, G.J. (1993) An empirical investigation of the effects of transformational and transactional leadership on organizational climate, attrition, and performance. In K.E. Clark, M.B. Clark and D.P. Campbell (eds) *Impact of Leadership.* Greensboro, NC: Center for Creative Leadership, pp. 177–88.

Deming, W. Edwards (1992) Quoted in *The Economist*, 1 February, p. 19.

DePree, M. (1989) *Leadership is an Art.* New York: Doubleday Dell.

DeVries, D.L. (1992) Executive selection: advances but no progress. *Center for Creative Leadership: Issues & Observations, 12*, 1–5.

Dienesch, R.M. and Liden, R.C. (1986) Leader–member exchange model of leadership: a critique and further development. *Academy of Management Review, 11*, 618–34.

Drucker, P.F. (1988) Leadership: more doing than dash. *Wall Street Journal*, 6 January, p. 14.

Ehrlich, S.B., Meindl, J.R. and Viellieu, B. (1990) The charismatic appeal of a transformational leader: an empirical case study of a small, high-technology contractor. *Leadership Quarterly, 14*, 229–48.

Emerson, R.M. (1962) Power-dependence relations. *American Sociological Review, 27*, 31–41.

Emler, N. and Hogan, R. (1991) Moral psychology and public policy. In W.M. Kurtines and J.L. Gewirtz (eds) *Handbook of Moral Behavior and Development*, Volume 3, *Applications.* Hillsdale, NJ: Erlbaum, pp. 69–93.

Erikson, E.H. (1975) *Life History and the Historical Moment.* New York: Norton.

Evans, M.G. (1970) The effects of supervisory behavior on the path–goal relationship. *Organizational Behavior and Human Performance, 5*, 277–98.

Fiedler, F.E. (1964) A contingency model of leadership effectiveness. In L. Berkowitz (ed.) *Advances in Experimental Social Psychology*, Volume 1. New York: Academic Press, pp. 149–90.

Fiedler, F.E. (1967) *A Theory of Leadership Effectiveness.* New York: McGraw-Hill.

Flanagan, J.C. (1954) The critical incident technique. *Psychological Bulletin, 51*, 327–58.

Fleishman, E.A. (1973) Twenty years of consideration and structure. In E.A. Fleishman and J.G. Hunt (eds) *Current Developments in the Study of Leadership.* Carbondale: Southern Illinois University Press, pp. 1–37.

Follett, M.P. (1949) The essentials of leadership. In L. Urwick (ed.) *Freedom and Coordination.* London: Management Publications Trust, pp. 47–60.

Freud, S. (1921) *Group Psychology and the Analysis of the Ego.* New York: Bantam.

Fromm, E. (1941) *Escape from Freedom.* New York: Rinehart.

Gabriel, R. and Savage, P. (1978) *Crisis in Command.* New York: Hill & Wang.

Gardner, J. (1990) *On Leadership.* New York: Free Press.

Gilbert, G.R. and Hyde, A.C. (1988) Followership and the federal worker. *Public Administration Review, 48*, 962–8.

Gouldner, A.W. (ed.) (1950) *Studies in Leadership.* New York: Harper.

Graen, G. (1975) Role-making processes within complex organizations. In M.D. Dunnette (ed.) *Handbook of Industrial and Organizational Psychology.* Chicago: Rand McNally, pp. 1201–45.

Greenwald, A. (1985) Totalitarian egos in the personalities of democratic leaders. Symposium Paper. *International Society of Political Psychology Annual Meeting*, Washington, DC (20 June).

Hackman, J.R. (ed.) (1990) *Groups that Work (And Those that Don't).* San Francisco: Jossey-Bass.

Heider, F. (1958) *The Psychology of Interpersonal Relations*. New York: Wiley.

Heider, J. (1982) The leader who knows how to make things happen. *Journal of Humanistic Psychology*, *27* (3), 33–9.

Hemphill, J.K. (1949) *Situational Factors in Leadership*. Columbus: Ohio State University, Personnel Research Board.

Hicks, J.P. (1992) The steel men with kid gloves. *The New York Times*, 3 April, p. D-1.

Hogan, R., Curphy, G.J. and Hogan, J. (1994) What we know about leadership: effectiveness and personality. *American Psychologist*, *49*, 493–504.

Hogan, R., Raskin, R. and Fazzini, D. (1990) The dark side of charisma. In K.E. Clark and M.B. Clark (eds) *Measures of Leadership*, West Orange, NJ: Leadership Library of America, pp. 343–54.

Hollander, E.P. (1958) Conformity, status, and idiosyncrasy credit. *Psychological Review*, *65*, 117–27.

Hollander, E.P. (1960) Competence and conformity in the acceptance of influence. *Journal of Abnormal and Social Psychology*, *61*, 361–5.

Hollander, E.P. (1961a) Emergent leadership and social influence. In L. Petrullo and B.M. Bass (eds) *Leadership and Interpersonal Behavior*. New York: Holt, Rinehart & Winston.

Hollander, E.P. (1961b) Some effects of perceived status on responses to innovative behavior. *Journal of Abnormal and Social Psychology*, *49*, 247–50.

Hollander, E.P. (1964) *Leaders, Groups, and Influence*. New York: Oxford University Press.

Hollander, E.P. (1965) Validity of peer nominations in predicting a distant performance criterion. *Journal of Applied Psychology*, *49*, 434–8.

Hollander, E.P. (1978) *Leadership Dynamics: A Practical Guide to Effective Relationships*. New York: Free Press/Macmillan.

Hollander, E.P. (1979) The impact of Ralph M. Stogdill and the Ohio State Leadership Studies on a transactional approach to leadership. *Journal of Management*, *5*(2), 157–65.

Hollander, E.P. (1985) Leadership and power. In G. Lindzey and E. Aronson (eds) *The Handbook of Social Psychology*, 3rd edition. New York: Random House, pp. 485–537.

Hollander, E.P. (1986) On the central role of leadership processes. *International Review of Applied Psychology*, *35*, 39–52.

Hollander, E.P. (1992a) The essential interdependence of leadership and followership. *Current Directions in Psychological Science*, *1*(2), 71–5.

Hollander, E.P. (1992b) Leadership, followership, self, and others. *Leadership Quarterly*, *3*(1), 43–54.

Hollander, E.P. and Bair, J.T. (1954) Attitudes toward authority-figures as correlates of motivation among naval aviation cadets. *Journal of Applied Psychology*, *38*, 21–5.

Hollander, E.P. and Julian, J.W. (1969) Contemporary trends in the analysis of leadership processes. *Psychological Bulletin, 71*, 387–97.

Hollander, E.P. and Julian, J.W. (1970) Studies in leader legitimacy, influence and innovation. In L.Berkowitz (ed.) *Advances in Experimental Social Psychology*, Volume 5. New York: Academic Press, pp. 33–69.

Hollander, E.P. and Julian, J.W. (1978) A further look at leader legitimacy, influence, and innovation. In L. Berkowitz (ed.) *Group Processes*. New York: Academic Press, pp. 153–65.

Hollander, E.P. and Kelly, D.R. (1990) Rewards from leaders as perceived by followers: further use of critical incidents and rating scales. *Annual Meeting of the Eastern Psychological Association*, Philadelphia, PA (30 March).

Hollander, E.P. and Kelly, D.R. (1992) Appraising relational qualities of leadership and followership. Paper presented at the *25th International Congress of Psychology*, Brussels, Belgium (24 July).

Hollander, E.P. and Offermann, L. (1990) Power and leadership in organizations: relationships in transition. *American Psychologist, 45*, 179–89.

Hollander, E.P. and Webb, W.B. (1955) Leadership, followership, and friendship: an analysis of peer nominations. *Journal of Abnormal and Social Psychology, 50*, 163–7.

Homans, G.C. (1961) *Social Behavior: Its Elementary Forms*. New York: Harcourt, Brace & World.

House, R.J. (1971) A path-goal theory of leader effectiveness. *Administrative Science Quarterly, 16*, 321–38.

House, R.J. and Shamir, B. (1993) Toward the integration of transformational, charismatic and visionary theories. In M.M. Chemers and R. Ayman (eds) *Leadership Theory and Research: Perspectives and Directions*. San Diego: Academic Press, pp. 81–107.

Howard, A. and Bray, D. (1988) *Managerial Lives in Transition: Advancing Age and Changing Times*. New York: Dorsey.

Howell, J.M. and Avolio, B.J. (1992) The ethics of charismatic leadership: submission or liberation? *Academy of Management Executive, 6*(2), 43–54.

Katz, D. and Kahn, R.L. (1978) *The Social Psychology of Organizations*, 2nd edition. New York: Wiley.

Katzenbach, J.R. and Smith, D.K. (1993) *The Wisdom of Teams: Creating the High-Performance Organization*. Cambridge, Mass.: Harvard Business School Press.

Kelley, R.E. (1988) In praise of followers. *Harvard Business Review*, Nov.–Dec., *88*(6), 142–8.

Kelly, D., Julien, T. and Hollander, E.P. (1992) Further effects of good and bad leadership revealed by critical incidents and rating scales. Paper presented at the Annual Meeting of the Eastern Psychological Association, Boston, Mass. (4 April).

Kipnis, D. (1976) *The Powerholders*. Chicago, IL: University of Chicago Press.

Kirkpatrick, S.A. and Locke, E.A. (1991) Leadership: do traits matter? *Academy of Management Executive, 5*(2), 48–60.

Kouzes, J.M. and Posner, B.Z. (1987) *The Leadership Challenge: How to Get Extraordinary Things Done in Organizations*. San Francisco: Jossey-Bass.

LeBon, G. (1897) *The Crowd: A Study of the Popular Mind*, 2nd edition. London: T.F. Unwin.

Lewin, K. (1947) Group decision and social change. In T.M. Newcomb and E.L. Hartley (eds) *Readings in Social Psychology*. New York: Holt, pp. 330–44.

Lewin, K., Lippitt, R. and White, R.K. (1939) Patterns of aggressive behavior in experimentally created 'social climates'. *Journal of Social Psychology, 10*, 271–99.

Likert, R. (1961) *New Patterns of Management*. New York: McGraw-Hill.

Lord, R.G. and Maher, K.J. (1990) Leadership perceptions and leadership performance: two distinct but interdependent processes. In J. Carroll (ed.) *Advances in Applied Social Psychology: Business Settings*, Volume 4. Hillsdale, NJ: Erlbaum, pp. 129–54.

McCall, M.W., Lombardo, M.M. and Morrison, A.M. (1988) *The Lessons of Experience*. Ashland, Mass.: Lexington Books.

McGregor, D. (1960) *The Human Side of Enterprise*. New York: McGraw-Hill.

Manz, C.C. and Sims, H.P. Jr (1987) Leading workers to lead themselves: the eternal leadership of self-managed work teams. *Administrative Science Quarterly, 32*, 106–28.

Marrow, A.J. (1969) *The Practical Theorist: The Life and Work of Kurt Lewin*. New York: Basic Books.

Mayo, E. (1933) *The Human Problems of an Industrial Civilization*. New York: Macmillan.

Meindl, J.R., Ehrlich, S.B. and Dukerich, J.M. (1985) The romance of leadership. *Administrative Science Quarterly*, *30*, 78–102.

Menzies, H.D. (1980) The ten toughest bosses. *Fortune*, *101*, 62–9.

Meyer, H.H. (1982) Whither leadership and supervision. *Professional Psychology*, *13*, 930.

Moreno, J.L. (1934) *Who Shall Survive?* New York: Beacon House.

Mulder, M. (1981) On the quantity and quality of power and the Q.W.L. Paper presented at the International Conference on the Quality of Work Life, Toronto.

Munsterberg, H. (1914) *Psychology, General and Applied*. New York: Appleton.

Ouchi, W.G. (1981) *Theory Z: How American Business can Meet the Japanese Challenge*. Reading, Mass.: Addison-Wesley.

Pfeffer, J. (1977) The ambiguity of leadership. In M.W. McCall, Jr and M.M. Lombardo (eds) *Leadership: Where Else Can We Go?* Durham, NC: Duke University Press.

Post, J.M. (1986) Narcissism and the charismatic leader–follower relationship. *Political Psychology*, *7*, 675–88.

Reich, R.B. (1987) Entrepreneurship reconsidered: the team as hero. *Harvard Business Review*, *65*(3), 77–83.

Roethlisberger, F.J. and Dickson, W.J. (1939) *Management and the Worker*. Cambridge, Mass.: Harvard University Press.

Sanford, F. (1950) *Authoritarianism and Leadership*. Philadelphia: Institute for Research in Human Relations.

Schmidt, K.O. (1975) *Tao te Ching*. Lakemont, GA: CSA Press.

Schwager, E.H., Kelly, D.R., Julien, T. and Hollander, E.P. (1993) What women and men perceive as good and bad leadership. *Annual Meeting of the Eastern Psychological Association*, Arlington, VA (19 April).

Shartle, C.L., Stogdill, R.M. and Campbell, D.T. (1949) *Studies in Naval Leadership*. Columbus: Personnel Research Board, Ohio State University.

Stewart, R. (1982) *Choices for the Manager*. Englewood Cliffs, NJ: Prentice-Hall.

Stogdill, R.M. (1948) Personal factors associated with leadership. *Journal of Psychology*, *25*, 35–71.

Stogdill, R.M. and Shartle, C.L. (1948) Methods for determining patterns of leadership behavior in relation to organization structure and objectives. *Journal of Applied Psychology*, *32*, 286–91.

Sundstrom, E., DeMeuse, K.P. and Futrell, D. (1990) Work teams: applications and effectiveness. *American Psychologist*, *45*(2), 120–33.

Tarde, G. (1903) *The Laws of Imitation* (translated from 2nd French edition by E.C. Parsons; original, 1890). New York: Holt.

Vanderslice, V.J. (1988) Separating leadership from leaders: an assessment of the effect of leader and follower roles in organizations. *Human Relations*, *41*, 677–96.

Vroom, V.H. and Yetton, P.W. (1973) *Leadership and Decision-making*. Pittsburgh, PA: University of Pittsburgh Press.

Weber, M. (1921) The sociology of charismatic authority. Republished in translation (1946) in H.H. Gerth and C.W. Mills (trans. & eds) *From Max Weber: Essays in Sociology*. New York: Oxford University Press, pp. 245–52.

Westerlund, G. (1952) *Group Leadership: A Field Experiment*. Stockholm: Nordisk Rotogravyr.

Whiteside, D.E. (1985) *Command Excellence: What It Takes to be the Best!* Washington, DC: Department of the Navy, Leadership Division, Naval Military Personnel Command.

Will, G. (1991) Corporate raiders. *Boston Globe*, 2 September, p. 15.

5 British businessmen abroad

Peter Collett

INTRODUCTION

For a long time it was assumed that commerce creates a uniform culture all of its own, and that what is good for business in one country is automatically right in others (cf. Haire *et al.*, 1966; England, 1975). This view has recently been challenged by scholars who have shown, not only that different cultural assumptions encourage different types of organizational structure (Tainio and Santalainen, 1983; Adler, 1991), but that even within the same country there are often enormous differences in 'corporate culture' (Deal and Kennedy, 1982; Furnham and Gunter, 1993).

The major exponents of this new, culturally relative school of thought are Laurent, Hofstede and Trompenaars. Laurent (1983, 1986) has shown that the values, beliefs and goals of managers differ markedly from one country to another. He has demonstrated, for example, that the assumptions of managers within a large multinational organization vary widely according to country, and that the variation in managerial assumptions is much greater between nations than between different organizations within the same country. Hofstede (1984, 1991) has also concluded that 'there are no universal solutions to organization and management problems'. Studying people in IBM, he discovered that management values can be distinguished cross-culturally according to four independent factors – which he calls 'Power Distance', 'Individualism', 'Uncertainty Avoidance' and 'Masculinity'. He has shown that nations can be scored on these four dimensions, and he has proposed that the scores can be related to indigenous styles of leadership, motivation and management.

Over the past four years, a great deal of attention has been paid to cross-cultural differences in management style. The research conducted in this area has covered a wide range of topics, such as attitudes to work (Graves, 1979), the Protestant work ethic (Furnham, 1990; Giorgi and Marsh, 1990), business conventions (Mole, 1991), what people look for in a job (Harding *et al.*, 1986) and the kinds of resources they use to deal with business problems (Smith *et al.*, 1993). Styles of social behaviour in different countries have also been compared (Hall and Hall, 1990; Collett, 1993). Although some of these comparisons lie outside business studies, they still have a bearing on the conduct of international business, if only because the way that people from different countries behave when they do business can have a dramatic effect on the outcome of their transactions.

However, two notes of caution should be struck. The first is that we need to guard against assuming that, just because two countries can be shown to differ in some respect, it automatically follows that the business worlds of those countries exhibit the same difference. Take the case of national stereotypes. You might decide, for example, that you want to find out how businesspeople from certain countries perceive each other. When you look through the literature, you discover that, while there are lots of studies on national stereotypes, there aren't any on businesspeople. So what do you do? Do you abandon the exercise altogether, or do you decide to use the studies you have located as a guide to the attitudes of businesspeople in those countries? The first option doesn't get you anywhere. The problem with the second option, however, is that it can lead you to draw quite the wrong conclusions. Just because two countries perceive each other in certain ways, it doesn't follow that the businesspeople in those countries will hold the same opinions as their compatriots. In fact, because of the nature of their work, and the opportunities that it provides for contact with foreigners, it is quite likely that businesspeople will entertain less stereotyped views of their counterparts in other countries. However, this, as we shall see later on, isn't always the case.

The other reason for caution concerns the inferences that are sometimes drawn from cross-cultural differences. Most of the research in culture-and-management has involved comparisons, rather than investigations of how the business representatives in different countries actually relate to each other. In other words, the research has been *cross-cultural* rather than *intercultural*. There is, of course, nothing wrong with cross-cultural research, except that it cannot be taken as a guide to what happens when representatives from different cultures meet. We cannot assume, just because people from two countries differ, that this is going to influence their transactions in any way. The only way to find out what does affect international business transactions is to study them *in vivo*, or, failing that, to ask people what it is like to do business in other countries.

The research on international business is extremely lop-sided, with most of the effort being devoted to the study of long-term rather than short-term contact with other countries. As Furnham and Bochner (1986) have shown, most of the research on the effects of foreign contact has focused on groups like students, aid workers and expatriates – all of whom have to face problems of adaptation, and who are liable to experience anxiety, cultural alienation and home-sickness. Furnham and Bochner point out that businessmen should experience less culture shock than other types of travellers, but they should still experience stress. It is very unlikely that that culture shock is a problem for the 'business commuter', who flies to Berlin or Paris in the morning and comes home that evening. He, too, is part of the patchwork quilt of international dealings, but the problems he has to deal with are very different from those of the expatriate.[1]

Because the business commuter's trips are short, he is not exposed to the roller-coaster swings of mood which characterize the adaptation process of people who visit other countries for extended periods of time. The business commuter seldom experiences 'culture shock' – partly because the countries he visits are usually close by, but also because he tends to be isolated from those aspects of the host country which might otherwise disturb him. It is not unusual for a business commuter to fly into a foreign capital, and to be whisked off to a meeting in a boardroom which is no different from any other. Apart from the cuisine, and the 'foreign-ness' of his hosts, there may be very little that strikes him as unusual or strange. Even his hotel, with its standardized fixtures and mid-Atlantic menu, is likely to create a feeling of familiarity and the illusion that home is never far away.

We still know very little about the business commuter, where he travels to, how long he spends abroad, how many cities or countries he visits and for what purpose. The nature of the problems that he confronts, and the way they differ from those associated with cases of extended international contact, also waits to be examined. We have yet to explore the perceptions that business commuters have of the countries they visit and how this relates to factors like their facility with the local language and the ease of doing business abroad. These are just a few of the issues which persuaded us to take a closer look at the business commuter. Instead of including all foreign destinations, we decided, however, to focus on British businessmen doing business on the continent – that is, on 'Eurocommuters' (Collett, 1994).

THE EUROCOMMUTER SURVEY

The survey was conducted in the departure lounges of Heathrow and Gatwick airports by a team of British Airport Authority interviewers. As the survey was concerned with the experiences of British businessmen in Europe, the interviewers concentrated on flights leaving for European cities. The interviewers were provided with a rough guide to how many businessmen they should try to interview going to each European country.

Statistics compiled by the Civil Aviation Authority show that 19 per cent of UK airline passengers to Europe travel to Germany and 18 per cent to France. The Netherlands comes next with 10 per cent, followed by Switzerland (9 per cent), Italy (8 per cent), Spain (7 per cent), Belgium (7 per cent), Eire (6 per cent), Sweden (3 per cent), Denmark (3 per cent), Norway (2 per cent) and Portugal (2 per cent). Taken together, these countries account for well over 90 per cent of the British air traffic to the continent. It was decided, therefore, to restrict the survey to these countries, and to exclude countries like Austria, Finland and Luxembourg, which are visited less frequently. However, because no eastern European countries appeared in the top twelve, it was decided, as a matter of interest, to include Russia. The final sample was planned to be in the region of 625 individuals, distributed so that they reflected the proportions of British travellers to each of the thirteen countries. Because so many British people visit Germany and France, we planned to interview 125 businessmen travelling to each of these countries. Fifty interviews were planned for businessmen travelling to the Netherlands, and to Switzerland, Italy and Spain, and 25 interviews for Belgium, Eire, Sweden, Denmark, Norway, Portugal and Russia. This gave us a total of 625 planned interviews.

The survey was conducted in the following way: the interviewers positioned themselves in the departure lounges of flights to the thirteen countries, leaving sufficient time to conduct one or two interviews before passengers started to board the plane. They approached people who looked as though they were travelling on business, and asked them, first, whether they were a British passport holder living in the UK and, second, whether they were travelling to Europe on business. These two filter questions were designed to exclude other nationals, as well as Britons who were going abroad for some other purpose.

The interviewer then asked where the person would be doing business and what were the purposes of the trip. Interviewees were asked whether they would be visiting a branch of their own company, another company or both. They were asked how often they had travelled on business in the past year, which European cities they had visited and how many years they had been travelling to Europe on business. Interviewees were also asked whether they spoke French, German, Italian, Spanish or any other European languages, and they were asked about their ability with each language.

If the list of business destinations that someone had visited in the past year included a European city, then this was selected by the interviewer to be the so-called 'Target City'. The country in which it was located became the 'Target Country'. If several European cities appeared on the list, the interviewer asked the person to nominate the European city and country which they felt most confident to talk about. The reason for selecting a target country and a target city was so that the interviewee could be asked about the problems of doing business in a particular country, rather than about the problems of European business in general.

Once a target city and target country had been identified, interviewees were asked a series of questions about typical travelling arrangements – for example, who actually makes the arrangements, how do they normally get to the airport, do they normally fly business class, what kind of transport do they use at the other end and where do they normally stay?

Following that, each interviewee was asked to compare the business climate of the target country with that of the UK. The criteria for comparison included characteristics like formality, competitiveness, arrogance, flexibility, humour, impulsivity, concern with rank, etc. There were fourteen of these criteria altogether.

Interviewees were asked to describe how difficult it is to do business in the target city, using a 7-point rating scale that went from 'Extremely difficult' to 'Extremely easy'. They were then presented with a list of twenty problems, such as 'The monotony of travel', 'Being away from the office', 'Strange foreign customs', etc., and asked to say whether each represented a 'big problem', a 'small problem' or 'no problem at all' when they were doing business in the target city. Following that, they were asked to say which European country they considered to be the most difficult to do business in, and why.

At this point, the interviewer changed gear slightly, and focused on just France and Germany. The reason for this is that these two countries attract such large numbers of British businessmen. Interviewees were asked whether they had done business in both France and Germany. If they had, they were then asked in which country they had the most business experience and which country they thought had a business climate most similar to that of the UK. They were also asked whether they found it more difficult to do business in France or Germany, and the main reason for this.

Interviewees were asked to rate the contribution that European business trips make to their job, using a 7-point rating scale that ran from 'Extremely negative' to 'Extremely positive'. Finally, they were asked about the main business of their company, whether it has branches in Europe, the title of their job and the main elements of the job. They also indicated which age group they fell into, and the interviewer recorded their sex.

The survey sample

The sample consisted of 634 individuals, 618 of whom were male (i.e. 97.5 per cent), and 16 of whom were female (i.e. 2.5 per cent). There were numerous reasons why people were travelling to Europe, but by far the most common purpose was to take part in a business meeting. This accounted for about half of the cases.

The interviewees were from a wide range of businesses, including agriculture, energy, mining, engineering, manufacturing, construction, transport and finance. In response to the question, 'Does your company have branches in Europe?', 72 per cent of the interviewees answered 'Yes', and 28 per cent answered 'No'. When they were asked whether they would be visiting their own company or another company, 10 per cent of the sample indicated that they would not be visiting any company; 30 per cent said that they would be visiting only branches of their own company, while 47 per cent said that they would be visiting another company, and 13 per cent said that they would be visiting branches of another company *and* their own company. In other words, 60 per cent of the people interviewed were destined for meetings in companies other than their own.

There were two measures of business experience. One involved a question about how many times the interviewee had travelled on business to the continent in the last twelve months, while the other asked how many years he had been travelling to Europe on business. Responses to these questions revealed that people had made an average of 15.2 business trips to the continent in the past year, and that, on average, they had been travelling to Europe on business for the past 10.6 years.

In designing the survey, an attempt was made to ensure that all thirteen countries were represented in the target countries, and that France and Germany had at least twice as many nominations as any of the other countries. This requirement was satisfied, because 21 per cent of the sample identified France as their target country, while 20 per cent of the sample chose Germany. The corresponding percentages for the other countries were as follows: Italy (9 per cent); Netherlands (8 per cent); Spain (8 per cent); Switzerland (7 per cent); Belgium (5 per cent); Eire (4 per cent); Sweden (4 per cent); Portugal (4 per cent); Denmark (4 per cent); Norway (4 per cent); and Russia (2 per cent).

Business climate

After the interviewees had nominated a target country, they were asked to compare the business climate in that country with the business climate in the UK in terms of attributes like formality, competitiveness, arrogance and so on. For example, if a businessman had nominated France as his target country, he was asked to say who was more formal in business – the British or the French – or were they the same? After that, the businessman was asked a similar question about competitiveness, and so on through a list consisting of fourteen attributes.

Figure 5.1 presents the 'Business Climate Scores' for those businessmen who nominated France or Germany as their target country. The left-hand side of the figure shows the business climate scores for France, and the right-hand side shows the corresponding scores for Germany. A separate business climate score was derived for each country on every attribute. This was done by taking the percentage who said that the target country had more of a particular attribute than the British, and adding half of the percentage who said that the British and the target country were the same on that attribute. In other words, each score was calculated by splitting the shared vote between the two countries, and adding it to the vote for the target country. For example, 36 per cent of the sample said that the French business climate is more formal than that of the British, 43 per cent held the opposite opinion, and 21 per cent said the business climate is the same in the two countries. The score for France on formality was derived by adding 36 per cent to half of 21 per cent. This produces a score of 46.

The left-hand side of Figure 5.1 shows that most informants saw the British business climate as being more flexible, humorous, organized and

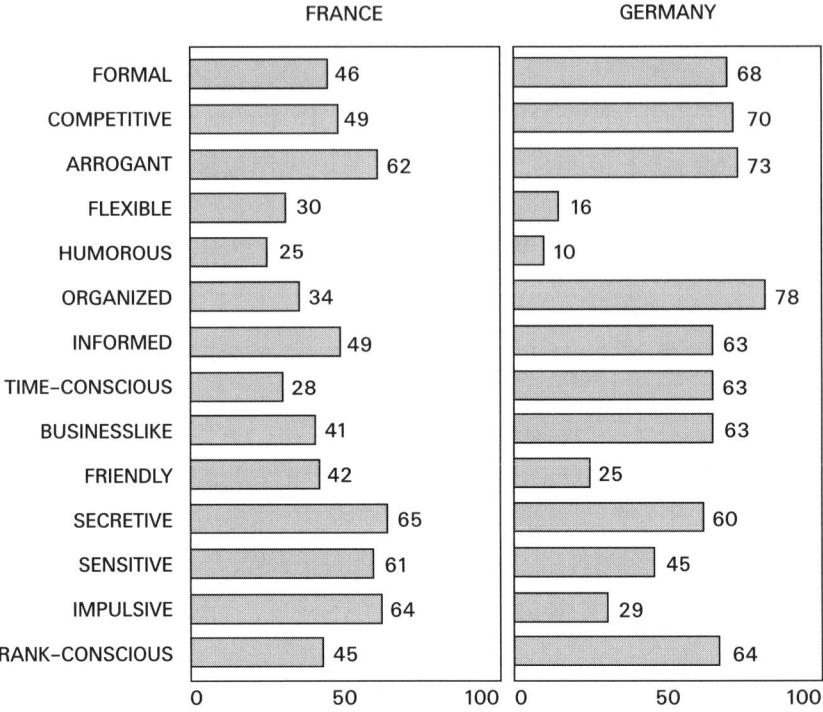

Figure 5.1 Business climate scores for France and Germany

time-conscious than that of the French, and that they saw the French business climate as being more arrogant, secretive, sensitive and impulsive than that of the British. The business climates of the two countries were seen as being similar with regard to attributes like being formal, competitive, informed, businesslike and friendly.

The corresponding results for Germany are very different from those for France. Here the British are seen as more flexible, humorous, friendly and impulsive than the Germans, and the Germans as being more formal, competitive, arrogant, organized, informed, time-conscious, businesslike, secretive and concerned about rank than the British. There was only one case, involving sensitivity, where most businessmen saw the two nations as being essentially similar. In general, people who took part in the survey regarded the British business climate as being more similar to that of the Germans than that of the French. This tendency to see the business climate of France as being very different to that of Britain emerged at various points in the study.

The full matrix of comparisons, of which Figure 5.1 is just a part, provides an enormous amount of information, not just on how British businessmen perceive the business climate of different European countries, but also on how the various business attributes are related to each other. If we take just formality, for example, we find that British businessmen regard the business climate in Britain as being more formal than that in Italy, Portugal, Eire, Denmark, Norway and Spain, but much less formal than in Germany, Switzerland, Sweden and Russia. Sense of humour also presents an interesting picture. Here we find that the respondents perceive the business climate to be more light-hearted in Britain than in every other country except Eire and Spain. The British are prepared to concede that the Irish are more humorous than themselves, and that the Spaniards are almost as humorous as themselves. The fact that Germany gets a 'humour score' of only 10 is consistent with the widely held stereotype of the British that the Germans have no sense of humour at all (Collett, 1993).

British businessmen perceive the business climate as being more competitive in Britain than in most other European countries. France and Holland are seen as being rather similar to Britain in this respect, but the scene in Germany is perceived as being more competitive than in Britain. The British are prepared to accept that they are much more arrogant than the Italians, the Portuguese, the Irish, the Norwegians and the Russians. The Germans, however, are regarded as even more arrogant than the British, and so are the French. The British tend to see themselves as much more flexible, or as equally flexible to most other countries, but Ireland is seen as having the most flexible business culture of all.

As far as organization is concerned, the British see themselves as being much more organized than most other European countries. They believe, however, that the Germans, the Dutch, the Swiss and the Scandinavians – in other words, the northern European countries – are much more organized than them. This cultural distinction is partly reflected in attitudes to time, because British businessmen believe that, while they are more time-conscious than most other European nations, and especially the Latins, they are not as time-conscious as the Germans, the Swiss and the Swedes. The Latin countries, however, get high marks for friendliness because, although the British perceive themselves as being more friendly than the Germans, the Swiss and the Swedes, they see themselves as less friendly than the Italians, the Portuguese, the Spaniards, the Danes and the Irish. The idea that Eire has a particularly friendly business culture is certainly consistent with the notion that the Irish have a highly developed sense of humour.

The Irish are also seen as much more impulsive than the British, and – as one might expect – so are the French, the Italians, the Portuguese and the Spaniards. The British also regard their own business climate as being rather low on sensitivity, because they do not regard themselves as significantly more sensitive than any other European country. They do, however, accept that the business climate in countries like Italy, Portugal, Spain and Russia is much more sensitive than their own. Finally, there is the issue of rank. British businessmen see more concern for rank in their own business climate than in the other European countries, except for Switzerland and Russia.

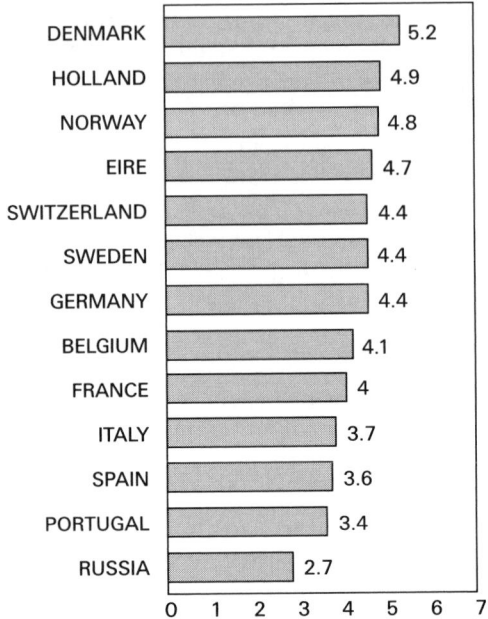

Figure 5.2 Ease of working in various countries

Ease of doing business abroad

Everyone who took part in the survey was asked to say how difficult they found it to do business in the target country they had nominated, using a 7-point scale that went from 'extremely difficult' to 'extremely easy'. Figure 5.2 presents the mean score for each target country. It shows that Denmark is regarded as the easiest country to do business in, closely followed by Holland, Norway, Eire and so on. There are several things worth noticing about the position of the countries. The first is that the Scandinavian countries – Denmark, Norway and Sweden – all appear in the top half of the list. The Latin countries, on the other hand, all appear near the bottom of the list – only Russia prevents them from being right at the bottom.

In addition to being asked which country is the easiest to do business in, the informants were also asked to say whether it is easier to do business in France or Germany. The reason for focusing on France and Germany is that a disproportionately large number of British businessmen have dealings with these countries. This part of the interview involved only individuals who had done business in France *and* Germany – in other words, people who had dealt with only one country, or neither, were excluded from this part of the study altogether. Those who satisfied this requirement were asked three questions:

1 In which country have you had most business experience?
2 Which country has a business climate most similar to the UK?

Which is more difficult to do business in?

		FRANCE	same	GERMANY	
More similar business climate to the UK?	FRANCE	4	4	13	21
	same	2	0	1	3
	GERMANY	61	9	6	76
		67	13	20	100

Which is more difficult to do business in?

		FRANCE	same	GERMANY	
More business experience in?	FRANCE	19	8	14	41
	same	11	4	3	18
	GERMANY	35	3	3	41
		65	15	20	100

Figure 5.3 Comparisons of France and Germany

3 Is it more difficult to do business in France or Germany?

For each question, informants were required to answer 'France', 'Germany' or 'About the same'.

The top half of Figure 5.3 shows the relationship between questions 2 and 3. The column totals show that, in response to the question about which country is more difficult to do business in, 67 per cent of the informants mentioned France, 20 per cent mentioned Germany and 13 per cent said that the two countries were about the same. The row totals show that in response to the question about which country has a business climate more similar to that of the UK, 21 per cent mentioned France, 76 per cent mentioned Germany and 3 per cent said that the two countries were the same. In other words, the vast majority of informants said that Germany is easier to do business in, and that its business climate is more similar to that of the UK. This is borne out by the cell entries, which show that 61 per cent of the sample expressed *both* opinions.

The bottom half of Figure 5.3 shows the relationship between questions 1 and 3. The column totals are very similar to those in the top half of the figure – 65 per cent of the sample thought that France was more difficult,

20 per cent thought that Germany was more difficult and 15 per cent thought that France and Germany were equally difficult to do business in. The row totals show that 41 per cent of the sample had more experience of France, 41 per cent had more experience of Germany and 18 per cent had equal business experience of France and Germany. On the basis of these percentages it appears that, overall, experience of working in these two countries has little effect on which is regarded as the more difficult to do business in. Inspection of the cell entries, however, reveals that those businessmen who had more experience of France did not perceive France as being any more difficult to do business in than Germany. However, there was a strong tendency among those businessmen who had more experience of Germany to say that France was the more difficult of the two countries, and it is this group of informants who are responsible for the general finding that British businessmen find it more difficult to do business in France than in Germany.

Everyone who took part in the survey was asked to rate the contribution that European business trips made to their job, using a 7-point scale which went from 'extremely negative' to 'extremely positive'. Most ratings were somewhere between 'positive' and 'extremely positive', which shows that, as a rule, British businessmen regard European business trips as making an important contribution to their job.

Those people who nominated Russia as their target country gave the top rating of 6.6, while those who named Norway gave the lowest rating of 5.9 to foreign business trips. The order of the countries on this criterion is rather different from the order of the countries on the ratings for 'ease', which suggests that there isn't a positive relationship between the ease of doing business abroad and the contribution that foreign business makes to one's job. This is borne out by further analysis, which shows that the correlation between the mean country scores for 'ease' and 'contribution' is -0.61 ($p < .025$) – in other words, people who find it easy to do business in a particular country also find that their business trips make less contribution to their job than do those people who experience greater difficulty in the country of their choice. This negative relationship between 'ease' and 'contribution' is certainly counter-intuitive. It shows that the ease of doing business abroad is not the only factor which influences people's perceptions of their time abroad, and that a difficult working environment can still yield benefits which make the experience worthwhile.

Business problems

The interviewees were presented with a list of 'business problems' that they might have encountered when doing business abroad. They were asked to say whether each represented 'a big problem', 'a small problem' or 'no problem at all' when they did business in the target country. Figure 5.4 presents the full list, and it orders the items according to the percentage of

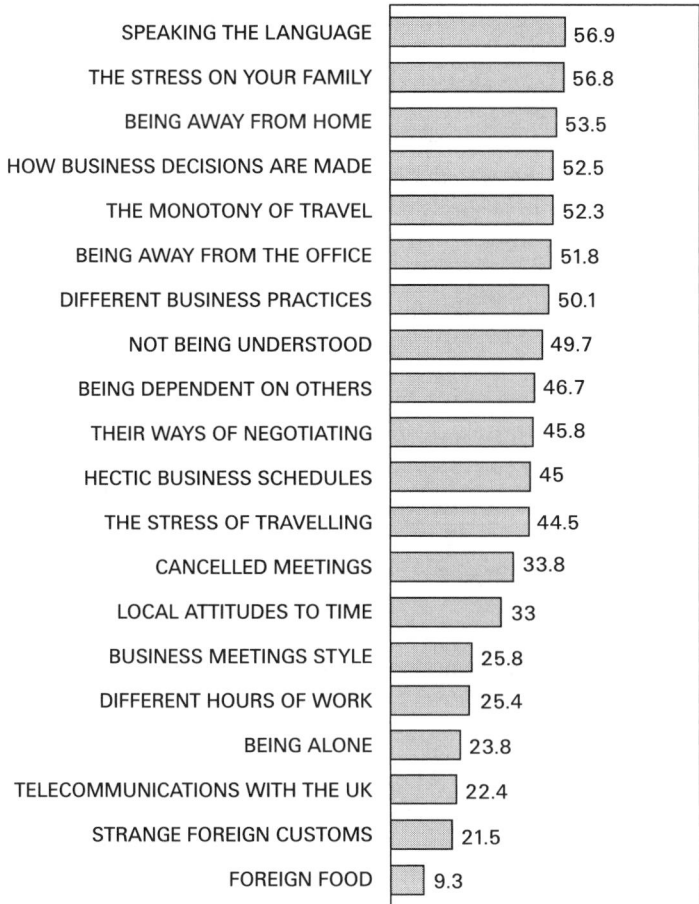

Figure 5.4 Problems experienced abroad

people who regarded each as a problem. Top of the list is 'Speaking the language', followed by 'The stress on my family'.

It is very interesting that language problems appear at the top of the list because the inability of British businessmen to speak the languages of their European colleagues is often regarded as a major obstacle to their effectiveness abroad. Whether or not this is the case, British businessmen regard the task of speaking the local language as the most serious of all the problems that they encounter.

The figure shows that the first seven items on the list were regarded as a problem by more than half of the people interviewed, but that there were also several items at the bottom of the list which were not regarded as a problem by many people. 'Foreign food', for example, was deemed to be a problem by less than 10 per cent of the sample. This figure seems surprisingly low, considering the attachment that the British have to their own cuisine and their negative attitude to 'foreign muck'. The accounts of travellers through the ages show that the British have had a long aversion to foreign food, particularly to the garlic of the French and the 'herbes and salats' of the Italians. However, the culinary tastes of the British have changed enormously over the past two decades, and this probably explains why so few British businessmen regard foreign food as a problem when they are working abroad. In fact, when we examine the evidence more closely, we discover an enormous amount of variation across the various countries: Portugal, for example, attracts not one complaint about its food, whereas, in the case of Russia, half the sample regards the local food as a problem.

Another interesting feature of Figure 5.4 is the order of the items on the list. If we look at those items which are specific to business, we find that there are eight altogether, namely:

1 How business decisions are made
2 Different business practices
3 Their ways of negotiating
4 Hectic business schedules
5 Cancelled meetings
6 How business meetings are conducted
7 Different hours of work
8 Telecommunications with the UK.

The other items, like 'The monotony of travel', 'Being away from home' and so on, are not exclusive to the world of business. Because they are also experienced by tourists and travellers who have no business purpose, we might legitimately regard them as 'non-business' problems. If we now look at the position of these two types of problems in Figure 5.4, we find that the 'business' and 'non-business' problems are scattered throughout the list. In fact, only three of the 'business' problems appear in the top half of the list – contrary to what one would expect, it is not the case that the most pressing problems confronting British businessmen abroad are those which are exclusively business in character. This is very revealing, because it shows that problems which have nothing to do with work, like 'The monotony of travel' and 'Being away from home', are just as crucial, and sometimes even more important, than those which arise directly out of an attempt to do business abroad. It suggests that, in an attempt to alleviate the difficulties that businessmen experience abroad, one should pay equal attention to problems that have nothing to do with business.

Just as difficulties can be ranked according to the percentages of people who deem them to be a problem, so too it is possible to rank countries according to the percentages of people who associate them with various problems. This can be done either by considering the potential problems

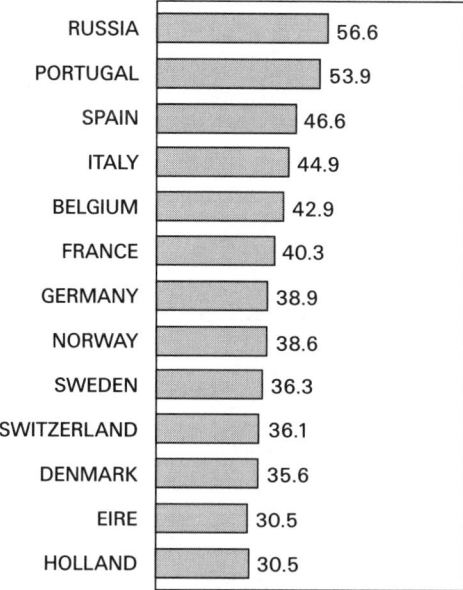

RUSSIA	56.6
PORTUGAL	53.9
SPAIN	46.6
ITALY	44.9
BELGIUM	42.9
FRANCE	40.3
GERMANY	38.9
NORWAY	38.6
SWEDEN	36.3
SWITZERLAND	36.1
DENMARK	35.6
EIRE	30.5
HOLLAND	30.5

Figure 5.5 Problem scores for various countries

one at a time or by deriving an average score across all the problems. Figure 5.5 shows the outcome of the second approach. It reveals, for example, that Russia obtained the highest 'problem score' overall. The figure shows that the Latin countries – Portugal, Spain and Italy – are grouped together once again, immediately after Russia, and that Belgium and France come next. The Scandinavian countries – Norway, Sweden and Denmark – are close together again near the bottom, and Eire and Holland are right at the bottom.

The ways in which countries are ordered with regard to specific problems is also extremely illuminating. Figure 5.6, for example, shows the percentages of businessmen who regarded the 'Local attitude to time' as a problem in the various countries. In this regard, Portugal is seen as the most problematic of all the countries, followed by Russia and then Spain. All three Latin countries appear in the top half of the list, with France and Belgium following closely on the heels of Italy. Norway comes much higher up in the list than one might anticipate, but Sweden and Denmark, the other Scandinavian countries, are near the bottom, where one would expect to find them. Germany, not surprisingly, presents the least problem of all the countries when it comes to local attitudes to time. Finally, it is worth pointing out that Eire is fifth in the list, ahead of Italy and France, both of which are reputed to have a rather flexible attitude to time (cf. Collett, 1993). The position of Eire on the list is quite consistent with the opinion, widely held among the English, that the Irish operate at a fairly slow pace

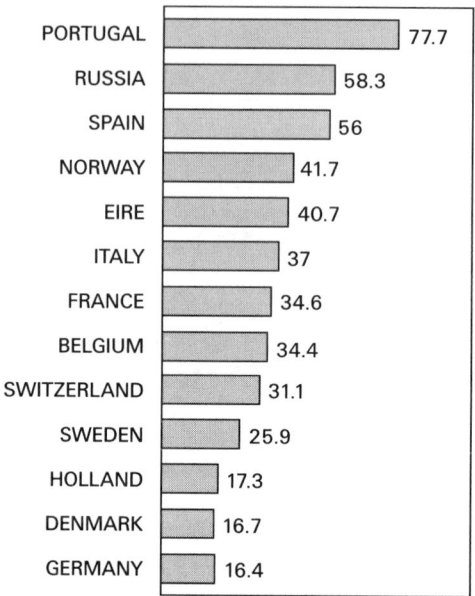

Figure 5.6 'Local attitude to time' – where it's a problem

and don't like to be rushed. It is sometimes said that the Gaelic dictionary doesn't have a translation for *mañana* because the Irish don't have a word that conveys the same degree of urgency!

Another problem which is of some interest is 'Speaking the language' of the host country. Figure 5.7 shows that Russia is, once again, regarded as the most problematic country in this respect, and that Spain, Italy and Portugal also present something of a problem to British businessmen. It is only when we get down to Norway, Belgium, Denmark and Holland – in other words, those countries where a large proportion of the local population can converse in English – that half or less of the sample regards language as a problem. Everyone in Eire speaks English, which explains why it is right at the bottom of the list. In spite of this, we still find 7.4 per cent of the businessmen who nominated Eire reporting that they have some difficulty 'speaking the language'. As the Irish do not conduct their business meetings in Gaelic, we can only assume that a small, but not insignificant, proportion of British businessmen have difficulty understanding the Irish accent.

Other European languages

In order to assess their competence in other European languages, informants were asked whether they spoke French, German, Spanish, Italian or any other European languages. For each language they were asked to say

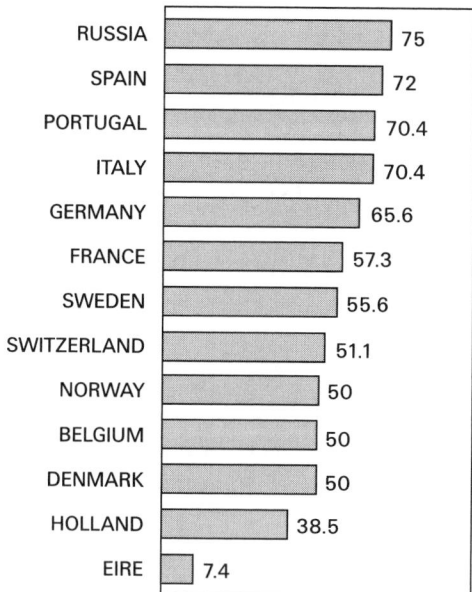

Figure 5.7 'Speaking the language' – where it's a problem

whether (1) they could not speak the language at all, (2) they could speak a little of the language but not enough to do business or (3) they could speak the language well enough to do business. We discovered that 36 per cent of the sample could not speak French at all, that 39 per cent could speak a little French and 25 per cent were sufficiently competent to do business in the language. Sixty-six per cent of the sample could not speak German, 23 per cent spoke a little German and 11 per cent could do business in the language. The results for Spanish and Italian were much worse. Only 10 per cent could speak a little Spanish and an additional 5 per cent could use it in their business dealings. The corresponding figures for Italian were 8 per cent and 4 per cent.

Although there are no comparable data on the linguistic abilities of continental businessmen, it is very likely that a much higher proportion are capable of using English than the British are of using other European languages in business. It is also likely that, as a group, British businessmen have less facility with other European languages than the sample we have studied, because this sample is bound to contain individuals who have either been pre-selected for their language skills or who have managed to improve them in the course of their business dealings abroad. There is in fact some evidence to support this notion, because, when we separate the informants into two groups on the basis of how many business trips they have made to the continent in the past year, we find that those who made eleven trips or more are able to speak significantly more European languages than those who made less than that number of trips in the past year. Ability to speak other European languages is clearly related to how often business-men travel to the continent on business, but whether this is due to selection or experience we do not yet know.

The British have a well-deserved reputation for being a nation of monoglots, and this is reflected in the fact that, even with this specialized sample, the ability to conduct business in other European languages is not terribly impressive. This, however, is not something of which British businessmen are unaware, because, when they are asked about the problems they encounter on the continent, 'Speaking the language' comes out at the top of their list.

DISCUSSION

Most of the research that has been done in the area of culture-and-manage-ment has looked at differences between managers from different countries in terms of their values, beliefs and motivations (Laurent, 1986; Hofstede, 1991; Trompenaars, 1993). Very little attention has been paid to the difficulties that managers from the same country encounter when they are doing business in another country, let alone in several other countries. The Eurocommuter Survey set out to fill this gap in our knowledge by tapping into the opinions and accumulated experience of British businessmen who deal with the continent. The study itself uncovered some interesting and hitherto unknown facts about this group of individuals – for example, the types of companies they visit, the various reasons for their trips, how often they travel abroad and how long they have been doing business on the continent.

The study explored the various problems that British managers encounter on the continent, and it showed that problems which are not exclusive to business are just as crucial as those which are of a specifically business nature. There is a tendency to assume that the problems that businessmen experience abroad are business related. The study reveals, however, that problems which have nothing to do with business can be just as pressing, and sometimes even more serious than those which are business related.

The study was designed so that the countries to which British businessmen travel could be compared with each other. This was done, first of all, by selecting those European countries which are the most common destinations of British businessmen and, second, by getting interviewees to focus on a country where they had business experience. By sampling interviewees so that they covered the major countries, we were able to compare countries in terms of the problems they pose, the characteristics of their business climate, the ease of doing business and the contribution that working in those countries makes to a person's job. Analysis of the relationship between these last two issues uncovered a negative relationship between the ease of working in a country and the contribution that working there makes to the job. Normally one would assume that those countries which are easiest to work in are also those that offer the greatest contribution to the job. We find, however, that this is not the case, and that countries like Russia, which pose enormous problems, nevertheless contribute a great deal to the individuals who do business there.

Business climate revealed an enormous amount of variation between countries. In this chapter we have been able to look at the business climates of only France and Germany, which were reported to be very different from each other, and that of the UK. Many of the opinions that British businessmen hold about the business climate in these countries are similar to the stereotypes that British people in general have about the French and the Germans – for example, that the French are impulsive, or that the Germans have no sense of humour. Another hallmark of stereotypes that emerges in people's opinions is the degree to which they appear to be self-serving – that is, they attribute positive qualities to the British and negative ones to other countries. For example, British businessmen regard their own business climate as being more flexible and more humorous than that of any other country, except Eire. However, many of the opinions that British businessmen hold are definitely not self-serving, because they recognize that the business climate of other countries is, in many respects, superior to that of the UK. The German business climate, for example, is regarded as much more competitive, organized, informed and businesslike than that of the British – a situation which British businessmen grudgingly acknowledge and, one assumes, would like to change.

When British businessmen are asked to compare France and Germany, two-thirds of them report that the French are more difficult to do business with than the Germans. However, these strong opinions are mitigated by at least two other factors. First of all, we find that businessmen who feel that France has a business climate more similar to that of the UK do not regard France as a more difficult country to do business in. Nor do people who have had more business experience in France. This suggests that strong, and particularly negative, opinions about the business environment and practices in other countries tend to be based on ignorance, or at least that positive attitudes are encouraged by personal experience. It would be very interesting to pursue this issue by extending this type of study to examine the stereotypes and opinions of British businessmen who do *not* do business abroad.

One of the theoretical issues raised by this study concerns the nature of the relationship between business motivations, on the one hand, and percep-tions of these motivations, on the other. In his enormous cross-cultural study of motivation, Hofstede found that the French have a much higher 'Power Distance' score than the British and the Germans – that is, they are more concerned about status differences. In our study of business culture we discovered that British businessmen see the French as being *less* 'concerned about rank' than the British, who, in turn, are less concerned about rank than the Germans. The findings from our study and Hofstede's research do not sit together very comfortably. On the one hand, we have the French being particularly concerned about status, while on the other we find that the British don't recognize this about the French. This raises the interesting question about what is more likely to affect the course of a meeting between a French and a British businessman – will it be the differences in motivation uncovered by psychologists or the culturally shaped perceptions that each person has about the other person's motivations? In other words, can the results of cross-cultural comparisons help us to anticipate the problems associated with international encounters, or do we need to study these encounters in their own right?

ACKNOWLEDGEMENTS

I would like to express my gratitude to the British Airport Authority for making this survey possible, and to the Economic and Social Research Council for their support. I would also like to thank Stan Maiden, David Field and Graham Campling at BAA, and Ian MacDonald and Kay Lattimore at Oxford, for their assistance with this chapter.

NOTE

1 'Business commuter' refers to both men and women. For convenience, the term 'businessmen' has also been used. It should be understood as applying to businessmen and businesswomen.

REFERENCES

Adler, N.J. (1991) *International Dimensions of Organizational Behaviour*. Boston, Mass.: Plus-Kent.

Collett, P. (1993) *Foreign Bodies: A Guide to European Mannerisms*. London: Simon & Schuster.

Collett, P. (1994) The Eurocommuter Survey. Unpublished report.

Deal, T.E. and Kennedy, A.A. (1982) *Corporate Cultures: The Rites and Rituals of Corporate Life*. Reading, Mass.: Addison-Wesley.

England, G.W. (1975) *The Manager and His Values: An International Perspective*. Cambridge, Mass.: Ballinger.

Furnham, A. (1990) *The Protestant Work Ethic*. London: Routledge.

Furnham, A. and Bochner, S. (1986) *Culture Shock: Psychological Reactions to Unfamiliar Environments*. London: Methuen.

Furnham, A. and Gunter, B. (1993) *Corporate Assessment*. London: Routledge.

Giorgi, L. and Marsh, C. (1990) The Protestant Work Ethic as a cultural phenomenon. *European Journal of Social Psychology*, *20*, 499–517.

Graves, D. (1979) The impact of culture upon managerial attitudes, beliefs and behaviour in England and France. In T.D. Weinshall (ed.) *Managerial Communication*. London: Academic Press.

Haire, M., Ghiselli, E. and Porter, L. (1966) *Managerial Thinking: An International Study*. New York: Wiley.

Hall, E.T. and Hall, M.R. (1990) *Understanding Cultural Differences.* Yarmouth, Maine: Intercultural Press.

Harding, S., Phillips, D.K. and Fogarty, M. (1986) *Contrasting Values in Western Europe.* London: Macmillan.

Hofstede, G. (1984) *Culture's Consequences.* London: Sage.

Hofstede, G. (1991) *Cultures and Organizations.* London: McGraw-Hill.

Laurent, A. (1983) The cultural diversity of western conceptions of management. *International Studies of Management and Organization, 13*(1/2), 75–96.

Laurent, A. (1986) The cross-cultural puzzle of human resource management. *Human Resource Management, 25*(1), 91–102.

Mole, J. (1991) *Mind Your Manners.* London: The Industrial Society.

Smith, P.B., Peterson, M.F., Jeslino, J., Hofmann, K., Koopman, P. and Ropo, A. (1993) European national cultures as defined by managerial behaviour. Paper presented at Conference on European Identities, Farnham Castle, UK, May.

Tainio, R. and Santalainen, T. (1983) Some evidence for the cultural relativity of organizational development programs. *Journal of Applied Behavioral Science, 20*(2), 93–111.

Trompenaars, F. (1993) *Riding the Waves of Culture: Understanding Cultural Diversity in Business.* London: Nicholas Brealey.

6 Pay satisfaction in America and Britain

Colin Fraser and Leonard Berkowitz

Although jobs can be rewarding in a variety of ways (Landy, 1989; Warr, 1987), we would expect the pay people receive for their work to be among the most significant of these benefits, and indeed pay can have a considerable influence on employees' behaviour. Empirical research has shown that pay can affect, among other things, their absenteeism and turnover (Lawler, 1971), and their personal well-being and mental health (Warr, 1987).

What is more interesting, however, is that the absolute level of pay may not be as all-important as common sense might have us think. In quite a few investigations of the correlates of pay satisfaction, the relationship between the amount of money employees received and their satisfaction with their pay, although usually positive, was relatively weak, or at best moderate. As Rice, Phillips and McFarlin (1990) have noted, this research has shown that 'in many cases, greater rewards do not provide greater contentment. Those with the highest pay are not always the most satisfied with their pay' (p. 386).

This relatively weak relationship between amount of pay and pay satisfaction clearly indicates that most employees consider factors in addition to the amount of money they are getting in deciding how satisfactory is their remuneration. What is much less certain, however, is just what these factors might be. Most theorists hold that the major additional consideration is a personal standard, some notion of what level of pay is deserved, and/or wanted, and/or expected. For example, in his well-known analysis of the role of pay in work settings, Lawler (1971) adopted what can be regarded as an elaborated equity theory perspective, proposing that people's satisfaction with their pay is determined largely by the difference between the amount they think they deserve and the amount they perceive themselves as receiving. The deserved level, in turn, is determined by, among other things, comparisons with the pay received by significant others.

There is good evidence that employees' satisfaction with their pay is greatly affected by the disparity between deserved and received pay. Thus, when Rice, Phillips and McFarlin (1990) studied a sample of mental health professionals, they found that this discrepancy was one of the most important predictors of how pleased the respondents were with their pay. Much the same results were obtained by Berkowitz *et al.* (1987) in their study of a random sample of male full-time employees in Madison, Wisconsin. In this case, the best predictor of pay satisfaction was a factor whose chief component was based on the difference between deserved and received pay relative to the pay they were getting.

However, with all of this evidence demonstrating that people consider the pay they believe they deserve in deciding how adequate is their pay, we can ask whether the deserved level is necessarily based on social comparisons, as most equity theories assume (e.g. Adams, 1965; Lawler, 1971). The multiple regression analyses carried out by Berkowitz *et al.* (1987) found no indication that social comparisons entered into the determination of deserved pay level. As they pointed out, people may arrive at some estimate of what they think they deserve on the basis of a number of relatively internal considerations, such as the nature of their job and the responsibilities they have (Jaques, 1961), and/or their self conceptions (Goodman, 1974), and/or what they have earned in the past (Messé and Watts, 1983).

Yet another question has to do with whether this internal standard is the only other factor, besides amount of pay, that influences their satisfaction with their pay. Do other considerations having little directly to do with pay also affect their sense that their pay is adequate? In the Madison, Wisconsin, study just mentioned (Berkowitz *et al.*, 1987), the respondents' job satisfaction, the fringe benefits provided by their job and the quality of their lives, among other things, also contributed to their satisfaction with their pay. Respondents appeared to consider a variety of gratifications in judging whether they were getting sufficient benefits in return for their work.

The present chapter is primarily a test of the generality of the Madison findings. A number of the interview measures employed in this US study were also used with a sample of men residing in Northampton, England, and we here ask whether there are the same predictors of pay satisfaction in the two samples. We are especially interested in the degree to which deserved pay level affected this satisfaction. Referring, in the interests of simplicity, to this deserved level as the pay the respondents considered to be fair, we established two somewhat different measures of the perceived fairness of the respondents' pay, and then inquired, through multiple regression analysis, whether pay fairness had the same influence on pay satisfaction in Northampton as in Madison.

In addition, this chapter also compares the Northampton and Madison samples on the degrees to which matters other than pay fairness entered into the determination of pay satisfaction. In particular, we look into the contribution made by job satisfaction and the material/economic benefits received from work. As was just noted, the US respondents' judgement of how satisfactory their pay was seemed to have been affected by several kinds of rewards obtained from their work, and this chapter asks whether this is the case in the British sample as well.

As with many other areas of the social sciences, most of the literature on pay and pay satisfaction is based on work carried out in the United States, even though conclusions and claims about pay satisfaction are by no means always confined to that country. The present chapter is intended as a modest contribution to the limited cross-national comparisons that exist in the field. In thinking of grounds for predicting American–British similarities and differences we could locate few systematic empirical or theoretical bases for predictions. That did not prevent us generating numerous, and frequently contradictory, speculations about possible national similarities and differences. Rather than lengthening this chapter unreasonably, however, we will first let the evidence speak for itself before, in the final section, airing some of our more relevant speculations, which may act as bases for hypotheses in the future.

THE TWO SURVEYS

This report will focus on two sets of issues. First, it will examine the relative contributions that each of four sets of variables makes to the prediction of pay satisfaction in two separate samples of full-time male employees, one from the US and the other from the UK. This examination will be based on multiple regression analyses of data collected in surveys conducted in Dane County, Wisconsin (i.e. the city of Madison, Wisconsin, and its surrounding areas), and in Northampton in the Midlands of England. After this, the second issue will be concerned with the question of whether job satisfaction and the material benefits people obtain from their work significantly affect the relationship between the perceived fairness of one's pay and pay satisfaction. Because of its relatively speculative nature, our attempt to answer this latter question will be based on a very conservative procedure, log-linear regressions.

The locations

Madison is a city of approximately 180,000 people in Wisconsin, in the north mid-west of the United States. It is a comparatively well-off community, with a relatively low rate of unemployment, approximately 4 per cent according to official US statistics at the time of the Madison survey (autumn 1981). As the state capital and the home of a large, leading American university, as well as the main service area for the county's residents, its economy is relatively stable and its labour force has a large white-collar and professional element.

Northampton, a city in the East Midlands of England, has a population of approximately 250,000. Although it, like Madison, is the administrative centre of its county, it is not a university community, higher education being represented by a large college of further education. Furthermore, at the time of the Northampton survey, the autumn of 1986, it had a much higher level of unemployment, about 12 per cent, close to the British national average. This unemployment rate, however, was lower than that in a number of other Midlands cities.

The surveys

The Madison study, which is described in detail by Berkowitz *et al.* (1987), generated a random sample of 248 male full-time employees, each of whom was interviewed by telephone for a little less than half-an-hour about their jobs and their pay. The Northampton Work Attitudes and Work History Survey was part of a large Social Change and Economic Life Initiative funded by the Economic and Social Research Council. The random sample used in this investigation consisted of just over 1,000 employed, unemployed and non-employed men and women, including 295 full-time employed males, who were interviewed in their homes for approximately one-and-a-half hours, on the average, about their jobs and their work history. However, since all of the respondents were not asked all of the same questions and because of missing data on one or another measure, the results to be reported here are based on only 196 cases.

The measures used

The measures employed in the analyses summarized here tap five different aspects of the work situation. Our dependent variable, pay satisfaction, was the extent to which the respondents were satisfied with their pay. The independent variables were the perceived fairness of the pay, the level of job satisfaction, the magnitude of the material/economic benefits obtained from the job and whether the respondents engaged in social comparisons regarding their pay.

Taking these up in order, the *pay satisfaction* question required the respondent to rate how dissatisfied or satisfied he was in general with his pay. Although this one question might appear to omit some relevant considerations, research indicates that the different aspects of pay satisfaction tend to be highly intercorrelated (e.g. Orpen, 1986). Thus, in the Madison study (Berkowitz *et al.*, 1987), a factor analysis of eight separate items asking about pay satisfaction yielded only a single factor.

Two *pay fairness* measures were used. The *qualitative fairness* measure consisted of a question asking the respondent to indicate the degree to which he believed his pay was less or more than he deserved. For the *quantitative fairness* index we computed the difference between (a) the annual pay the respondents said they should be getting, and (b) the annual pay they reported receiving, and then divided this difference by their annual pay. There were eight *job satisfaction* questions; seven measured satisfaction

Table 6.1 Comparable measures in the Madison and Northampton surveys

Measures	Source of difference		
Dependent variable			
Satisfaction with total pay	m		s
Predictor variables			
3 measures of *material benefits*			
Annual gross pay	m		
Annual net household income	m		
Satisfaction with household standard of living		f	s
2 measures of *perceived fairness of pay*			
Qualitative fairness: pay more or less than deserved		f	
Quantitative fairness:			
deserved pay – annual pay / annual pay	m		
1 question of *use of social comparisons*			
Do you ever compare your pay with the pay of others?			
8 questions on *job satisfaction*			
Overall job satisfaction			s
Work interesting	m	f	s
Satisfaction with hours	m	f	s
,, ,, job security	m	f	s
,, ,, use of initiative	m	f	s
,, ,, promotion chances	m	f	s
,, ,, supervisors	m	f	s
,, ,, fringe benefits	m	f	s

Notes

m signifies minor difference in wording.

f signifies difference in question format because of telephone vs. face-to-face interview procedures.

s signifies response scale difference: 1–10 in Madison, 0–10 in Northampton.

with different facets of the job and one measured overall job satisfaction. The *material benefits* measures were the respondents' annual pay, the total income in their household that they reported, and how satisfied they said they were with their household's income. And finally, to assess the respondents' *use of social comparisons*, they were asked, simply, whether they ever ('yes' or 'no') compared their pay with the pay of other individuals or groups.

Table 6.1 lists all fifteen of the measures, together with a specification of the comparability of the Northampton and Madison measures. In addition, it should be noted, as was made clear above, that there were differences relating to the locations, timing of surveys and nature of the interviews. Clearly, the comparability of the surveys and the measures used in the present analysis is less than ideal and considerable caution must be exercised

Table 6.2 Significant predictors of pay satisfaction in the two samples

Measures		Beta	T	Sig.
Northampton, UK sample				
Qualitative fairness		.44	7.51	< .0001
Overall job satisfaction		.29	4.98	< .0001
Use of social comparisons		− .15	2.58	.02
	Multiple R = .65			
	Adjusted R² = .41			
Annual pay¹		.13	1.99	.06
Madison, US sample				
Qualitative fairness		.38	7.51	< .0001
Quantitative fairness		− .23	4.66	< .0001
Satisfaction with fringe benefits		.20	4.30	< .0001
Overall job satisfaction		.17	3.03	.003
Work is interesting		.14	2.57	.02
Annual pay		.10	2.11	.04
	Multiple R = .73			
	Adjusted R² = .52			

Note

1 In each sample, after the initial forward regression analysis had identified which measures predicted pay satisfaction at the .05 level or less, the remaining measures were then entered into the prediction equation in order to determine if other measures also tended to contribute to the prediction of the dependent variable at a near-significant level. This analysis showed that only annual pay in the UK sample was of borderline significance (p < .10).

in interpreting apparent differences in the predictors of pay satisfaction in the two samples.

Nevertheless, fifteen very similar questions were asked of two good quality random samples and we believe the comparability is sufficient for exploratory purposes. Moreover, we could argue, we can have greater confidence in the results if the findings in the two studies are similar despite the methodological differences.

FINDINGS

Regression analyses with all measures as predictors

In the first phase of this investigation multiple regression analyses were carried out separately for the two samples using all fourteen measures as the possible predictors of pay satisfaction. In doing this, a forward regression analysis was first conducted to identify those variables that predicted the dependent measure significantly at at least the .05 level. Then, since this study was exploratory in nature and might suggest hypotheses worthy of further examination, all of the remaining measures were forced into the prediction in order to determine which of them had relationships with pay satisfaction that were of borderline significance. Table 6.2 summarizes the results for the Northampton and Madison data taken separately.

As can be seen in the table, there are marked similarities in the results from the two samples, although there are some obvious differences as well. One of the measures of perceived fairness of pay – the degree to which the respondents thought they were getting the pay they deserved (here termed qualitative fairness) – was the most important predictor of pay satisfaction for both the British and US respondents (beta = .44 in Northampton; and beta = .38 in Madison). And, furthermore, overall job satisfaction was also a significant predictor of satisfaction with one's pay in both groups (beta = .29 in Northampton; and beta = .17 in Madison). Yearly pay also contributed to pay satisfaction: at a borderline level in Northampton (beta = .13, p = .06) and to just a significant degree in the slightly larger US sample (beta = .10, p < .04).

The differences in results seem modest in comparison to these similarities. Thus, we find that those respondents who reported comparing their pay with others tended to have lower pay satisfaction in the British sample (beta = − .15, p < .02), whereas this relationship did not approach significance in Madison, although it was in the same negative direction (beta = − .08, p > .10). On the other side, our second perceived fairness measure, quantitative fairness, was significantly related to pay satisfaction in the US group (beta = − .23), but did not contribute significantly to the prediction of pay satisfaction in the Northampton group. (Note that the negative beta here does in fact indicate a substantively positive relationship between fairness and satisfaction.) Finally, we can also see in the table that the men's satisfaction with the fringe benefits provided by their job, their rating of their work as interesting and their annual pay predicted pay satisfaction in the Madison sample (betas = .20, .14 and .10), whereas these measures were not reliable predictors of the dependent variable in the British sample.

Using indices to reduce the number of measures

With the number of measures employed in this preliminary analysis, fourteen independent variables plus one dependent measure, it is of course possible that some of the findings just reported had achieved statistical significance by chance. Furthermore, we would argue (Berkowitz *et al.*, 1987) that a combination of theoretical ideas and prior empirical research suggests that the somewhat confusing array of fourteen separate predictors partially conceals four particularly plausible sets of predictors of pay satisfaction. We therefore carried out another series of regression analyses with a reduced number of predictor measures using indices established to reflect those four domains. One was the *Pay Fairness Index*, the sum of the standardized scores on the two pay fairness measures, qualitative and quantitative fairness (changing the direction of the latter measure so that a

Table 6.3 Beta weights obtained in regression of the four indices on pay satisfaction in the UK and US samples

Index		Northampton	Madison
Pay fairness		.36**	.52**
Job satisfaction		.34**	.27**
Material benefits		.08	.19*
Use of social comparisons		− .13*	− .06
	Adjusted R²	.35	.48

*   p < .10
**   p < .0001

high index score indicates high perceived fairness). A second was a *Material Benefits Index* consisting of the sum of the standardized values for annual pay and satisfaction with the household's standard of living. The *Job Satisfaction Index* was more complex and was based on a factor analysis of all eight job satisfaction items in each of the two samples. Six of these items loaded highly on a single job satisfaction factor in both samples so that our index score was based on the sums of the standardized values on each of these six measures: overall job satisfaction, how interesting the work was, satisfaction with job hours, the opportunity to use initiative, promotion chances and supervision. Finally, we have a *Social Comparison Use Index* consisting only of the single comparison item mentioned above: whether the respondent ever compared his pay with others' pay.

Table 6.3 reports the beta weights obtained when these indices were regressed on pay satisfaction, again using the Northampton and the Madison data separately. As can be seen, here too the results appear more similar than different in the two samples, while simplifying but remaining compatible with the findings in Table 6.2. The respondents' assessment of the fairness of their pay was the most important predictor of how satisfied they were with their pay in both the British and US groups, but this perceived fairness seems to have been less important for the UK men than for their US counterparts (beta weights of .36 and .52 respectively). In addition, job satisfaction made a somewhat smaller, but still significant, contribution to pay satisfaction in both groups than did pay fairness (betas = .34 and .27 for the Northampton and Madison samples respectively).

On the other hand, we can also see that there were some weak differences between the Northampton and Madison results: (a) The use of social comparisons had a near significant negative relationship with the dependent measure in the British sample, whereas the effect did not come close to significance in the US group (betas = − .13 and − .06), and (b) the material benefits index was not a significant predictor of pay satisfaction in Northampton but was nearly significant in Madison (betas = .08 and .19 respectively).

The table also shows that the four indices accounted for considerably less of the variance in pay satisfaction in the Northampton sample than in the Madison data (35 per cent as compared with 48 per cent), largely because the perceived fairness of one's pay was somewhat less important to the British respondents than to their US counterparts.

Taking all the findings together, the results seem to be more similar than different in the two communities. In both samples they highlight the overriding importance of the degree to which the men believed their pay was fair (i.e. that they were paid what they thought they deserved) in predicting how satisfied they were with their pay. But, in addition to this, the findings for both the British and the US men indicate that job satisfaction was also a major contributor to pay satisfaction. As Berkowitz *et al.* (1987) had suggested in their report of the Madison results, job satisfaction's positive effect could have come about through either a generalization or a compensation process. In the first case, the pleasure the respondents obtained from their work might have generalized to their pay; happy with one, the men became happy with the other. The second possibility is a bit different. Here, the respondents might have cognitively traded off rewards they received on their job against other considerations, such as income.

Whatever the explanation for these particular findings, the results have a fairly clear implication. Contrary to what might have been expected from a strictly economic perspective, subjective factors, particularly those dealing with (a) the belief that one's pay is fair and (b) the psychological gratifications obtained from work, appear to play a greater role than the magnitude of the economic benefits derived from the job in predicting, and conceivably in determining, the level of pay satisfaction.

Examining interactions in the combined sample

The analyses reported so far leave a number of interesting questions unanswered. For one thing, they have not tested whether the relationships between the predictors and pay satisfaction differ significantly in the two samples. And furthermore, regardless of any sample differences, they also have not determined whether there are any interactions among the predictor variables in affecting the respondents' satisfaction with their pay. More specifically, we might ask if the contribution of pay fairness to the prediction of pay satisfaction varies with how satisfied the respondents were with their job and/or with the magnitude of the material benefits they obtained from it. It is possible, for example, that the greater the satisfaction the men receive from their work the less the importance of their pay's fairness. But would higher economic rewards also reduce the importance of pay fairness?

A log-linear analysis was conducted to investigate these matters using the four indices described above as well as the pay satisfaction measure. Since the samples differed in the range of their scores, it was deemed advisable to employ only dichotomous scores in combining the data from the Northampton and Madison samples. The distribution on each measure was first divided at the variable median for each sample so that we then had the classes 'Northampton' vs. 'Madison' as well as the scores 'above' or 'below the median' on each measure. The total N was 406 cases, 202 from the UK and 204 from the US, providing usable data. Log-linear regressions were then used to predict the probability that pay satisfaction was above the median, with pay fairness, job satisfaction, material benefits, social comparison use and nationality as explanatory variables.

The initial log-linear analysis revealed, not surprisingly, that both pay fairness and job satisfaction led to highly significant log likelihood chi squares (termed 'deltaG' in Britain): 58.3, $p < .0001$, and 32.9, $p < .0001$, respectively. Much more interesting, though, are the significant interactions also obtained in this analysis: the interaction of pay fairness with material benefits (log likelihood chi square $= 4.7$, $p < .05$) and the interaction of pay fairness with job satisfaction (log likelihood chi square $= 5.1$, $p < .05$). Note that nationality had no significant effect in the prediction of pay satisfaction, either alone or in interaction with the other variables.

We have summarized the above significant interactions in Table 6.4. The table reports the 'odds ratios' in each of the eight cells formed by the combinations of the above and below the median categories on the three variables, pay fairness, job satisfaction and material benefits, as derived from the log-linear model. Simply put, the figure given in any one cell is the ratio of (a) the number of individuals with *high pay satisfaction* for (b) every one with *low pay satisfaction*, as predicted by the model.

Consider first the difference between the low and high pay fairness groups within each of the four combinations of high and low job satisfaction and high and low material benefits. As you can see, in all four of these instances the odds that there would be a person with high pay satisfaction is greater under high than low pay fairness.

But, going further, we can then get an idea of the relative importance of pay fairness in each of these four conditions by computing, in each group, the ratio of (a), the odds of having a person with high pay satisfaction in the high fairness group, with (b), the odds of having a person with high pay satisfaction in the low pay fairness category. Thus, as the table indicates, the high-to-low pay fairness odds ratio is greater under low job satisfaction (odds ratios of 4.82 and 15.36) than when the respondents were more satisfied with their jobs (odds ratios of 1.67 and 5.32). This means that the men's belief that their pay was fair (i.e. that they were receiving the pay they deserved) was a relatively more important predictor of pay satisfaction when they were *not* deriving much satisfaction from their work. Looked at another way, those who were highly satisfied with their jobs seemed to be somewhat less concerned with fairness in deciding how satisfied they were with their pay.

Another examination of the odds ratios provides us with an estimate of how material benefits affected the pay fairness–pay satisfaction relationship.

Table 6.4 Odds of a respondent being high in pay satisfaction in relation to perceived pay fairness, job satisfaction and level of material benefits

		Low material benefits			High material benefits		
		Pay fairness	*Odds ratios*		*Pay fairness*	*Odds ratios*	
Job satisfaction							
			(1)	*(2)*		*(1)*	*(2)*
		High	0.88		High	2.31	
	Low			4.82			15.36
		Low	0.18		Low	0.15	
		High	1.81		High	4.74	
	High			1.67			5.32
		Low	1.08		Low	0.89	

Notes
The odds given in Col. 1 refer to the number of respondents above the median in pay satisfaction for every person with below median pay satisfaction as predicted by the log-linear model.

The odds shown in Col. 2 refer to the odds that a respondent high in perceived pay fairness will also be above the median in pay satisfaction relative to the odds that someone low in pay fairness will have high pay satisfaction.

Again as the table shows, we can see that the high-to-low pay fairness odds ratio is higher for men who obtained greater material benefits from their job (odds ratios of 15.36 and 5.32) than for those receiving fewer such benefits (odds ratios of 4.82 and 1.67). In other words, the possession of relatively substantial economic benefits heightened the importance of perceived fairness in influencing pay satisfaction, rather than reducing it as common sense might have suggested.

In summary then, this conservative analysis of the combined samples: failed to find any national differences; confirmed yet again the predictive power, regarding pay satisfaction, of both pay fairness and job satisfaction as main effects, but not material benefits or social comparisons; found that pay fairness as a predictor of pay satisfaction is more important for men with lower job satisfaction than for men with higher material benefits.

SPECULATIONS AND CONCLUSIONS

Our findings, in general, reveal both similarities between the American and British samples and differences, with, on the whole, the former being more reliably demonstrated than the latter. Let us first ruminate about the tentative and sometimes borderline differences that were suggested by the multiple regressions before turning to the similarities.

As Tables 6.2 and 6.3 show, measures of annual pay, satisfaction with fringe benefits and material benefits had some significant predictive power in Madison but not Northampton. To British common sense, and perhaps American too, this might not seem surprising. British popular stereotypes and commonly invoked beliefs appear to accept that, although Britons are becoming more materialistic and consumerist, they still have some way to go before they equal Americans in those respects. In Britain, the US is believed to be an even more materialistic society than the UK, and we suspect that many Americans might reluctantly concede the 'truth' of such claims. The greater effectiveness of material benefits in the US, then, would seem quite compatible with common sense. It is not so clear, though, that it fits with received wisdom in the social sciences, where the writings of theorists such as Maslow and Inglehart suggest that material benefits will loom larger for people with a lower material standard of living. Since on most, possibly all, economic indicators the general standard of living in the UK is lower than that in the US, we would expect that material benefits, including pay itself, should be better predictors of pay satisfaction in Britain than America. Our findings then suggest a small victory for common sense and stereotypes over social science.

Tables 6.2 and 6.3 also show that engaging in pay comparisons has significant, or borderline significant, predictive power in the UK but not in the US. Relevant speculations, here, might well have predicted an outcome along those lines. British trade unions organize a higher percentage of the labour force than US labour unions do. A key element in union strategies in pay negotiations is frequently the use of arguments and evidence regarding 'differentials', that is, the use of collective or categorical or fraternalistic types of social comparisons. Furthermore, it has been claimed that age-related, status-related and other forms of systematic pay differences are more readily acknowledged in Britain than in the US. So, British employees will be more accustomed than their American counterparts to using fraternalistic social comparisons in evaluating their pay. The position regarding egoistic or inter-individual pay comparisons is unclear but consensus seems to have emerged from the social comparison literature (e.g. Olson, Herman and Zanna, 1986; Smith and Gaskell, 1990) that fraternalistic comparisons are considerably more likely than egoistic comparisons to have real consequences. Thus the apparently greater relevance in the British sample of social comparisons for pay satisfaction seems to be understandable.

The recurring finding that our measures of perceived fairness of pay are even more powerful predictors of pay satisfaction in the US than in the UK suggests to us two alternative possible explanations. The first relies on the fact that the particular measures of fairness used asked the individual about what he himself felt he deserved. That might be thought of as a somewhat individualistic conception of fairness; a more collectivist approach to assessing fairness might have asked about the fairness of the pay of people doing the same job as the individual or the fairness of the pay system more generally. If we assume, as we did above in discussing social comparisons regarding pay, that a British workforce may have somewhat more collectivist values than an American one, the personal deservingness measures of fairness may have been better measures of the American employees' sense of fairness of pay than of the British employees'. An alternative explanation, however, is suggested by the somewhat counter-intuitive finding from the log-linear analyses, which we will consider in more detail shortly, that pay fairness is more powerfully associated with pay satisfaction in the case of higher paid rather than lower paid employees. The fact that the Madison sample both absolutely and relatively was, on average, somewhat better paid than the Northampton sample might explain the even greater predictive power of pair fairness in the US sample.

Thus, our speculations regarding such differences as we did observe assume that materialistic and individualistic values are even more culturally acceptable in the US than in the UK, together with the possibility that the higher average income of the American sample may also be relevant. Two major caveats, however, are necessary. First, all three apparent differences emerged from separate multiple regression analyses where, because of minor incompatibilities in the data in the two samples, direct assessment of the statistical significance of differences was not possible. We believe that the differences are sufficiently plausible and just sufficiently robust to be worth further examination but, for the moment, some caution must be called for.

Second, even if we assume that widespread stereotypes and beliefs in both countries do represent the US as the more individualistic and materialistic, we must recognize that popular views would also recognize that Britain, for a considerable period of time and particularly since the advent of Thatcherism in 1979, has been moving steadily in the same direction. If differences of degree in espousing certain widespread values leads to limited differences in the predictors of pay satisfaction, general similarities in underlying values should lead to marked similarities regarding people's thoughts about satisfaction and dissatisfaction with their pay. And that is what we have found.

In all of our analyses both overall job satisfaction and pay fairness emerged as highly significant predictors of pay satisfaction in both samples. It is commonly accepted that pay satisfaction is one major predictor and determinant of job satisfaction but, as Berkowitz *et al.* (1987) pointed out, the equally plausible reverse relationship is usually ignored. Why should satisfaction with one's job in general – and our findings recurrently show that intrinsic satisfaction with the work itself is heavily implicated – be related to pay satisfaction? Two rather different possibilities have occurred to us. Perhaps affect-based generalization explains the relationship, such that, if you feel positive, or negative, about one, that feeling tends to be carried over to the other. Or, a more cognitively based trade-off may be in operation: if, like the archetypal academic, you recognize your good fortune in having work of such high intrinsic interest, you decide that you are content not to accumulate the material benefits that your talents might otherwise have brought you; if you are being paid to read, and sometimes even write, books, it would be greedy to expect to be paid a great deal. Those two alternative hypotheses need to be explicitly pitted against each other in order to help clarify not only how individuals evaluate their pay but how they think about their jobs as well.

It is our conviction that *the* issue concerning individuals' beliefs and feelings about their pay that most urgently requires better understanding is the issue of how people assess the fairness or unfairness of their pay. As social psychologists, we have been guilty of confounding the general notion of fairness with one particular conception of fairness, namely equity (e.g. Eiser, 1986, p. 253; Walster, Walster and Berscheid, 1978), thereby ignoring other powerful conceptions of how resources might be fairly distributed, including notions that they should be distributed equally or, again, that they should be distributed in terms of people's needs. Technically, an equity analysis claims that the allocation of resources is fair if the ratio of an individual's outcomes or rewards to her or his inputs equals the outcomes/inputs ratio of the individual's key comparison other. But, as McClintock, Kramer and Keil (1984) have very convincingly argued, such a notion of what is fair is only one of numerous ways of assessing fairness. The unjustified equating of fairness with equity usually also ignores the possibility that the perceived fairness of a pay system (cf. Heneman, 1985), in addition to the personal rewards of the individual, may colour individuals' evaluations of their pay. It is possible that different individuals, groups and perhaps even nations may use different criteria for assessing what is fair or unfair. A broader and richer view of fairness seems necessary to enhance our understanding of the psychology of pay, and that in turn could encourage a more comprehensive study in social psychology of fairness and justice.

Our findings, via log-linear analyses, of interactions among predictors of pay satisfaction push the study of pay fairness a little further forward. Pay fairness, it emerges, is a more powerful predictor of pay satisfaction for men who receive above average, rather than below average, material benefits from their jobs and for men who experience below average, rather than above average, job satisfaction.

Intuitively, the second of those findings seems to make an obvious kind of sense in that someone experiencing lower job satisfaction may well, in a trade-off fashion, be more likely to assess the fairness or unfairness of another source of satisfaction, his pay. One might have expected an analogous finding with regard to material benefits and fairness, i.e. the worse paid would be more inclined to think about the fairness of their pay and that would play a larger role in their sense of satisfaction or dissatisfaction. But it is, in fact, the better paid for whom pay fairness is a more important predictor regarding satisfaction. Perhaps it is only the better paid who can indulge in the relative 'luxury' of giving a great deal of thought to how fair their pay is. Making the fairness of their pay so central to their thoughts and feelings about pay may be harder for the less well paid who may be rather more concerned about the magnitude than the fairness of their pay. And that argument might be extended to account for the finding, noted earlier, that fairness of pay was not quite as powerful a predictor of pay satisfaction in the British sample as it was in the somewhat better paid American sample.

We can generate additional post hoc speculations about these subtle interrelations by considering both interactions together. Pay fairness looms largest as a predictor of pay satisfaction for men who are better paid but receiving lower job satisfaction and is of least concern for those receiving higher job satisfaction but lower pay. Relatively good pay coupled with the absence of job satisfaction was held by Goldthorpe *et al.* (1968) to characterize employees with an instrumental attitude towards their work, i.e. they were doing their job for the material benefits it brought and didn't expect to find their work particularly satisfying. It may be that our higher paid/ lower job satisfaction employees have traded off the likelihood of job satisfaction in return for higher pay, in which case it makes sense that they should be particularly concerned in evaluating how fair their pay really is. If, on the other hand, you have traded off pay in return for higher job satisfaction, then too close an examination of the fairness of your pay could be disruptive to your sense of well-being. In this context, an analysis of personal satisfactions in terms of trade-offs among different facets of the whole may offer a more obvious, albeit highly speculative, explanation than one derived from generalizations of gratifications.

In both the UK and the US it appears that, currently, the most likely strategy for increasing pay satisfaction is to increase employees' perceptions of pay fairness rather than to increase their pay. Money isn't everything. Social psychologists still have a lot of work to do.

ACKNOWLEDGEMENT

The authors are very grateful to Peter Treasure and Brendan Burchell for statistical assistance and advice.

REFERENCES

Adams, J.S. (1965) Inequity in social exchange. In L. Berkowitz (ed.) *Advances in Experimental Social Psychology*, Volume 2. New York: Academic Press.

Berkowitz, L., Fraser, C., Treasure, F.P. and Cochran, S. (1987) Pay, equity, job gratifications, and comparisons in pay satisfaction. *Journal of Applied Psychology*, 72, 544–51.

Eiser, J.R. (1986) *Social Psychology*. Cambridge: Cambridge University Press.

Goldthorpe, J.H., Lockwood, D. *et al.* (1968) *The Affluent Worker in the Class Structure*. Cambridge: Cambridge University Press.

Goodman, P.S. (1974) An examination of referents used in the evaluation of pay. *Organizational Behaviour and Human Performance, 12*, 170–95.

Heneman, H.G., III (1985) Pay satisfaction. In K.M. Rowland and G.E. Ferris (eds) *Research in Personnel and Human Resources Management*, Volume 3. Greenwich, Conn.: JAI Press.

Jaques, E. (1961) *Equitable Payment*. New York: Wiley.

Landy, F.J. (1989) *Psychology of Work Behaviour*. Pacific Grove, CA: Brooks/Cole.

Lawler, E.E., III (1971) *Pay and Organizational Effectiveness*. New York: McGraw-Hill.

McClintock, C.G., Kramer, R.M. and Keil, L.J. (1984) Equity and social change in human relationships. In L. Berkowitz (ed.) *Advances in Experimental Social Psychology*, Volume 17. New York: Academic Press.

Messé, L.A. and Watts, B.L. (1983) Complex nature of the sense of fairness: internal standards and social comparison as bases for reward evaluation. *Journal of Personality and Social Psychology, 45*, 84–93.

Olson, J.M., Herman, C.P. and Zanna, M.P. (eds) (1986) *Relative Deprivation and Social Comparison*. New York: Erlbaum.

Orpen, C. (1986) Correlates of pay satisfaction. *Psychological Reports, 59*, 1205–6.

Rice, R.W., Phillips, S.M. and McFarlin, D.B. (1990) *Journal of Applied Psychology, 75*, 386–93.

Smith, P. and Gaskell, G. (1990) The social dimension in relative deprivation. In C. Fraser and G. Gaskell (eds) *The Social Psychological Study of Widespread Beliefs*. Cambridge: Cambridge University Press.

Walster, E., Walster, G.W. and Berscheid, E. (1978) *Equity: Theory and Research*. Boston, Mass.: Allyn & Bacon.

Warr, P. (1987) *Work, Unemployment, and Mental Health*. Oxford: Oxford University Press.

7   Work and well-being among offshore oil employees

Katharine R. Parkes

INTRODUCTION

The work conditions of North Sea oil employees, and their lifestyle more generally, have been widely studied by researchers from a variety of disciplines, including occupational medicine, psychiatry, sociology, psychology and physiology. Issues of work characteristics, health and safety and psychosocial factors in the offshore environment have therefore been addressed from several different perspectives.

Areas of particular relevance to psychologists include social networks, the lifestyles of oil employees and their families, the home–work interface and the 'intermittent husband syndrome' (Clark *et al.*, 1985; Lewis *et al.*, 1988; Morrice, 1981; Morrice *et al.*, 1985; Solheim, 1988; Taylor *et al.*, 1985); psychosocial aspects of offshore work, including the perceived work environment, social support, personality, mental health and job satisfaction (Gann *et al.*, 1990; Hellesoy, 1985; Sutherland and Cooper, 1986); work design (particularly, shift patterns, work/rest schedules, task allocation and the implications of confined work and living space), some aspects of which are reviewed by Sutherland and Cooper (1989); and risk perception, safety attitudes and accident involvement (Marek *et al.*, 1987; Rundmo, 1992a, 1992b; Sutherland and Cooper, 1991; Wagenaar *et al.*, 1993).

All these topics have some bearing on the present chapter, but the main focus of the work described here is on the health (particularly, mental health) of offshore personnel, as compared with similar employees onshore, and the psychosocial characteristics of the North Sea work environment. Links between psychosocial work characteristics and mental and physical health have been widely reported in the research literature (e.g. Cohen *et al.*, 1986; French *et al.*, 1982; House, 1981; Karasek and Theorell, 1990). However, very little empirical research in this area relates specifically to the offshore environment; available literature is reviewed in the following sections.

Mental health of offshore employees

Mental fitness is an important factor in medical screening for offshore work, not least because serious mental disturbance may necessitate medical evacuation (Norman *et al.*, 1988). However, offshore workers may also experience a range of less severe mental health problems, such as anxiety, depression and job dissatisfaction; whether such problems are more prevalent offshore than in comparable groups onshore merits research attention, particularly if offshore work conditions play a causal role in psychological distress.

To date, it appears that only two studies have examined the mental health of employees on North Sea installations in the UK sector, as compared with that of onshore groups. One study was based on questionnaire data obtained from employees of a 'major offshore personnel service company' (Cooper and Sutherland, 1987; Sutherland and Cooper, 1986). The other study was carried out more recently in a multinational oil company (Gann *et al.*, 1990). The authors of the two studies, using different methods, measures and sample populations, came to different conclusions. Thus, Sutherland and Cooper concluded that offshore workers had higher rates of anxiety and obsessional symptoms than comparable onshore groups, while Gann *et al.* found no differences between onshore and offshore employees in symptoms of anxiety and depression.

In view of the discrepancies in the findings, it is of interest to examine the basis of the conclusions reached in each of these studies. Sutherland and Cooper's data were collected by means of questionnaires mailed to potential respondents at their homes; the questionnaire included the Crown–Crisp Experiential Index (Crown and Crisp, 1979), a symptom checklist. As no comparison group of onshore employees was studied, the conclusion that free-floating anxiety and obsessionality were high relative to onshore groups was based on comparisons with 'normative' data taken from several different sources, including General Practice patients, an industrial sample and psycho-neurotic out-patients.

A number of methodological aspects of this study are relevant in assessing its findings. First, the response rate was low (26 per cent), raising questions as to the extent to which the sample was representative. Second, no onshore comparison group was included in the study. Thus, conclusions about levels of anxiety and obsessionality among offshore employees depended on comparing the offshore data with published values; the suitability of the comparison groups is therefore relevant to the conclusions reached. In particular, it should be noted that both the industrial sample (age range 42–56 years) and the General Practice sample (age range 35–70 years) cited by Sutherland and Cooper were considerably older than the offshore group (80 per cent under 40 years). Anxiety tends to decrease with age (Crisp *et al.*, 1978); therefore, higher anxiety reported by the offshore group could be at least partially attributable to age. These and other methodological problems need to be taken into account in evaluating the conclusions reached in Sutherland and Cooper's (1986) book.

The more recent study by Gann *et al.*. (1990) provided further information about relative symptom levels in onshore and offshore groups. Gann *et al.* administered anxiety and depression scales (Goldberg *et al.*, 1988) to employees undergoing routine medical examinations. Both onshore and offshore personnel were included; there were 796 participants in the sample, representing an almost complete sequence of consecutive attenders. The data were analysed with particular reference to job level, age and the onshore/offshore comparison. At each job level, onshore/offshore differences failed to reach the .05 significance level for either anxiety or depression, with one exception (which would be expected from the number of significance tests carried out).

The scope of Gann *et al.*'s study was more limited than that of Sutherland and Cooper but the methodology was more rigorous, although the fact that medical examination was compulsory for offshore employees but voluntary for those onshore raises some questions as to the comparability of the two groups. Also, data collection by company personnel in the context of a medical examination may have led to an under-reporting of symptoms among offshore employees, through concern that their continued employment might be jeopardized by adverse medical reports.

On the basis of these two studies, the view that offshore workers show less favourable mental health than their onshore counterparts is not well supported. However, even if significant differences were clearly demonstrated, their underlying causes could not be established without research into the psychosocial environment offshore and its implications for mental health. Indeed, it is inherently difficult to establish the direction of causal effects in work stress research. None the less, studies which throw light on the nature of the stressors encountered in offshore work, and their associations with well-being, are potentially important.

The offshore work environment and its implications for well-being

Descriptive accounts of offshore work, including problems that may arise from the work environment itself and, more generally, from the lifestyle associated with offshore work, have appeared in a number of publications (e.g. Cox, 1987; Solheim, 1988; Sunde, 1983). The potential sources of stress described include confined work and living conditions; lack of privacy; living in close proximity to others in a mixed community of very different types of people; noise and other physical environment stressors, including potential hazards; shift patterns; monotonous work in which periods of boredom are interspersed with periods of intense activity; work which may provide little opportunity for developing new skills.

The emphasis put on these different aspects of offshore work depends on the particular interests of the authors concerned. From a medical perspective, for instance, aspects of offshore work which may have adverse effects on health are a major concern (e.g. Cox, 1987; Sunde, 1983). However, Sunde also notes features of offshore work which are potentially favourable to the health and well-being of those concerned, including enhanced pay rates and long periods of leave, careful monitoring of health, restrictions on smoking and alcohol, the availability of offshore medical services and a lower retirement age.

From a sociological viewpoint, the problems raised by offshore employment are seen as extending beyond individual concerns to wider social and economic issues (e.g. House, 1985; Rosen and Voorhees-Rosen, 1978). Solheim (1988), commenting more specifically on the job characteristics of offshore employees, notes that the value of a job offshore is seen not to lie in the work itself, but in the release from it; thus, intrinsic job satisfaction tends to be sacrificed in favour of external rewards of money and leisure at home. A similar point is made by Alvarez (1986) in *Offshore: A North Sea Journey*, a vivid account of his observations of offshore oil employees and their work conditions: 'During the time you are offshore, you are defined solely in terms of your work, and if the work does not satisfy you there are no other compensations' (p. 113).

Psychologists concerned with offshore work focus primarily on its individual and interpersonal implications, including effects on marriage and family interactions; on the leisure patterns of oil workers; and on the work demands and constraints it imposes (Butler and Smith, 1986; Clark and Taylor, 1988; Morrice *et al.*, 1985). The offshore work environment, and its consequences for the well-being of the offshore workers and their families, lends itself to inter-disciplinary research, but few wide-ranging studies of this kind have been reported. One exception is a study carried out among personnel on the Statfjord platform in the Norwegian sector of the North Sea (Hellesoy, 1985). The Statfjord study surveyed several different occupational groups working on the platform (including contractors' personnel and those employed directly by the operating company), using interviews and questionnaires. The main set of data (collected in 1980) was based on the questionnaire responses of some 450–500 individuals (numbers varied for different questions), corresponding to response rates of approximately 64–71 per cent. In addition, archival data (e.g. records of visits to the sick bay) were analysed.

In their report on this study, Hellesoy and his colleagues present a wide range of descriptive data, together with analyses linking perceptions of the work environment (including work characteristics, safety, hazards and risks, physical environmental factors, social support and other aspects of the work situation) to self-reports of well-being, including work satisfaction, physical health and psychosomatic problems. These results are augmented by analyses of records maintained by the occupational health service (including frequency of contacts and diagnostic evaluation).

The Statfjord study adopted the 'Michigan model' of work stress (see, for instance, House, 1981) as a conceptual framework, and in this context particularly emphasized the role played by social support from supervisors and work-group members in promoting safety, efficiency and well-being. Less attention was given to the role of individual differences, particularly in personality, which may also have a significant impact on relations between the work environment factors and outcome measures. Furthermore, as the study was cross-sectional (data being collected at a single point in time), no causal inferences could be made. None the less, the research made a significant contribution to identifying potentially important psychosocial factors in the offshore work environment, and in documenting their associations with well-being.

In considering work conditions offshore and their implications for mental health, findings from the Sutherland and Cooper (1986) study noted earlier are also relevant. In addition to assessing mental health, these authors assessed job stressors (i.e. sources of stress in the job situation), work satisfaction and personality traits, including Type A behaviour and locus of control. Using these data, they examined relations between the perceived job stressors and symptom levels, and the extent to which the personality characteristics contributed to mental health independently of work conditions.

The authors concluded that poor relationships at home and at work were of major importance as predictors of dissatisfaction and distress, and that Type A behaviour merited further investigation in the context of offshore work. While these conclusions are consistent with the more general work stress literature, the magnitude and statistical significance of the relationships observed may have been inflated by methodological problems. In particular, the possible confounding effects of 'negative affectivity' (i.e. the tendency of some individuals to perceive themselves, their health and their environment negatively) are ignored by Sutherland and Cooper. As Brief *et al.* (1988) demonstrated, negative affectivity inflates relations between self-reported stressors and well-being; such effects could account to a large extent for the correlations observed by Sutherland and Cooper.

While less directly applicable to offshore work, studies of several other occupational groups who work away from home, in a confined physical environment and under demanding work conditions, also merit note in the present context. For instance, Sutherland and Flin (1989) draw attention to the similarities between work conditions in the fishing industry and those in the offshore oil industry. Studies carried out among sailors and submariners, astronauts and others whose work necessitates extended periods away from home are also relevant (e.g. Beckman *et al.*, 1979; Binkley, 1990; Eastman *et al.*, 1990; Mederer and Weinstein, 1992). A particular feature of these occupations is the psychosocial impact on families of the husband's frequent absence from home, and the adaptive demands imposed on wives by this pattern of work.

The present study

Over the past decade, the technology of oil and gas extraction, the design of oil platforms, the regulations relating to offshore safety and the economic climate in which the oil industry operates have changed considerably. Thus, the extent to which the findings of the studies reviewed above reflect the current conditions and concerns of UK sector employees is uncertain.

The present study attempted to overcome some of the limitations of earlier work, albeit in a relatively small-scale study. The main aims of the work were to compare measures of mental health and perceptions of the work environment in onshore and offshore groups; to identify the combinations of factors which characterize onshore and offshore work settings, and those associated with particular platforms and installations; to examine the roles played by work perceptions and personality in relationships between onshore/offshore environments and mental health; and to examine factors predictive of work satisfaction, including perceptions of workload and work-related social support.

The major features of the research approach adopted were as follows:

- Data were collected both onshore and offshore, thus allowing a more precise evaluation of the impact of offshore work conditions than is possible if research is carried out only among offshore personnel.
- The employees studied were control-room operators and other personnel carrying out similar tasks in the production areas. Whether located onshore or offshore, these operators are responsible for a variety of monitoring, control and communication tasks. Effective performance of these tasks is of critical importance to the production process; thus, the well-being and alertness of controllers is inherently of interest and concern. Furthermore, the present study allowed direct comparison between groups carrying out similar work onshore and offshore, an important methodological consideration.
- All data were collected on site, whether onshore or offshore, thus meeting the point made by Sutherland and Flin (1989) who noted that collecting data during leave periods (rather than in the work environment) may influence the responses obtained.
- The study was designed to obtain as high a response rate as realistically possible so as to avoid the inherent limitations of research in which many potential participants fail to respond.

Some aspects of this study have been reported in more detail elsewhere (Parkes, 1992, 1993a). A technical report is also available (Parkes, 1993b). The present contribution seeks to present a more descriptive account of the findings relating to well-being (including affective and somatic symptoms, sleep problems and minor health complaints) and job satisfaction among oil industry employees onshore and offshore.

RESEARCH METHOD

A total of 172 oil company personnel participated in the research. In the offshore group, there were eighty-four control-room operators (including some supervisors) drawn from three North Sea installations. For the purposes of this report, the installations involved were designated A1, A2 and A3. They differed in several respects. Thus, A1 had a complement of approximately 150 personnel, while A2 was larger (200 personnel) and of more recent design and construction. The remaining participants were employed on A3, which was smaller in size than the other two installations and had more limited recreational facilities.

A comparison group of eighty-eight operators and supervisors carrying out control-room tasks at six onshore sites (four located in Scotland and two in north-east England) also took part. Data from two small sites were combined, resulting in five onshore locations (designated B1, B2, B3, B4 and B5). All the participants worked as control-room operators or carried out similar control and monitoring tasks in the production areas. Both operators and supervisors were included. Only men were involved in the study, as no women were employed in these roles at the installations involved. A high level of co-operation was received from those concerned; only twelve individuals declined to participate (including one entire shift team which made a collective decision not to be involved). Overall, the data set included more than 90 per cent of the intended sample.

Questionnaires were administered on site, either individually or in small groups, with an experimenter present; completion of the questionnaires (which took place during working hours, but away from the immediate workplace) required 45–60 minutes. All individual data were treated as confidential to the researchers and, in particular, were not disclosed to any company personnel.

Measures

The questionnaires were divided into three main sections covering, respectively: general background information; personality and mental health; perceptions of the work situation and work satisfaction.

Demographic and background information

The first section included demographic information; present job level and tenure; preference for onshore versus offshore work; ratings of sleep quality and duration when working different shifts; and minor health problems (using the checklist devised by Vaernes *et al.*, 1988).

Personality and health measures

The second section consisted of inventories assessing personality characteristics known to predict well-being and, more particularly, responses to work-related demands. Measures of current mental health and of minor health complaints were also included. The main measures reported here are described below.

- *Extraversion/introversion* and *neuroticism* were assessed using an abbreviated version of the Eysenck Personality Questionnaire (Eysenck *et al.*, 1985).
- *Mental health*. The measure of current symptom levels used was the 'General Health Questionnaire' (GHQ) (Goldberg, 1978). The version used included a 12-item general scale of psychological symptoms, recommended for occupational and organizational research (Banks *et al.*, 1980), and separate 7-item scales assessing somatic symptoms, anxiety and social dysfunction, as developed by Goldberg and Hillier (1979). Likert-scale scoring was used here, each item being scored on a 0–1–2–3 scale.
- *Minor physical health problems*. Reports of minor health complaints (including headaches, neck pain, shoulder pain, back pain, indigestion, heartburn and stomach upset) and sleep problems experienced during work periods in the previous six weeks were assessed with a checklist previously used in a study of process-control workers in the chemical industry (Vaernes *et al.*, 1988).

Job satisfaction

Seventeen items were used to assess satisfaction with pay, hours of work and shifts, physical working conditions, skill and variety in tasks, status and perceived importance of the job and management. Factor analysis identified three main dimensions: general satisfaction (seven items), organizational satisfaction (three items, concerned with satisfaction with management, people and physical working conditions) and status satisfaction (three items relating to the extent to which supervisor, other work-group members and the individual himself perceived the job as important). Two of the remaining four items which did not fall clearly on any of the three scales (satisfaction with pay and satisfaction with working hours and shift patterns) were treated as single item measures.

RESULTS

Characteristics of the sample

The initial analyses examined differences between the onshore and offshore groups in demographic characteristics and other background measures, including preferences for onshore versus offshore work.

There were few *demographic* differences between the onshore and offshore groups. The main exception was age: onshore employees were significantly older (average, 44.5 ± 7.8 years, range 29–59 years) than their offshore counterparts (average, 40.9 ± 6.8 years, range 28–57 years). However, as compared with the Sutherland and Cooper (1986) sample (in which 80 per cent of participants were aged under 40 years), the higher mean age of the present offshore group is consistent with the fact that, as the offshore oil industry has itself become more mature, so the average age of offshore employees has increased, a change that has important implications for work performance, health and safety.

Other background variables, such as *marital status* and *education*, did not show significant differences between the two groups. Overall, 92 per cent of the respondents were married, the proportions in the onshore and offshore groups being 90 per cent and 95 per cent respectively. Thus, in this sample, there was no evidence to suggest that offshore work tends to attract disproportionate numbers of single or divorced men or to give rise to high rates of marriage breakdown relative to comparable onshore work. The range of educational qualifications was also similar in the onshore and offshore groups: 30 per cent reported no formal qualifications, 21 per cent reported GCE passes at O- or A-level; and 49 per cent reported technical certificates, diplomas or degree-level qualifications.

For the offshore employees, average *job tenure* (i.e. the length of employment in their present jobs) was nearly seven years, while for those onshore it was about a year less. The offshore personnel in particular appeared to be a very stable workforce; almost all respondents thought that they would still be in the same job in a year's time. In the onshore group, 91 per cent expected to stay in their jobs. In terms of past work experience, the great majority of respondents (87 per cent) had been employed on *shiftwork* prior to their present job; on average, respondents had a career total of more than eighteen years' experience of shiftwork.

Preference for working onshore or offshore

Preference for working onshore or offshore was assessed on a 5-point scale, ranging from '*definitely prefer onshore*' through '*no preference*' to '*definitely prefer offshore*'. There was a highly significant difference between the onshore and offshore groups in these preference ratings (Mann–Whitney test, U = 2346.5, Z = 4.30, p < .0001). Almost all the onshore respondents favoured onshore work; only 5.7 per cent of them expressed any preference

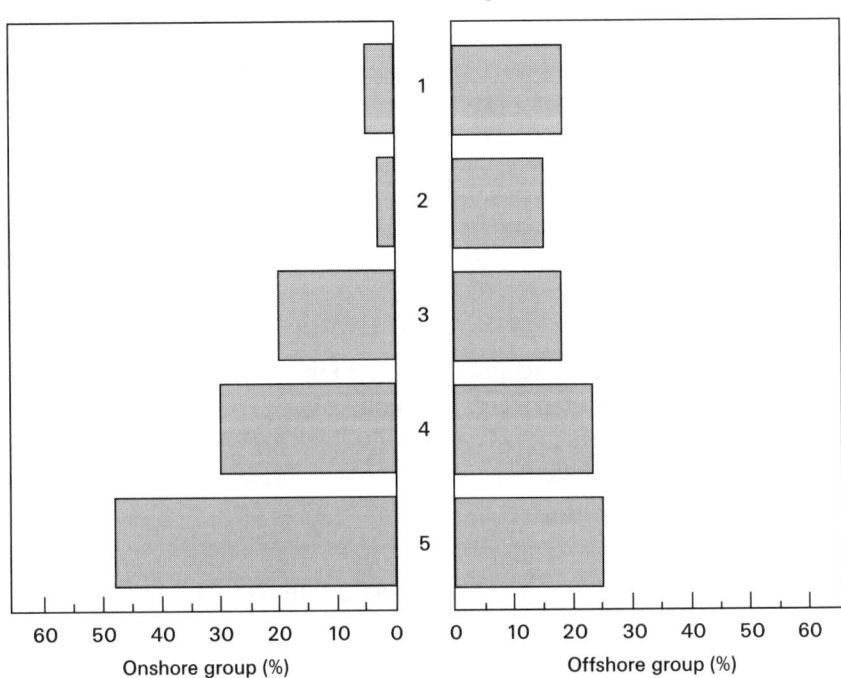

Preference ratings

Preferences were scored on a 5-point scale
1 = definitely prefer offshore
3 = no preference
5 = definitely prefer onshore

Figure 7.1 Preferences for onshore versus offshore work in the onshore and offshore groups

for working offshore. Among the offshore group, the pattern of responses was less clear-cut: 48.8 per cent of the respondents indicated that they would prefer to work onshore, 17.9 per cent were neutral, while 33.3 per cent expressed a preference for offshore work. The distributions of the preference responses for the onshore and offshore groups are shown graphically in Figure 7.1.

The main reasons given by offshore employees for not working onshore were lack of employment opportunities near their homes and pay rates. More positively, offshore respondents valued the relatively long leave periods spent with their families.

Minor health complaints and sleep problems

Minor health complaints (including headaches, neck pain, shoulder pain, back pain, indigestion, heartburn and stomach upset) and sleep problems

Table 7.1 Percentages of onshore and offshore groups reporting minor health problems

	Onshore	Offshore	Significance of difference
Headaches	34%	43%	ns
Sleep problems	36%	54%	p < .04
One or more of the other minor problems	67%	54%	(p = .11)

were assessed with a checklist previously used in a study of process-control workers in the Norwegian chemical industry (Vaernes *et al.*, 1988). In general, the present findings were similar to those reported by Vaernes *et al.* The main results are summarized in Table 7.1.

- With the exception of concerns about sleep, headaches were the most frequently reported health problems. Thus, 42.8 per cent of the offshore group and 34.4 per cent of the onshore group reported headaches; the difference between these rates was not significant. However, of those who did endorse the headache item, onshore personnel were more likely to report moderate or severe headache problems whereas, among offshore respondents, mild problems were more commonly reported.
- Sleep problems were reported by nearly half the respondents overall, but the distribution of responses was significantly different for onshore and offshore groups (chi^2 = 4.59, df = 1, p = .032). Both mild and moderate problems were more frequently reported by offshore personnel (54 per cent) than by those working onshore (36 per cent). In contrast, only 24.7 per cent of the sample of onshore shift-workers in the Vaernes *et al.* (1988) study reported sleep problems.
- Each of the other health complaints included in the checklist was reported by less than 25 per cent of respondents. When responses in these minor categories were summed, it was found that the onshore group was more likely to report problems than the offshore group (66.7 per cent as compared with 53.6 per cent). This difference did not reach the .05 significance level, but its direction is consistent with the higher medical standards required of offshore employees, and with their younger average age.

Neuroticism in relation to health problems onshore and offshore

Minor psychosomatic complaints such as headaches and sleep problems are more likely to be reported by individuals high in neuroticism than by those low in this characteristic (Watson and Pennebaker, 1989). Furthermore, the

Table 7.2 Neuroticism in relation to health problems onshore and offshore

		Onshore n = 88	Offshore n = 84	Chi-square
Headaches	Low N	30%	28%	ns
	High N	38%	57%	p < .10
Sleep problems	Low N	22%	50%	p < .01
	High N	48%	57%	ns

impact of neuroticism on reported health problems may be more marked under stressful work conditions. It was therefore of interest to determine whether disproportionately high incidences of minor health problems were reported by high neurotic individuals working offshore. In these analyses, the onshore and offshore groups were divided into subgroups on the basis of high (scores of 3 or more) or low (scores of 2 or less) neuroticism, and separate chi-squared tests carried out. The results are shown in Table 7.2.

Among those low in neuroticism, there was no significant difference in the proportions of onshore and offshore groups reporting headaches, but in the high neuroticism group those working offshore were more likely to report headaches than those working onshore (chi^2 = 3.13, df = 1, p <.10). Thus, only the combination of offshore work and high neuroticism resulted in disproportionately high levels of reported headaches. However, for sleep problems, the pattern of results was different. In this case, the reported incidence of sleep problems was relatively high in all subgroups, except for individuals low in neuroticism working onshore (chi^2 = 6.55, df = 1, p = <.01).

Mental health

In the initial analysis of the GHQ-12 symptom scores, the onshore and offshore groups were directly compared; mean scores for both groups were then compared with published data. The results showed that the onshore and offshore samples in the present study differed significantly (p < .05) in GHQ-12 scores, offshore personnel reporting higher symptom levels (8.75 ± 3.76) than those onshore (7.64 ± 2.94). This difference remained significant after controlling for age, job level and neuroticism. The GHQ-12 scores of the onshore and offshore employees in the present sample were also compared with published data from a representative sample of engineering employees (Banks *et al.*, 1980) (see Figure 7.2).

These comparisons showed that mean symptom levels among offshore personnel were closely similar to the published values, while among onshore personnel they were significantly lower than the published values (p <.01). Thus, there was no evidence to suggest that the offshore group showed

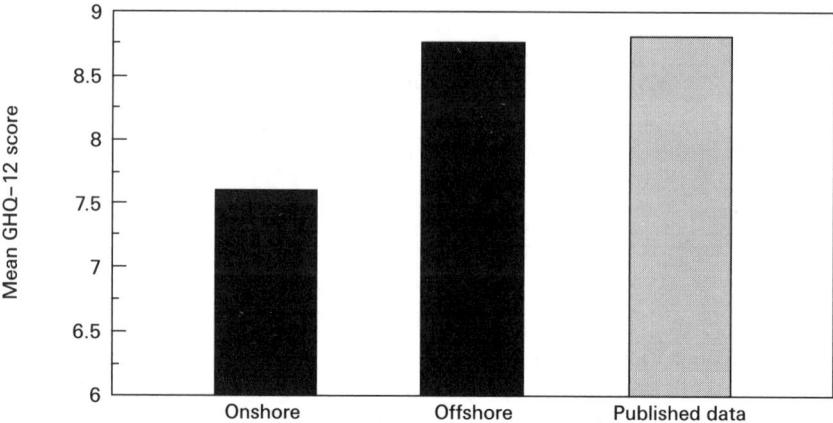

Figure 7.2 Mean GHQ scores in the onshore and offshore groups as compared with published data

higher symptom levels than the engineering employees (the most appropriate published data available for comparison purposes). However, the conclusion which might be drawn from this result, that the mental health of the offshore group gave no cause for concern while that of the onshore group was better than would be expected, does not stand up to more rigorous examination. As discussed by Parkes (1992) in a more detailed examination of these data, two factors are particularly relevant in interpreting the findings:

(a) Offshore employment requires a high standard of physical and mental health; thus, medical and psychiatric conditions which would not necessarily be a bar to onshore employment are not acceptable for offshore personnel (UK Offshore Operators Association, 1986). Furthermore, in addition to a pre-employment medical examination, further medical checks at regular intervals are compulsory for offshore personnel. It is also relevant that, although offshore workers with health problems may transfer to onshore work, poor health is never a reason for a transfer from onshore to offshore work. Thus, offshore workers are an unusually 'healthy worker' group who would be expected to show better mental and physical health than a cross-section of onshore industrial employees.

(b) The personality characteristics of both onshore and offshore employees in the present study were such that both groups would be expected to have favourable mental health relative to the general population (see Figure 7.3). Thus, in terms of neuroticism and extraversion (personality measures which are strongly predictive of mental health), the present sample tended to show greater emotional stability (i.e. lower neuroticism), and to be more active, sociable and adaptable (i.e. higher

Figure 7.3 Mean extraversion and neuroticism scores in the present sample as compared with general population males

extraversion) than general population males (Eysenck and Eysenck, 1975). However, as noted above, only the onshore group showed low GHQ-12 scores relative to the published comparison data; the expected low scores were not observed in the offshore group.

Taken together, these findings strongly suggest that the offshore group in the present study reported higher symptom levels than would have been expected in comparable onshore employees. However, use of the GHQ-12 scores for comparison purposes (appropriate published data were available only for this measure) did not allow any analysis of onshore/offshore differences in specific types of symptoms. Further analyses were therefore carried out to compare the onshore and offshore groups in terms of scores on the three GHQ subscales (anxiety, somatic symptoms and social dysfunction). The results showed clearly that the elevated levels of symptoms among those working offshore were attributable solely to significantly higher anxiety ($p < .01$) in the offshore group (3.62 ± 3.42) as compared with the onshore group (2.43 ± 2.18). In contrast, onshore/offshore differences in somatic symptoms and in social dysfunction scores were nonsignificant. Mean job satisfaction scores also showed no difference between the two groups. Controlling for age, job level and neuroticism did not markedly alter these results.

DISCUSSION

In highlighting the link between offshore employment and anxiety, the present study does not support the conclusion of Gann *et al.* (1990) that onshore and offshore workers do not differ in symptom levels. Conversely, the present results are consistent with previous findings suggesting that anxiety is relatively high among offshore workers (Sutherland and Cooper, 1986). However, in the present study, it was possible to make direct comparisons of reported symptom levels in offshore and onshore personnel employed in very similar jobs. This direct comparison eliminated several explanations of anxiety differences between onshore and offshore groups which could not be precluded in the Sutherland and Cooper study.

The possibility that the high anxiety in the offshore group existed prior to their employment offshore cannot be entirely ruled out in a cross-sectional study. However, it is improbable that anxious individuals would be particularly likely to seek, or to be selected for, offshore employment; furthermore, the high medical standards required of offshore employees, and their tendency to show 'stable extravert' personality characteristics, suggest that this explanation is implausible. Also, the elevated scores of the offshore group applied only to anxiety symptoms; somatic symptoms and social dysfunction levels did not differ significantly between the onshore and offshore groups.

The alternative, and more likely, explanation is that the offshore environment plays a causal role in anxiety among offshore employees. This explanation implies that, if individuals in the offshore group were employed in similar jobs onshore, they would show lower anxiety levels than they reported in the present study; such an interpretation is consistent with the evidence outlined above. In this context, it is of interest to note that the particular symptoms which most strongly differentiated the offshore group from those working onshore reflected feelings of being *'constantly under strain'* and being *'strung up and nervous all the time'*, together with *'getting scared or panicky for no good reason'*. Thus, it appears that the offshore environment is associated with feelings of pervasive tension and apprehension, rather than with more specific aspects of anxiety.

The nature of North Sea employment exposes offshore personnel to a variety of psychosocial and physical environment stressors which may be causally linked to the levels of anxiety and tension observed. Relevant factors include the constraints and potential hazards of offshore work; the possibility of sudden emergencies; fatigue and sleep problems associated with the demanding shift patterns worked by offshore employees (Parkes, 1993a); helicopter travel to and from the shore; physical stressors offshore (e.g. confined space, isolation, noise, vibration and adverse weather conditions); and psychosocial factors, including lack of privacy, the proximity of workmates out of working hours, isolation from family and friends, and the family problems which may result from 'intermittent husband absence'. The present study did not attempt to identify the relative importance of these different factors in relation to elevated anxiety levels. However, in general terms, the findings are consistent with theoretical approaches to stress (e.g. Lazarus and Folkman, 1984) in which the perception of physical or psychological threat is seen as playing a central role in anxiety; more specifically, among offshore workers, previous research has demonstrated empirical links between perceived risk and anxiety (Hellesoy, 1985), and between perceived risk and more general strain outcomes (Rundmo, 1992b).

A further issue which merits consideration is whether all offshore employees experience higher anxiety than they would do if working onshore, or whether particular personality characteristics predispose some individuals to respond to the offshore environment with elevated anxiety while others remain unaffected. The work of Sutherland and Cooper (1986, 1991) suggests that Type A personality is likely to be particularly relevant in this context; data obtained in the present study tended to confirm the significance of Type A as a significant underlying factor in the elevated anxiety levels reported by offshore employees (see Parkes, 1993b). However, other personality and attitudinal factors may also be important; further studies in which longitudinal data are used to compare cohorts of onshore and offshore employees are required to establish the extent to which personality and environmental characteristics combine to influence the performance and health of offshore workers. Such research can provide an important basis for the promotion of well-being and job satisfaction among offshore employees; more generally, human factors research is a vital part of wider efforts to ensure efficiency, productivity and, above all, safety on offshore oil and gas installations.

REFERENCES

Alvarez, A. (1986) *Offshore: A North Sea Journey*. London: Hodder & Stoughton.

Banks, M.H., Clegg, C.W., Jackson, P.R., Kemp, N.J., Stafford, E.M. and Wall, T.D. (1980) The use of the General Health Questionnaire as an indicator of mental health in occupational studies. *Journal of Occupational Psychology, 53*, 187–94.

Beckman, E., Marsella, A.J. and Finney, R. (1979) Depression in the wives of nuclear submarine personnel. *American Journal of Psychiatry, 135*(48), 524–6.

Binkley, M. (1990) Work organization among Nova Scotian offshore fishermen. *Human Organization, 49*, 395–405.

Brief, A.P., Burke, M.J., George, J.M., Robinson, B.S. and Webster, J. (1988) Should negative affectivity remain an unmeasured variable in the study of job stress? *Journal of Applied Psychology, 73*, 193–9.

Butler, R.W. and Smith, D.C. (1986) Recreational behavior of onshore and offshore oil industry employees in Newfoundland, Canada. *Leisure Sciences, 8*, 297–318.

Clark, D. and Taylor, R. (1988) Partings and reunions: marriage and offshore employment in the British North Sea. In J. Lewis, M. Porter and M. Shrimpton (eds) *Women, Work and Family in the British, Canadian and Norwegian Offshore Oilfields*. London: Macmillan.

Clark, D., McCann, K., Morrice, K. and Taylor, R. (1985) Work and marriage in the offshore oil industry. *International Journal of Social Economics, 12*, 36–47.

Cohen, S., Evans, G.W., Stokols, D. and Krantz, D.S. (1986) *Behavior, Health and Environmental Stress*. New York: Plenum.

Cooper, C.L. and Sutherland, V.J. (1987) Job stress, mental health, and accidents among offshore workers in the oil and gas extraction industries. *Journal of Occupational Medicine, 29*, 119–25.

Cox, R.A.F. (1987) *Offshore Medicine: Medical Care of Employees in the Offshore Oil Industry*, 2nd edition. London: Springer-Verlag.

Crisp, A.H., Ralph, P.C., McGuinness, B. and Harris, G. (1978) Psychoneurotic profiles in the adult population. *British Journal of Medical Psychology*, *51*, 293–301.

Crown, S. and Crisp, A.H. (1979) *Manual of the Crown–Crisp Experiential Index.* London: Hodder & Stoughton.

Eastman, E., Archer, R.P. and Ball, J.D. (1990) Psychosocial and life stress characteristics of Navy families: Family Environment Scale and Life Experiences Scale findings. *Military Psychology*, *2*, 113–27.

Eysenck, H.J. and Eysenck, S.B.G. (1975) *Manual of the Eysenck Personality Questionnaire.* London: Hodder & Stoughton.

Eysenck, S.B.G., Eysenck, H.J. and Barrett, P. (1985) A revised version of the psychoticism scale. *Personality and Individual Differences*, *6*, 21–9.

French, J.R.P., Caplan, R.D. and Harrison, R.V. (1982) *The Mechanisms of Job Stress and Strain.* Chichester: Wiley.

Gann, M., Corpe, U. and Wilson, I. (1990) The application of a short anxiety and depression questionnaire to oil industry staff. *Journal of the Society of Occupational Medicine*, *40*, 138–42.

Goldberg, D. (1978) *Manual of the General Health Questionnaire.* Windsor: NFER.

Goldberg, D.P. and Hillier, V.F. (1979) A scaled version of the General Health Questionnaire. *Psychological Medicine*, *9*, 139–45.

Goldberg, D., Bridges, K., Duncan-Jones, P. and Grayson, D. (1988) Detecting anxiety and depression in general medical settings. *British Medical Journal*, *297*, 897–9.

Hellesoy, O.H. (ed.) (1985) *Work Environment: Statfjord Field.* Bergen, Oslo: Universitetsforlaget.

House, J.S. (1981) *Work Stress and Social Support.* Reading, Mass.: Addison-Wesley.

House, J.D. (1985) *Working Offshore: The Other Price of Newfoundland's Oil.* Memorial University of Newfoundland: Institute of Social and Economic Research.

Karasek, R. and Theorell, T. (1990) *Healthy Work: Stress, Productivity, and the Reconstruction of Working Life.* New York: Basic Books.

Lazarus, R.S. and Folkman, S. (1984) *Stress, Appraisal and Coping.* New York: Springer.

Lewis, J., Porter, M. and Shrimpton, M. (eds.) (1988) *Women, Work and Family in the British, Canadian and Norwegian Offshore Oilfields.* London: Macmillan.

Marek, J., Iversen, E. and Hellesoy, O.H. (1987) Risk, organization and safety on an oil platform. In W.T. Singleton and J. Hovden (eds) *Risk and Decisions.* Chichester: Wiley, pp. 123–37.

Mederer, H.J. and Weinstein, L. (1992) Choices and constraints in a two-person career: ideology, division of labor, and well-being among submarine officers' wives. *Journal of Family Issues*, *13*, 334–50.

Morrice, J.K.W. (1981) Psychosocial problems in the oil industry. *Update*, 1 January, 27–34.

Morrice, J.K.W., Taylor, R.C., Clark, D. and McCann, K. (1985) Oil wives and intermittent husbands. *British Journal of Psychiatry*, *147*, 479–83.

Norman, J.N., Ballantine, B.N., Brebner, J.A., Brown, B. *et al.* (1988) Medical evacuations from offshore structures. *British Journal of Industrial Medicine*, *45*, 619–23.

Parkes, K.R. (1992) Mental health in the oil industry: a comparative study of onshore and offshore employees. *Psychological Medicine*, *22*, 997–1009.

Parkes, K.R. (1993) *Human Factors, Shift Work, and Alertness in the Offshore Oil Industry. Part I. A Survey of Onshore and Offshore Control-Room Operators. Part II. Alertness, Sleep, and Cognitive Performance.* Report OTH 92–389. ISBN 0–11–8821350. London: HMSO.

Parkes, K.R. (1994) Sleep patterns, shift work, and individual differences: a comparison of onshore and offshore control-room operators. *Ergonomics, 37,* 827–44.

Rosen, D.H. and Voorhees-Rosen, D. (1978) The Shetland Islands: the effects of social and ecological change on mental health. *Culture, Medicine and Psychiatry, 2,* 41–67.

Rundmo, T. (1992a) Risk perception and safety on offshore petroleum platforms – Part I: Perception of risk. *Safety Science, 15,* 39–52.

Rundmo, T. (1992b) Risk perception and safety on offshore petroleum platforms – Part II: Perceived risk, job stress and accidents. *Safety Science, 15,* 53–68.

Solheim, J. (1988) Coming home to work: men, women and marriage in the Norwegian offshore oil industry. In J. Lewis, M. Porter and M. Shrimpton (eds) *Women, Work and Family in the British, Canadian and Norwegian Offshore Oilfields.* London: Macmillan.

Sunde, A. (1983) Psychosocial aspects of offshore work. In *Safety and Health in the Oil and Gas Extractive Industries.* London: Graham & Trotman for the Commission of European Communities.

Sutherland, K.M. and Flin, R.H. (1989) Stress at sea: a review of working conditions in the offshore oil industry and fishing industries. *Work and Stress, 3,* 269–85.

Sutherland, V.J. and Cooper, C.L. (1986) *Man and Accidents Offshore – an Examination of the Costs of Stress among Workers on Oil and Gas Rigs.* Colchester: Lloyd's of London Press.

Sutherland, V.J. and Cooper, C.L. (1989) Occupational stress in the offshore oil and gas industry. *International Reviews of Ergonomics, 2,* 183–215.

Sutherland, V.J. and Cooper, C.L. (1991) Personality, stress and accident involvement in the offshore oil and gas industry. *Personality and Individual Differences, 12,* 195–204.

Taylor, R.C., Morrice, K., Clark, D. and McCann, K. (1985) The psychosocial consequences of intermittent husband absence: an epidemiological study. *Social Science and Medicine, 20,* 877–85.

UK Offshore Operators Association (1986) *Medical Aspects of Fitness for Offshore Work: A Guide for Examining Physicians.* London: United Kingdom Offshore Operators Association.

Vaernes, R.J., Knardahl, S., Romsing, J., Aakvaag, A., Tonder, O., Walther, B. and Ursin, H. (1988) Relations between environmental problems, psychology and health among shift-workers in the Norwegian process industry. *Work and Stress, 2,* 7–15.

Wagenaar, W.A., Groeneweg, J., Hudson, P.T.W. and Reason, J.T. (1993) Promoting safety in the oil industry. The Ergonomics Society Lecture, presented at the Ergonomics Society Annual Conference, Edinburgh, 13–16 April 1993.

Watson, D. and Pennebaker, J.W. (1989) Health complaints, stress and distress: exploring the central role of negative affectivity. *Psychological Review, 96,* 235–54.

8   Job demands and anxiety

Donald Broadbent

INTRODUCTION

Different effects of 'stress'

Some jobs are less desirable than others. But there is no simple rank order, with the same jobs at the bottom regardless of the measure one takes. If that were so, each unpleasant aspect of the job would contribute in the same way. Making that assumption I assessed a number of jobs in a National Health Service laundry, and gave 'stress points' for each feature that seemed undesirable (Broadbent, 1981). The total number of points correlated significantly with the number of clinical symptoms of anxiety or depression.

This chapter focuses on various different dimensions of unhappiness at work (Argyle, 1987). Being sluggish or lethargic is not the same as being tense or alarmed, just as being relaxed and calm is different from being excited or alert. Two broad dimensions of experience have now been replicated by a very large number of researchers (e.g. Thayer, 1967; Russell, 1980; Mackay *et al.*, 1978; Warr, 1990a, 1990b; see Argyle, 1987; Thayer, 1989; Warr, 1987, 1990a, 1990b for reviews). One of these dimensions is broadly the scale from 'happy' to 'sad' while the other is from 'aroused' to 'sleep'.

In the same way, the extreme forms of distress that appear as symptoms of anxiety are associated with certain jobs, and yet those jobs may not be associated with especially high depression or even low job satisfaction (Broadbent and Gath, 1979, 1981; Broadbent, 1985; Hesketh and Shouksmith, 1986; Warr, 1990a, 1990b). Perhaps therefore it is too simple to assume a single dimension to stressfulness in the style of Broadbent (1981). In assessing jobs, we should try and separate factors that predict anxiety from those that predict depression or least job satisfaction.

The dimensions of jobs

Just as emotional experience does not lie on a single dimension, so too people's descriptions of their jobs are complex. Large-scale surveys have found that people describe their jobs in two broad dimensions: one relating to the sheer amount they have to do ('demand') while the other relates to the choice, variety or skill of their decisions within the job ('discretion') (Karasek, 1979, 1981). The work of a successful lawyer may well be high on both these dimensions, while that of an assembly-line worker is high only on demand, and that of a janitor low on both (Karasek *et al.*, 1988). Broadly, both high demand and low discretion are associated with distress. There is a good deal of debate about whether the two dimensions act independently or interactively, and especially about the nature of 'discretion'; but it is now widely agreed that both ought to be taken into account (see Kasl, 1989, for a critical review).

A tempting hypothesis is that these two dimensions of jobs might be linked with the two dimensions of human distress. That is, perhaps demand is associated with high 'arousal' and thus with anxiety rather than depression. Discretion on the other hand might not relate simply to anxiety, but perhaps to depression or low job satisfaction. If this were the case, then attempts to avoid job-related anxiety ought to concentrate on the demand dimension rather than other aspects of the job.

There is now a plausible amount of evidence for this linkage. For instance, two early studies found higher anxiety among assembly-line workers as compared with people doing similar low-variety jobs without the element of pacing (Broadbent and Gath, 1981; Broadbent, 1981). The paced workers did not differ in depression, or even in job satisfaction, from their colleagues. Later studies showed that there was a relationship between anxiety and demand among electricity workers (Broadbent, 1985) but no overall linkage of anxiety and discretion. There was also an association of anxiety and demand in veterinary work (Hesketh and Shouksmith, 1986). Carayon-Sainfort (1992) obtained similar results for office work with computers. On a large scale, and across a variety of jobs, Warr (1990a, 1990b) has found that reports of high tension or anxiety relate to job demand. Depression and sluggishness on the other hand do not.

It is less clear what the relation is between discretion and job satisfaction or depression; but in general those people who say their jobs are high in demand are also those who report symptoms of anxiety. We can now take this as a broad conclusion.

Cause and effect

There is, however, a problem with all the papers quoted above: they are cross-sectional studies that look at the people who happen to be in various jobs at a certain time. But suppose the people who choose a job, or who stay in it, differ in anxiety from those who go elsewhere? Perhaps if a job is unpleasant the anxious people stay in it rather than risk unemployment. Furthermore, in some cases the assessment of demand is simply through the person's own perception of the work. The judgement of demand is contaminated by the personality of the individual. Perhaps the work may not really be very demanding, but anxious people may see it as such. Thus people could become anxious because of family or constitutional changes, and then perceive their work as high in demand simply because they are anxious. This radical possibility is ruled out in some of the studies, because the definition of the job as demanding came from objective, non-self-report measures; but it might affect those investigations that relied on the person's own rating.

One cannot therefore assume that the demand causes the anxiety; it might be the other way round. This theoretical issue makes a big difference to any practical decision about reducing the bad impact of jobs. If demand causes anxiety, we need to concentrate on changing the job. If anxiety causes perceived demand, or makes people stay in demanding jobs, then we should start with the individual rather than the job. Of course, it could be that the two interact in a pattern of reciprocal causation.

To distinguish the theories, we need to follow events in the same people over a period of time. We need to be able to relate change in demand to changes in anxiety, in the same person; and we need to know who stays in jobs and who leaves them. That is much more difficult than cross-sectional studies, which is why longitudinal studies are rare. This chapter attempts to start providing such evidence; some of the difficulties will appear.

The question of individual vulnerability

Some individuals may be more vulnerable to stresses. For instance, there is some evidence that people with high scores on the Cognitive Failure Questionnaire (CFQ) may show larger effects of the job (Broadbent *et al.*, 1982; Smith *et al.*, 1989). This relationship is consistent with results of Clegg and colleagues (Clegg *et al.*, 1987; Clegg and Wall, 1990). On the other hand, the relationship was not found by Fisher and Hood (1987), considering the stress of going to university for the first time.

Yet susceptibility to cognitive failure may itself change with changes in demand or discretion. Broadbent (1991, unpublished paper) found no differences in CFQ scores between different groups of car workers, even though they differed in anxiety and depression. But Fisher and Hood did find a change after the move to university; and Morse *et al.* (1991) measured changes as a function of premenstrual tension and of therapy for that condition. The Cognitive Failure Questionnaire was therefore included in the present study, to see whether the scores change with time, and whether they predict vulnerability.

OUTLINE OF THE STUDY

The study took place in a single large supermarket, on the outskirts of a substantial British city. The supermarket used the methods of organizing the work that were then the most recent, some individuals working the check-outs with a variety of automatic aids that speed the process while making it more routine, other individuals restocking shelves as they become depleted, and so on. Many potential workers would not have experienced a similar situation before, even if they had worked in the retail trade.

Over a period of about six months, every person being recruited to the supermarket was asked to respond to a series of questionnaires; these looked primarily at their state on entry, including anxiety and depression, but also asked about their perceptions of their previous employment. Six weeks later the same individuals were approached to find their perceptions of work in the supermarket itself. Finally, they were approached six months after entry, to see what had happened to them by that time.

Naturally a proportion of the original sample had left the job by six weeks and even more after six months. It was therefore possible to assess what kind of individuals left and what kind stayed. Among those who stayed, it was possible to relate changes in anxiety over the six-month period to change in the demand they experienced between their previous work and the supermarket job. From these measures, it is possible to shed some light on the cause–effect relationship between anxiety and demand.

Procedure

At entry 200 people were approached to complete the questionnaire, which they did during the induction procedure. In all 196 (98 per cent) agreed to take part and provided data. The high response rate naturally reflects the fact that questionnaires were completed in work time. It was also because, for ethical reasons, the respondents were told very clearly that they need not complete any individual question if they were unwilling to do so. In fact, a number of cases arose in which they were unwilling to respond either to perceptions of the job or to the more intrusive questions about symptoms.

The main measures taken were:

- Middlesex Hospital Questionnaire (MHQ: Crown and Crisp, 1966, as modified by Broadbent *et al.*, 1984). This provides measures of anxiety and depression; and also of obsessional and somatic symptoms and obsessional personality, though those will be of less interest.
- Ratings of job satisfaction in the previous job. This was done by a single question with a scale of possible responses from 0 to 7.
- Ratings of demand and discretion in the previous job. These were

assessed by giving the respondent fourteen questions taken from those of Karasek (1979), seven for each scale, and asking for a response between 1 and 4 for each question in terms of its applicability to the job.

- 'Want From Job' (WFJ). This measure was designed to elicit differences in motivation. The question takes the form 'In a word, what do you look for in a job?' The first and second words elicited were recorded; it has been found previously that there are interesting differences between, e.g., those who say 'money' and those who say 'satisfaction' (Broadbent, 1985).

- The Cognitive Failure Questionnaire (CFQ: Broadbent *et al.*, 1982) was given in a shortened form: only the twelve questions showing highest item–total correlation in the original paper were included.

In addition, records were kept on the sex and marital status of the worker, and of whether they had previous retail experience, as well as of distance and method of travel to previous work.

At the six-week point only 141 (70 per cent) of the entrants were still employed; both they and those who had left were provided with questionnaires and asked to return them. For the first eighty of the employees the approach was made in the store, but, as there was no 'set-aside' working time comparable to the induction period, later approaches (as to all those who had left) were made by mail to the last known address. Questionnaires were accompanied by a reply-paid envelope, and those who responded were reimbursed for that trouble by provision of a £1 telephone card.

The questionnaire at this point repeated the job satisfaction, demand, and discretion scales. On this occasion, they were to be answered about the work done at the store rather than in previous employment.

A set of scales of social support, based on House (1981), was also administered. These give separate measures of support from supervisor, co-workers, spouse and friends; since only some of the respondents had spouses, two derived measures were scored. One was the average support for all scales completed, so that the unmarried had an average excluding the spouse scale. The other measure was a score of availability of spouse support, which was the House scale for spouse support but with a score of 0 for the unmarried.

There were also some direct questions about particular aspects of work in the store. These included the attitudes to the supervisors; one particularly important point, for the analyses given later, was the number of hours/week actually worked. A number of the respondents were employed part-time rather than full-time.

Replies were received from 102 of the 141 employees (72 per cent) and eight from those who had left (15 per cent). The very low rate of return from those who had left the job is scarcely surprising, but means that few separate analyses could be done on them; the drop in response rate for the employees is reasonable given the greater burden on their own time.

Table 8.1 Means from the first questionnaire, for all entrants to the study and for those who were still present after six months

	Scales	
	Whole original sample (Mean)	Survivors at 6 months (Mean)
Personality details:		
Age	26.65	30.07
Anxiety	2.41	2.58
CFQ	15.55	15.43
Previous job:		
Demand 1	17.86	17.51
Discretion 1	16.30	15.64
Job satisfaction	4.52	4.44
Distance to work	3.2	3.29
(For store job after six months, for comparison)		
Demand 3		17.85
Discretion		12.41
Satisfaction 3		4.50
Proportions:		
Male	.30	.24
Retail experience	.56	.56
Want from job:		
Money	.61	.74
Satisfaction	.41	.39
Achievement	.10	.06

Note
People were allowed to give two words for 'what they look for in a job', so proportions sum to more than one. A number of less common choices exist, such as 'contact with people'.

At six months those who had still been employed at time 2 were all contacted again; 56 were still employed and 40 of these responded (71 per cent). Of the 38 who had left, 20 responded (53 per cent).

At this time the MHQ and CFQ were measured again, together with current job satisfaction, and the social support and specific task questions about the work in the store.

RESULTS

Predicting who leaves

Table 8.1 shows the means for the first questionnaire on the whole sample, before they had started work in the store. It also gives the same measures, before starting work, for the much smaller group who survived after the end of six months.

It is worth noting that the original entrants were used to work that had much the level of demand found in the store; but the survivors judged the work to have lower discretion than they had met previously.

The survivors differ from the original sample in a number of ways, being older, more likely to be female, having had jobs of less discretion previously, and thinking of different words to describe what they look for in a job; in the original sample roughly 60 per cent mention 'money', but among the survivors this rises to over 70 per cent. But are these differences due merely to chance? One cannot rely on tests of each variable separately, because the various measures are correlated with each other. For instance, the younger, the male and those previously in higher discretion jobs all have significantly higher levels of job satisfaction with the previous work.

Three discriminant functions distinguish those who had left from those still in employment. In this form of analysis each factor is added considering only its significance after the factors already in the function have been taken into account. Factors were added in order of their success in prediction.

Two of the analyses used the largest possible sample, those who answered all questions in the original session. One of these analyses discriminated between those who had stayed six weeks and those who had not, while the other discriminated those who lasted a full six months from everybody else. The large loss took place very early, but possibly a different kind of person left later.

Both these analyses however are limited because they could take into account only pre-existing features of the person. The third analysis therefore used the smaller sample that stayed at least six weeks and gave judgements about the work in the store itself.

The immediate loss

If we use the usual criterion of accepting only variables reaching the 0.05 level of significance, then there is only one that predicts the loss in the first six weeks. That is, whether the person mentions 'achievement' as a factor in their choice of job. If, instead, one adopts that very lax criterion of accepting any variable with $p < 0.50$ then the predictors of departure before six weeks include also age (the older go at this stage), less obsessional personality, higher demand in the previous job and higher satisfaction in the previous job. The picture is one of people leaving who have been used to jobs of higher status.

The long-term loss

(a) Still using only variables from questionnaire 1, and thus looking at the total wastage from the start for six months, the discriminant function gives only one variable as a predictor of departure at the usual criterion of 0.05. That is discretion in the previous job, higher values increasing the probability of leaving. Another variable is border-line (0.05, p < 0.10); this is the response 'money' to the 'want from job' question. Giving that response makes leaving less likely.

By the lax criterion of p < 0.50, departure is predicted by low irritability and high depression, high cognitive failure, higher demand in the previous job and previous experience in the retail sector. It is interesting to note that, if all these variables are entered, discretion is then eliminated as adding nothing to them. That is, people who report high discretion in their previous job are people with other characteristics of endurance.

(b) Using the smaller sample who were still available after six weeks, the loss between then and six months is predicted by more variables, many of them derived from work in the store itself. Only previous retail experience, a mention of money as a motive and obsessional symptoms (another MHQ score) come from the first session of testing. Departure is also predicted by low social support from the immediate superior at the store, by long distance of travel to work and by high demand 2, that is, at the store. All these variables are significant by the strict criterion; the only additional ones entering by the lax criterion were irritability, depression and mentioning 'satisfaction' as a motive.

In both these analyses it is again notable that anxiety does not predict departure even by the lax criterion. It seems to be unrelated to the chances of leaving the job.

There is no evidence in any of these results that either anxious or non-anxious people tend to leave. Those who go, do so because the job is not satisfying their goals. That is, they look for achievement or they are people for whom money is relatively unimportant. They also regard their past job as high in discretion, while the group consensus is that jobs in this store are not.

This result casts doubt on one possible explanation of the anxiety/demand relation; but, of course, it considers only the chances of leaving the store altogether. It is still possible that the anxious people might leave some particular jobs within the store, and not others, which will now be considered.

Predicting later judgements from those in previous work

Table 8.2 shows the correlations between judgements of demand in previous work, judgements of anxiety on entry to the store and the corresponding judgements at times 2 and 3. The latter can of course be obtained from the survivors of the whole six months, but a separate set of correlations for times 1 and 2 only is given for the larger sample still present after six weeks.

Clearly, reports of anxiety are quite stable; those individuals who were anxious at the end of the study were also likely to be those anxious at the beginning. Less markedly but still reliably, people who thought their previous work high in demand also judge the new work in the store as being similarly high. It is tempting to see the latter relationship as a chronic bias of judgement rather than anything objective. If so, other people may not think that individuals worked as hard as they themselves think. The correlation might however be genuine, and due to a tendency to drift towards similar jobs when one changes one's employer.

Whatever the reasons, the pre-existing biases of individuals are having an influence on the present judgements. Cross-sectional correlations, looking at the people who happen to be in jobs at one time, do indeed have a possible error due to this cause. However, previous anxiety is not correlated with later demand, in either the large or the restricted sample. There is no sign that previously anxious people judge jobs as more demanding. In addition, we cannot say that they tend to stay in demanding jobs and thus leave a correlation among the survivors. (That is, the correlation of anxiety 1 and demand 2 is negligible for both groups.)

What is more worrying is that the correlation of anxiety 3 and demand 3, though positive, is not significant. The effect found in other studies does not appear, cross-sectionally, in this one. As we shall see, the reason is that the pre-existing biases happen to have worked *against* the finding in this case. To show this, we need to look at anxiety 3 and demand 3 after correcting them for the other contaminating factors.

Predicting final state

The measures at time 3 are of course available only from the smallest sample; all the following analyses are therefore conducted only on that group.

Individual correlates of the measures of final state

Table 8.3 shows the correlations of final anxiety, depression and job satisfaction, with all the other variables that are significant with at least one of the three. This table illustrates the point made by Argyle (1987) about the distinction needed in assessing emotion; no outside factor is significant

Table 8.2 Correlations of earlier and later measurements

	n	Mean (SD)	Anx 3 (n)	Dem 1 (n)	Dem 2 (n)	Dem 3 (n)
In small sample still in at time 3:						
Anxiety 1	45	2.58	.609***	− .014	.001	.067
		(2.46)	(44)	(38)	(45)	(45)
Anxiety 3	45	3.51		.054	.018	.168
		(3.04)		(39)	(45)	(45)
Demand 1	39	17.51			.306	.375*
		(4.13)			(39)	(39)
Demand 2	46	17.93				.669***
		(3.93)				(46)
In larger sample available at time 2:						
Anxiety 1	92	2.51		− .031	− .160	
		(2.20)		(78)	(92)	
Demand 1	80	17.51			.317**	
		(4.19)			(80)	
Demand 2	94	18.17			−	
		(3.91)				

***p < 0.001
** p < 0.01
* p < 0.05

with all three, even though anxiety is correlated with both depression and low satisfaction.

Satisfaction is related to age; to discretion both now and at both earlier times; to social support, whether from superiors, workmates or friends; and to a low tendency for supervisors to 'talk down to staff'. Yet neither of the symptom scales is significant with those factors.

Depression is linked both to low contemporary support from the spouse; and to initial depression and anxiety. Satisfaction shares the first but not the second relation.

Finally, both anxiety and low satisfaction are linked to a low tendency for superiors to help new workers, but anxiety alone is related to the hours of work. The direction of the effect should be noted; it is those who work longer hours who are less anxious. This may conflict with any prior assumption that long hours mean excessive overtime; in fact, the main distinction is between full-time and part-time workers. The latter tend to be female (r = 0.33, p <0.05) and to have jobs of lower discretion (r = 0.32, p <0.05), as well being more anxious.

Thus, anxiety does seem to be influenced by factors largely different from those that lower satisfaction. Although it seems to share something with depression (perhaps pre-existing neuroticism or negativity), the other correlates of each are also separate. If, however, the measures of anxiety in the

Table 8.3 Correlations with final anxiety, depression and satisfaction

	Anxiety 3	Depression 3	Satisfaction 3
Pre-existing factors:			
Age	− ·210	− .091	.328**
Disc 1	.033	.075	.328*
Anx 1	.069***	.425**	− .035
Dep 1	.339*	.516***	.001
From questionnaire 2:			
Hours of work	− .364*	.114	.177
Satisfaction 2	− .197	− .119	.541***
Disc 2	− .214	− .028	.397**
Social support:			
immed. super.	− .237	− .216	.369*
other workers	− .085	− .115	.310*
spouse	− .132	− .273	.235
friends/rels	− .184	− .171	.307*
Supervisors:			
help new staff	− .316*	− .230	.508***
'talk down'	.185	.132	− .447**
From questionnaire 3:			
Hours of work	− .277	.136	.054
Anx 2	−	.725***	− .392**
Dep 3	.725***	−	.237
Satisfaction 3	− .392**	− .237	−
Disc 3	− .197	− .098	.570***
Social support:			
immed. super.	− .191	− .203	.603***
other workers	.002	.066	.258
spouse	− .33	− .408*	.622***
Supervisors:			
help new staff	− .307*	− .236	.609***
'talk down'	.227	.094	− .483

***p < 0.001
** p < 0.01
* p < 0.05

present job are being contaminated by other factors, such as pre-existing neuroticism, then it becomes important to assess their effects, corrected for the pre-existing level and for other possible influence.

Effects correlated for contaminating variables

The final and most important analyses therefore are multiple regressions. In these the effect of, say, final level of demand on final anxiety is assessed only after a number of other variables have been introduced into the equation. These include the possible role of CFQ in increasing 'vulnerability' either to demand or to discretion.

The pre-existing level of anxiety does have an important effect on final anxiety; that is sure even after all the other variables have been inserted (Beta 0.71, p <.001). Further, most of these other variables have no satisfactorily significant effect on final anxiety once initial anxiety is considered. But, when all these corrections have been made, the final level of demand is related to final anxiety (Beta 0.43, p <.01).

The apparent absence of effect in the cross-sectional analysis is due to the fact that pre-existing anxiety and judgements of demand are each correlated with the final judgements, but not with each other. To show the link of final demand to final anxiety, one needs to eliminate these contaminating factors.

On the other hand, demand does not relate to depression or satisfaction. Final depression is predicted by initial depression (Beta 0.61, p <.01) and by nothing else. Satisfaction is predicted as we might expect by previous satisfaction (Beta 0.45, p <.05) and also by final discretion (Beta 0.52, p <.01). So, the same individuals do show rises in anxiety when job demand rises and in satisfaction when discretion rises. In addition, there is no evidence in these results of depression being affected by these changes. This pattern agrees with the claims based on cross-sectional studies.

Part-time and full-time workers

We saw that people working short hours were more anxious than those working longer ones; this factor was not used in the regression analyses because it is associated with sex and discretion. It is undesirable to extract too many variables from a relatively small sample such as this.

As sex did not show much relation to anxiety in the regression analysis and further analyses showed that sex did not alter the size of other effects, it was removed from the final analyses. Instead, hours of work are inserted; and also the interactions of other factors with hours of work. This allows us to see if the relations were the same in full-time as in part-time staff. To keep the number of variables down, the ratings of demand and discretion in the previous job were removed; though not that of initial demand and discretion in the store. It is still true that final discretion predicts final satisfaction; and that depression is affected by neither final demand nor final discretion.

For anxiety, however, the overall effect of final demand is replaced by an interaction of demand with hours of work. There seems, in other words, to be a difference between full-time and part-time workers. Separate analyses for the two groups were performed to analyse the interaction but they are somewhat suspect because of the low numbers. So far as they can be trusted, they show that for those working at least 20 hours a week final demand had a significant effect. For the remaining part-time workers final demand gave no significant effect. Interestingly, the 'over-20 hour' group showed no other effects, not even for initial anxiety. For the 'less than 20 hour' group, the main predictor of final anxiety was initial anxiety.

This finding is important for conclusions about the causal direction of the link between anxiety and demand. If high anxiety makes a person rate the job as demanding, then there is no obvious reason why the length of exposure to the job should matter. But if the job rating is accurate, and demanding jobs cause high anxiety, then it is reasonable that a longer exposure should give a larger effect. Cherry (1984) reported that women in part-time jobs showed less effects of the nature of the job. Before concluding that, however, it is important to check that there is no other explanation. Part-time workers may be different in some other way and this might lie behind the interaction with hours of work.

Other moderating factors

Part-time workers seem likely, *a priori*, to have different family situations from full-time workers and also rather different motivations. Both these possibilities are confirmed when one looks at the inter-correlations. The hours worked correlate -0.27 ($0.05 < p < 0.10$) with the mean social support from all sources; and -0.31 ($p < 0.05$) with saying 'money, first' in response to the 'want from job' question. That is, the full-time workers report less social support and are less likely to be working for money. Either of these factors therefore, rather than sheer length of exposure to the job, might conceivably be the cause of the rise in anxiety under high demand. To clarify the point, each factor in turn was substituted for hours worked. Briefly, social support cannot be the explanation of the effect of hours; but motivation might be.

In the analysis of social support, there was no interaction whatever of support and demand ($p > 0.30$), whether overall average support was taken or marital support. But there was an interaction with *discretion* at time 2 in each case ($p < 0.01$). That is, people in a job of chronic low discretion do seem to be protected against anxiety by the presence of social support. This is interesting in itself, but quite different from the effects of demand.

When people who gave 'money' as their first response were contrasted with all others, this factor behaved like hours worked: the interaction with demand gave Beta $= 0.66$, $p < 0.05$. That is, the effect is much the same as that of hours. As a further step an analysis was performed in which CFQ and its interaction were omitted, but both 'wanting money' and 'hours worked' were included. Whichever was first extracted gave a significant interaction with final demand; but when the second interaction was inserted both became insignificant. That is, the effect is totally confounded between motivation and hours of work, and it is impossible to separate further.

The question of cognitive failure

In the tables, there is no evidence of CFQ score acting as a 'vulnerability' factor; the interaction terms of the analyses are all insignificant. This does not support the suggestions of Broadbent *et al.* (1982), Clegg *et al.* (1987, 1990) or Smith *et al.* (1989). Possibly the problem may lie in the further moderating effect of hours of work; the size of the sample is so low that the power becomes too weak to establish triple interaction of CFQ, hours and demand or discretion. Alternatively, it may be that the range of tasks is not large enough. But at present this result joins that of Fisher and Hood (1987) as a failure to show the 'vulnerability' effect of CFQ in a longitudinal study.

If final CFQ score is used as the dependent variable in a regression, it is of course predicted by initial CFQ. That is, the score is reliable over time as has been reported before. It is not predicted however by initial anxiety once initial CFQ has been entered. None of the measures of demand or discretion show any effect upon it, thus supporting the view that these job factors do not change it. But final anxiety does relate to it (Beta 0.43, $p < 0.05$). Since this effect is correlated for initial anxiety and CFQ, it must mean that some change in the individual is altering both scores together.

Thus, in support of Fisher and Hood, some factors do change CFQ score. CFQ has been found to change in response to factors other than job (Morse *et al.*, 1991), and external factors may have been acting here. But reported demand and discretion do not seem to alter CFQ, which supports earlier research.

CONCLUSION AND DISCUSSION

The main conclusion is that a causal relation, in which demand raises anxiety rather than merely being associated with it, now seems rather more probable. In the first place, anxiety does not seem to predict staying or leaving in this type of job; there are no grounds for thinking that the cross-sectional finding is an artefact of selective resignations. In the second place, there are certainly biases that make the same person judge successive jobs in a similar way, and report a similar level of anxiety of successive occasions. But this does not explain the relation between final anxiety and demand. Rather, the relation became significant when those biases were corrected, and did not even appear until that was done.

In addition, people who are exposed to the job for more of the week show the relationship more strongly. Unfortunately we cannot tell whether it is sheer length of exposure that matters or the reasons the individual has for working. The statistics will not separate them, and both are quite plausible on general grounds. A high demand could reasonably have a smaller effect when it is encountered only for a few hours or when the person needs money and finds it reassuring that the work will continue because there is a lot to do. In either case, however, it is hard to conceive of an explanation in which the anxiety is caused by something outside the job and then distorts the perception of demand. The causal relation seems likely to be the opposite: the job is seen as demanding and this raises anxiety in the full-time workers who are less motivated by money.

Longitudinal studies do indeed present serious practical difficulties and this one is clearly strongest on the prediction of those who leave the job. The numbers remaining at the end are small considering the number of factors to be extracted in the regressions. The survivors are furthermore a very selected population. The results on change of demand and change of anxiety need therefore to be replicated in a different situation, where the wastage is less and the sample of work wider. A study of this kind is already under analysis.

With this caution, there is certainly evidence of biases in self-report of demand. Yet, when such biases have been corrected, there is also evidence for an increase in anxiety as demand increases. The distinction between anxiety and other forms of distress reinforces, yet again, Argyle's emphasis on the multi-dimensional nature of human emotion.

ACKNOWLEDGEMENTS

The collection and analysis of the data were primarily undertaken by Margaret Broadbent; both she and the author were employed by the Medical Research Council. Thanks are due not only to the respondents, but also the management and other staff of the company concerned, whose help and insight were invaluable. Many of the better points in the chapter result from suggestions made by Dr Katharine Parkes.

REFERENCES

Argyle, M. (1987) *The Psychology of Happiness*. London: Methuen.

Broadbent, D.E. (1981) Chronic effects from the physical nature of work. In B. Gardell and G. Johansson (eds) *Working Life*. Chichester: Wiley, pp. 39–51.

Broadbent, D.E. (1985) The clinical impact of job design. *British Journal of Clinical Psychology*, 24, 33–44.

Broadbent, D.E. and Gath, D. (1979) Chronic effects of repetitive and non-repetitive work. In C.J. Mackay and J. Cox (eds) *Response to Stress: Occupational Aspects*. London: Independent Publishing Company, pp. 120–8.

Broadbent, D.E. and Gath, D. (1981) Symptom levels of assembly line workers. In G. Salvendy and M. Smith (eds) *Machine Pacing and Occupational Stress*. London: Taylor & Francis, pp. 243–52.

Broadbent, D.E., Broadbent, M.H.P., Male, J.C. and Jones, M.R.L. (1985) Health of workers exposed to electric fields. *British Journal of Industrial Medicine, 42,* 75–84.

Broadbent, D.E., Broadbent, M.H.P., Phillpotts, R.J. and Wallace, J. (1984) Some further studies on the predicting of experimental cold in volunteers by psychological factors. *Journal of Psychosomatic Research, 28,* 511–23.

Broadbent, D.E., Cooper, P.F., Fitzgerald, P. and Parkes, K.R. (1982) The cognitive failures questionnaire (CFQ) and its correlates. *British Journal of Clinical Psychology, 21,* 1–16.

Carayon-Sainfort, P. (1992) The use of computers in offices: impact on task characteristics and worker stress. *International Journal of Human–Computer Interaction, 4,* 233–61.

Cherry, N. (1984) Women and work stress: evidence from the 1946 birth cohort. *Ergonomics, 27,* 519–26.

Clegg, C. and Wall, T. (1990) The relationship between simplified jobs and mental health: a replication study. *Journal of Occupational Psychology, 63,* 289–95.

Clegg, C., Wall, T. and Kemp, N. (1987) Women on the assembly line: a comparison of main and interactive explanations of job satisfaction, absence and mental illness. *Journal of Occupational Psychology, 60,* 273–87.

Crown, S. and Crisp, A.H. (1966) A short self-rating scale for psycho-neurotic patients. *British Journal of Psychiatry, 112,* 917–23.

Fisher, S. and Hood, B. (1987) The stress of transition from home to university. *British Journal of Psychology, 78,* 425–41.

Hesketh, B. and Shouksmith, G. (1986) Job and non-job activities, job satisfaction and mental health among veterinarians. *Journal of Occupational Behaviour, 7,* 325–39.

House, J.S. (1981) *Work Stress and Social Support.* Reading, Mass.: Addison-Wesley.

Karasek, R.A. (1979) Job demands, job decision latitude and mental strain: implications for job redesign. *Administrative Science Quarterly, 24,* 285–306.

Karasek, R.A. (1981) Job socialisation and job strain: the implications of two related mechanisms for job design. In B. Gardell and G. Johansson (eds) *Working Life.* Chichester: Wiley, pp. 75–94.

Karasek, R.A., Theorell, T., Schwartz, J.E., Schnall, P.L., Pieper, C.F. and Michela, J.L. (1988) Job characteristics in relation to the prevalence of myocardial infarction in the US Health Examination Survey (HES) and the Health and Nutrition Survey (HANES). *American Journal of Public Health, 78,* 910–18.

Kasl, S.V. (1989) An epidemiological perspective on the role of control in health. In S.L. Sauter, J.J. Hurrell Jr and C.L. Cooper (eds) *Job Control and Worker Health.* New York: Wiley, pp. 161–89.

Mackay, C.J., Cox, T., Burrows, G.C. and Lazzarini, A.J. (1978) An inventory for the measurement of self-reported stress and arousal. *British Journal of Social and Clinical Psychology, 17,* 283–4.

Morse, C.A., Dennerstein, L., Farrell, E. and Varanvides, K. (1991) A comparison of hormone-therapy, coping skills training, and relaxation for the relief of premenstrual-syndrome. *Journal of Behavioural Medicine, 14,* 469–89.

Russell, J.A. (1980) A circumflex model of affect. *Journal of Personality and Social Psychology, 89,* 1161–78.

Smith, A., Peck, D. and Clatworthy, T. (1989) After-effects of working at visual display units. *Work and Stress,* (3) 2, 195–201.

Thayer, R.E. (1967) Measurement of activation through self-report. *Psychological Reports, 20,* 663–78.

Thayer, R.E. (1989) *The Biopsychology of Mood and Arousal.* New York: Oxford University Press.

Warr, P.B. (1987) *Work, Unemployment and Mental Health*. Oxford: Clarendon Press.

Warr, P.B. (1990a) Decision latitude, job demands and employee well-being. *Work and Stress*, *4*, 285–94.

Warr, P.B. (1990b) The measurement of well-being and other aspects of mental health. *Journal of Occupational Psychology*, *63*, 193–210.

9 Socializing work

David D. Clarke

INTRODUCTION

Michael Argyle's (1967) motor skill model of social behaviour, later known simply as 'the social skill model', marked a turning point in experimental social psychology, and in the systematic study of human relations and human working practices in general. It likened the way that people deal with one another to the way they deal with other complex entities in the world, especially the tools and machines they have to work with. The inspiration for this came from the realization that the problems of work seem to fall into two categories: problems of skill with the 'objects' of work themselves and problems of skill with people; and the further recognition that those may be just two aspects of the same general problem of skilled management of actions in a complex world. Furthermore, since there was already a good model for the analysis of physical skill, based on cybernetics, or the principle of self-regulation using negative-feedback loops, it was a logical step to extend that to serve as a model of people dealing with other people, according to their motives or goals, the discrepancies they detected between their goals and the current course of events, and the actions they could perform to reduce those discrepancies. This in turn gave rise to a more systematic study of the encoding and de-coding of interpersonal signals, and gave a unifying structure to the then burgeoning field of non-verbal communication research.

However, the social skill model was still a model of the individual in a social world or a social context. The processes of interest remained intra-psychic. The goals, the plans, the evaluation of performance and the correction of error were all carried out by each person 'internally', with other people playing the role of the problem or task domain on which these operations were carried out. This was a world in which a person could work with or upon others, but that was not quite the same as people working together, collectively setting goals, monitoring performance and all the rest, as part of their ongoing discourse, constructing interactively those same cognitive functions that the social skill model ascribed to the mind of each individual.

For a long time, the same view prevailed in the world of work. Key tasks were the responsibility of individuals. Duties and lines of accountability had to be laid down in advance. Plans were to be made explicit, and usually had to be completed and finalized before their execution began. Corporate procedures had to be followed, and evaluated according to criteria which were stated in advance. However, we are now coming to realize that, far from capitalizing on the strengths of our 'natural way of doing things', many of these ideas are disablingly contrary to them. Nowhere is this seen more clearly than in the accepted practices for funding and administering research. Often a 'research proposal' has to be stated in so much detail, and so long before the particulars of cases and data sets become known, that certain kinds of flexible exploratory work are virtually precluded as the price we pay for public accountability and the principles of careful planning which are known to enhance *some* kinds of activity.

A particular focus for these concerns, as science-intensive industries become more collegial in their approach to work, has been the problem of building effective teams and maximizing their performance. Once again, there has been a growing awareness that, in the natural ecology of human behaviour, there are forms of mutual action to be understood and exploited which are very different from the mere 'interaction' of self-contained, autonomous 'individuals' with memories, imagination and powers of decision that work in a hidden intrapsychic realm and share their products but not their process.

The aim of this paper is to sketch out a simple model for this newer, more socialized conception of collective work, drawing examples from a recent empirical project carried out at the University of Nottingham, funded by the Joint Research Councils' Initiative on Cognitive Science and HCI (Human–Computer Interaction). It aimed to 'socialize work' in two senses: (1) by introducing a new collectivist perspective into the study of everyday tasks and what it means to perform them *jointly*, drawing on the concepts and concerns of both cognitive and social science; and (2) by using expert groups as the means of doing collaborative research work on the topic of collaborative everyday work. The field of human–computer interaction in general, tied in as it is with issues of interface design and software development, especially for the office environment, has an overall orientation towards the analysis and support of working practices, although the collectivization of computer-based work in the real world has tended to outstrip the collectivization of HCI research priorities.

We were trying to integrate the information available on the nature of jointly conceived and executed actions, from different disciplines in cognitive science and neighbouring fields. We wanted to bring ideas and advances that any of them could suggest to bear on issues which they *all* found problematic. The immediate aim was to extend the range of the cognitive sciences beyond the actions of individuals, which they had always considered, to the problems of joint action, which they had tackled less often and with less success. The further aim was to lay the conceptual groundwork for a kind of information technology which could act in collaboration with people, rather than by responding to (or else issuing) their instructions to act. We had in mind a technology which may one day share with people the initiative, and perhaps even the responsibility, for jointly made plans, policies, decisions and actions.

Cognitive science has yet to develop adequate theoretical vocabularies with which to describe – let alone explain – the complex patterns of joint action and interaction which engage individuals in a variety of everyday settings. Joint action includes any activity where several individuals execute some common task. While the importance of joint action has been noted often enough before (for example, by Winograd and Flores, 1986; and Hutchins, 1987), progress has been hampered by the tendency of different cognitive science disciplines to work with incommensurable examples, concepts and units of analysis. Additionally, as different disciplines have tended to operate with different interests, priorities and commitments, each approach has made progress on some issues at the cost of continuing silence on others. In the absence of a multidisciplinary dialogue and debate, little overall impression of the nature of joint action and interaction has been obtained. Specific problems connected with the co-ordination of actions in co-operative and/or collaborative settings have tended to be marginalized. This is particularly unfortunate, however, as co-operative group working is becoming an increasingly salient context for computer use – as can be seen, for example, from the proceedings of specialist conferences on Computer-Supported Co-operative Work such as 'CSCW '86' (1986), and 'CSCW '88' (1988). Additionally, studies of interaction and planning within cognitive science have typically employed a 'microworlds' research strategy in which a very restricted, 'low-level' setting is studied in a simplified, decontextualized way. Models, formalisms and theoretical insights obtained from the study of one setting rarely transfer to others and frequently become unstable or untenable if the context is enlarged so that actions and plans within the microworld are seen as components embedded within longer-term plans or strategies. For instance, a detailed analysis of mouse movements and keystrokes made by people working with a spreadsheet package, as part of a particular task set by an experimenter, may have little relevance to their way of using the same software when writing a report (and doing several other things at once) in a busy office environment. Complex, joint action and interaction in everyday and work settings must become an important focus for theoretical and practical work in cognitive science if HCI is ever to address adequately the needs of distributed, collaborating groups, or to support the development of knowledge-based systems which function as colleagues rather than mere instruments. This might mean the creation of systems which can take a creative role in design teams or decide the division of labour between the people and the machines involved in a task.

Very often, it is the setting or situation *itself* which is the source of the complexity and contingency which participating agents have to manage jointly. Suchman (1987) documented some of the many ways in which users, jointly operating a complicated photocopier, manage the contingency and uncertainty of their interactions with each other and with the machine. In such cases, individuals are confronted not merely with the problem of making sense of each other's actions, but of doing so in an environment which is changing in ways which they cannot adequately predict or control. Along with other students of social action, Suchman sees this as a much more general case than 'the planning model' would lead us to believe. Far from springing forth in realization of a pre-formed cognitive plan, action is typically *ad hoc* or 'situated', being intimately bound up with the exigencies of a situation undergoing moment-by-moment change.

Studies of action planning, and for that matter problem solving, in cognitive science have generally investigated situations where the participants' goals are defined explicitly, in advance, and by someone else (often as part of the demands of the task in an experimental setting). Actions are then conceived of and evaluated in terms of the extent to which they contribute as *means to the end* of satisfying the required goal or some intermediate subgoal. Indeed, this understanding of action seems appropriate to the kinds of task most typically studied in HCI where single individuals interact with a machine, and to the standard conceptions of work and its analysis, outlined above. However, many theorists of social action (such as Habermas, 1984) have argued that joint action and interaction cannot be entirely reduced to instrumental, means–end relationships, particularly when issues of mutual understanding and interpretation are at stake – or at least cannot be so reduced in any non-trivial way. While goals are sometimes set externally in everyday activities, it is important to understand the other possibilities: goals set by participants themselves at the outset and then followed; goals which participants attribute to themselves after the event; and goals which are never distinguished from the execution of the task. On this view, the articulation of goals for joint action may sometimes be a retrospective rationalization of a course of action determined in some non-instrumental way (or even, in a sense, in a non-rational way).

METHOD

In order to cover the ground as systematically as possible, we started by dividing up the 'problem space' of possible joint-action types using twenty-four binary features, such as whether a particular activity was technologically mediated or not, linguistically mediated or not, recorded or reported, co-operative or competitive, and so on (see Table 9.1), and we collected a range of examples covering the presence and absence of all the features (although not, of course, all their possible combinations). We concentrated

Table 9.1 Twenty-four dichotomies defining the problem space

1	natural situations	unnatural situations
2	pre-specified goals	emergent goals
3	division of labour	equality of labour
4	pre-planned division of labour	emergent division of labour
5	mediated interactions	unmediated interactions
6	local communication	non-local communication
7	synchronous communication	asynchronous communication
8	goal is agreement	goal is obtaining correct beliefs
9	conflictful interactions	collaboration
10	joint actions running smoothly	joint actions going 'wrong'
11	linguistic tasks	non-linguistic tasks
12	physical tasks	abstract tasks
13	pre-planned actions	non-pre-planned actions
14	accounts of joint actions	joint actions themselves
15	one subject	more than one subject
16	work-oriented joint actions	daily tasks done jointly
17	protracted joint actions	short/real-time joint actions
18	divisions of expertise	no division of expertise
19	standard cognitive science materials	non-standard materials
20	task materials ambiguous	task materials with single clear meaning
21	use of artefacts in task	no artefacts
22	macro-structured interactions	interactions with only conversational structure
23	pre-specified time limit for interaction	no pre-specified time limits
24	seeded discussions or interviews	non-seeded interactions

on the joint performance of memory tasks, problem solving, decision making, planning, writing and natural language comprehension, predicting and forecasting, aesthetic judgement and causal attribution, that is, on the joint performance of activities that are usually seen as involving individual *cognition*, since the potential applications to theory and practice seemed most immediate in these domains, and they illustrate the kinds of generic tasks and skills that make up much of the working routine of most managerial and professional people.

We created a range of discussion and problem-solving situations, exemplifying different combinations of these features, in which volunteer subjects were placed, video-taped and audio-recorded (in stereo, for ease of later transcription). Examples included a joint memory task in which subjects met a week after watching a twenty-minute video clip together, to construct an agreed account of what it showed; a joint attribution task in which subjects discussed a report on homelessness, to arrive at an explanation for what had happened to the individuals in question; and a joint aesthetic task in which subjects were asked to place twelve works of art in an agreed preference order. Analysis was carried out mainly from transcripts, but with reference to the original taped materials as well.

We had already assembled a group of eleven researchers, mostly from the academic staff of Nottingham University, representing AI, cognitive, social, developmental, organizational and applied psychology, psychiatry and linguistics. The panel included specialists in joint planning, HCI, communication studies, experimental pragmatics and discourse analysis, sequence analysis, action theory, CAL, knowledge elicitation and various areas of computational, mathematical and formal modelling. Some of the analysis sessions which followed also involved members of the 'Action Analysis Group' from the same department, who had been exploring machine-learning techniques as methods for detecting hidden regularities in behavioural descriptions and recordings, and methods for forecasting the action choices of individuals using 'expert panel' methods like those used for this project. The subsequent analyses of project materials were done in small groups of about five people, drawn from the panel as a whole.

The exact process varied from occasion to occasion, but a common starting point was for the panel members to be sent selected extracts about a week before they were to meet, on video and in transcription, to study and to think about from the perspectives of their own respective fields. Then the meeting could begin with a brief commentary from each panel member in turn on the points of interest, concern or difficulty they had found. This led on to a more focused discussion of the features that were agreed to be of the greatest interest and relevance. We were very mindful, of course, of the fact that in arriving at these shared priorities we were exemplifying just the kind of collective cognition we were meeting to study. This allowed us, more or less at will, to switch into the role of 'participant observers' as a part of our research method.

In general, then, the strategy for panel analysis with each set of examples was to see which features of the cases could be accounted for (a) by the disciplines present in similar ways; (b) by each discipline in different ways; (c) by some disciplines and not others; and (d) by none of the explanatory concepts available at the time. These outcomes then set the scene, respectively, for (a) corroboration and consolidation between disciplines; (b) comparison and evaluation of explanations; (c) knowledge transfer between fields; and – most importantly – (d) the proposal, development and evaluation of *new* explanatory possibilities, getting the group to focus the union of their different theoretical domains onto the intersection of their problems.

The analysis groups met regularly over a period of about eighteen months, evolving the procedures for their meetings as they went along. On the whole, the problems we had expected did not arise (incommensurability of terms and perspectives between disciplines, for example), while *unexpected* difficulties arose initially with the pacing of meetings, the coherence of discussion and the appropriate circumstances in which to use the group and individual forms of analysis. These problems were overcome, partly by changing the format of the group meetings and partly by the introduction of other methods, such as discourse analysis, in parallel with the group work. We found it as important not to over-manage the meetings as it was not to under-manage them, and to this end we worked from a shared 'menu' of analytical strategies and stages rather than a rigid agenda. This and other reflexive aspects of the project forced us to deal with the relation between planned and situated action in our own activities as well as in the materials we were looking at. The various strands of the project were all complementary, with group analysis, for example, incorporating findings from, and providing further transcribed materials for, the discourse analytic part of the work.

We tried to pick out and concentrate upon specific instances of problems that all of the disciplines recognized, but none of them could yet solve. We felt that this was an area of research which did not need a testing ground for current ideas so much as a breeding ground for new ones, and that was mainly what this project aimed to provide.

We believed that the use of 'professional judgement' as a research tool (with suitable feedback and evaluation) would help to develop the skills and the conceptual repertoire of participants in a way that more objective methods often do not. The approach we chose fitted the problem especially well, because the greatest source of understanding we could draw upon concerning the nature of joint action, besides the knowledge we already had explicitly as individual people and disciplines, was the knowledge that was left unrecognized and unused because it was still implicit and distributed. We felt we should need to resort to other research procedures only when *that* had been drawn out and put to use.

GENERAL RESULTS

A number of recurrent themes emerged from the analysis sessions. These included:

The influence of the prior relationship between individuals engaged in joint actions, their personalities and the initial conditions of the task

For instance, we had examples of people doing our tasks who were used to working together, and for whom it seemed to be assumed from the outset that one of them would create a task structure which the other would follow. This is the normal situation in an organization, where colleagues approaching a new task are likely to have a prior conception of their areas of expertise and authority, which does not have to be worked out as an early stage of structuring the group and the work.

The social construction of 'facts' from previously disputed claims

For example, in a joint memory task, the way in which events which one person thought they recalled and others were uncertain about were later referred to as 'things that had happened', even when no explicit agreement had been reached in the meantime.

The non-linear organization of joint activities in time

Participants would often pick up and continue a 'loose end' of discussion from some way back, with no explication of what they were doing, but other participants would still typically identify the link and respond correctly.

The role of shared materials or representations of the task in creating an implicit consensual view of goals, action possibilities and the changing state of the task

For example, if the task was presented as a number of cards to be sorted into a shared order of preference, all participants would take the arrangement across the table of the cards that had been dealt with already and the size of the remaining pile, as indications of how far they had got with the task, and what they should do next. In this case they would take the next card from the ungraded pile and find a position for it in the array of cards ranked so far, without any discussion of the merits of this strategy, and in a way that would not have occurred had the task been presented as, say, a list against which they had to write numbers to indicate their order of preference.

The role of task material as a medium as well as an object of communication

The arrangement of task materials could serve as an act of communication as well as something to communicate about, depending on the conditions of shared knowledge. Subjects in different rooms with their own sets of materials and a telephone link between them would have to say 'I think we should put example A above B'. After some discussion, the participants might all agree, and all rearrange their materials accordingly. In a face-to-face situation, however, with one shared set of task materials, one person might make the change, and the others agree to it, without anything being said at all.

The occurrence of 'topic drift'

Often topic changes were gradual, rather than abrupt and clearly marked. A discussion of why someone was homeless might turn into a discussion of why they were jobless, with no clear line of division or conversational 'work' to negotiate the topic change. This meant that, as is so often the case in the analysis of verbal materials, it was not possible to divide the transcripts into sections according to topic as a part of the analysis. It also illustrated quite nicely the ephemeral nature of much of what interested us about joint action – everyone would change topic, and everyone would realize they had changed topic, without anyone in particular doing anything in particular to bring it about.

The tendency for certain views or courses of action to emerge as 'agreed upon', more by the absence of dissent than the presence of explicit support

If a point of view had been aired, and no-one had objected, it would later be referred to as something that the group all believed or had agreed to, even if no supporting comments had ever been made.

The different ways in which task elements are moved between forms of representation as a function of such things as consensus

The most obvious case of this occurred in group discussions where one member was asked to act as a 'scribe', to make notes of anything that would help the group in their deliberations. The rule (without prior discussion or explicit agreement) seemed to be that unagreed talk remained talk, but agreed talk was turned into writing. In another instance, materials were spread on the table between participants, with a central array used for relations that had agreed upon, and separate satellite arrays used for provisional structures that were still under discussion. An implication of this for computer network design might be that different notations, or different 'windows', might be needed for information according to the degree of agreement or certainly it had attained.

The way in which the structures of problem solving, interacting with co-actors, and producing deliverable products are influenced by each other, and by the technology and other artefacts involved (the nature of the 'product' would depend on the nature of the particular meeting or collaboration, but may take the form of a design, a verdict, a plan, a decision, a report, a prototype and so on)

In arriving at an agreed design, say, using a networked graphics package, there would be a three-way interplay between the nature of the thing being designed; the requirements of the package, perhaps only one 'pen' with one operator could be active at a time in the shared design space; and the roles of the different designers (such as creating sub-teams to work on sub-assemblies).

A PARTIAL MODEL AND SOME EXAMPLES

We went on to develop a simple model of one kind of joint action which was common in our materials. It has several distinct features and stages.

- The virtual absence of explicit initial planning, goal setting or task analysis, and very little macro-structure in the interactions which ensue. Instead, the starting point tends to be specific, detailed and seemingly arbitrary. So, when the task was to construct a joint preference ordering for a set of pictures, for example, the first substantive contribution tended to be something like 'I quite like this one', rather than, for instance, 'Shall we each make our own order and compare?' A strategy of abduction from one element of the task to the rest seemed more common in practice than the more likely seeming alternatives of working from an agreed task framework to the particular details, or else the reverse.

- A shared representation of the task state was then created. In the present task this might be done by setting the picture in question at the end of a row, to represent its provisional position in an, as yet incomplete, rank order. This kind of thing is an almost inevitable part of computer mediation, since, in interfacing the machine to the user, designers, almost unwittingly, create the media for users of interface with each other. By contrast, traditional face-to-face meetings, seldom supported by flip-charts and the like, can leave each participant with a quite idiosyncratic 'mental map' of the structure of the task domain, and their discourse about it.

- This means that all participants then have similar access to the current state of the task, as well as the end state they were aiming for, the discrepancy between the two, and the range of actions that would reduce the discrepancy.

- Each participant could contribute (in turn) while monitoring changes in the state of the task and adjusting their actions accordingly, so the task itself co-ordinated their actions and mediated their interactions. Again, computers (can) play a special role in this process. 'Physical' work, like building a wall, requires all contributors to orient to the same version of what they are doing, how they are doing it and how far they have got, in this case the partly built wall as it takes shape over time. 'Abstract' work, like planning a project, on the other hand, does not necessarily assemble participants around any concrete realization of the schemata they all have in mind. Computers embody (in a sense *are*) physical realizations of abstract ideas, and as such they impose some of the productive characteristics of wall building on abstract activities like planning.

The examples which follow are drawn mainly from one particular task, in which pairs of subjects were given two identical sets of twelve postcards, showing a variety of paintings in different styles, and were asked to produce a joint rank ordering from most to least liked. The twelve pictures were labelled, and are referred to in the following extracts, by the letters A to L.

The extracts which are quoted do not convey, much less constitute, 'the analysis'. They are more like isolated extracts of raw data to show concretely the kinds of things that emerged as consistent patterns and strategies when many examples were screened by a number of different observers from a number of different perspectives. Note, too, that the discourse analysis which made up part of the project was a separate strand from the analysis-group meetings, and it is the concerns of the latter which are mainly illustrated here.

The main characteristics of the 'abduction' process can be seen in the following instance of initial 'bootstrapping', from early on in one of the sessions.

P: Have you got an immediate favourite out of all these?[1]
S: No
(6.0)
P: ⟨whispered⟩ What's it say something to do with Venus isn't it
S: I don't like these
P: You don't like which ones?
S: Those two
P: Right
S: At all
P: You don't like those two at all?
S: No
P: It's funny cos I was gonna pick that one I like that one (.) not probably not the most but but out of all them I like it quite a lot um that's a I like that one Dali (3.0) which ones do you really hate?
S: E::r those two
P: Right (2.0) yeah okay I'll tell you the ones I don't like much that one
S: Yeah I'm not keen on that it's alright but I don't particularly like it =
P: = Number have to tell them number (.) H H letter H and I don't like that one much (.) I don't know what that is who's it by? ⟨laughter⟩ I certainly don't like it
S: Oh no I don't like it

After this, the strategy was accepted (although never discussed and agreed) of finding items which one or other participant disliked, so that they could be set aside while those which were 'popular by default' were discussed further.

This approach to joint action is heavily dependent on the creation and modification of shared representations. Often this was achieved by setting out the task materials in particular ways that all participants could see and alter. This was of course an ever-changing representation, standing for 'where we have got to, in doing the task, *now*', rather than the overall task, its goal or its end point. We called this the 'task state'. Once again, a parallel can be drawn with the properties of a shared computer interface, even though in that case the people involved could be sitting side-by-side at the same screen, or thousand of miles apart with identical screens and control options before them.

s: let me see I like em (1.5) I like the Van Gogh as well (1.0) I dunno [but they're all

v: [where's van Gogh no I must admit I I like Van Gogh but (?)

s: but I think I actually prefer the one beside that the er (.) number 1

v: that's beautiful isn't it

s: isn't that lovely

v: that is beautiful (.) I like I and I like J very much

s: I J well it would be good do em I then next for second

v: okay

s: yeah

v: yeah (2.5) and do you want to put John the Baptist which is F before J

s: e:m (1.0) I don't know (.) do you have any strong feeling about it either way

v: I like I prefer J to John the Baptist

s: you prefer Van Gogh

v: yeah

s: okay

v: okay so we'll put them in that order then

s: right (.) so that's three is number J (1.0) and four is number

v: F

s: F

v: yeah

Also:

s: Well Okay let's construct a provisional list of what we've we have agreed on

p: What shall we stick em all over there

s: Yeah (.) right (1.5) what else have we got then that one (3.0) the difficulty with this is that we haven't left spaces to insert any others BUT okay (.) so what we got left now we've got =

p: = These two were actually reasonably close

s: Yes Okay well do you want to bring those together then =

p: = And they're reasonably at the bottom so it should go there

Shared representations also have to be repaired. In the following example, two participants, S and V, have duplicate sets of objects from which to create a shared preference order. They have begun by producing their own separate orderings, and are now working by elimination – that is, by finding items to which they have both given a low rank to go in the bottom part of the agreed ranking. They have not kept any notes – their only record of the task is the current position of the materials, and their assumption is that, when they have finished, all the items from their independent arrangements will have been moved into the agreed arrangement. Something has gone wrong, and they have noticed that they have different numbers of items left. This threatens the validity of their joint arrangement as a true representation of their joint opinion. So they have to postpone the completion of the task while they backtrack and unpick the problem to the point where they can accept the pattern before them as an accurate product of the combination heuristic they were attempting to follow.

v: okay shall we start doing some more worst ones rather than better ones what do you think
s: well I've only got five left now
v: five I've got six (.) oh god right we've A I J F and then your second worst is E and your worst is H
s: and B was third worst I thought
v: oh right yeah sorry
s: yeah
v: yeah
s: okay (.) so that leaves (.) C D G K and L

There is also a need for local problems to be solved as they arise, without reference to explicit global plans. In the following extract, consensus suddenly breaks down, after a period in which participants had taken turns to make suggestions which were always agreed. One participant picks out a 'worst item' which the other rather likes. He recovers by suggesting his second worst, which they both turn out to dislike, and the previous procedure resumes. The point of interest is not that they solve the problem in this way, but that they both understand that this is what they are both doing, without any need to make it more explicit, or to reflect on the strategy they had been using until then, and the way it had failed.

s: yeah that's better much better (.) okay what's your worst one then
v: oh well surely it's got to be E
s: A B C D E well no I like Kandinsky
v: how about H that's pretty gross
s: E F G H (.) yeah yeah
v: yeah
s: yeah H [is last
v: [so that's the worst one
s: okay
v: okay then so you didn't find that too bad (.) how about your next worse one then

s: the next worst one (1.5) er postcard which do I like (.) aesthetic appeal
     (1.0) I'd say er the Dali one number two
v: what is it your worst
s: no my second worst
v: second worst

One of the features of the project was a deliberate element of recursiveness
or self-reference. Our meetings were self-consciously applying joint action
to the task of understanding joint action. Therefore the analysis groups also
recorded and analysed their own meetings. Here too the element of *ad hoc*
problem solving can be seen. In the next extract the group members are
finishing off one meeting by trying to find a time for the next. There is a
problem about the time, but *no* problem about how to deal with that
problem. Nor is there any set procedure being followed which the speakers
were aware of, or could have stated in advance. Here we escape the
dreadful bureaucratic regress of having a procedure for every task, and a
procedure to produce every procedure; an evaluation of every process, and
an evaluation of every evaluation.

D: Paul is it right that your work is less seasonal than ours and that one
     week has about the same sort of problems as another
P: yes the week of the if you only talk Fridays the twenty eighth of June
     is a good day because I don't have to teach my students Friday lunch
     time and early afternoon
JD: that's not a very good one for me I think it's the end of term I think
     we have to do various things
P: the nineteenth is actually our students exam and the Friday the 21st
     and then [the first week of their attachment I'm freer
JD: [beginning of July
J: I'm in the States for two months from the first of July

Of course, even given the view of how joint action works outlined earlier,
there is also some recourse to explicit planning, although it is surprisingly
rare, and some elaborate feats of co-ordination are performed without
anything of the kind.

P: Okay so have to sort out which ones we like (6.0) I'll just write down
     our order of preference in a second (.) okay so which ones do we agree
     on we don't like then?
s: U::m
P: We both don't like that one is that right?
s: Yeah

And:

T: Um (.) well I mean I just I suggest we both construct a list ourselves
     independently to start with =

R: = Yeah
T: And then and then we'll see try and merge them
R: Okay

CONCLUSIONS

Although only part of the work can be illustrated here, the findings of the project as a whole have a number of implications.

Theories of action, planning and problem solving in cognitive science and social psychology need to attend to the persuasive, argumentative aspects of joint action. We believe that this need exceeds the limits of current descriptions of the nature and role of mutual knowledge and the models which actors are thought to have of each other. It is not just a matter of adding a component called 'rhetoric' to standard cognitive architectures, or of relying on mutual knowledge of the 'I believe that she believes that I believe that . . .' sort, as that still fails to capture the persuasive orientation of much of the joint action in our study.

Accounts of joint action need to address the role of external representations and the media which support them (conversation, writing, technical artefacts). Indeed, much of the co-ordination involved in joint action can best be explained in relation to their properties, including their physical, material properties. To take an obvious example: in a face-to-face dialogue, previous utterances are a matter of memory and dispute, whereas in an electronic bulletin-board exchange, previous turns are a matter of record, which all participants can check and none can deny. In that sense, 'what has been accomplished' by the end of a meeting may mean two very different things: in one case where the discussion 'ended up'; and, in the other case, every point of view and potential course of action that was mentioned as it went along, all of which are still equally 'present'.

Models of action and planning which suppose that actors extensively pre-plan their action and interaction find little support in this work. Many of our studies suggest that action and interaction are locally managed and respond to the exigencies of changing situations. This is not to say, however, that all joint action is of this sort. Accordingly, hybrid models which give equal emphasis to the locally managed and the pre-planned aspects of joint action may need to be formulated. It was not our intention to produce programs or formal models as such, but guidelines and suggested methodologies for programmers and modellers, created by the panel and the project staff, and tested to some extent in their various other areas of research. The phenomena we identified have implications for such things as the affordances of different task materials and representations, the procedural importance of tacit agreement, the differentiation of labile and stable information and the identification of implicit goals.

'The medium is the message.' Computer-mediated work is not just a familiar kind of work which remains largely unchanged despite having a computer as mediator; it is a new kind of animal, in which the linking technology has the power to potentiate or to damage the fabric of the human connections it supports.

The project also enabled us further to develop the 'structured judgement methods' we have been allocating for applied social psychological and HCI research for some time. Based in part on developments in the judgemental forecasting literature, these methods offer a useful and potentially powerful middle way between the restrictions of closed formal techniques and the dangers of undisciplined intuition.

The ideas presented here seem in many ways to be a natural outgrowth and extension of the Argyle model of socially skilled activity including collaborative work, but the emphasis is changed somewhat to incorporate more of the sense of people working jointly on a task besides each other, in part a more 'discourse analytic' style of enquiry, and the idea of systematized professional judgement as a permissible instrument of social psychological research.

ACKNOWLEDGEMENTS

I am most grateful to the Joint Research Councils' Initiative on Cognitive Science and HCI for funding, to my co-investigator John Bowers and our research assistant Kate Iwi, who helped to gather and prepare much of the material for this chapter, and to all the members of the 'panel of experts' from which the groups for particular analysis sessions were drawn. They were Professors David Wood, Ian Howarth, Tom Cox and Nigel Shadbolt, Drs Mike Burton and Han Reichgelt, and the two principal investigators, Drs David Clarke and John Bowers (all of whom worked at the time at the Nottingham University Department of Psychology), Dr Paul Ryley (Department of Psychiatry), Dr Brigitte Nerlich (Department of Linguistics) and Dr Judy Ellis (formerly of the Social and Applied Psychology unit, Sheffield, later at Cardiff University).

NOTE

1 *Transcription conventions*
   P: and S: two of the participants dealing with this task, and speakers in this transcript. Likewise other letters in other extracts.
   (6.0) A pause of six seconds.
   (.) A pause of less than a second.
   [These words said by one speaker, concurrent with . . .
   [these words said by another.
   . . . . Separates non-consecutive lines of transcript.
   U::m Extended pronunciation.
   = Next speaker takes over / interrupts with no gap.
   (?) Speech unclear / transcription uncertain.

REFERENCES

Argyle, M. (1967) *The Psychology of Interpersonal Behaviour*. Harmondsworth: Penguin.

'CSCW '86' (1986) *CSCW '86: Proceedings of the Conference on Computer-Supported Co-operative Work, September 23–25, Austin, Texas*. New York: ACM.

'CSCW '88' (1988) *CSCW '88: Proceedings of the Conference on Computer-Supported Co-operative Work, September 26–28, Portland, Oregon*. New York: ACM.

Habermas, J. (1984) *The Theory of Communicative Action*, Volume 1. Cambridge: Polity.

Hutchins, E. (1987) *In Search of the Navigators*. New York: Wiley.

Suchman, L. (1987) *Plans and Situated Actions*. Cambridge: Cambridge University Press.

Winograd, T. and Flores, F. (1986) *Understanding Computers and Cognition*. Norwood, NJ: Ablex.

10 How environmental variables influence behaviour at work

Robert A. Baron

It was the summer of 1979, and I had just joined the staff at the National Science Foundation, where I was the new Program Director for Social and Developmental Psychology. As the most junior program director in my division, I was – naturally! – assigned to the smallest and least attractive office. Since I was a member of the professional-level staff, it was a private office with a window, but those were the office's only amenities. It was long and thin, and, when the necessary filing cabinets and bookshelves were in place, there was not much room to move around. The carpet was dingy, and the walls were badly in need of a fresh coat of paint. The view from the only window, too, was quite dismal: it looked directly at the blank wall of the building next door, which was separated from the NSF building by a narrow alley. My office was located near the copy room, so there was the 'chunk-chunk-chunk' of copies being made all day long. The fluorescent lights gave off an unpleasant greenish light, and were so glaring that I often left them off altogether. Perhaps worst of all, the room was located at the very end of the cooling and heating ductwork. As a result, the thermometer on my desk regularly recorded temperatures of over 85°F. It was so hot that I had to place a fan on my desk and work directly in its cooling stream of air; whenever I moved outside this artificial breeze, I began to drip perspiration onto whatever documents I was handling at the moment. And in the winter, opposite conditions prevailed: temperatures rarely rose above 60°F, and my fingers literally turned blue as I attempted to type all the government forms that were a basic part of my job. There was little or no air flow, so the office smelled slightly stale and smoky all the time.

The effects of these unpleasant working conditions on my performance were soon apparent. As the heat of the day increased, I became more and more lethargic. In fact, by mid-afternoon, I felt as though I were working in some kind of trance. All my reactions slowed down and my error rate went through the roof. After a few weeks, I found it necessary to schedule my day so that I worked on all 'thought' problems and issues early in the morning and left the afternoons for routine tasks. But drops in productivity were not the only problems I faced. As the days passed, I found myself becoming increasingly irritable and short-tempered. I became impatient with my secretary, and snapped at my wife when I returned home in the evening. Soon, I began to wonder: was it continued exposure to the unpleasant physical conditions in my office – the heat, glare, dinginess and stale, unmoving air – that was reducing my productivity and changing my personality? My own research on environmental factors, plus that of many colleagues, suggested that this might well be so. Here, in short, was a case in which social psychological theory and findings came face-to-face with my own life.

If there is one aspect of work settings that most people tend to take for granted it is certainly the *physical environment*. Most of the time, lighting, temperature, air quality and other aspects of the physical surroundings in which we work are definitely 'ground' rather than 'figure' in our perceptual worlds. Only when these factors depart from standard, acceptable levels, as in the incident described above, do they receive much overt attention. This does not imply, however, that the physical conditions under which we work are unimportant. On the contrary, a growing body of evidence suggests that many aspects of work-related behaviour are affected to an appreciable degree by such factors (e.g. Bell *et al.*, 1990; Sundstrom and Sundstrom, 1986). Moreover, large-scale surveys reveal that, for many people, the quality of their work surroundings *is* an important consideration. For example, in one survey of more than a thousand office workers in the United States, approximately 40 per cent rated physical working conditions as a *very important* factor in evaluating in their jobs (Harris, 1978, cited in Sundstrom and Sundstrom, 1986).

At present, it is widely taken for granted that organizations will provide reasonably safe, healthy and comfortable physical environments for their employees. And in developed countries, this assumption is backed by the full force of the law which seeks to guarantee such conditions for all employees. Yet, even a brief glance at recent history reveals that this has not always been the case. Until fairly recent times, most factories and offices provided anything *but* the kind of pleasant, sanitary surroundings most people now expect as a matter of course. Consider the following description of a typical office at the turn of the present century (MacCord, 1894):

Imagine a room with its floor some steps below the level of the sidewalk; a small and sultry room ill-lighted by an abortive skylight and two windows upon one side; worse ventilated by one door opening into an equally dismal office, and another communicating directly with the foundry whence drifted in a dull and heavy air, laden with smoke and evil odours, ornamented with. . .cobwebs, thrice magnified by accumulated grime and soot.

Currently, few employees in developed nations confront such dismal conditions. Most modern offices and factories are relatively clean and comfortable places in which to work. Yet, even today, environmental conditions vary considerably from office to office and from factory to factory. Indeed, even within a given facility employees are often aware of substantial differences in such factors from one location to another. (I was certainly aware of such differences when I compared my office with that of more senior program directors!) Do such differences, and perceptions of them, influence behaviour at work? Growing evidence suggests that they do. It appears that even relatively modest variations in temperature, lighting, air quality, noise, crowding and a host of other environmental factors do indeed exert appreciable effects on task performance, work-related attitudes and interpersonal relations among employees (cf. Bell *et al.*, 1990). It is upon such effects that the present chapter will focus.

Systematic research on effects of the physical environment of work settings has proceeded for several decades (e.g. Hollingworth and Poffenberger, 1926; Vernon, 1919), so there is a wealth of empirical data on which to draw. In order to provide a useful overview of this vast body of evidence, therefore, the present chapter will proceed as follows. An initial section will examine the crucial question of precisely *how* various aspects of the physical environment can affect work-related behaviour. In other words, potential mechanisms through which variables such as lighting, temperature and air quality can, potentially, influence behaviour in work settings will be considered. Next, empirical evidence relating to the impact of several physical aspects of work settings will be reviewed. Included among these factors are *lighting*, *noise*, *air quality* and *temperature*. In a final section, a theoretical model for understanding the impact of environmental variables on performance and interpersonal relations in work settings will be presented.

HOW ENVIRONMENTAL VARIABLES INFLUENCE BEHAVIOUR AT WORK: SOME POTENTIAL MECHANISMS

Anyone who has worked in a factory or office in which the air conditioning failed during a steamy summer day or who has tried to concentrate on a complex task in the presence of loud, extraneous noise is well acquainted with the fact that many aspects of work-related behaviour can be influenced by environmental variables. Task performance, current mood, relations with others – all, it seems, are affected by the physical conditions around us. But precisely *how* do such effects occur? One possibility is that environmental variables exert their effects directly, through purely physical or physiological means. In extreme cases, this may well be so. Prolonged exposure to very high temperatures can raise core body temperature above normal levels, and so induce *heat exhaustion* and *heat stroke* – physiological reactions that greatly alter behaviour (Bell *et al.*, 1990). Similarly, very low levels of lighting may make it impossible for individuals to perform various tasks simply because their visual systems do not receive sufficient physical stimulation to function properly. Apart from such extremes, however, it seems clear that environmental variables affect performance and behaviour through their impact on various *psychological* mechanisms. Several of these will now be considered.

Heightened arousal

One way in which several environmental variables may affect behaviour is through the induction of *heightened arousal*. While the explanatory value of the concept of arousal has recently been questioned by some scientists (Neiss, 1990), many researchers continue to believe that it is of use with respect to understanding the impact of several environmental factors on behaviour (cf. Bell *et al.*, 1990). Arousal refers to an individual's general state of alertness or excitation, both psychological and physiological (Scott, 1966), and growing evidence suggests that several environmental variables tend to induce increments in this respect. In particular, uncomfortably warm or cool temperatures (Bell, 1981), very bright or glaring illumination (Biner, 1991) and noise (Klein and Beith, 1985) have all been found to increase arousal among persons exposed to these conditions.

How might such environmentally induced heightened arousal affect behaviour in work settings? Potentially in several different ways. First, consider task performance. Research conducted over the course of several decades offers support for the view that the relationship between arousal and task performance is curvilinear in nature. As arousal rises, task performance first increases but then, beyond some point, falls. Thus, for a given task, performance is generally maximal at some intermediate level of arousal. This relationship is known as the *Yerkes–Dodson Law*, and has been confirmed for a wide range of tasks, and across a broad range of arousal (Broadbent, 1971; Hebb, 1972). Additional findings suggest that the inflection point is lower, along the dimension of arousal, for relatively complex tasks and higher for relatively simple ones. However, in both cases, the general curvilinear function applies.

In addition to its impact on task performance, heightened arousal also affects cognition. Specifically, when individuals experience increased arousal, they attempt to label such feelings, and to identify their source. In other words, they engage in *attributional processes*, attempting to determine the causes of their own reactions and behaviour. This process can have important implications for interpersonal behaviour in work settings. For example, consider a situation such as the one mentioned above, in which air conditioning has failed on a hot and steamy day. Individuals exposed to such conditions may experience heightened arousal but may not necessarily (or clearly) attribute such feelings to the elevated temperatures in which they work. Thus, they may attribute their increased arousal to other sources, such as irritating remarks or actions by others. The result: they react more strongly than would otherwise be the case to provocation, and interpersonal friction is increased (cf. Zillmann, 1988). In sum, heightened arousal is a useful mechanism for interpreting the impact of several environmental variables on behaviour in work settings.

Information overload

A key finding in the study of human cognition is as follows: human beings possess limited information-processing capacity. In other words, we can perceive, recognize, understand and interpret only a finite quantity of information at any given time. This finding has important implications for the impact of environmental variables on behaviour, for, in combination, such factors can produce a state of *overload* in which basic information-processing capacities are exceeded. Consider, for example, a situation in which an individual is attempting to perform a complex task requiring careful attention but is (1) working in a crowded office surrounded by many other persons, and (2) is exposed to a high level of noise from telephones, copy machines and others' conversations. Clearly, in such a case, information overload may occur, and performance on the complex task will suffer.

Information overload affects more than current task performance, however. Additional evidence indicates that, when information-processing capacity is exceeded, individuals develop a kind of 'tunnel vision', in which they focus all available attentional resources on only a part of the information reaching their senses. While this may be adaptive from the point of view of completing specific tasks, it may cause individuals to ignore potentially important and relevant information. As a result, their overall effectiveness may be impaired. Returning to the situation described above, the individual in question may, by focusing attention on the task at hand, manage to maintain at least a moderate level of performance. However, at the same time, this person may fail to process important communications from others adequately, with negative consequences for future performance and interpersonal relations.

Adaptation level

Information overload is usually an unpleasant state of affairs – one that most individuals seek to avoid or terminate. However, the opposite situation, in which individuals receive too little stimulation from the external environment, can also be aversive (Wohlwill, 1966). The annoying quality of such *understimulation* is well captured by the following statement: 'Boredom is the hardest job of all; it's impossible to take a break.' Together, the negative reactions of most people to both overload and understimulation suggest that, generally, human beings seek an intermediate, and optimal, level of stimulation from the environment. This view is a central component of a theoretical approach known as *adaptation level theory* (Helson, 1964; Wohlwill, 1974). According to this theory, all individuals seek an optimal level of stimulation and will engage in efforts either to increase or to reduce environmental stimulation in order to attain this level. The theory further suggests that this optimal level of stimulation, known as adaptation level, reflects individuals' previous experience. Thus, a person from a very cool climate may find temperatures in the high 70s Fahrenheit unpleasantly warm, while someone from a very hot climate may find the same temperatures a bit too cool.

Adaptation level theory has important implications for understanding the impact of environmental variables on behaviour. Specifically, it suggests that individuals will attempt to remain within their preferred range of stimulation whenever possible. This can be accomplished in two distinct ways. First, individuals can engage in overt actions designed to alter the amount of environmental stimulation they receive; this is known as *adjustment*. Second, it involves shifts in the adaptation level itself – changes that can occur in a relatively automatic manner without conscious effort on the part of the persons involved. For example, an individual accustomed to working in a very quiet office may gradually adapt to noisier conditions on a new job so that, over time, he or she no longer perceives this increased level of noise as objectionable. Conversely, an individual accustomed to working in a noisy office may adapt to a quieter one, so that he or she no longer perceives it as *too* subdued.

Affective reactions

In one sense, the most obvious impact of environmental variables on individuals involves their influence on current moods or *affective states* (e.g. Isen, 1987). Various environmental conditions are capable of inducing positive or negative affective reactions among the persons exposed to them. On the one hand, negative affect is generated by such conditions as excessively high or low temperatures (Bell, 1981), loud and unpredictable noise (Bell, 1980), polluted air (Zillmann, Baron and Tamborini, 1981), crowding (Baum and Paulus, 1987) and lack of privacy (Sundstrom and Sundstrom, 1986). On the other hand, positive affect is generated by contrasting environmental conditions involving moderate temperatures (Baron, 1978), clean air containing a high concentration of negative ions (Baron, 1987b), pleasant fragrances (Warm *et al.*, 1991), warm white versus cool white indoor lighting (Baron, Rea and Daniels, 1992) and low levels of crowding (Baum and Valins, 1977). In sum, several physical aspects of work settings can strongly influence the affective states of the persons in them.

A large body of evidence indicates that shifts in affective states, in turn, can have important effects upon many aspects of work-related behaviour. To mention just a few recent findings, it has been reported that people experiencing positive affect, as compared to those experiencing negative affect: (1) set higher personal goals and demonstrate higher levels of motivation (Baron, 1990); (2) are more likely to offer aid to co-workers and engage in other forms of prosocial organizational behaviour (George, 1991); (3) assign higher evaluations to others in a performance-appraisal context (Baron, 1987a, 1993); (4) attain higher performance on tasks involving creative problem solving (Isen and Daubman, 1984); (5) accept higher levels of risk under conditions where potential costs of risk taking are minimized (Isen, Nygren and Ashby, 1988); and (6) express stronger preferences for resolving interpersonal conflict through co-operation and collaboration, but weaker preferences for resolving such conflicts through avoidance and competition (Baron *et al.*, 1990). Given the scope of these findings, it seems clear that environmental conditions can exert important effects upon a wide range of behaviours in work settings.

Environmental stress

A final mechanism through which environmental conditions can influence organizational behaviour is that of *stress*. Considerable evidence indicates that unpleasant environmental conditions can serve as an important source of stress. To the extent they do, such conditions produce the physiological, cognitive and behavioural effects associated with stress regardless of its specific source (Roskies, 1987). It is important to note that it is not necessary for environmental conditions to reach extreme levels in order to generate stress reactions. On the contrary, growing evidence suggests that prolonged exposure to even moderately unpleasant environmental conditions can produce such effects (Rotton, 1991).

As is true for all sources of stress, aversive environmental conditions in work settings will serve as stressors only to the extent that they are perceived (*appraised*) as threatening and potentially harmful by the people involved. Once they are so interpreted, however, they may interfere with task performance (Kahn, 1992; Motowidlo, Packard and Manning, 1986), reduce individuals' ability to cope with other sources of frustration or annoyance (Cohen, 1980) and adversely affect personal health (Cohen and Williamson, 1991).

PHYSICAL ASPECTS OF WORK SETTINGS: EFFECTS OF TEMPERATURE, NOISE, LIGHTING AND AIR QUALITY

While many different aspects of the physical environment could, potentially, influence behaviour in work settings, a relatively small number have been the focus of most research to date. These variables include temperature, air quality, noise and lighting.

Temperature

One of the most obvious physical aspects of work settings is ambient temperature. Complaints about temperatures that are too high or too low are among the most common voiced by employees concerning the physical environments in which they work (BOSTI, 1981). Temperature itself is a physical variable that can be measured with great precision. However, feelings of personal comfort are not related in a simple or linear fashion to ambient temperature. Rather, they appear to reflect a combination of air temperature, humidity and air movement (Sundstrom and Sundstrom, 1986). These factors are captured in an index of *effective temperature* developed during the 1920s (Houghten and Yaglogu, 1923).

Effects of temperature on task performance

With respect to task performance, the effects of temperature appear to be relatively clear. Temperatures individuals find uncomfortably warm tend to reduce performance on cognitive tasks requiring considerable mental effort (e.g. recording and decoding signals; using them in further calculations: Fine and Kobrick, 1978), on motor tasks requiring eye–hand co-ordination (e.g. Bell, Loomis and Cervone, 1982), clerical tasks (e.g. number checking) and vigilance tasks, in which individuals must stay alert to detect changes in events or displays (Pepler, 1958). Additional evidence suggests that these reductions stem, at least in part, from reductions in arousal. However, the negative affect generated by unpleasantly hot conditions may also play a role, distracting individuals from the task at hand and reducing their level of motivation (e.g. Bell and Fusco, 1990).

Relatively little research has focused on the effects of unpleasantly cool temperatures, but available data suggest that low temperatures may also produce decrements in performance (Bell, 1981).

Temperature and interpersonal relations

Informal observation suggests that many individuals become irritable and short-tempered when exposed to temperatures they find unpleasantly warm, and a substantial body of empirical evidence offers support for this view. Several laboratory studies indicate that individuals report less favourable reactions to others and rate them lower in the context of unpleasant heat or cold than is true in more moderate environmental conditions (Byrne, 1971; Bell and Baron, 1976). Turning to overt aggression, many studies conducted in both the laboratory and field indicate that, as temperatures rise, many people do indeed become more irritable, are more easily provoked and are more likely to lash out, in some fashion, against others (Anderson, 1989; Baron, 1978; Bell and Baron, 1991). A remaining question, still unanswered by such research, involves the issue of whether the relationship between ambient temperature and anger or aggression is linear or curvilinear in nature. The linear hypothesis suggests that anger and aggression continue to increase as temperature increases, at least until the point at which people are overcome by heat exhaustion or heat stroke (Anderson, 1989; Anderson and DeNeve, 1992). The curvilinear hypothesis, in contrast, suggests that anger and aggression increase with temperature up to the point at which individuals become so uncomfortable that escape from the present discomfort becomes a dominant tendency – one stronger than the tendency to vent anger against others (Baron, 1978; Bell, 1992). This view is based upon the suggestion that there is an underlying curvilinear relationship between negative affect and aggression; that is, tendencies to lose one's temper increase with negative affect up to some point, but then decrease as negative affect rises still further. At present, existing evidence is insufficient to warrant clear choice among these two models.

Practical implications

Implications of research findings with respect to ambient temperature seem relatively straightforward. First, from the point of view of task performance, it is important that employees work in an environment in which temperature (and other components of *effective temperature* – humidity and air movement) is regulated so as to fall within a range that will facilitate both output and accuracy. Second, from the perspective of interpersonal relations, excessive heat should be avoided, since such conditions do appear to exert adverse effects on interpersonal relations. In short, an appropriate thermal environment appears to be one necessary condition for both individual and organizational effectiveness.

Noise

Noise, defined as unwanted sound, is an inescapable part of many work settings. Few persons enjoy the luxury of being able to work in a noise-free environment, undisturbed by ringing phones, conversations in adjoining areas and various machinery. On the contrary, these are an integral part of most offices and factories. Given this fact, it seems important to understand the impact of noise on various aspects of organizational behaviour, and a substantial body of evidence provides insight into these effects.

Before turning to this research, two preliminary points should be noted. First, noise must be distinguished from physical *sound*. Sound refers to physical energies detectable by our auditory sensors. In contrast, noise refers only to sounds to which individuals have a negative affective response –that is, sounds that they find distracting or annoying. This implies that the same sound can be interpreted as noise by one individual but not by another (Bell *et al.*, 1990).

Second, a distinction is often drawn between *predictable* and *unpredictable* noise. Predictable noise occurs with temporal regularity, so that individuals know approximately when it will occur. In contrast, unpredictable noise occurs in a variable or random manner; thus, individuals cannot predict when it will be present. Existing evidence suggests that most people find

Table 10.1 The magnitude (in decibels) of various common sounds

Source	Level (decibels)
Jet takeoff at 200 feet	120
Auto horn at 3 feet	110
Motorcycle	100
Shout at 0.5 feet	100
Heavy truck at 50 feet	90
Pneumatic tools at 50 feet	85
Freight train at 50 feet	80
Freeway at 50 feet	70
Air conditioners at 20 feet	60
Typical living room	45
Library	35
Whisper at 15 feet	30
Broadcasting studio	10

unpredictable noise to be more aversive and distracting than predictable noise (Kryter, 1970).

Noise and task performance

All sounds, including noise, are measured physically in terms of *decibels*. The zero point on this scale is the smallest sound pressure (energy) that can be detected by a young adult, and equals about 0.0002 microbars (i.e. dynes per square centimetre). The decibel scale is a log scale, so that an increase of 20 decibels represents a tenfold increase in sound pressure. Thus, a sound of 40 decibels is ten times stronger than one of 20 decibels. Table 10.1 reports the intensity, in decibels, of a number of common sounds.

With this basic information in place, the impact of noise upon task performance can be considered. Turning first to predictable noise, some findings indicate that moderate levels of predictable noise can actually enhance performance on simple clerical, cognitive and motor tasks (e.g. detecting specific numbers, multiplying two numbers, turning over blocks: Koelega and Brinkman, 1986; Sundstrom and Sundstrom, 1986). Such effects may stem, at least in part, from modest increments in arousal. However, predictable noise interferes with more complex and demanding tasks, especially when it is quite loud (e.g. 100 decibels).

In contrast, the effects of unpredictable noise appear to be uniformly negative. Such noise interferes with clerical, cognitive, motor and vigilance tasks, primarily by interfering with the careful concentration and attention required by such tasks (e.g. Davidson, Hagmann and Baum, 1990; Nagar and Pandey, 1987). Unpredictable noise also appears to exert an additional negative impact on task performance. Such noise produces adverse *after-effects* – decrements in performance that occur after cessation of the noise.

In addition, tolerance for task-related frustration appears to be reduced by prior exposure to unpredictable noise (Sherrod *et al.*, 1977). Specifically, individuals previously exposed to unpredictable noise often give up sooner than people not exposed to such noise when subsequently asked to work on difficult tasks.

Noise and interpersonal behaviour

If noise is a source of negative affect, it would be predicted that, in its presence, individuals will express less favourable evaluations of others. In fact, this appears to be the case (Matthews, Canon and Alexander, 1974). The only exception to this general rule involves situations in which mutual exposure to unpleasant noise induces feelings of 'shared suffering'; in such cases, individuals exposed to noise actually express enhanced liking for one another (Kenrick and Johnson, 1979).

Noise also appears to exert appreciable effects on willingness to offer aid to others. In several studies, the presence of noise has been found to reduce the likelihood that individuals will help strangers in need of their assistance (e.g. Matthews and Canon, 1975; Page, 1977).

Not surprisingly, noise also seems to increase the likelihood that individuals will lose their tempers in the face of provocation from others (Geen and O'Neal, 1969). This is especially likely to be so when noise is both unpredictable and uncontrollable (Donnerstein and Wilson, 1976).

Why does noise reduce ratings assigned to others, decrease helping and increase aggression? One possible explanation involves the fact that noise often generates negative affect among the persons exposed to it. Previous research indicates that negative affect, in turn, can contribute to each of the effects described above (cf. Isen, 1987; Isen and Baron, 1991). In sum, noise may exert adverse effects upon various forms of interpersonal behaviour because it serves as an environmental source of negative affect.

Practical implications

Given that noise (especially unpredictable noise) reduces task performance and exerts adverse effects on interpersonal behaviour, it appears that efforts to reduce its presence in work settings are well justified. Many different techniques can be employed to attain this goal. These include the use of sound-absorbent surfaces such as acoustical ceilings, carpeting, draperies and fabric-covered panels. Another approach, and one that may prove far less costly and thus more practical in many work settings, focuses on the use of *masking* sounds to reduce the intensity of noise. Such sounds, which are generated by fans and other components of ventilation systems, as well as by equipment specifically designed for this purpose (see Figure 10.1), generate complex waveforms consisting of many different sound frequencies. These sounds then physically counter the energy contained in the

Figure 10.1 One product designed to mask noise in work environments through the production of modified white noise

sound waves of noise, thus producing a significantly quieter work environment. In sum, the technology required to modulate noise in many work settings already exists; it only remains to convince responsible parties in organizations that the benefits of using such technology can be quite substantial.

Lighting

Thousands of research projects have been conducted to investigate the impact of the physical environment on work-related behaviour. Of these, however, the best known is certainly the famous *Hawthorne studies* conducted in the 1920s (Roethlisberger and Dickson, 1939). As readers of this chapter already know, these studies began with a simple question: would increments in level of illumination produce corresponding improvements in productivity? Results, of course, led the investigators to focus on a host of other issues relating to employee motivation and the social nature of work groups. Still, it is interesting to note that concern with the effects of one environmental variable (lighting) was present at the very dawn of systematic organizational research.

Lighting and task performance

In the decades since those early studies, much additional research has examined the impact of lighting on behaviour in work settings. Not surprisingly, most of this work has been conducted within what might appropriately be termed the *visual processing* perspective: efforts to identify specific levels of illuminance required for the performance of various tasks (e.g. Boyce, 1981; Rea, 1988). This is certainly appropriate, for, unless employees are provided with sufficient light to carry out work tasks, performance will, indeed, suffer. The results of such research indicate that for a wide variety of tasks that require attention to visual details (e.g. typing, proof-reading, number verification), performance does rise with increasing illumination (Boyce *et al.*, 1989; Smith, 1978). However, these benefits are greatest at relatively low levels of illuminance, and decrease in magnitude as illuminance rises to moderate and then high levels. Further, it has been found that gains in performance are larger for relatively complex tasks than for relatively simple ones. Finally, gains in performance at higher levels of illuminance are greater for older than for younger employees (Hughes, 1976).

Indirect effects of lighting

Performance of vision-related tasks is not the entire story where the impact of lighting is concerned, however. In recent years, researchers have begun to address the possibility that changes in illumination can exert somewhat wider-ranging effects on behaviour in work settings (e.g. Biner, 1991; Boyce *et al.*, 1989). Such research is based on the suggestion that changes in indoor lighting can induce corresponding shifts among employees in current affect (i.e. mood) and in arousal (Biner *et al.*, 1989; Flynn, 1977). To the extent this is so, then important alterations in several forms of behaviour might well be expected to follow.

At present, relatively little evidence exists with respect to the impact of lighting upon arousal, although a few studies suggest that high levels of illuminance (considerably brighter than those encountered in most offices; approximately 1,750 lux) do induce higher levels of arousal than more moderate levels of illuminance (350 lux) (Biner, 1991; Veitch, Gifford and Hine, 1991). Additional research offers support for the suggestion that lighting can exert appreciable effects on current moods or *affective states* (e.g. Flynn *et al.*, 1973; Nelson, Nilsson and Johnson, 1984). Perhaps the most detailed research on this topic to date is that conducted recently by Baron, Rea and Daniels (1992).

These researchers sought to investigate the hypothesis that certain lighting conditions would induce higher levels of positive affect than other, contrasting lighting conditions. More specifically, they predicted that higher levels of positive affect would be induced by (1) relatively low versus relatively high levels of illuminance and (2) by 'warm white' light (i.e. light containing relatively more red, yellow and orange hues) versus 'cool white' light (i.e. light containing relatively more blue and green hues). These predictions were based on previous research indicating that relatively low illuminance and 'warm white' light received higher affective ratings from subjects than high illuminance and 'cool white' light (e.g. Nelson, Nilsson and Johnson, 1984).

It was further predicted that to the extent various lighting conditions induced positive affect among participants, these conditions would also influence behaviour and cognition in a manner consistent with the findings of previous research on the impact of positive affect (cf. Isen, 1987). Thus, it was anticipated that lighting conditions that generated high levels of positive affect would: (1) raise evaluations of neutral stimuli (Isen and Shalker, 1982), including evaluations of strangers' performance (Baron, 1987a, 1993), (2) increase self-set goals and reported confidence in one's ability to perform various tasks (Locke and Latham, 1990), (3) enhance reported preference for resolving interpersonal conflict through relatively constructive means such as collaboration or co-operation (Baron *et al.*, 1990), and (4) increase willingness to offer help to others (Cunningham *et al.*, 1990; Isen, 1970).

To test these predictions, several studies were conducted in which two key aspects of indoor lighting – level of illuminance and spectral distribution (warm white versus cool white) – were systematically varied. In each experiment, a between-subjects design was employed, so that participants performed several different tasks in the presence of a single combination of these lighting variables (e.g. high illuminance–cool white light; low illuminance–warm white light, etc.). The tasks selected were ones found, in previous research, to be sensitive to changes in current affect (cf. Isen and Baron, 1991). Levels of illuminance were set at 150 and 1,500 lux, respectively, in the low and high illuminance conditions. Subjectively, 150 lux is a level of lighting somewhat more subdued than that found in most office settings, while 1,500 lux is a level of lighting somewhat brighter than that found in most offices. Spectral distribution was varied by changing the fluorescent lamps in the experimental rooms: these were either cool white or warm white, depending on lighting conditions.

Results offered clear support for predictions derived from the suggestion that lighting conditions influence individuals' affective states. In two separate studies, participants in the low illuminance group assigned higher performance appraisals to a fictitious employee than those in the high illuminance group (see Figure 10.2). In another investigation, subjects exposed to warm white light reported stronger preferences for resolving interpersonal conflicts through collaboration and weaker preferences for resolving conflicts through avoidance than subjects exposed to cool white light. In addition, in the presence of warm white light, participants in the low illuminance condition reported greater ability to perform a clerical

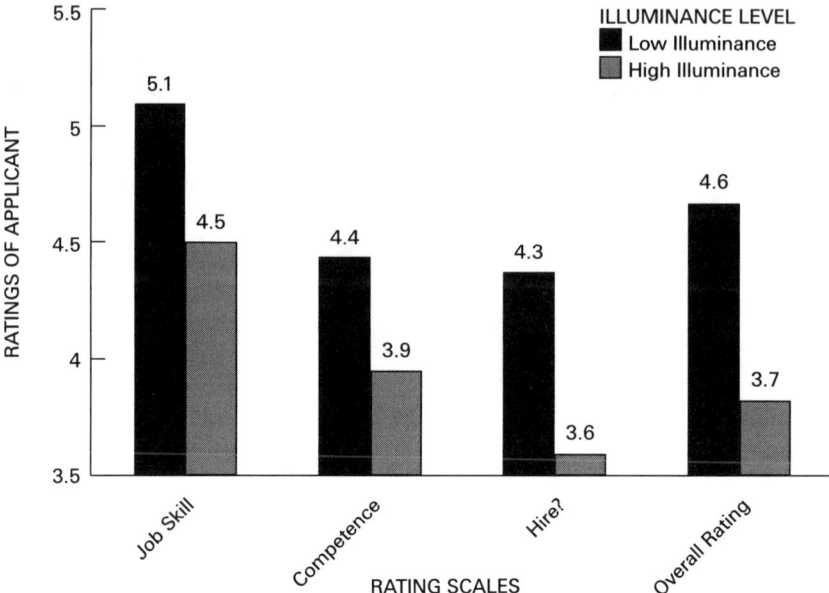

Figure 10.2 Ratings of a fictitious applicant on four dimensions as a function of illuminance level (based on data from Baron, Rea and Daniels, 1992)

coding task than those in the high illuminance condition. Finally, in a third study, subjects exposed to warm white light volunteered more of their time to help the researchers without compensation than those exposed to cool white light. Additional findings offered some support for the view that all these effects were, indeed, mediated by lighting-induced shifts in participants' affective states.

In sum, the findings of this research indicate that lighting conditions can indeed influence individuals' current moods, and hence important aspects of work-related behaviour. Given that interior designers and architects have long sought to match lighting conditions to the functions for which indoor spaces are used, these findings are hardly surprising.

Practical implications

Research on the effects of lighting indicates that this environmental variable has appreciable effects on the performance of tasks involving visual processing. Thus, it is obviously crucial that employees performing such tasks be provided with sufficient levels of illuminance to complete them successfully and without visual strain. Additional evidence indicates that certain aspects of lighting can also influence employees' affective states. Given the fact that affective states influence tasks (Sinclair, 1988) and also influence several forms of interpersonal behaviour (Carnevale and Isen, 1986), further efforts to delineate the precise nature of these effects would appear to be well justified.

Air quality

Concern over the harmful effects of polluted air has risen dramatically during the past two decades. Indeed, air pollution, and its potentially catastrophic effects on world climate, was a major topic of discussion at the Rio Conference on the global environment held in 1992. Unfortunately, individuals in many work settings find themselves at double risk where polluted air is concerned. First, they are exposed to pollutants found in the air of the geographic location of their office or factory. Second, they are exposed to pollutants directly connected to processes and equipment operating in these work settings. It is far from surprising, then, to learn that more than 50 per cent of factory workers report that they are exposed to hazardous air pollution in their work settings (Quinn and Staines, 1979). Even among office workers, approximately 25 per cent describe their offices as too smoky or smelly on at least some occasions (BOSTI, 1981).

Air pollution and task performance

That breathing polluted air has adverse effects on personal health is a well-established fact. Relatively high concentrations of such pollutants as *carbon monoxide, photochemical smog, airborne particulate* and *oxides of nitrogen and sulphur* are common in the air of major cities, and all these substances have been found to exert a harmful impact on health. For example, physicians have identified an *air pollution syndrome* caused by combinations of pollutants, and involving headache, fatigue, insomnia, irritability, depression, back pain, impaired judgement, gastro-intestinal problems and burning or itching of the eyes (Hart, 1970). To the extent that various pollutants are found in higher concentrations in work settings than elsewhere, employees are definitely at serious risk from the perspective of personal health.

Turning to performance, considerable evidence indicates that several pollutants can reduce output or accuracy on many tasks. For example, exposure to carbon monoxide at concentrations commonly found along major roads (25 to 125 parts per million) has been found to slow human reaction time significantly and to reduce manual dexterity (Briesacher, 1971). Since these are key components of many jobs, these findings suggest that performance may well be adversely affected by conditions prevalent in many urban locations. Similar findings have been reported for other constituents of polluted air such as those listed above (i.e. oxides of nitrogen and sulphur).

Air pollution and interpersonal behaviour

Many forms of air pollution are invisible to the eye and have little if any odour. Other forms, however, can be readily detected and are characterized by highly unpleasant aromas. The results of several studies indicate that such pollution can produce high levels of negative affect, and that such negative affect, in turn, can exert appreciable effects on interpersonal relations (Bell *et al.*, 1990). Specifically, several types of malodorous pollution have been found to reduce attraction between strangers (Rotton *et al.*, 1978) and, at least at moderate levels, to increase aggression (Rotton *et al.*, 1979). Interestingly, aggression appears to decrease in the presence of very high concentrations of malodorous pollutants – a finding consistent with the suggestion of a curvilinear relationship between negative affect and aggression described above in connection with the impact of temperature. In sum, certain types of pollution appear to produce negative shifts in interpersonal relations as well as reductions in task performance, and such effects appear to be mediated by the negative affect they induce.

Cigarette smoke

One type of air pollution that many people find especially objectionable is *cigarette smoke*. Growing evidence indicates that *passive smoking* – mere exposure to smoke exhaled by others – may be almost as harmful to personal health (perhaps just as harmful) as smoke that is directly inhaled from cigarettes (Surgeon General's Report, 1986, cited in Bell *et al.*, 1990: 221). Thus, it is not surprising that legislation restricting smoking in public places and in many work settings has been passed in many locations. Nonsmokers exposed to high concentrations of cigarette smoke report increased feelings of irritation, fatigue and anxiety (Jones, 1978), and some findings indicate that their performance on various tasks may be reduced by such feelings (Stone, Breidenbach and Heimstra, 1979). Finally, exposure to cigarette smoke appears to increase feelings of anger and actual hostility on the part of nonsmokers (Zillmann, Baron and Tamborini, 1981). Taken together, these findings suggest that the costs of permitting cigarette smoking in work settings may, at least for nonsmokers, be very high indeed.

Other aspects of air quality: air ions and artificial fragrances

While most attention with respect to the impact of air quality has focused on pollutants, additional research has examined the possible effects of two other components of the air we breathe: *air ions* and *artificial fragrances*.

Air ions

Air ions are a form of atmospheric electricity created when air molecules acquire small positive or negative electric charges. Both positive and negative ions are normally present in all air, but certain weather conditions and specific industrial processes and equipment can produce wide shifts in the number and relative concentrations of these particles. For example, high concentrations of positive ions are often present in the vicinity of high-voltage wires, while the concentration of negative ions is sharply reduced by several types of electronic equipment (e.g. VDT screens: Charry, 1984). High concentrations of positive ions are also generated by recurrent weather patterns found in certain parts of the world – especially by hot, dry winds that blow from mountainous regions into the plains below (e.g. the Foehn in Switzerland, the Santa Anna in the Rocky Mountain region of the United States and the Sharav in Israel). In contrast, the concentration of negative ions often rises sharply after thunderstorms.

Epidemiological (correlational) studies indicate that high concentrations of positive ions are associated with increases in the incidence of traffic and industrial accidents, and even some types of violent crimes (Sulman, Pfeifer and Hirschman, 1964). For example, such effects occur in several countries when the warm, dry winds mentioned above are present. Needless to add, because such research is correlational in nature, it is impossible to determine whether these effects are caused by these winds and the elevated levels of positive ions they produce or by other factors.

Laboratory studies, in which the concentration of ions has been systematically varied, indicate that high concentrations of *negative ions* produce quicker reaction times (Hawkins and Barker, 1978), reports of pleasant feelings (affect) (DeSanctis, Halcomb and Fedoravicius, 1981), and enhanced task performance (Baron, 1987b). In contrast, high concentrations of *positive ions* have been linked, in such studies, with reduced performance, negative moods and irritability (Charry and Hawkinshire, 1981). The magnitude of such effects is relatively small, but, taken as a whole, they appear to be consistent with the conclusions that, at least up to moderately high levels, increased concentrations of negative ions increase arousal and alertness, while increased concentrations of positive ions produce opposite effects. Given the relative paucity of systematic research on the effects of air ions, however, these conclusions should be viewed as preliminary in nature.

Artificial fragrances

Human beings have used fragrances to enhance the quality of their environments for thousands of years. Recently, however, several large companies have developed equipment designed to release pleasant fragrances into work environments, through the heating-ventilation-air-conditioning systems of large buildings (Shimizu, 1990). The rationale for the use of such

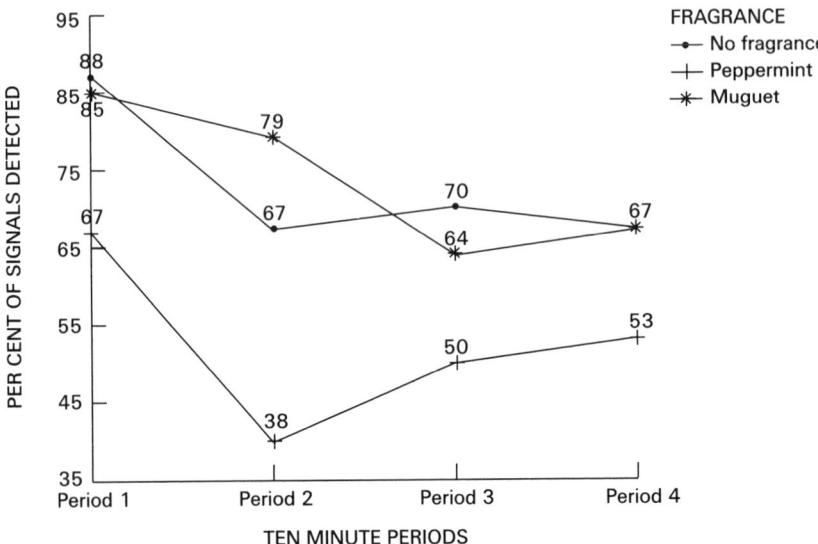

Figure 10.3 Performance on a vigilance task as a function of exposure to two fragrances. (Based on data from Warm *et al.*, 1991)

equipment is straightforward: these manufacturers claim that certain fragrances produce beneficial effects on productivity. Specifically, they assert that certain fragrances enhance alertness and arousal while others exert a calming influence, helping people recover from the adverse effects of work-related stress. Are such claims actually justified? To date, relatively little systematic research has been conducted to examine these claims. However, the studies that have been completed offer something of a mixed picture (cf. Baron, 1990; Warm, Dember and Parasuraman, 1991).

First, the results of these investigations indicate that fragrances rated as pleasant by participants can influence performance on at least some tasks. For example, in one carefully conducted experiment, Warm, Dember and Parasuraman (1991) examined the effects of two distinct fragrances, muguet (Lily of the Valley) and peppermint, on performance of a vigilance task. The task involved detecting when two lines that were repeatedly presented with a separation of 10 mm were, occasionally, presented with a separation of 12 mm. Results indicated that both fragrances enhanced performance to a comparable degree relative to a no-fragrance control condition (see Figure 10.3).

That the effects of artificial fragrance are not restricted to vigilance tasks, or even to task performance generally, is suggested by the findings of additional research conducted by the present author. In these laboratory studies, commercial products (e.g. air fresheners) rated by judges as pleasant were sprayed or not sprayed into rooms where individuals performed a variety of tasks. Results indicated that presence of these fragrances increased subjects' self-set goals on a clerical coding task, enhanced their preference for resolving conflicts with others through collaboration but reduced their preference for resolving such conflicts through avoidance and actually increased the number of concessions they made during simulated negotiations (Baron, 1990).

In more recent experiments (Baron and Thomley, in press), pleasant fragrances have been found to enhance task performance under highly stressful conditions and to increase willingness to comply with requests for both immediate and delayed helping. In addition, these recent studies provide direct support for the view that pleasant fragrances exert their impact on work-related behaviour primarily through increments in positive affect. Two major forms of evidence point to this conclusion. First, path analyses reveal that pleasant fragrances do generate increments in positive affect and that such increments, in turn, increase task performance. Second, pleasant fragrances and receipt of a small gift influence several aspects of behaviour (e.g. task performance, helping) in virtually identical ways. Since many previous studies indicate that receipt of a small gift induces positive affect, the fact that pleasant fragrance induces highly similar effects suggests, through the method of *converting operations*, that these contrasting procedures influence behaviour through the same (or similar) underlying mechanisms.

Finally, it should be noted that additional evidence concerning the effects of pleasant fragrance offers little support for the view that the behavioural effects of pleasant fragrance stem from increments in arousal (Baron and Bronfen, in press, Study 3). In an experiment specifically designed to test this suggestion, participants worked on a complex word-construction task in either the presence or the absence of pleasant fragrance and after receiving or not receiving a small gift (see Figure 10.4). During this period, they were presented with a request for assistance on the task from a co-worker. Finally, at the end of the session, the experimenter gave participants a questionnaire, and asked them to complete it at home and to return it through campus mail. It was reasoned that increments in both arousal and positive affect could, potentially, increase compliance with the request for immediate help. However, because increments in arousal dissipate rapidly, it was further reasoned that only increments in positive affect could increase compliance with the request for delayed help. Such effects, if they occurred, would be consistent with the findings of several previous studies indicating that positive affect at the time information is encoded into memory can influence later recall, increasing the likelihood that positive information will be brought into consciousness (Isen, 1987).

Results indicated that both exposure to pleasant fragrances and receipt of a small gift increased performance on the word-construction task and also increased compliance with the request for immediate help. In addition, both pleasant fragrance and receipt of a small gift also increased compliance

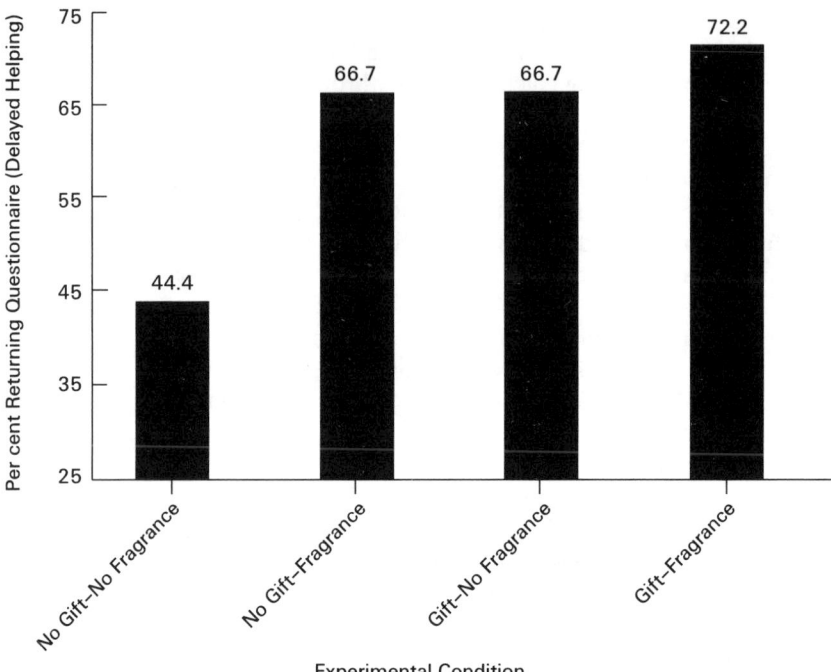

Figure 10.4 Percentage of participants in each condition who engaged in delayed
helping (i.e. returned the questionnaire). (Based on data from Baron
and Bronfen, in press)

with the request for delayed help. Taken together, these findings provide
further evidence for the suggestion that the effects of pleasant fragrance are
mediated by increments in positive affect, but are inconsistent with the view
that such effects stem primarily from increments in arousal.

Practical implications

Given that polluted air impairs task performance and exerts negative effects
upon several forms of interpersonal behaviour, it would appear that removing various pollutants from the air circulating in work settings is an
important and worthwhile task. Fortunately, highly effective equipment for
accomplishing this task currently exists. For example, air filtration equipment employing HEPA filters (High Energy Particular Arresting Filters) is
now readily available. Such filters remove up to 99.75 per cent of airborne
particulate matter, down to 0.3 microns in diameter – a size smaller than
many bacteria. In addition, they are highly effective at removing several
components of cigarette smoke. Other filters, highly efficient in removing
airborne gases such as carbon mononxide and formaldehyde, have recently
been developed. Given the ready availability of such equipment, plus

increasingly stringent legal requirements with respect to clean air in work environments, air quality is one environmental variable certain to receive increasing attention from many organizations in the immediate future.

ENVIRONMENTAL VARIABLES AND ORGANIZATIONAL BEHAVIOUR: AN INTEGRATIVE MODEL

Research on the physical environment of work settings encompasses a vast array of variables, topics and processes. Such diversity is an obvious strength of research in this area, but it also poses a theoretical dilemma: can this broad range of data and findings be encompassed within a single integrative framework? Clearly, the basic requirements for such a model are stringent. Not only must it incorporate all aspects of the physical environment of workplaces; it must also consider the role of individual perceptions, experience and information processing *and* the mechanisms through which environmental variables exert their impact on task performance and interpersonal behaviour. This is a daunting task, but measurable progress in theory building, as in any other worthwhile activity, can be obtained only through effort. Thus, the model presented in Figure 10.5 is offered here as a first step in this process.

As shown by Figure 10.5, the model suggests that various aspects of the physical environment of work settings (temperature, crowding, air quality, noise, humidity, fragrance and so on) ultimately influence three crucial aspects of work behaviour: *task performance*, *interpersonal behaviour* and *work-related attitudes*. Such effects are not produced in a direct manner, however; rather, they result from the impact of environmental variables on a wide range of mediating mechanisms and processes occurring within individuals (*individual processes*). These processes, in turn, may impinge directly on key aspects of work-related behaviour or, alternatively, can influence such outcomes through their impact on intervening processes occurring within groups (*group processes*). Since discussion in this chapter has already focused on the nature of environmental variables and the individual processes that may mediate their effects, attention here will be focused on the potential role of *group processes*.

Environmental variables and group processes

The integrated model presented in Figure 10.5 proposes that environment-induced shifts in individual processes (i.e. in arousal, affect, cognitions and so on) can also influence important aspects of work behaviour through their impact on various group processes. Among the most important of these are potential effects on *group decision making* and *group performance*.

With respect to group decision making, it is proposed that environmental conditions may contribute to the occurrence of *groupthink* (Janis, 1982). According to several models of this process, groupthink is most likely to

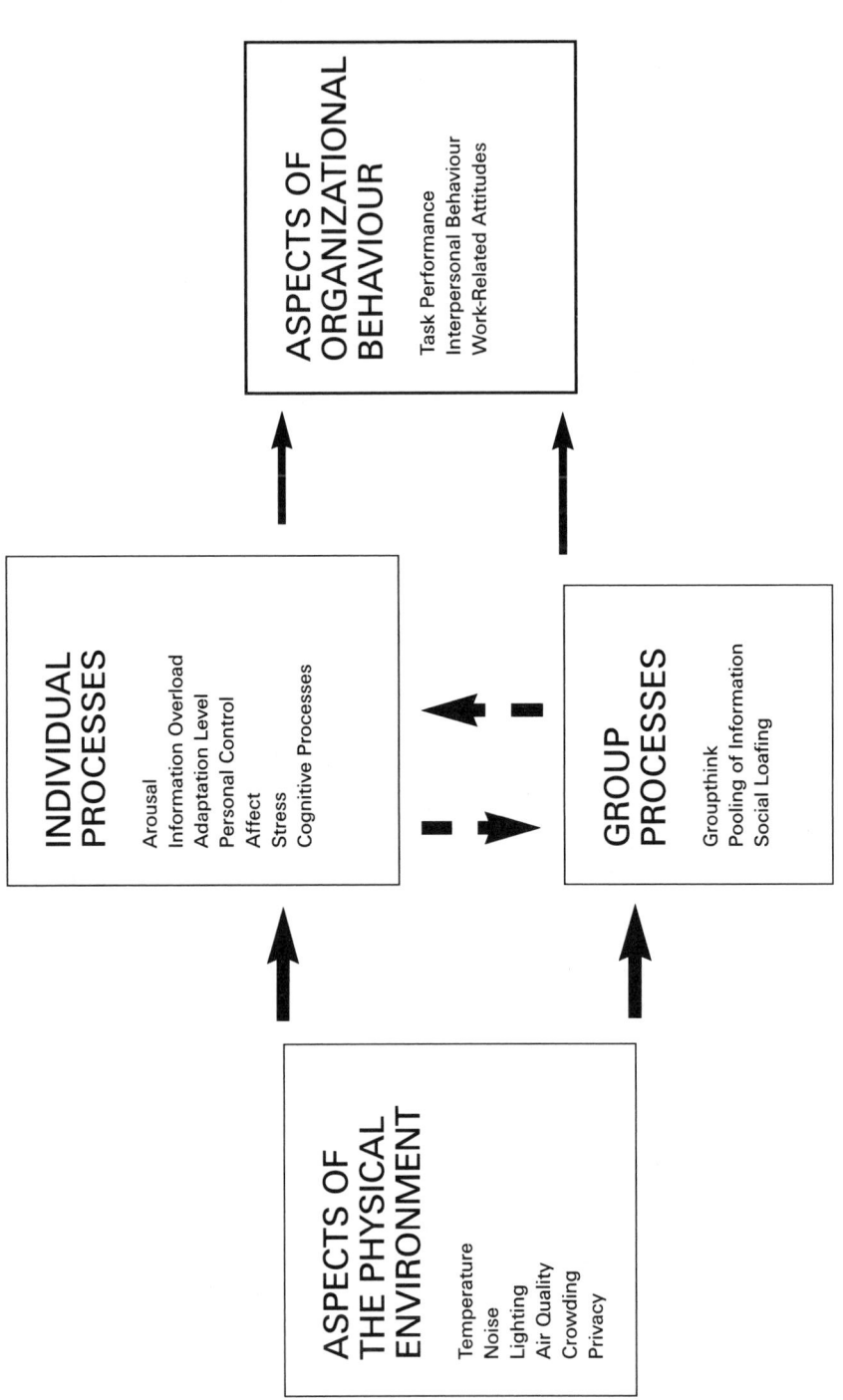

Figure 10.5 Integrated model of the effects of environmental variables on task performance, interpersonal behaviour and work-related attitudes

develop under conditions where groups are highly cohesive, suffer from structural and procedural flaws that limit their capacity to obtain and evaluate information relevant to their decisions, and face a provocative situational context in which members believe that their very survival is threatened (Tetlock *et al.*, 1992). It seems possible that environmental conditions serving to generate high levels of arousal, information overload, negative affect and stress can facilitate or intensify tendencies towards groupthink, with all the negative consequences for decision making this implies.

Second, certain environmental conditions may adversely affect group task performance by increasing the magnitude or likelihood of *social loafing* by group members (Harkins and Szymanski, 1988; Weldon and Mustari, 1988) or by reducing the propensity of group members to exchange unshared information (Stasser, 1992). Social loafing refers to the tendency of group members to exert less effort on a task when working together with others than when working on the same task alone. It derives, at least in part, from members' beliefs that their individual contributions cannot be evaluated and that, if they engage in social loafing, other group members will take up the slack – an assumption that appears to be valid in many cases (e.g. Williams and Karau, 1991). It seems possible that certain environmental conditions – especially ones serving to generate high levels of negative affect and perceptions of lack of personal control, and information overload – may increase tendencies towards social loafing. This would be the case because such conditions would tend to strengthen the perception that individual contributions cannot be assessed, and also because such conditions tend to weaken cohesiveness and commitment to the group.

Finally, it seems possible that unpleasant environmental conditions might magnify the tendency of group members to discuss shared information rather than unshared information. For example, the high levels of arousal generated by such conditions may intensify group members' tendencies to state – and restate – the information they know best (i.e. dominant responses). Similarly, such tendencies might also be increased by high levels of environmentally induced stress, stimulus overload and negative affect (cf. Bell *et al.*, 1990). To the extent such effects occur, environmental variables would exert negative effects on an important aspect of group decision making, and hence on key aspects of organizational behaviour.

CONCLUDING COMMENT

The integrative model presented in Figure 10.5 is based on a large body of research evidence concerning (1) effects of the physical environment on individual and group processes, and (2) the effects of such processes on important aspects of work-related behaviour. However, its ultimate value, from both a theoretical and a practical perspective, can be determined only by additional research. Such research must, of necessity, focus on many different issues and employ a wide range of strategies – laboratory simulations, long-term field investigations, survey techniques. Is the required effort justified? For practical as well as scientific reasons, the answer must be a definite *yes*. Continuing public concern with environmental issues virtually assures the occurrence of further attempts to improve the physical quality of work settings. In the absence of a solid foundation of scientific theory and data such efforts – and legislation relating to them – will rest largely on guesswork and political expediency. Such outcomes, it is suggested here, are potentially as dangerous as they are fallacious.

REFERENCES

Anderson, C.A. (1989) Temperature and aggression: ubiquitous effects of heat on occurrence of human violence. *Psychological Bulletin, 106,* 74–96.

Anderson, C.A. and DeNeve, R.M. (1992) Temperature, aggression and the negative affect escape model. *Psychological Bulletin, 111,* 347–51.

Baron, R.A. (1978) Aggression and heat: the 'long hot summer' revisited. In A. Baum, S. Valins and J.E. Singer (eds) *Advances in Environmental Research,* Volume 1. Hillsdale, NJ: Erlbaum.

Baron, R.A. (1983) The control of human aggression: a strategy based on incompatible responses. In R.G. Geen and E.I. Donnerstein (eds) *Aggression: Theoretical and Empirical Reviews.* New York: Academic Press.

Baron, R.A. (1987a) Mood of interviewer and the evaluation of job candidates. *Journal of Applied Social Psychology, 17,* 911–26.

Baron, R.A. (1987b) Effects of negative ions on cognitive performance. *Journal of Applied Psychology, 72,* 131–7.

Baron, R.A. (1990) Environmentally-induced positive affect: its impact on self-efficacy, task performance, negotiation, and conflict. *Journal of Applied Social Psychology, 20,* 368–84.

Baron, R.A. (1993) Interviewers' moods and evaluations of job applicants: the role of applicant qualifications. *Journal of Applied Social Psychology, 23,* 253–71.

Baron, R.A. and Bronfen, M.I. (in press) A whiff of reality: empirical evidence concerning the effects of pleasant fragrances on work-related behavior. *Journal of Applied Social Psychology.*

Baron, R.A., Fortin, S.P., Frei, R.L., Hauver, L.A. and Shack, M.L. (1990) Reducing organizational conflict: the potential role of socially-induced positive affect. *International Journal of Conflict Management, 1,* 133–52.

Baron, R.A., Rea, M.S. and Daniels, S.G. (1992) Effects of indoor lighting (illuminance and spectral distribution) on the performance of cognitive tasks and interpersonal behavior: the potential mediating role of positive affect. *Motivation and Emotion, 16,* 1–33.

Baron, R.A. and Thomley, J. (in press) A whiff of reality: positive affect as a partial mediator of the effects of pleasant fragrances on task performance and helping. *Environment and Behaviour.*

Baum, A. and Paulus, P.B. (1987) Crowding. *Handbook of Environmental Psychology, 1,* 533–70.

Baum, A. and Valins, S. (1977) *Architecture and Social Behavior: Psychological Studies of Social Density.* Hillsdale, NJ: Erlbaum.

Bell, P.A. (1980) Effects of heat, noise stress, and provocation on retaliatory evaluative behavior. *Journal of Social Psychology, 40,* 97–100.

Bell, P.A. (1981) Physiological comfort, performance, and social effects of heat stress. *Journal of Social Issues, 37,* 71–94.

Bell, P.A. (1992) In defense of the negative affect escape model of heat and aggression. *Psychological Bulletin, 111*, 342–6.

Bell, P.A. and Baron, R.A. (1976) Aggression and heat: the mediating role of negative affect. *Journal of Applied Social Psychology, 6*, 18–30.

Bell, P.A. and Baron, R.A. (1991) The role of affect in aggression and conflict. In A. Isen and B. Moore (eds) *Affect and Social Behavior*. New York: Springer, pp. 64–88

Bell, P.A. and Fusco, M.E. (1986) Linear and curvilinear relationships between temperature, affect, and violence: reply to Cotton. *Journal of Social Psychology, 16*, 802–7.

Bell, P.A. and Fusco, M.E. (1990) Heat and violence in the Dallas field data: linearity, curvilinearity, and heteroscedasticity. *Journal of Applied Social Psychology, 19*, 1479–82.

Bell, P.A., Fisher, J.D., Baum, A. and Green, T.E. (1990) *Environmental Psychology*, 3rd edition. New York: Holt, Rinehart & Winston.

Bell, P.A., Loomis, R.J. and Cervone, J.C. (1982) Effects of heat, social facilitation, sex differences, and task difficulty on reaction time. *Human Factors, 24*, 19–24.

Biner, P.M. (1991) Effects of lighting-induced arousal on the magnitude of goal valence. *Personality and Social Psychology Bulletin, 17*, 219–26.

Biner, P.M., Butler, D.L., Rischer, A.R. and Westergren, A.J. (1989) An arousal optimization model of lighting level preferences: an interaction of social situation and task demands. *Environment and Behavior, 21*, 3–16.

BOSTI (1981) *The Impact of Office Environment on Productivity and Quality of Working Life: Comprehensive Findings*. Buffalo, NY: Buffalo Organization for Social and Technological Innovation.

Boyce, P.R. (1981) *Human Factors in Lighting*. New York: Macmillan.

Boyce, P.R., Berman, S.M., Collins, B.L., Lewis, A.L. and Rea, M.S. (1989) *Lighting and Human Performance: A Review*. Lighting Equipment Division National Electrical Manufacturers Association and Lighting Research Institute.

Brickner, M., Harkins, S. and Ostrom, T. (1986) Personal involvement: thought provoking implications for social loafing. *Journal of Personality and Social Psychology, 51*, 763–9.

Briesacher, P. (1971) Neuropsychological effects of air pollution. *American Behavioral Scientist, 14*, 837–64.

Broadbent, D.E. (1971) *Decision and Stress*. New York: Academic Press.

Byrne, D. (1971) *The Attraction Paradigm*. New York: Academic Press.

Carnevale, P.J.D. and Isen, A.M. (1986) The influence of positive affect and visual access on the discovery of integrative solutions in bilateral negotiation. *Organizational Behavior and Human Decision Processes, 37*, 1–13.

Charry, J.M. (1984) Biological effects of small air ions: a review of findings and methods. *Environmental Research, 34*, 358–89.

Charry, J.M. and Hawkinshire, F.B.W.V. (1981) Effects of atmospheric electricity on some substrates of disordered social behavior. *Journal of Personality and Social Psychology, 41*, 185–97.

Cohen, S. (1980) Aftereffects of stress on human performance and social behavior: a review of research and theory. *Psychological Bulletin, 87*, 578–604.

Cohen, S. and Spacapan, S. (1978) The aftereffects of stress: an attentional interpretation. *Environmental Psychology and Nonverbal Behavior, 9*, 559–72.

Cohen, S. and Williamson, G.M. (1991) Stress and infectious disease in humans. *Psychological Bulletin, 109*, 5–24.

Cunningham, M.R., Shaffer, D.R., Barbee, A.P., Wolff, P.L. and Kelley, D.J. (1990) Separate processes in the relation of elation and depression to helping: social versus personal concerns. *Journal of Experimental Social Psychology, 26*, 13–33.

Davidson, L.M., Hagmann, J. and Baum, A. (1990) An exploration of a possible physiological explanation for stressor aftereffects. *Journal of Applied Social Psychology*, *20*, 869–80.

DeSanctis, M., Halcomb, C.G. and Fedoravicius, A.S. (1981) Meteorological determinants of human behavior: a holistic environmental perspective with special reference to air ionization and electrical field effects. Unpublished manuscript, Texas Tech University, Lubbock, TX.

Donnerstein, E. and Wilson, D.W. (1976) Effects of noise and perceived control on ongoing and subsequent aggressive behavior. *Journal of Personality and Social Psychology*, *34*, 774–81.

Evans, G.W., Jacobs, S.V. and Frager, N. (1979) *Human Adaptation to Petrochemical Smog*. Paper presented at the meetings of the American Psychological Association, New York.

Fandt, P.M. and Ferris, G.R. (1990) The management of information and impressions: when employees behave opportunistically. *Organizational Behavior and Human Decision Processes*, *45*, 140–58.

Fine, B.J. and Kobrick, J.L. (1978) Effects of altitude and heat on complex cognitive tasks. *Human Factors*, *20*, 115–22.

Flynn, J.E. (1977) A study of subjective responses to low energy and nonuniform lighting systems. *Lighting Design and Application*, *7*, 6–15.

Flynn, J.E., Spencer, T.J., Martyniuk, O. and Hendrick, C. (1973) Interim study of the procedures for investigating the effect of light on impression and behavior. *Journal of the Illuminating Engineering Society*, *3*, 87–94.

Forgas, J.P. (1991) Affect and social perception: research evidence and an integrative theory. In W. Stroebe and M. Hewstone (eds) *European Review of Social Psychology*. New York: Wiley.

Geen, R.G. and O'Neal, E.C. (1969) Activation of cue-elicited aggression by general arousal. *Journal of Personality and Social Psychology*, *11*, 289–92.

George, J.M. (1991) State or trait: effects of positive mood on prosocial behaviors. *Journal of Applied Psychology*, *76*, 299–307.

Harkins, S. and Szymanski, K. (1988) Social loafing and self-evaluation with an objective standard. *Journal of Experimental Social Psychology*, *24*, 354–65.

Hart, R.H. (1970) The concept of APS: air pollution syndromes. *Journal of the South Carolina Medical Association*, *66*, 71–3.

Hawkins, L.H. and Barker, T. (1978) Air ions and human performance. *Ergonomics*, *21*, 273–8.

Hebb, D.O. (1972) *Textbook of Psychology*, 3rd edition. Philadelphia: Saunders.

Helson, H. (1964) *Adaptation Level Theory*. New York: Harper & Row.

Hollingworth, H.L. and Poffenberger, A.T. (1926) *Applied Psychology*. New York: Appleton.

Houghten, F.C. and Yaglogu, C.P. (1923) Determining lines of equal comfort. *Transactions of the American Society of Heating and Ventilating Engineers*, *29*, 163–76.

Hughes, P.C. (1976) Lighting the office. *The Office*, *84*(3), 127ff.

Isen, A.M. (1970) Success, failure, and reaction to others: the warm glow of success. *Journal of Personality and Social Psychology*, *15*, 294–301.

Isen, A.M. (1987) Positive affect, cognitive processes, and social behavior. In L. Berkowitz (ed.) *Advances in Experimental Social Psychology*, Volume 20, New York: Academic Press, pp. 203–53.

Isen, A.M. and Baron, R.A. (1991) Affect as a factor in organizational behavior. In B.M. Staw and L.L. Cummings (eds) *Research in Organizational Behavior*, Volume 14, Greenwich, Conn.: JAI Press, pp. 1–53.

Isen, A.M. and Daubman, K.A. (1984) The influence of affect on categorization. *Journal of Personality and Social Psychology*, *47*, 1206–17.

Isen, A.M. and Shalker, T.E. (1982) Do you 'accentuate the positive, eliminate the negative' when you are in a good mood? *Social Psychology Quarterly, 4,* 245–9.

Isen, A.M., Nygren, T.E. and Ashby, F.G. (1988) Influence of positive affect on the subjective utility of gains and losses: it is not just nor worth the risk. *Journal of Personality and Social Psychology, 55,* 710–717.

Janis, I.L. (1982) *Victims of Groupthink,* 2nd edition. Boston, Mass.: Houghton Mifflin.

Jones, J.W. (1978) Adverse emotional reactions of nonsmokers to secondary cigarette smoke. *Environmental Psychology and Nonverbal Behavior, 3,* 125–7.

Kahn, R. (1992) Stress and behavior in work settings. In M.D. Dunnette (ed.) *Handbook of Industrial and Organizational Psychology,* 2nd edition. Palo Alto, CA: Consulting Psychologists Press.

Kenrick, D.T. and Johnson, G.A. (1979) Interpersonal attraction in aversive environments: a problem for the classical conditioning paradigm. *Journal of Personality and Social Psychology, 37,* 527–79.

Kirkpatrick, S.A. and Locke, E.A. (1991) Leadership: do traits matter? *Academy of Management Executive, 5*(2), 48–60.

Klein, K. and Beith, B. (1985) Re-examination of residual arousal as an explanation of aftereffects: frustration tolerance versus response speed. *Journal of Applied Psychology, 70,* 642–50.

Knowles, E.S. (1983) Social physics and the effects of others: tests of the effects of audience size and distance on social judgments and behavior. *Journal of Personality and Social Psychology, 45,* 1263–79.

Koelega, H.S. and Brinkman, J.A. (1986) Noise and vigilance: an evaluative review. *Human Factors, 28,* 465–81.

Kroner, W., Stark-Martin, J. and Willemain, T. (1992) Control of work environment and productivity. Unpublished manuscript, Rensselaer Polytechnic Institute.

Kryter, K.D. (1970) *The Effects of Noise on Man.* New York: Academic Press.

Locke, E.A. and Latham, G.P. (1990) *A Theory of Goal Setting and Task Performance.* Englewood Cliffs, NJ: Prentice-Hall.

Lorenzen, H.J. and Jaeger, D. (1968) The office landscape: a 'systems' concept. *Contract, 9*(1), 164–73.

Louis Harris & Associates (1978) *The Steelcase National Study of Office Environments: Do They Work?* Grand Rapids, MI: Steelcase.

MacCord, C.W. (1894) The modern mechanical drawing-room. *The Engineering Magazine, 7*(6), 855–63.

Matthews, K.E. and Canon, L.K. (1975) Environmental noise level as a determinant of helping behavior. *Journal of Personality and Social Psychology, 2,* 571–7.

Matthews, K.E., Canon, L.K. and Alexander, K. (1974) The influence of level of empathy and ambient noise on the body buffer zone. *Proceedings of the Association Division of Personality and Social Psychology, 1,* 367–70.

Motowidlo, S.J., Packard, J.S. and Manning, M.R. (1986) Occupational stress: its causes and consequences for job performance. *Journal of Applied Psychology, 71,* 618–29.

Nagar, D. and Pandey, J. (1987) Affect and performance on cognitive task as a function of crowding and noise. *Journal of Applied Social Psychology, 17,* 141–57.

Neiss, R. (1990) Ending arousal's rein of error: a reply to Anderson. *Psychological Bulletin, 107,* 101–5.

Nelson, T.M., Nilsson, T.H. and Johnson, M. (1984) Interaction of temperature, illuminance, and apparent time on sedentary work fatigue. *Ergonomics, 27,* 89–101.

Oldham, G.R. (1988) Effects of changes in workspace partitions and spatial density on employee reactions: a quasi-experiment. *Journal of Applied Psychology, 73,* 253–8.

Oldham, G.R., Kulik, C.T. and Stepina, L.P. (1991) Physical environments and employee reactions: effects of stimulus-screening skills and job complexity. *Academy of Management Journal, 34,* 929–38.

Page, R.A. (1977) Noise and helping behavior. *Environment and Behavior, 9,* 559–72.

Paulus, P.B. (1980) Crowding. In P.B. Paulus (ed.) *Psychology of Group Influence.* Hillsdale, NJ: Erlbaum, pp. 245–90.

Paulus, P.B., Annis, A.B., Seta, J.J., Schkade, J.K. and Matthews, R.W. (1976) Crowding does affect task performance. *Journal of Personality and Social Psychology, 34,* 248–53.

Paulus, P.B., McCain, G. and Cox, V. (1981) Prison standards: some pertinent data on crowding. *Federal Probation, 15,* 48–54.

Pepler, R.D. (1958) Warmth and performance: an investigation in the tropics. *Ergonomics, 2*(1), 63–8.

Quinn, R.P. and Staines, G.L. (1979) *The 1976 Quality of Employment Survey.* Ann Arbor, MI: Institute for Social Research.

Rea, M.S. (1988) Proposed revision of the ISENA illuminance selection procedure. *Journal of the Illumination Engineering Society, 17*(1), 20–8.

Roethlisberger, F.J. and Dickson, W.J. (1939) *Management and the Worker: An Account of a Research Program Conducted by the Western Electric Company, Hawthorne Works, Chicago.* Cambridge, Mass.: Harvard University Press.

Roskies, E. (1987) *Stress Management for the Healthy Type A.* New York: Guilford Press.

Rotton, J. (1991) Individuals under stress. In C.E. Kimble (ed.) *Social Psychology: Living with People.* New York: W.C. Brown.

Rotton, J., Barry, T., Frey, J. and Soler, E. (1978) Air pollution and interpersonal attraction. *Journal of Applied Social Psychology, 8,* 57–71.

Rotton, J., Frey, J., Barry, T., Milligan, M. and Fitzpatrick, M. (1979) The air pollution experience and interpersonal aggression. *Journal of Applied Social Psychology, 9,* 397–412.

Saavedra, R. and Earley, P.C. (1991) Choice of task and goal under conditions of general and specific affective inducement. *Motivation and Emotion, 15,* 45–66.

Sanders, G.S. (1983) An attentional process model of social facilitation. In A. Hare, H. Bumberg, V. Kent and M. Davies (eds) *Small Groups.* London: Wiley.

Scott, L. (1905) Better conditions for workers. *World's Work, 10*(3), 6408–13.

Scott, W.E. (1966) Activation theory and task design. *Organizational Behavior and Human Performance, 1,* 3–30.

Sherrod, D.R. (1974) Crowding, perceived control, and behavioral aftereffects. *Journal of Applied Social Psychology, 4,* 171–86.

Sherrod, D.R., Armstrong, D., Hewitt, J., Madonia, B., Speno, S. and Fenyd, D. (1977) Environmental attention, affect, and altruism. *Journal of Applied Social Psychology, 7,* 359–71.

Shimizu, Inc. (1990) *Aromanity: Creating a Pleasant Environment with Fragrance,* Tokyo, Shimizu Ltd.

Sinclair, R.C. (1988) Mood, categorization breadth, and performance appraisal: the effects of order of information acquisition and affective state on halo, accuracy, information retrieval, and evaluations. *Organizational Behavior and Human Decision Processes, 42,* 22–46.

Smith, S. (1978) Is there an optimum light level for office tasks? *Journal of the Illuminating Engineering Society, 7,* 255–8.

Stasser, G. (1992) Pooling of unshared information during group discussion. In S. Worchel, W. Wood and J.H. Simpson (eds) *Group Process and Productivity.* Newbury Park, CA: Sage, pp. 48–67.

Stasser, G. and Stewart, D. (1992) Discovery of hidden profiles by decision-making groups: solving a problem versus making a judgment. *Journal of Personality and Social Psychology, 63*, 426–4.

Stone, J., Breidenbach, S. and Heimstra, N. (1979) Annoyance response of non-smokers to cigarette smoke. *Perceptual and Motor Skills, 9*, 907–16.

Sulman, F.G., Pfeifer, Y. and Hirschman, M. (1964) Effect of hot dry desert winds (sharav) and application of ionizing treatment to weather-sensitive patients. *International Journal of Biometeorology, 18*, 393.

Sundstrom, E. and Sundstrom, M.G. (1986) *Work Places: The Psychology of the Physical Environment in Offices and Factories.* London: Cambridge University Press.

Tetlock, P.E., Peterson, R.S., McGuire, C., Change, S. and Feld, P. (1992) Assessing political group dynamics: a test of the groupthink model. *Journal of Personality and Social Psychology, 63*, 403–25.

Thomas, K.W. (1992) Conflict and negotiation. In M.D. Dunnette (ed.) *Handbook of Industrial and Organizational Psychology*, 2nd edition. Chicago: Rand McNally.

Thomley, J. and Baron, R.A. (1992) Influence of environmentally-generated positive affect on behaviour, performance, and helping. Unpublished manuscript, Rensselaer Polytechnic Institute.

Veitch, J.A., Gifford, R. and Hine, D.W. (1991) Demand characteristics and full spectrum lighting effects on performance and mood. *Journal of Environmental Psychology, 11*, 87–95.

Vernon, H.M. (1919) The influence of hours of work and of ventilation on output in tinplate manufacture. Industrial Fatigue Research Board Report No. 1. London: HMSO.

Warm, J.S., Dember, W.N. and Parasuraman, R. (1991) Effects of olfactory stimulation on performance and stress in a visual sustained attention task. *Journal of the Society of Cosmetic Chemists, 42*, 1–12.

Weldon, E. and Mustari, L. (1988) Felt dispensability in groups of coactors: the effects of shared responsibility and explicit anonymity on cognitive effort. *Organizational Behavior and Human Decision Processes, 41*, 330–51.

Williams, K.D. and Karau, S.J. (1991) Social loafing and social compensation: the effects of expectations of co-worker performance. *Journal of Personality and Social Psychology, 61*, 570–81.

Wohlwill, J.F. (1966) The physical environment: a problem for a psychology of stimulation. *Journal of Social Issues, 22*, 29–38.

Wohlwill, J.F. (1974) Human response to levels of environmental stimulation. *Human Ecology, 2*, 127–47.

Zillmann, D. (1988) Cognition–excitation interdependencies in aggressive behavior. *Aggressive Behavior, 14*, 51–64.

Zillmann, D., Baron, R.A. and Tamborini, R. (1981) Social costs of smoking: effects of tobacco smoke on hostile behavior. *Journal of Applied Social Psychology, 11*, 548–61.

11 Social skills and work

Peter Trower and Henk T. van der Molen

INTRODUCTION

Almost every facet of work involves some kind of social activity (Argyle, 1989). Every organization is a social system (Katz and Kahn, 1966), virtually every work group is a social group and every work role has a social aspect, from chief executive through to manager, supervisor, professional, skilled or unskilled worker. Often this social aspect is a formal part of the job or even the main focus, as in face-to-face personnel work or selling, or it may be an informal, subsidiary component, as in getting on with one's co-workers. It follows that how people perform interpersonally in an organization is a major determinant of how effective and productive that organization is, not to mention of the well-being of the employees themselves. Indeed, according to organization development theory (Beer and Walton, 1990), the 'human-process approach' is one of the two strategies for improving organizational effectiveness and employee well-being, the other being the 'technostructural approach' (i.e. systems-level structures).

According to Beer and Walton (1990), the human-process approach involves employees in examining interpersonal, group and intergroup processes and planning changes (in them) that will improve effectiveness. The goal is to examine dysfunctional behaviour practices openly and to develop consensus about desired group and organizational behaviour. The philosophy behind this is participative 'normative re-educative' change rather than the coercive top-down change that is typically practised in organizations.

One important approach within this human-process approach framework is to identify and facilitate the best forms of interpersonal behaviour required to achieve organizational and individual goals. We shall focus in this chapter on one way of achieving this at the individual level, namely by assessing and, if necessary, 'developing' individuals in such a way as to improve their social interaction skills in their given roles. We shall see later that different kinds of social interaction can have significant negative and positive effects on various measurable outcomes.

The success of this approach depends upon progress in the second strategy described by Beer and Walton (1990), namely the technostructural approach, which assumes that motivation and behaviour are powerfully influenced by job design and its underlying technology, organization structure and control, and information and reward systems. In other words, this approach works by analysing and, if necessary, changing the working environment in such a way as to facilitate the right amount and type of interaction. This may involve local changes, for example in setting up or changing the structure of work groups, or it may involve organizational restructuring such as decentralization, industrial democracy, systems analysis, etc. There is a considerable body of research on the effects of such changes on the social behaviour of people and consequent effects. For example, cohesive groups can be facilitated by the right kind of organizational structure, and this leads in turn to interpersonal co-operation. Co-operation in such cohesive groups leads to greater productivity than either competition or individual motivation (Johnson *et al.*, 1980) and other studies have shown reduced labour turnover and absenteeism.

Clearly each approach – the human-process approach or the techno-structural approach – is complementary to the other. Improving social relations in a work group will not work very well in long assembly lines or automated plants which make social contact very difficult.

In this chapter we shall focus on the first approach – assessing and developing individual skills – but the reader needs to refer to literature elsewhere that reviews the second, namely the environmental conditions that would be necessary for the first approach to succeed (e.g. Hackman and Oldham, 1980; Cooper, Cooper and Eaker, 1988) and other individual difference factors that would influence social interaction in the workplace (e.g. Furnham, 1992).

The chapter will consist of two main parts. In the first we will outline the social skills approach and review its application, including some of the areas in the work setting where this and similar approaches have been used or where they may have potential. In the second we shall provide an account of one such programme, including an empirical evaluation of the programme and a detailed description of one of the core training modules.

SOCIAL SKILLS THEORY AND APPLICATION

Social interaction problems

Wherever people interact in an organization there is potential for interactional problems. A brief consideration of these problems shows how serious their effect can be. It includes all types of interview, such as selection of key people, appraising people's work goals, achievements and motivation; all kinds of meetings, such as planning, management decisions, bargaining and negotiation; supervisory relationships, such as team building and leading, supervision, inspection; co-operative relationships, such as parallel or sequential co-operation over similar or different tasks; one-to-one relation-ships such as those between professional and client, seller and customer, involving such skills as assessment, information and advice giving, problem solving and persuasion; teaching and training.

Effective and ineffective skills

The work situations listed above all require social skills, and these can be assessed in terms of effective or ineffective skills. Indeed, there is consider-able evidence that good social skills are important, indeed vital, and where these are lacking or inadequate there are specifiable negative consequences. Some examples follow.

Supervisory skills

A number of studies have shown the impact of poor supervisory skills in organizational settings on such factors as output, job satisfaction, labour turnover and absenteeism. For example, Likert (1961) reported studies showing large differences – at least 78 per cent – in the productivity of similar departments whose supervisors used different styles of supervision, e.g. democratic versus autocratic. This was even more marked when employ-ees felt hostile to their supervisors.

Fleishman and Harris (1962) found a ratio of about 8 to 1 in the number of complaints made under different kinds of supervision. Too much 'initiat-ing structure' or too little 'consideration', and the grievance rate rose and job satisfaction fell. Very low levels of consideration produced a similar pattern in labour turnover.

A number of studies obtained similar effects for absenteeism, with absent-eeism dropping to as much as one-fifth following improved supervision styles (Argyle, 1989).

Interviewing skills

Doctor–patient interviews

Maguire (1986) reported a number of studies which showed disturbingly poor interviewing and communication skills in the medical profession, including among medical students, experienced doctors, paediatricians and surgeons. In one study, Maguire and Rutter (1976) found that the majority of medical students nearing the end of their training were rated as 'poor' or 'very poor' at a number of fundamental skills in the interview situation: such as the ability to cover personal topics like feeling depressed or suicidal, marital problems or sexual adjustment; failure to pick up on leads; talking too much; using leading questions that biased the patient's answer; and even such basic skills as putting the patient at ease at the outset of the interview. Weiner and Nathanson (1976) found experienced doctors showed exactly the same pattern of deficiencies. A typical problem was the failure to find out what patients were worried about.

Selection interviews

It is well known that selection interviews have relatively low validity and reliability, and that they are susceptible to bias and distortion. There is good indirect evidence that a contributory factor to this is likely to be inadequate interviewer skills (Alban Metcalfe and Wright, 1986).

The social skills model

Argyle (1969, 1989) has developed a model of social skills and pioneered a system of social skills assessment and training which has been influential worldwide and has been empirically evaluated in numerous studies. It is important to have such an explanatory model of the process of social skills acquisition if one is to develop procedures to bring about beneficial change. In this model the performer is *motivated* to influence *others' social responses* (the performer's goal) and emits a stream of *social responses* (and initiating actions) which are corrected continuously as the result of *feedback*, which is *perceived* and *translated* into appropriate corrective action (Argyle, 1969, 1983). It is by virtue of this corrective feedback process that skills are acquired and continuously refined. Problems can arise at any of these points in the process. Although other more elaborate information-processing models of social skill have been subsequently developed (see Trower, in press), this was the first, formative and most parsimonious model of its kind.

Social skills components

In addition to the process of social skill acquisition, it is equally important to have an understanding and knowledge of the actual component skill behaviours. Argyle has also pioneered work in this area, namely on identifying the non-verbal and verbal skill elements and the way that they are organized into learned sequences. He identifies the main skill components as follows.

Verbal skills

These include instructions and advice, questions, listener responses, such as paraphrasing and reflection of feeling, information and informal chat. There are subtle differences between orders, suggestions and instructions which are important in effective supervision. They can be given with differing degrees of persuasiveness, by listening to the other's point of view and incorporating it where possible, by explaining the reasons for the instruction, by making explicit the reasons and advantages or what will happen if it is not carried out. The sequence and choice of elements is different for various tasks, such as negotiating, selling and interviewing. In trying to influence the other person, the interviewer may, for example, take corrective action, as described by the social skills model, by getting the candidate to talk more or to give more appropriate answers.

Non-verbal skills

The verbal elements are expressed in the context of non-verbal skills, which have several important functions.

First, interpersonal attitudes such as friendly–hostile, inferior–superior and sexual attraction are much more powerfully expressed and usually less consciously attended to when they are expressed non-verbally. This again is an important area, for example for supervisors, who should try to express both friendliness and dominance – a difficult combination.

Second, emotional states can be unintentionally expressed via leakage cues in the face and body posture, despite awareness of appropriate 'display rules'.

Third is the area of self-presentation or impression management, i.e. sending messages about the self – as manager, doctor, etc.

Social skills training

Given the components and process of social skills, they can be combined into a training technology. The format of social skills training is now well known, and on this assumption the following description will be kept very brief. The general principle is that the individual is taught the skills in laboratory-based practice sessions and then uses them in the situations where the difficulties occur.

The training *procedure* generally consists of the following components.

1 *Instruction.* A particular skill or skills theme is taken and its function in social interaction described. The skill is then broken down into a sequence of behavioural elements so that the trainee can see exactly what has to be done.
2 *Modelling.* Learning by observing others, or modelling, is a very efficient way of acquiring complex new skills, since the trainee can see the entire sequence carried out as a whole and can judge for himself its effectiveness (Bandura, 1986). The best method is to get a model who is similar to the trainee in age, sex and class and who gives a 'coping' rather than a 'mastery' performance. All these factors help the trainee to associate himself with the model and encourage emulation.
3 *Rehearsal.* After instruction and modelling, the trainee is ready to try the

new skill in role play with a role partner. As in the analogy with rehearsing lines for a play, each successive attempt should approximate more closely to the final desired effect. Sometimes trainers get their clients to practise covert rehearsal first – that is to go through the behavioural sequence in their imagination.

4 *Coaching, feedback and reinforcement.* In the ongoing process of rehearsal, the trainee gets information on how he is doing so that he can rectify his performance. Feedback can be given via audio or video replay and verbally. Skilful handling of feedback is vital to successful training, and should be based on positive reinforcement.

5 *Homework.* Training is preparation, and the next step is for the trainee to implement the new skill in the work situation. Homework assignments are set very concretely, and subsequent training sessions spend a good deal of time dealing with homework implementation difficulties.

There are many other forms of staff training, some of which contain some of the components of social skill training, but which may have a specific purpose, for example to gain insight.

Training applications

Social skills training approaches have been developed in recent years for a wide variety of settings, tasks and roles. One way of organizing these applications is in terms of levels, as follows.

First is the level of the core skills. Those listed in Hargie (1986) as having been extensively researched include non-verbal communication, questioning, reinforcement, reflecting, opening and closing, explaining, self-disclosure and listening. Other authors have included instruction, ordering, explicit and implicit requests and advising. We have included some of these and some others (see below). Each of these core skills can be further broken down into finer elements, some of which will be described below.

At the next level are the higher-order sequences of skills that go to make up complete definable tasks such as interviewing, chairmanship, negotiating and bargaining, and self-presentation/impression management. Argyle (1989) lists the selection interview, the appraisal interview (for evaluation of progress, providing information and setting targets and arousing motivation), the personnel interview (for problems with performance and problem solving), skills of chairing a committee and presenting material to an audience. Millar, Crute and Hargie (1992) include counselling, selection, research, medical and appraisal interviews in their practitioner book on professional interviewing.

Finally, at the third level are the work roles such as manager, supervisor, doctor, nurse, etc. So, while tasks can be broken down into the skill elements, roles can be analysed in terms of the component tasks. For example, Alban Metcalfe and Wright (1986) list some of the skills at the task level that a manager needs to master as including the counselling interview, selection interview, appraisal interview, negotiation skills and leadership skills. Argyle (1989) identifies an intermediate level of complex task skills for supervisors as 'initiating structure' (which focuses on the jobs that have to be done), 'consideration' (which focuses on the needs of the group members) and 'participatory leadership' (which enables subordinates to participate in decision making). Other authors have developed comparable programmes for the helping professionals. For example, Maguire (1986) has developed training for doctor–patient interviews, Kagan (1985) developed training applications for nurses and Lang *et al.* (1990) for psychologists. Research continues to evaluate the best combinations of such skills.

AN ILLUSTRATIVE CASE: THE PERSONAL PROBLEMS (PERSONNEL) INTERVIEW

Background

To illustrate the social skills training approach from a practitioner's point of view we shall in this section describe in some detail a training module for the personal problems (personnel) interview. It forms part of a comprehensive social skills training package developed at the University of Groningen Department of Personality and Educational Psychology. We have chosen this particular interview, not only because it is representative of the social skills training approach, but because it plays such a crucial role in improving the dysfunctional interactional practices described by Beer and Walton (1990).

The personal problems interview training formed part of a course entitled 'Professional Communications Skills Training for Work Situations' for graduates at Groningen University intending to enter a career in work and organizational settings. The training has also been further developed and used for middle managers in Solihull Health Authority.

The main goal of the whole communications course is to offer insight and skills training in both first-level core skills and second-level task skills. The length of the course is fourteen sessions. Each training group consists of twelve trainees and two trainers. The training method is based on the model described earlier and also draws on Ivey's micro training method (Ivey, 1971). Perhaps the most important part of the training is the role play. This happens in triads – one of the trainees plays the role of the manager, one that of the employee and one that of the observer. After the 'interview' the manager gets feedback from the observer about the way he or she dealt with the situation and applied the skills. Here audio-visual feedback is used.

The course consisted of six modules as follows:

1 Basic core skills. These included attending behaviour (comprising such

elements as use of eye contact, attentive body language and verbal following); 'minimal encouragements' (small listener feedback responses to reinforce the speaker), reflection of feeling, paraphrasing of content, open and closed questions; 'concreteness' (a compound skill designed to obtain specific information) and summarizing. In addition, there were two meta-level skills: role explanation (for clarifying misconceptions about the manager's role) and thinking aloud (expressing aloud thought the manager has at difficult moments in the interview).

2 The selection interview
3 The appraisal interview
4 Breaking bad news interview
5 The personal problems interview
6 Giving advice on organizational problems.

Each skill is broken down into component parts and each part modelled, practised in role play and feedback given in the manner of the social skills training procedure described earlier. For example, in the role plays, trainees have to deal with simulations of real situations and use the skills in the way taught. Apart from feedback during the training, the behaviour of the candidates is also assessed by a number of trained assessors from pre- and post-training role-play tests. The pre-training tests are also used to obtain a profile of the trainees' strong and weak points. The purpose of this is for the trainer and trainee together to sort out learning points for the trainee before the start of the course, so that the weakest skills can be given particular attention during the training.

The effectiveness of the course was investigated by van der Hoek and van der Molen (1989). In a pre-test–post-test only design, the investigators found that blind assessors, trainers and trainees all rated the trainees significantly improved ($p < .01$) on all six categories of skill measured, namely conversational structuring, stimulating listening, interpersonal sensitivity, ability to deal with stress, ability to take decisions and oral communication. The items and the categories were scored on a 5-point scale, with score 1 meaning weak execution of the skill, 3 reasonable execution of the skill, 5 good application of the skill. Based on the ratings of the independent assessors, who were blind to the order of the pre-post video-taped tests and had no contact with each other, the trainees' mean total score improved from 2.25 pre-test to 3.97 post-test. Unexpectedly, the independent assessors judged the change to be greater than did either the trainers or trainees. As a measure of the magnitude of the change, the authors used a modified version of the effect size formula of Shapiro and Shapiro (1982) and derived an effect size of 2.82, which is very large compared to other studies and metanalysis (Shapiro and Shapiro reported an effect size of .85).

The personal problems (personnel) interview

Fictional case

> Carl Carpenter, who is in charge of the project group 'commercial and industrial building', has been under the impression that one of his foremen, Bert Builder, is not functioning as well as usual. Bert looks tired, and is often absent-minded during meetings. Remarks arising from Bert's team of construction workers have made it clear that Bert has been rather irritable. If, for example, they are a day behind schedule, Bert gets into a state, even if the delay is caused by bad weather. Because of this, Bert's relationship with his team is deteriorating. Carl is wondering what's wrong. Things cannot go on like this, something has to be done. Carl is not looking forward to talking with Bert; he knows Bert is very touchy and very private when it comes to personal affairs. Nevertheless, he decides to invite Bert for a personal interview. Bert arrives at the pre-arranged time.

In this case we see that Carl Carpenter is under the impression that Bert Builder might be having some personal problems which affect his work. Carl is about to undertake a special and difficult part of his task as supervisor: conducting an interview with an employee about suspected personal problems. Carl takes the initiative for this interview, which in itself is difficult since he will have to state his reasons. Whether Bert wants this interview remains to be seen. If employees in an organization experience personal problems, they will not usually flaunt them. We are not suggesting they should. Everyone has problems, and everybody should decide for himself if and with whom they choose to discuss them. Therefore we make a clear distinction between personal problems that do not and those that do (or seem to) affect work. In the latter case it might be in the interests of both employee and organization to discuss personal problems openly. Often the initiative for such a discussion should be taken by the person in charge. Sometimes, however, employees will voluntarily approach either their superior or a colleague.

Two interview styles

We will now discuss two styles which the supervisor can use in the personal problems interview. In order to explain both styles we will use our fictional case. We will present two dialogue samples, in which both styles become clear.

Sample 1

> 1. CARL: 'Bert, I've asked you in for a chat, because I have a feeling your work's not going well. Do you have any ideas about this?'
>   BERT: 'What do you mean "not going well", can you explain?'

2. CARL: 'Come on Bert, don't tell me you haven't noticed. But if you insist, I'll give you some examples. During our last meeting I noticed you weren't as involved as usual, as if your mind is somewhere else. And then the men in the team tell me you're unreasonably short with them. Well, it's made me think. I could be wrong, but I thought there might be a problem.'

BERT: 'Yeah, I see what you mean. It's true, I've done better.'

3. CARL: 'Has anything happened here on the job?'

BERT: 'No, nothing special, although we are behind schedule.'

4. CARL: 'True, and that's a nuisance, but it's no reason to walk around with a long face.'

BERT: 'I guess not.'

5. CARL: 'So, has anything happened between you and one of the men, or something else here at work?'

BERT: 'No, not that I know of.'

6. CARL: 'Well, then that's not it.' (looks pensive)

BERT: (waits)

7. CARL: 'Hm, let's see, are you having more trouble concentrating than before?'

BERT: 'No, not really.'

8. CARL: 'Everything all right at home, Bert?'

BERT: 'Sure, everything's fine. . .'

The conversation continues along these same lines: Carl asks the questions, Bert gives short answers and waits for the next question. Carl tries to find out why Bert is not functioning well, but Bert does not seem to co-operate. The idea behind Carl's behaviour (and of a lot of people wanting to help another) is that the easiest way to find the true cause of a problem is to ask a lot of questions. Then, it is thought, sound advice can be appropriately given. We call this the diagnosis–prescription interview style. Such an interview is very similar to an interview with a doctor: he asks a lot of questions, makes a diagnosis and writes out a prescription.

This kind of interview is not always doomed to fail. In some cases the nature and cause of the problem can be found. Whether a solution can be found is another matter. There are, however, some serious drawbacks to this method when dealing with personal problems. First, the person experiencing personal problems cannot always pinpoint the cause. Usually there are several causes. Second, in such a conversation it is very difficult to talk about problems in one's own way. In the sample above we see Bert more or less submissively answering the questions and waiting for the next one. A consequence of this direct questioning method is the difficulty in establishing a relationship of trust. We see Bert answering questions, usually in the negative, but there is no space for him to come forward with things he may find very difficult to talk about. Thus, the diagnosis–prescription style makes it easy for the other person to remain silent about difficult subjects.

The diagnosis–prescription style has certain disadvantages. Is there another method? Let's have a look at the next sample, in which Carl uses the co-operation style.

Sample 2

1. CARL: 'Bert, I've asked you in for a chat, because I have the feeling your work's not going well. At meetings for instance you seem to be absent-minded, and from the men in your team I hear you can be very hard on them. I'm worried about it, and I'd like us to talk about it. What do you think?'

   BERT: (somewhat hesitant) 'Well eh, . . . yes it's not going that well.'

2. CARL: 'I see you're hesitating. Firstly, anything said here is just between you and me. And of course there's no need to tell me things you don't want to. Now, I have one hour; what I would like to do is see if we can find out, together, what the problem is. Then we'll see if we can come up with some solutions. What do you think?'

   BERT: (a little less hesitant) 'Sure, sounds like a good idea. . .'

3. CARL: 'Right. Now, as I said, I'd like to hear what you think of it.'

   BERT: 'Well, you're right about me being absent-minded during meetings. . .'

4. CARL: 'Hm hm' (looks at Bert questioningly)

5. BERT: 'It's not that I'm not interested, I am. It's just that I'm having a hard time concentrating. . .'

6. CARL: 'Do you have any idea why?'

   BERT: 'No, I'm not sure, there are all kinds of things. . .'

7. CARL: 'All kinds of things . . . Can you give me an example?'

   BERT: 'Well, one of the things I'm wondering about is whether I should be moving on. I've been here for nine years now and I won't be getting any promotion. . .'

8. CARL: 'Go on. . .'

   BERT: 'This is very difficult, you're not going to tell anyone, are you?'

9. CARL: 'No, I'm not, I've already told you. But I understand it's difficult to talk about.'

   BERT: 'Well, okay. This isn't really about not getting promoted. Things aren't too good at home. . .'

10. CARL: 'What's wrong?'

    BERT: 'I don't talk about it much, but my wife left me sometime ago. She's got someone else. . .'

11. CARL: 'That must have been very upsetting. How long has this been going on?'

    BERT: 'Well, things hadn't been good for sometime. About six

> months ago she met this bloke and two months ago she moved in with her sister, because she wants to think things through. She doesn't know if she wants to stay with me or with that bloke. I feel so powerless.'

12. CARL: 'Hm, I can imagine, you're just waiting to see what they come up with.'

BERT: 'Right. And I might as well tell you the rest of it: because I don't know what to do. I often go to the pub at night and I don't stop at three beers, if you know what I mean. Anyway, because of all this I'm not doing too well on the job and I know I'm too hard on the men but before I know it I've done it again. . .'

Comparing the beginnings of the two samples, we notice a difference right away. In the first sample Carl almost immediately starts asking questions like some sort of detective. In the second sample he also tells Bert why he has invited him for this interview, but he includes a couple of concrete examples, and he makes his own feelings clear: 'I'm worried about it. . .'.

This is, however, only half the basis needed for a co-operative relation. In order to establish the other half, Carl asks Bert explicitly if he wants to talk. Thus Bert is given the role of equal partner. You could say a contract is negotiated in which both parties agree to the interview. In the second sample we see Bert's hesitant reaction. This might be caused by Carl's last question: 'What do you think?' We do see him admit to the problem. Carl takes up Bert's hesitation and, by acknowledging it (reaction 2), he shows understanding. But he does more than that. First he isolates this interview from the rest of the company ('Anything said here is just between you and me'). This is of importance to the confidentiality of the interview. It's important to Bert, who might think that whatever he says will spread through the company like wildfire. Then Carl tells Bert that he need not say anything unless he wants to. This puts Bert more at ease. In contrast to the events in the first sample, there's no pressure on Bert. In the course of sample two we see the positive effect that this has. If people do not try to force something out of you, but give you a chance to decide for yourself, you are often more willing to talk.

Prior to giving Bert a chance to talk, Carl makes a few things clear. First, he mentions the amount of time available for the interview. Of course there's always the possibility of further interviews should they be necessary. Then he explains to Bert what kind of conversation he would like this to be: 'What I would like to do is see if we can find out, together, what the problem is. Then we'll see if we can come up with some solutions. What do you think?' Thus the basic outline of the interview is marked, Bert knows what he's in for and is given another opportunity to make up his mind. We realize that not everybody will lose their inhibitions, and open up after such a beginning, but the chance of co-operation increases if the other person feels he has an equal say in the matter, and is taken seriously.

In sample two (reaction 2) we see Bert's hesitation decreasing. He realizes he's not going to be put on the spot, but he decides to hold back a while longer. Once the basis for co-operation has been formed, Carl decides to begin with a general open question: 'I'd like to hear what you think of it' (reaction 3). He does not ask a series of questions in order to confirm his own suspicions, as in sample 1, but he gives Bert some space. Then Bert starts to talk, slowly and falteringly at first. Carl restricts himself to listening, giving minimal encouragements (4, 7, 8), asking open questions (6, 10), asking one direct question (11) and showing understanding by means of reflecting emotions and paraphrasing content (9, 11, 12). This causes Bert to lose some of his inhibitions and to talk more openly. By the end it becomes clear that his absent-mindedness and his temper towards the men are caused by the situation at home.

Here we see a major difference between the diagnosis–prescription style and the co-operation style. In the former, the questions follow from Carl's preconceived ideas. In the latter Carl connects as much as he can to what Bert says. Bert is given the opportunity to tell his own story.

There are clearly several advantages to the co-operation style over the diagnosis–prescription style. First, the employee is encouraged to think actively about his problem. Thus an appeal is made to his responsibility. This results in a clearer view of the factors influencing the problems. Second, the relationship between supervisor and employee is explicitly confidential. And, third, there is no need to be as directive as in diagnosis–prescription style, which makes it easier to listen attentively.

Last but not least we want to mention some scientific evidence supporting the co-operation style. Research shows that diagnosis–prescription advice is rarely taken (Lewin, 1958; Korsch and Negrete, 1972). The same research shows that clarity and openness in the approach to the parties concerned, and their involvement in the recommendation, led to a higher percentage of people acting on the recommendations. The co-operation style is clearly preferable for personal problems interviews with employees. We will now proceed to show how to conduct such an interview by presenting a dialogue style which can be seen as a concretization of a more general co-operation style.

The co-operation style in practice

The skills-based method presented below is derived from Egan (1994). The function of this interview model is to arrange the various interview goals with their respective means, thus keeping a clear view of the situation.

Before discussing the different phases of the model, some preliminary remarks. Dealing with someone else's personal problems is treading on dangerous ground. The interviewer needs to be continually aware that they are not a professional counsellor or psychotherapist. However, offering assistance within the workplace does have its advantages. For employees it might be easier to talk to a familiar person. Moreover, the supervisor knows part of the employee's situation. When the problems result from work-related factors, knowledge of specific situations can be very useful. It is easier to understand the nature of the problem, and possibly simpler to take quick and concrete steps to eliminate the problem, e.g. by mediating in a co-workers' conflict.

Phase 1: problem clarification

In the first phase of an interview both supervisor and employee are supposed to get a clear view of the problem. It is important for the supervisor to have a basic attitude of respect and acceptance of the employee as a person. Since personal problems are not easily discussed, the beginning of the conversation is often hesitant and careful, as we have seen in sample two. It is the supervisor's task to clarify the procedure, and to invite the employee to talk. The supervisor listens; the employee recognizes that he can talk freely or, if he'd rather, he can stall for a bit.

Once rapport has been established, the supervisor encourages the employee to speak more freely. The main goal in this phase is to have a good view of factors contributing to the problem, and of the thoughts, feelings and behaviour of the employee. At this point our goal is not making choices, establishing the exact nature of the problem or finding solutions. If it appears, in the course of the interview, that the employee is having problems at home and as a consequence is drinking heavily, as in our fictional case, the supervisor at this stage does not come forward with suggestions.

At this stage the supervisor's task is to listen carefully, to try to create some order in the interview, and to make vague statements concrete. The supervisor should try to search the employee's story for clues to solutions, which he keeps to himself for the time being.

Skills in phase 1

In order to achieve the above goals, the supervisor needs regulating skills, such as situation clarification at the beginning of the interview (e.g. explaining why he has invited the employee for an interview, indicating the amount of time available and the structure of the interview). In addition, listening skills are especially important. In order to show the employee that he is interested, the supervisor has to make use of skill components such as 'attending behaviour', 'minimal encouragements', open and closed questions, paraphrases of content, reflections of feeling and concreteness. In order to give some structure to the story it is necessary to use summarizing skills.

Phase 2: formulating an action plan

If phase 1 has led to a clarification and clear description of the problems we can move on to phase 2. Action in phase 2 means actively looking for a solution to the problem. In Bert's case: 'How can we make sure your work does not suffer from your home situation?' or 'How can we make your home situation easier?' In short, the goal in phase 2 is to do something about the problem.

The employee should decide which problem to tackle first. If possible, he should also choose the means to achieve this goal. If this is not possible, the supervisor should play an important role in this. Often people know what their problem is, but they don't know how to change it. And, even if they do know how to change it, it doesn't mean they can bring about this change. In short, in a number of cases the supervisor will have to advise the employee.

Next, the supervisor will have to determine, after consultation with the employee, how to achieve the desired goal and which (new) behaviour is necessary. Supplying ways to deal with the problem is not enough, however. The supervisor will have to check what happens to the employee in his attempts to deal with the problem. Is it working? There will have to be another meeting to evaluate progress. In the problem-clarification phase it may become clear that the supervisor is not equipped to deal with this problem. In the action phase he will then have to find possibilities for referral.

Action programme steps

We will now briefly discuss nine separate steps of an action programme. Each step will be illustrated by means of our fictional case.

Step 1: problem clarification

In the preceding part we have said enough about problem clarification. Perhaps the supervisor will initiate an action programme or the interview will have cleared the air and the existing situation be accepted. During their first interview Carl summarizes Bert's problems and lists them as follows:

- Bert's wife is having a relationship with someone else, and is trying to decide what to do.
- Bert feels abandoned and powerless.
- He drinks more than is good for him.
- Consequences: lack of concentration, worrying and short-tempered with the workmen.
- Separate problem: lack of promotion opportunity.

Step 2: priorities

There often prove to be several problems or one problem of a complex nature. Which problem should be dealt with first? Supervisor and employee are not able to deal with all the problems at the same time. Therefore a certain order has to be established. It is not wise to begin with the 'worst' problem, since this is usually the most difficult to deal with. In order to promote self-confidence and the chance of success, it is advisable to start with a relatively simple (sub)problem.

The problem Bert wants to tackle first is the situation at work. No matter how bad the situation is at home, he does want to do well on the job. To him the most important part is his relationship with the men; meetings aren't that frequent. Although he wants to cut down on his drinking more than usual, he is not (yet) an alcoholic.

Step 3: goals

Following the choice of problems, supervisor and employee should formulate goals which will lead to a reduction of those problems.

The goal is to improve the relationship between Bert and his construction workers. After all, they are a day behind schedule, and a bad relationship does not encourage them to make it up.

Step 4: means

The next step is to make a list of the means available to the employee to reach his goal. What can he do, what kind of help can he get? If there are several opportunities, it might help to list the pros and cons of each possibility.

How does Bert improve the relationship with the construction workers? During his conversation with Carl, Bert suggests the possibility of offering his apologies about his behaviour to the guys during their break. The reasons for this behaviour he prefers to keep to himself.

Step 5: criteria

Supervisor and employee decide together what results their actions should have in order to be called successful. These criteria are a further concretization of the (sub)goals that were set.

Carl and Bert decide that Bert will try to achieve two things in the next week. First, the relationship with the men: there's hardly any communication. Second, maybe less important from a personal, but more so from the business point of view, they will try to catch up with their schedule.

Step 6: execution

The most important step, after discussing and organizing the action, is the execution of the plans. The employee will have to do something. Together they decide on the actual steps to be taken.

Bert will do what they agreed on, the very next day. There's no time like the present.

Step 7: evaluation

The employee returns for another interview, and discusses his experiences with the supervisor. What worked, what didn't; what else happened; to what extent, according to the criteria set in step 5, did he reach his goal? Also, what to do next, in view of the results?

> One week later Carl and Bert have their next interview. They have reached their goal on relationship improvement, since the men have accepted and appreciated Bert's apologies. However, he did not manage to keep his personal affairs out of it, since one of the men asked him what was wrong. He decided it might be better to tell them a bit more, and mentioned his marital problems; he did not tell them about his drinking. They have not managed to get back on schedule, because it has been raining all week. The important thing is that he and the men are getting along. But there is more to be done; Bert is still drinking heavily.

Step 8: a new start

Based on the evaluation, the employee continues his course of action if necessary. It is also possible to tackle another problem. Depending on the progress of clarification one of the first five steps can be taken again.

> In another interview Carl and Bert start dealing with Bert's alcohol problem. Their goal is to reduce Bert's use of alcohol. They also discuss the lack of promotion opportunities; although Carl does not see any immediate possibilities for Bert, they do decide he will take a refresher course in 'management'.

Step 9: conclusion

If the various goals have been reached, supervisor and employee can conclude their task as far as personal problems are concerned.

> When Carl thinks Bert is working up to standard, the interviews about personal problems can be concluded. Of course Carl cannot make Bert's wife return: in view of the situation that would be best. Bert would not feel abandoned any more, and he would not feel the need to go to the pub every night. However, Carl can help Bert to deal with his situation, whichever turn it takes.

Giving advice

An important skill in the action phase is giving advice. Although the co-operation strategy is based on co-operation between supervisor and employee, there are situations in which the supervisor has more skills to deal with certain aspects of a problem. In those cases the supervisor should take on a more directive role. If Bert Builder's only problem were choice of further education, and Carl Carpenter, with his more extensive experience, could give him sound advice, then he should. Advice should be given in plain terms, and it should be well argued and succinct.

A special case of giving advice is recommending 'referral'. As we have said before, supervisors should be well aware that they are not professional counsellors. If Bert Builder's drinking problem is a case of alcoholism, Carl Carpenter should refer him to a clinic for alcohol and drugs abuse. More generally, but equally relevant, supervisors should consider very carefully whether they are dealing with work-related or purely private problems. If a supervisor decides he is not competent enough to deal with the problem, or that there is no relation to the work situation, he will have to clarify the situation and refer the case.

Dealing with reactions to advice

When giving advice, the supervisor should pay close attention to the employee's reaction. After giving advice he should once again become a careful listener. Sometimes an employee may have doubts about the feasibility of the advice or he may feel a strong resistance to the advice. The supervisor can respond to such reactions by paraphrasing content or reflecting emotions. Thus the employee knows he is being taken seriously, and the resistance may even wane. Responses of this kind are certainly better than insisting on the advice given. In relation to this it is worth mentioning the $E = Q \times A$ formula, where E stands for Effect, Q for Quality and A for Acceptance. In other words: the Effect of advice does not just depend on its Quality, but also on Acceptance. No matter how sound the advice, if the employee does not accept it, the effect is zero. The formula also leads to the conclusion that the effect will be maximal if the quality of the advice is sound and the employee accepts it and acts on it. Of course an employee has the right to ignore any advice. If he does accept it, it is important to try and make concrete arrangements. In another interview supervisor and employee can decide if the advice has been beneficial.

REFERENCES

Alban Metcalfe, B.M. and Wright, P. (1986) Social skills training for managers. In C.R. Hollin and P. Trower (eds) *Handbook of Social Skills Training: Clinical Applications and New Directions*, Volume 2. Oxford: Pergamon.

Argyle, M. (1969) *Social Interaction*. London: Methuen.

Argyle, M. (1983) *The Psychology of Interpersonal Behaviour*, 4th edition. Harmondsworth: Penguin.

Argyle, M. (1989) *The Social Psychology of Work*. Harmondsworth: Penguin.

Bandura, A. (1986) *Social Learning Theory*. Englewood Cliffs, NJ: Prentice-Hall.

Beer, M. and Walton, E. (1990) Developing the competitive organization: interventions and strategies. *American Psychologist*, *45*, 154–61.

Cooper, C.L., Cooper, R.D. and Eaker, L.H. (1988) *Living with Stress*. Harmondsworth: Penguin.

Egan, G. (1994) *The Skilled Helper*, 5th edition. London: Brooks-Cole.

Fleishman, E.A. and Harris, E.F. (1962) Patterns of leadership behavior related to employee grievances and turnover. *Personnel Psychology*, *15*, 43–56.

Furnham, A. (1992) *Personality at Work: The Role of Individual Differences in the Workplace*. London: Routledge.

Hackman, J.R. and Oldham, G.R. (1980) *Work Redesign*. Reading, Mass.: Addison-Wesley.

Hargie, O. (1986) *A Handbook of Communication Skills*. London: Croom Helm.

Hoek, B.J. van der and Molen, H.T. van der (1989) Effectmeting van de cursus professionele gespreksvoering in bedrijfssituaties (Effects of a professional communication skills training for work situations). *De Psycholoog*, *24*, 550–7.

Ivey, A.E. (1971) *Microcounselling: Innovations in Interviewing Training*. Springfield, IL: Charles C. Thomas.

Johnson, D.W., Maruyama, G., Johnson, R. and Skon, L. (1980) Effects of cooperation, competition, and individualistic goal structures on achievement: a meta-analysis. *Psychological Bulletin*, *89*, 47–62.

Kagan, C.M. (ed.) (1985) *Interpersonal Skills in Nursing: Research and Applications*. London: Croom Helm.

Katz, D. and Kahn, R.L. (1966) *The Social Psychology of Organizing*. New York: Wiley.

Korsch, B.M. and Negrete, V.F. (1972) Doctor–patient communication. *Scientific American*, *227*, 66–74.

Lang, G. and Molen, H.T. van der, with Trower, P. and Look, R. (1990) *Personal Conversations: Roles and Skills for Counsellors*. London: Routledge.

Lewin, K. (1958) Group decision and social change. In E. Maccoby, T. Newcomb and E. Hartley (eds) *Readings in Social Psychology*, 3rd edition. New York: Holt, Rinehart & Winston, pp. 197–211.

Likert, R. (1961) *New Patterns of Management*. New York: McGraw-Hill.

Maguire, P. (1986) Social skills training for health professionals. In C.R. Hollin and P. Trower (eds) *Handbook of Social Skills Training: Clinical Applications and New Directions*, Volume 2. Oxford: Pergamon.

Maguire, P. and Rutter, D. (1976) History taking for medical students. I – Deficiencies in performance. *Lancet*, *2* (7895), 556–8.

Millar, R., Crute, V. and Hargie, O. (1992) *Professional Interviewing*. London: Routledge.

Shapiro, D.A. and Shapiro, D. (1982) Meta-analysis of comparative therapy outcome studies: a replication and refinement. *Psychological Bulletin*, *92*, 581–604.

Trower, P. (in press) Adult social skills: state of the art and future directions. In W.T. O'Donohue and L. Krasner (eds) *Handbook of Psychological Skills Training*. New York: Allyn & Bacon.

Weiner, S. and Nathanson, M. (1976) Physical examination: frequently observed errors. *Journal of the American Medical Association*, *236*, 852–5.

12 Putting practice into psychology

David Pendleton

INTRODUCTION

Michael Argyle's contribution to psychology has been essentially pioneering. He has opened up new fields of research and made valuable contributions within them. In so doing, he has stimulated the interest of others who have become the settlers in the field. Their task has been to refine, to qualify, redefine and make new distinctions, by which time Michael has usually moved on. This is the contribution of an original thinker. A generation of psychologists has every reason to be grateful for his contribution and social psychology in the UK has to acknowledge his role as a founding father and elder statesman.

In general, his work has sought to deal with real issues rather than artefacts. By this I mean that he has tended to find his research issues in the world of people rather than in the academic literature. It may even be that much derives from his reflections on his own experience of life. His work on social skills, on long-term relationships and on happiness are typical. The work on social situations is unusual in this respect, originating as it did from an essentially academic source.

Since most of his work begins with human experience, it is to be expected that much will be readily applied. The work on social skills, for example, has transformed much professional training (e.g. Pendleton *et al.*, 1984). But for how much of psychology can the same be said?

Social psychology should satisfy Alexander Pope's poetic recommendation that 'the proper study of mankind is man', but the search for social psychological contributions which have the same applicability as Michael Argyle's work can be frustrating. Much seems to begin and end in the literature rather than in human experience and so it stays in the literature rather than finding broader expression and application.

It is not my intention here to enter into a debate about the purpose of academic endeavour or to seek to quantify the fortuitous contributions made by 'blue sky' research. Rather, I intend to explore why it is that a great deal of academic endeavour does not make much of a difference beyond the laboratory or the classroom, and why those who are academically trained may find the transition to the world of professional practice a difficult one to make – despite their having received a training which should equip them to do so. The explanations for these difficulties are to be found, I believe, in the nature of academic activity and its essential differences from professional practice.

THE ACADEMIC AND THE PROFESSIONAL

Those who have worked in both the academic world and in that of professional practice will be struck by their differences and by the extent to which those differences are both intriguing and disturbing. They certainly make the transition from one world to the other far from straightforward. Initial reflections on this subject were, for this author, entirely personally motivated – to seek to make sense of personal experience. Subsequently, in the context of attempting to account for the poor uptake of continuing professional education by the medical profession, the same reflections became relevant.

Doctors are trained and qualify just once. From that point on in their careers, they can take life and death decisions with no attempt being made to reassess their continuing competence. As medical knowledge moves on, the matter of keeping their professional knowledge and skills up to date is left to the voluntary arrangements of Continuing Medical Education (CME). Inducements are made in the form of payment for attending a minimum of sessions, but this is not compulsory.

Given the seriousness of their role and the potential for calamity, we might expect their eager attendance at CME. Yet this is not the case. Most doctors do the minimum. It is not that they are poorly motivated, but rather that there appears to be a mismatch between their needs and the education that is provided. Essentially, CME is academically based, but their needs are professional. Other cases drawn from professional practice can be used to illustrate the key differences between the academic world and the professional.

Adrian Furnham and I have been fascinated by these differences for some time and have written about them often (e.g. Furnham and Pendleton, 1991). Many of the important differences are outlined in Table 12.1.

The most important difference between the two worlds is that their *aims* are different. The academic is seeking insight – to understand the nature and causes of things, irrespective of the use to which that insight may be put. It is sufficient in and of itself. The professional is interested only in that subset of understanding which is relevant to the problem which he or she is currently seeking to solve or manage.

Academics are rarely concerned about the *time* their endeavours may take since other considerations take priority. It would be far better for an academic to rewrite a book completely, for example, and go beyond a publisher's deadline than to have the book flawed by a (perceived) lack of

Table 12.1 Some differences between the academic and the professional

	Academic	*Professional*
Major aim	Insight and knowledge	Action to solve a problem
Urgency	Low	High
Cost–benefit analysis	Irrelevant	Crucial
Principal quality criterion	Elegance	Practicality
Usual source of insight	Own research, others' experience	Others' research, own experience
Level of complexity	High	Low
Means of persuasion	Theory backed by data	Data backed by argument
Preferred medium of presentation	Written	Face-to-face
Personality type most valued	Introvert	Extravert
Method for dealing with uncertainty	Statistical	Personal

quality. The professional is expected to balance both quality and time and deliver both to an agreed quality standard and an agreed budget of time and money. Faced with the same dilemma as the academic, the professional would be expected, first, to give priority to the client's perception of quality, second, to negotiate how the overrun of time and money was to be managed and, third, to resist the temptation to raise the quality of the end result beyond that required by the circumstances.

Cost–benefit analysis is also dealt with differently. When the aim is insight or understanding, greater understanding is better by definition and any incremental improvement is worth having. To distinguish between any two matters is appropriate, however small the distinction may be. Cost involved and time taken are relatively unimportant. The professional world requires that the cost of activity is either borne directly by the client or absorbed by the professional. The latter represents an opportunity cost. Thus the relationship between cost and benefit has to be faced at all times and may lead to very different actions being taken.

The *principal quality criterion* in each world differs. The academic world has many well-defined quality criteria which are a part of its history and philosophy. Academic quality criteria include logical consistency, precision and verifiability. The quality criterion which tends to be uniquely emphasized, however, is the principle of parsimony which is well understood and favours contributions which are elegant. Professionals are generally employed to help find solutions or to help manage a situation more effectively. Above all, their contributions must work. After that, there are considerations of cost, time and the quality of communication between the professional and the client. But the principal consideration is practicality.

The academic gains *insight* from his or her research, whether this is literature research or empirical research. The researcher is typically a third person, dispassionate and uninvolved (despite the emergence of participant observation). The personal experience which informs academic endeavour is usually that of other people. In the professional world, the reverse is true. Generally, the professional is drawing on a great deal of personal experience and has to guard against becoming almost totally anecdotal by checking his or her experience against the available research literature.

Falsifiability is a key academic principle which inevitably produces *complexity*. Once an idea, theory or hypothesis has been proposed, the required task of all academic contributors is to show that all or part of it is false. This tends to complicate that which was originally simple. Kuhn's (1962) ideas about the progress of science suggest that there will indeed be simplicity again as the original idea or theory becomes so complex that it is unsustainable and it is discarded in favour of a new theory or idea. But the state of complication lasts a good deal longer than that of re-simplification with the consequence that, at any given point of academic endeavour, the current state of a theory or idea will be complex. The professional world has a low tolerance for complexity, not simply for that which is untrue.

Persuasiveness is a property of the theory and the data for the academic. The ideas persuade, not the individual. This has not always been so. Those who have wandered through the Oxford Examination Schools will have noticed the existence of the School of Astronomy and Rhetoric, implying that the force of argument may have been all that the early astronomers had at their disposal when astronomical measurement was crude. The professional is frequently to be found in the same position as the early astronomers. They typically have to offer careful research done elsewhere, simple research data gathered for the client in a short space of time and a keen argument to support their recommendations.

It is not surprising, therefore, that the professional's *preferred medium of presentation* is face-to-face, where the full power of the argument can be experienced. The academic publishes, hoping that those whom he or she wishes to influence will read the journals. If the academic audience has a dispute with the originator of a paper, they will write to the journal or publish a contradictory paper. The professional, having to compete with other pressing demands on the client's time, has to deal with objections as they arise so that a solution may be implemented quickly.

Not surprisingly, the academic's preferred *personality type* is introverted, and better suited to scholarship. The professional world favours extraverts, better suited to dealing with people.

The most painful difference, however, is the *method of dealing with uncertainty*. The academic deals with uncertainty by addressing it explicitly and setting limits to it. The doubt which surrounds the applicability of an academic research study to the general population can be estimated and the confidence intervals can be calculated. That having been done, the matter is dealt with. The professional is frequently in a different position. The quantity and quality of the available information brought to bear on a problem is weighed carefully but there is rarely a simple deduction which will solve the problem or manage it more effectively. The professional's judgement is sought by the client and any doubt, whether or not it is discussed, is largely dealt with by the professional personally. It is the principal source of stress in professional life.

If we examine several cases drawn from the author's professional practice as an applied psychologist, we shall see how many of these differences work. The cases also indicate the potential benefits to be gained from drawing the academic and professional worlds closer together.

CASE 1: THE PROBLEMS OF CONTINUING MEDICAL EDUCATION

This case illustrates the specific issue of the role of *cost–benefit analysis* in the professional world and also shows how the academic basis of education may be unsuitable to professional development.

Continuing Medical Education is poorly attended and the medical journals are merely skimmed, at best, by most doctors. These facts have led the government to introduce a new contract for medical practitioners in the National Health Service which requires them to attend CME in order to earn a small proportion of their salary.

Principally concerned with professional matters, most doctors want to improve the quality of their actions (their practice) as directly as possible. They are concerned to maximize the return on their investments – in this case, their investment of time. They will inevitably be more interested in investing an hour in CME, the faster and the broader its likely impact on their practice. This is a matter of cost–benefit analysis based on the likely yield of the activity.

A typical cost–benefit (yield) analysis in continuing medical education is provided in Table 12.2 (Pendleton, 1990; King, Pendleton and Flew, in preparation). Maximum yield is defined here as having a low cost in terms of time and broad benefit or impact on practice. Video-based skills training makes a difference on every consultation after it has been taken, and requires just three days – a sound investment, and it has been extremely well received. Large numbers have taken part, it is now a feature of most vocational training schemes in General Practice and books on this topic sell well.

Balint training is a form of psychotherapeutically based reflection on practice in peer groups with a leader. It has a broad effect on practice but

Table 12.2 Cost–benefit (yield) analysis for Continuing Medical Education

	Time cost high	*Time cost low*
Narrow benefit	Reading most articles in medical journals or attending most postgraduate lectures	Reading review articles or attending update lectures
Broad benefit	Attending Balint training	Video-based skills

the training typically lasts for years. It has a following and a society exists for its adherents. Its yield, being broad but slow, would be classified as medium. Similarly, medium yield would describe attendance at update lectures or reading review articles in journals. But, since the absolute time involved in this activity is low compared with Balint training, more people take part in it.

The lowest yield of all is that which is associated with the most common media for Continuing Medical Education – journal articles and postgraduate lectures which are usually so narrow in their focus that it takes a great deal of time and effort to cover significant areas of a doctor's work. Thus, not surprisingly, CME is poorly attended and most journals are poorly read. This is not a failure of motivation on the part of the doctors, it is a failure of insight on the part of the providers of CME. They have based their activity on the traditional academic aims, media and methods, when their audience is professional. They have also omitted the cost–benefit analysis of their work as perceived by their potential audience.

CASE 2: THE FINANCIAL INSTITUTION

Principally, this case demonstrates how the professional has to deal with uncertainty personally. It also shows how the classification of psychological concepts and knowledge is less helpful to the practitioner than it might be.

The Regulators of the London Stock Exchange are charged with ensuring that the interests of shareholders are as well protected as possible. They carry out their task by formulating and enforcing rules by which applications for a listing on the London Exchange are judged. Companies requesting a listing have to submit documents which are carefully studied by the Regulators and this service takes time and costs money. A listing in London is a prize worth winning, however, since it is the principal market in Europe and this has allowed the London Exchange's Regulators to enforce high standards.

The advent of the Single European Market in 1992 changed matters considerably, since any company which is listed on any European Exchange is able, through mutual recognition, to apply for a listing in London. Currently, if the London Regulators are to continue to set and enforce high standards, the basis of their influence can no longer be their ability to deny a company access to the London Exchange. Instead, they will have to alter their relationship with the stockbrokers who represent the companies and become more like consultants who add value, and less like policemen.

The social psychological literature has much to say on related matters. The practitioner could look at such topics as attitude change, stereotypes, influence and leadership. But the time scales for action required and the budgets available meant that a programme of action was required which was relatively brief and tightly focused. The literature was conceptually rich and laden with studies, but not case studies which showed how similar problems had been tackled before. The practitioner has to assemble the relevant psychological approaches piecemeal from a classification that is academic.

The approach we took was to cast the central issue as a leadership problem in which the Regulators and their management had to begin to think and act differently, with respect both to the task and to their relationships with their clients and colleagues.

The steps taken were:

- measure the stockbrokers' perceptions of the Regulators and regulatory activity by questionnaire study and interview study
- use the data with the Regulators to think through procedural changes which would lead to a more appropriate service
- institute a leadership development programme for the management team
- institute a customer service development programme for the front-line professional and support staff
- train the professional staff in how to run meetings with brokers more effectively and more co-operatively
- measure customer reaction for a second time.

The programme led to a 20 per cent improvement in customer perception after the year which the programme took to implement. But was this enough for the investment? Was it the best possible course of action? Would other psychological models have been more appropriate? The clients were satisfied but we shall never know for sure and we live with the uncertainty despite having given the client our best judgement.

CASE 3: HONG KONG AFTER 1997

This case demonstrates the professional preference, for persuasive purposes, of data backed by argument, face-to-face presentation and the extraverted personality type.

Cathay Pacific Airways is Hong Kong's airline and is committed to staying in Hong Kong after the territory reverts to Chinese rule in 1997. Despite the contents of the Basic Law which sets out the Chinese government's agreement to allow Hong Kong to manage its own affairs for fifty years after the handover, concerns run high in all of Hong Kong's businesses. Cathay Pacific wished to launch its mission statement for the 1990s and to persuade its employees of the soundness of its position on Hong Kong's future. How should this be done?

Their position was based on their company values, their understanding of the Chinese, their contacts with the Chinese government, their investigations of the Chinese Special Economic Zone (SEZ) just north of the Hong Kong border in Shenzen and their fierce determination to make the arrangement work. It might be thought appropriate, therefore, to produce a closely argued case and set it out in all of the airline's languages for all to read and digest at their own pace. This would be the academic way.

We became involved with Cathay in organizing day-long conferences for their 700 managers in groups of eighty. These conferences used television technology to create a sense of occasion, computerized voting to establish and work with the views of those attending and a question-and-answer format with no holds barred so that the most difficult questions could be put to the directors and managing director.

These conferences were able to offer only snapshots of the complete arguments, only extracts from the data, but they demonstrated the unanimity of the directors and, more than anything, they demonstrated effectively the force of their convictions

This approach to the problem required mastering a format which is more comfortably located in the broadcast media: ensuring that visual materials and presentations by the consultants and directors were of the highest order to sustain the jet-lagged attention of the audience for a day and speaking with passion rather than just precision. None of these skills would be learned in an academic institution in the United Kingdom but the effectiveness of the consulting intervention required them all in order to communicate the messages well.

The principles of communication are well understood by social psychologists, but they are not practised in British academic institutions. In the USA, there is much more emphasis on communication: the subject is taught in its own right along with the practical skills associated with it. The problem is not that the academic teachers do not understand these matters, it is that their aim is insight and understanding rather than skill acquisition in the field. The problem which this gives to the practitioner is that he or she may know what needs to be done but may be unable to do it, having been trained in a more scholarly, introverted tradition where self-presentation is virtually irrelevant and the written word is the favoured medium.

THE RELATIONSHIP BETWEEN THEORY AND PRACTICE

It has become received wisdom that 'nothing is as practical as a good theory' but this implies that the direction of influence is from theory to practice. It is also, presumably, a tautological observation in which only theory which is practical is considered to be good. The relationship between theory and practice should, however, be reciprocal, since a theory which fails to work in practice needs to be re-examined, but many theories apparently continue to be held without having to pass the test of practice. Hence the use of the term 'academic' as a criticism meaning '*of purely theoretical or speculative interest – an academic argument*'.

Doctors can now be trained clinically. This means that they are introduced to patients without first having studied clinical medicine. They are encouraged to analyse the patient's problems until they can proceed no further. They report their conclusions to their tutor who then sends them off to complete a laboratory course, to read several relevant chapters of a clinical medicine text and to learn how to conduct an appropriate clinical procedure. They return to the patient to advance their investigations. The clinical course progresses in this manner until it is completed.

Increasingly, universities and colleges are emphasizing the practical nature of their courses. The new University of Westminster (formerly the Polytechnic of Central London) advertises its courses in the following terms:

> Our students deal with real world problems set by major employers so they begin their careers ready to make practical contributions.

This is an emphasis which is to be expected from an institution which was set up for essentially vocational purposes. But could such an emphasis be developed in a subject like psychology and in the most academic institutions? Could it be developed without reducing the quality of their work? Indeed, could it even enhance that quality?

The matter seems to hang on one's understanding of the nature of psychology. It has never entirely convinced others of its status as a science since both science and arts degrees can be obtained in the subject at institutions which maintain that distinction. But, if it is a science, can it be better understood and taught as an applied science or as a pure science?

The scientist-practitioner is emerging in the field of clinical psychology. This is an innovation which seeks to bring out the science in practice: to make practice more scientific. What I am posing is the possibility that the opposite may be at least as helpful, namely, to set out deliberately to make the science of psychology more practical, particularly in those domains connected with work.

PUTTING PRACTICE INTO PSYCHOLOGY

The field of psychology is broad and diverse. Some of it is potentially very useful but it would be difficult to know this by examining the subject index of most psychology texts. Subjects are to be found such as perception, learning, memory, motivation, personality and so on. Those practitioners who seek to apply psychology do not think in these terms and so require a

CONCEPTUAL CLASSIFICATION

	Learning	Perception	Personality
Ensuring quality in medical care			
Coping with change in organizations			
Commun-icating commitment			

PRACTICAL CLASSIFICATION

Figure 12.1 Comparing a conceptual and practical classification for occupational psychology

different classification. An improvement would be to see such matters classified as bereavement, divorce, counselling, recruitment, leadership and so on. But closer still to the practical application of the subject would be to teach by cases. This would mean, not the replacement of the psychological classification, but supplementing it with another means of accessing the wealth of useful material which the subject has created. Figure 12.1 shows how such a classification might work for occupational psychology.

In Figure 12.1, the classifications are simply different ways of accessing the material. In the cells of the table would be found the content of occupational psychology, but it is made significantly more accessible to the practitioner by the classification based on cases. The practical classification can be used both for creating texts in the subject and also for teaching. Such an approach would also suggest gaps in the curriculum which may need to be filled, such as the teaching of much-needed skills. It would also show potential areas for theoretical and research contributions which do not yet exist in the field.

CONCLUSION

As psychological endeavour continues to develop, it is interesting to specu-late on the forces which will shape it in the twenty-first century. One of the more compelling influences may well be the pressing need for practical solutions to real problems. These may create political pressure to influence the criteria for supporting research and for continuing to fund academic institutions and units. But, whether or not structural changes are brought about in the institutions which govern psychological research and teaching, the demands of the increasing numbers of practitioners seeking to use psychology are likely to have an effect on the topics it addresses, the classifications it uses, the content of its curricula and the settings in which it is taught.

REFERENCES

Furnham, A. and Pendleton, D. (1991) The academic consultant. *Journal of General Management*, *17*(2), 13–19.

King, J., Pendleton, D. and Flew, R. (in preparation) In practice: shaping the future of a general practice partnership. In D. Pendleton and J. Hasler *Professional Development in General Practice*. Oxford: Oxford University Press.

Kuhn, T. (1962) *The Structure of Scientific Revolutions*. Chicago: University of Chicago Press.

Pendleton, D. (1990) The educational process: methods and opportunities. Paper presented at BMS Conference on Continuing Medical Education in General Practice, Dublin, February 1990.

Pendleton, D., Schofield, T., Tate, P. and Havelock, P. (1984) *The Consultation: An Approach to Learning and Teaching*. Oxford: Oxford University Press.

13 Age and work

Peter Warr

A decline is widely expected over the next two decades in the proportion of young people in the labour market, and a corresponding increase will occur in the percentage of older men and women. That trend is represented in simplified form in Table 13.1.

It can be seen that in Europe as a whole the proportion of people aged between 55 and 64 will increase by some 23 per cent between 1990 and 2020. That shift will be less in Eastern Europe, but it will be very substantial in parts of the West. For instance, Germany, Sweden and the United Kingdom will all see increases in excess of 30 per cent. Of course, not all of those older people will be seeking jobs, and there has in recent years been a marked decline in the proportion of older people who are active in the labour market. However, making allowance for that fact, there will nevertheless be a significant change in the age composition of the labour force in the next two decades (e.g. Department of Employment, 1992; Warr, 1994a).

Against that background, this chapter will examine two issues in the area. How does ageing affect work behaviour and well-being? And (much less frequently investigated) the reverse question of how work affects ageing: are there particular aspects of jobs which accelerate or slow down specific aspects of physiological or psychological ageing?

Table 13.1 Increases in the proportion of people aged 55–64 between 1990 and 2020

All Europe	23%
France	24%
Germany	39%
Hungary	3%
Poland	21%
Sweden	33%
United Kingdom	33%

Source: International Labour Office.

WORK PERFORMANCE

The relationship between an employee's age and his or her work perform-ance has been investigated by a number of researchers. For example, Waldman and Avolio (1986) and McEvoy and Cascio (1989) have presented meta-analyses of studies published in the past four decades. The average association between age and job performance was in both cases almost zero; for example, in the second (larger) analysis the mean correlation was found to be 0.06. There are wide variations between individual studies, with age–performance correlations in the McEvoy and Cascio analysis ranging from −0.44 to 0.66.

In interpreting those findings, a number of issues need to be considered, with more detailed information sought in future investigations. First is the usual problem about potential unreliability and invalidity of the criteria. Job performance has been scored either in terms of measured output or through ratings made (most commonly) by a person's supervisor. In both cases, variance in scores is likely to be limited by the fact that clearly unacceptable performance would have led already to the voluntary or involuntary removal of low-performing employees. Ratings of performance are open to several biases and inaccuracies, and it is possible that raters' age stereotypes sometimes influence results to the disadvantage of older people (e.g. Stagner, 1985).

A second problem concerns the numbers and characteristics of older employees in a study. Many investigators have drawn attention to the relatively small numbers of over-50s in samples which purportedly cover all age groups within a single job (e.g. McEvoy and Cascio, 1989; Sparrow and Davies, 1988). That imbalance arises from the fact that in many occupations people are likely to move into alternative work in their later years. It seems likely that the people moving out will often be less able to cope than those who remain, although in some cases the leavers may be the better employees who are promoted to more responsible positions.

Third, in some circumstances it is important to consider maximum possible performance, as well as typical levels. Data in terms of average output or supervisors' ratings might accurately represent a person's typical behaviour, but people can often lift their performance substantially above its normal level in cases of emergency or special need. Such elevated performance can be maintained for considerable periods through increased personal effort. In cases where an age difference is observed in typical work performance, we do not know whether age is also related to maximum possible performance; that is sometimes the more important piece of information.

A fourth issue concerns the causal factors which might underlie any observed age difference in job behaviour. Different influences are likely to be important in different kinds of work. For example, where job perform-ance is positively associated with increased age, learning through experience on the job (or in similar contexts) may be a key underlying feature. Previous relevant experience has been shown by several investigators to be significantly correlated with rated job performance, and sometimes entirely accounts for positive associations between age and performance. For example, Schwab and Heneman (1977a) observed a correlation of 0.29 between age and output in a sample of American assembly workers; after partialling out years of experience in the firm, that value dropped to 0.04.

Fifth, in making inferences from correlational data about age and performance, we need to consider the possible non-linearity of relationships. The use of only linear coefficients of correlation rules out the possibility of finding curvilinear associations between age and job performance. For example, increasing but negatively accelerating curves or an inverted-U pattern might sometimes be expected, in addition to linear relationships of the kind described above (e.g. Doering, Rhodes and Schuster, 1983; Warr, 1994a, 1994b).

We may draw the following general conclusions. There is no single relationship between age and job performance; negative, positive and inverted-U patterns are observed. On average the relationship is around zero, and in most cases the negative or positive influence of chronological age is small or non-existent. However, much research has examined only the two variables, age and performance, rather than also including other factors that might account for any association that is observed.

There remain a number of ambiguities in the available data, and more complex research designs and theorizing are needed. In particular, it would be helpful to develop models which can explain why different relationships with age occur in different kinds of jobs. An outline possibility of that kind is summarized in Table 13.2. Activities are placed into groups according to the importance of age-related capacity limitation or potential enhancements through experience.

Let us think in terms of four main types of activities, recognizing that the variations are in fact continuous rather than discrete in this simplified manner. The four categories can be defined in terms of the presence or absence of two features, concerned with either basic capacities or relevant experience.

In the first case (column 2), we should ask whether task requirements exceed basic capacities that are known to decline with age. Those basic capacities ultimately derive from physiological processes, which tend to deteriorate over the years; examples include speed of information processing or effectiveness of sensory mechanisms. These declines in capacity are likely to be more influential after the age of 60 or 70; our concern here is with the years of paid employment. Second, we should consider whether the acquisition through experience of knowledge and skills is likely to improve performance with increasing age (column 3). Some activities benefit from accumulated experience, and others do not; in the former case, more experienced (and thus on average older) employees are likely to be more effective.

Table 13.2 Four categories of job activity and expected relationships of performance with age

Task category	Task requirements more exceed basic capacities with increasing age	Performance can be enhanced by relevant experience	Expected relationship with age	Illustrative job content
1. *Age-enhanced activities*	No	Yes	Positive	Knowledge-based judgements with no time pressure
2. *Age-impaired activities*	Yes	No	Negative	Continuous, paced data processing; rapid learning; heavy lifting
3. *Age-counteracted activities*	Yes	Yes	Zero	Skilled manual or cognitive work
4. *Age-neutral activities*	No	No	Zero	Relatively undemanding activities

In many cases, job performance will be a function of both accumulated experience and declining raw capacities, and any observed relationship with age will reflect the relative strength of the two types of age-related influences. There are, of course, empirical problems of specifying in advance for any one task the relative importance of each type of influence. And a single job may be made up of tasks in more than one category, so that age may have different associations with different aspects of performance in the same job.

In reviewing research evidence in this field, let us start with the category of activities for which a *positive* age gradient is expected. Category-1 activities (at the top of Table 13.2) are those which remain within basic capacities despite advancing age and in which performance benefits from experience. As indicated in the table, these may be referred to as 'age-enhanced' activities. For example, positive associations between age and job performance are likely in settings that are relatively stable, where knowledge and skills can continue to be developed by older workers (e.g. Maher, 1955). The acquisition of social knowledge and interpersonal skills through accumulated experience was particularly emphasized by Perlmutter, Kaplan and Nyquist (1990). In their study of food-service employees between 20 and 69, age was correlated 0.36 with performance effectiveness.

Research from several non-occupational standpoints has shown that certain types of cognitive functioning tend to improve with age during the working years. For example, scores on some tests of intellectual ability are regularly found to be higher among older people (e.g. Berg and Sternberg, 1985). Those tests measure what has been referred to as 'crystallized' intelligence (e.g. Horn, 1970), covering cognitive processes and primary abilities that are embedded in learned cultural meanings. Crystallized intelligence (as opposed to 'fluid' intelligence, to be discussed later) is measured through tests of verbal comprehension, analogies and vocabulary; it benefits through practice and new learning. For example, in Stankov's (1988) study of Australians aged between 20 and 70 crystallized intelligence was correlated 0.27 with age, whereas for fluid intelligence that value was -0.31.

Models of age-related gains in cognitive performance are sometimes presented in terms of 'selective expertise' (e.g. Salthouse, 1985b). The work performance of older employees may remain within an area of maintained expertise, being embedded in familiar contexts, although individuals might have more difficulty with new and complex activity. Positive associations with age (category 1 in Table 13.2) are thus often expected.

Other situations in which older employees are likely to be viewed as more effective than younger ones include those demanding personal characteristics which are more often found in older people. For example, Walker (1964) observed in a study of mail sorters a steady increase in consistency, with less variation in output from week to week, across groups from under 25 years to 60 and over. Bowers (1952) reported more positive appraisals of conscientiousness and attendance for older workers, in a sample where ages extended into the late-60s.

Second, let us consider category 2 of Table 13.2, activities described as 'age-impaired'. A negative relationship with age is expected in tasks where basic capacities are exceeded (and more exceeded for older people) and experience cannot help. That possibility includes continuous rapid information processing or strenuous physical activity of a kind which becomes more difficult with advancing years.

There are many studies illustrating this negative association outside specifically occupational settings. Some of those deal with sensory processes of visual and auditory functioning, others with motor activity and muscular strength (e.g. Verrillo and Verrillo, 1985), but most research of interest to this chapter has concerned cognitive processes. Non-occupational research into age-impaired activities may be roughly divided into investigations with psychometric tests and studies of particular components of information processing, such as reaction time and learning.

The psychometric tests of interest in this section are those introduced above as tapping 'fluid' intelligence, concerned with performance in situations where new material has to be processed, often under time pressure. Tests are usually made up of abstract, non-verbal problems, and are sometimes referred to as measuring 'non-verbal intelligence'. It has long been established that older people within the working population (and of course beyond that) perform less well on these tests than do their younger counterparts (e.g. Dixon *et al.*, 1985; Salthouse, 1985b).

Reaction time in a wide range of tasks is known to be longer as people become older. Salthouse (1985a) illustrated this by presenting more than fifty correlations between age and speed of performance on laboratory tasks (single and choice reaction time, card sorting, digit-symbol substitution, etc.); the median correlation was -0.45, with a range from -0.15 to -0.64. Reduced speed of information processing with increased age is potentially able to account for a wide range of apparently diverse findings. Older people's slower handling of information may give rise to poorer performance on any task that requires rapid cognitive processing. That is obvious in the case of reaction time and similar activities, but can also be expected in situations where active mental rehearsal, comparison between alternatives and temporary storage in memory are needed. Cognitive capacities are limited, and there is need to pass information through the system as rapidly as possible before it is lost or overtaken by other material. Particularly complex tasks, requiring a larger number of processing steps, are especially likely to be susceptible to cognitive slowing (e.g. Myerson *et al.*, 1990); those tasks include conventional tests of fluid intelligence (e.g. Vernon, Nador and Kantor, 1985).

What about age differences in learning and memory? Cross-sectional age impairment is regularly observed. For example, Salthouse (1985b, ch. 11) collated findings from several dozen studies (of digit span, free recall of lists, spatial memory, paired associate learning, etc.); these consistently indicate a negative relationship with age. Particular interest has recently been paid to the notion of 'working memory' (e.g. Baddeley, 1986; Salthouse, 1990). Much information processing requires that operations are carried out on one set of material, while retaining in temporary storage (one's 'working memory') some information which has to be brought into active operations later in the activity. For example, in a laboratory investigation of working memory, people might be presented with a list of words to hold in mind, then asked to carry out a task of logical reasoning, before recalling the original list.

Mental activities of that kind (involving simultaneous storage and processing of information) are very common in daily life, in problem solving, mental arithmetic and many forms of reasoning; and the demands frequently exceed available cognitive capacity. It is known that older people perform less well than younger ones in situations where working memory is heavily loaded (e.g. Campbell and Charness, 1990; Gick, Craik and Morris, 1988). That differential effectiveness may underlie age-related decrements in many types of information-processing activities, including those in tests of fluid intelligence (e.g. Salthouse, 1991).

Within specific jobs, age impairment (category 2 in Table 13.2) is expected where job content is changing rapidly, so that previous knowledge and skills can become obsolete. For example, Dalton and Thompson (1971) reported a marked (cross-sectional) decline in the performance of professional engineers after the age of about 40, as their technical knowledge became increasingly out-of-date. This process was viewed in part as a negative spiral: an older engineer who lacks current knowledge receives poorer appraisals and less challenging assignments, so that he or she comes to feel discouraged and less willing to make an effort for retraining; that discouragement in turn leads to more negative appraisals and further discouragement.

Many other job activities fall within category 3 of Table 13.2, referred to there as 'age-counteracted'. Older people may have increasing difficulties in some areas because of a decline in information-processing or physical capacities, but they are able to counteract that decline in various ways. This possibility is addressed by models of 'selective optimization with compensation' (Dixon *et al.*, 1985; Baltes and Baltes, 1990b). Those are based on the fact that, as people age, they are able to increase their effectiveness in areas of specialization. Continued interest and practice in a limited number of areas permit the growth of knowledge-based competence; and individuals are sometimes able to learn how to compensate as necessary for limitations arising from deteriorating basic capacities.

Relevant experience may benefit people in at least four different ways. First is the all-round development of expertise, in the sense of enriched job knowledge and skills, as discussed above in terms of age-enhanced activities. Such expertise (associated with years of experience, but not necessarily linearly) permits more appropriate responses to new situations, generates more rapid and accurate decisions, and also frees cognitive capacity to cope with particularly demanding stimuli (e.g. Charness and Bosman, 1990; Glaser, 1988).

Second in respect of category-3 activities, older individuals may be able to counteract specific limitations through learned behaviours or other gains. For example, an older person may take written notes to compensate for possible memory limitations; Birren (1969) has described how middle-aged managers may have learned how to conserve their energy by operating through day-to-day tactics which reduce cognitive and affective load; older people may simply work harder for brief periods in order to keep up with their younger colleagues; and spectacles, hearing aids, etc., can reduce the problems of sensory deterioration.

Older people's successful compensation in cognitive activities has been documented in relation to transcription typing by Salthouse (1984). He examined the performance of experienced typists aged between 19 and 72. Consistent with findings summarized above in relation to type-2 activities, older typists were found to respond more slowly in a reaction-time task and in digit-symbol substitution. However, there was no age difference in actual typing speed. By experimentally manipulating the length of preview available (the number of characters visible ahead of the current position), Salthouse showed that older typists in this experienced group looked further ahead than their younger counterparts. It was that additional preparation time which permitted them to type as rapidly as their younger colleagues.

A third possible consequence of relevant experience is behavioural accommodation, in which a person alters his or her activities in order to avoid situations which might reveal defects. For example, older employees may have progressed into positions from which they can delegate tasks in which they are less effective than previously. In extreme cases, accommodation can be seen in selective migration of older workers out of jobs which they come to find difficult.

Finally, processes of cognitive 'compilation' may occur with increased experience, as higher-order or more automatic skills are assembled to become relatively independent of difficult lower-order procedures; age-related declines in the latter may occur in parallel with the maintenance of effective higher-order skills. For example, only about one third of the speed-up with practice that Charness and Campbell (1988) observed in a two-digit mental squaring task was due to faster execution of elementary arithmetic operations; most of the speed-up was due to learning how to chain together the subgoals quickly and efficiently.

The precise outcomes from the opposed influence of declining capacities and increasing experience in category-3 activities will depend on the relative strength of each variable in the particular behaviour under study. Research into this category is rather limited. Nevertheless, in many employment situations age declines are likely to be of the category-3 kind, counteracted by relevant experience, rather than of category-2, in which case experience cannot compensate for impaired capacities.

Last in Table 13.2 are the many 'age-neutral' activities in category 4. Work is routine and non-problematic, requiring either limited skill or skill that is firmly established such that behaviour is fairly automatic. In those circumstances, age differences in task performance are not expected. Within laboratory studies, this uniform performance at different ages is regularly found in easy tasks. For instance, 'primary' memory is apparently unaffected by age; older people are as able as their younger counterparts to hold in memory small amounts of information (within their span of primary memory) that are being used in uncomplicated cognitive activities (e.g. Poon, 1985). Furthermore, while increased age is associated with slower learning of new material (see above), it is unrelated to the speed of forgetting of material after it has been acquired (Rabbitt and Maylor, 1991).

The four-part framework summarized in Table 13.2 draws attention to the fact that category-2 activities (those for which we might expect age impairment) comprise only a minority of job behaviours. Some job tasks are certainly of that kind, but many jobs are made up primarily of the other three types of activity: age-enhanced, age-counteracted or age-neutral. Furthermore, in considering the relationships between age and *overall* job performance, evaluative combinations have to be made across a number of component activities. Only in cases where performance is impaired by age in the majority of job components (or in those which are especially salient) will an overall evaluation be lower for older workers; such a situation is likely to be relatively uncommon.

JOB-RELATED WELL-BEING AND VALUES

Most investigations in this next area have focused on the relationship between age and job satisfaction. As with other constructs, satisfaction may be viewed at different levels of generality. 'Overall' job satisfaction reflects a person's feelings about his or her job as a whole, whereas 'facet' satisfactions concern specific features of that job. Research into age and satisfaction has most often dealt with the more general construct.

Overall job satisfaction is typically found to be significantly higher among older workers (e.g. Glenn, Taylor and Weaver, 1977; Doering *et al.*, 1983; Rhodes, 1983), although the positive correlation is not high, usually falling between 0.10 and 0.20. The pattern of association is often said to be linear, although the review of early research by Herzberg *et al.* (1957) pointed to a U-shaped relationship. Their conclusion was that overall job satisfaction was likely to be high for the youngest group of adults, when novelty encourages positive feelings about a job. However, between the ages of 20 and 30 increasing boredom and perceptions of reducing opportunities may lead to some reduction in satisfaction. In due course, it was suggested, a person comes to terms with his or her job (perhaps having moved out of relatively unrewarding positions), and some increase in satisfaction is observed. Such a pattern was demonstrated by Clark, Oswald and Warr (1994), with a minimum job-satisfaction level at age 31.

A cross-sectional increase in job satisfaction after the age of about 30 is widely observed, but many investigators have failed to find evidence of raised satisfaction in very young employees. That discrepancy in results may be due to limited sampling at young ages in certain studies. Furthermore, there may be no decline in satisfaction among those young workers who receive training and advancement early in their career; variations in those aspects of a job may determine the results from any one study.

More focused satisfaction, with a specific job facet, is related to age in various ways, depending on the facet under investigation. It is generally found that satisfaction with the nature of the work itself is greater in older groups. This relationship remains significant after controlling for job or organizational tenure (e.g. Schwab and Heneman, 1977b) and a range of job characteristics and work values (Clark *et al.*, 1994). Satisfaction with pay is often found to be positively associated with age (e.g. Rhodes, 1983; Kacmar and Ferris, 1989; Clark *et al.*, 1994), but an age gradient is usually absent in relation to extrinsic satisfaction, and in relation to satisfaction with promotion, with co-workers and with supervision. That does not exclude the possibility that significant age relationships are sometimes present, and findings about facet satisfaction are likely to depend on the nature of the sample, the organization and the measures investigated.

As in other parts of this chapter, we might expect factors associated with age, such as income or job level, to account for some of the variance in the relationship between age and job satisfaction. The specific characteristics of a job and their desirability or undesirability are likely to be particularly important in that relationship. Wright and Hamilton (1978) focused on workers' preferences for different job features at different stages in their life, showing that employees were more concerned early in their career with promotion opportunities and income, and later in their lives with security and pleasant social relations. They analysed national survey data to suggest that older workers are more likely to have moved into jobs whose characteristics they value, and that those differences in personally desirable job content can partly explain the positive association between overall job satisfaction and age (see also Kalleberg and Loscocco, 1983).

A second important dimension of job-related well-being covers feelings of anxiety or strain associated with the job. Although these have often been examined in relation to specific job stressors, there is only limited information about age differences. Maslach and Jackson (1981) found that older members of their human service sample reported lower levels of burnout in terms of emotional exhaustion and depersonalization. Warr (1992) observed an inverted-U relationship between age and job anxiety, with employees between 25 and 34 reporting most anxiety. In seeking possible explanations of that relationship, additional variables were included in multiple regression analyses. A significant negative correlation between age and job-related anxiety was retained after controlling for differences in job tenure, job level, decision latitude, work demands, working conditions, income, employment commitment, education and other potentially relevant variables.

It thus appears that, after controlling for the fact that older people have moved into better jobs, there is still a positive age gradient in occupational well-being. It may be possible to account for more variance in that relationship by including additional occupational variables, but part of the age gradient in job-related affect is likely to be attributable to non-job differences between older and younger people. For example, there is a small but significant cross-sectional increase with age in general measures of life satisfaction (Diener, 1984); and there is generally less non-job anxiety (Warr, 1990) and depression (Ryff, 1989) among older members of the workforce. The fact that older employees report higher job satisfaction and other forms of occupational well-being than younger people is likely to be partly attributable to broader differences of those kinds; the causes of the positive age gradient are not entirely occupational.

Turning to specific work values that have been investigated, it is usually found that involvement in one's current job is greater among older employees, with a median correlation with age of about 0.25. However, an independent age effect does not always remain after controlling for job and organizational factors (Hanlon, 1986; Rhodes, 1983). Similar conclusions are appropriate in relation to the broader notion of organizational commitment. Measures of organizational commitment are usually associated positively with employee age; the average correlation was 0.20 in the meta-analysis reported by Mathieu and Zajac (1990).

Key elements of the Protestant work ethic have been measured through a number of scales. These cover, for instance, the importance of work as an end in itself, the moral value of disciplined activity and the possible harmful effects of excessive leisure (Furnham, 1990a). Scores on these scales tend to be positively associated with age, and those relationships remain after partialling out income, job level, tenure and education (e.g. Furnham, 1990b). Over and above any possible cohort effects, we are again left with the question: what aspects of growing older, above those that have been included in previous analyses, are responsible for changed values of those kinds? A broad examination of personal, family, social and occupational experiences over the life course is required to answer that question.

THE INFLUENCE OF JOBS ON AGEING

Studies reviewed in earlier sections have focused primarily on the ways in which age-related processes can have effects on behaviour and attitudes at work: what age differences exist at work, and how can those be explained? Causal processes in the reverse direction are also important: how do jobs affect the processes of ageing? The emphasis here is upon inter-individual variation arising from extended exposure to the different conditions of employment.

This emphasis is becoming more important in gerontological research as a whole. Ageing, as evidenced by changes in physiological and psychological functioning, is not determined solely by a standard set of intrinsic factors giving rise to an unalterable rate of change; changes during the life course are influenced by social and physical environments and by psychological processes underpinning a person's interactions with those environments. Some environments are more conducive to 'successful ageing' than are others (Baltes and Baltes, 1990a).

Environmental differences are likely to contribute to the increased variability in cognitive performance between people that is regularly observed with increasing age. In cases where a negative age gradient exists in terms of average values, the older sub-sample necessarily contains more low scorers; but it is not unusual for some older people to be as effective as the best young person (e.g. Rabbitt, 1991). This increased inter-individual variability is likely to have developed slowly over a number of years.

In examining possible influences upon the pace of ageing, we are in part concerned with the consequences of long-term exposure to certain forms of environmental demands and opportunities. The centrality of paid employment in most people's life means that certain features of jobs can have substantial impacts upon mental health and development (e.g. Warr, 1987). However, jobs are located in the broader network of a socio-economic structure, and it is of course difficult to disentangle occupational influences from those arising from a person's place in that structure.

Evidence about the long-term influence of jobs on ageing thus tends to be indirect. However, significant positive associations between extended job experience and individual expertise have been demonstrated in several studies (see above). It is also beyond dispute that short-term training interventions can improve intellectual functioning, and that some job holders are exposed to more intellectual stimulation throughout their career than are others.

One source of inter-individual variability has been discussed in terms of the 'environmental complexity' provided by different jobs. Complex environments expose a person to more varied stimuli, require more decisions and contain greater ambiguity than do simple environments (e.g. Schooler, 1987). By presenting more challenges and requiring complex information-processing, complex environments embody the types of experience and training that have been shown to assist cognitive functioning across the life-span.

Cross-sectional and longitudinal research has pointed to the causal importance of this aspect of jobs. Kohn and Schooler (1983) have summarized an extensive programme in which several forms of 'intellectual flexibility' were found to be influenced by the complexity of a person's current job and that held ten years previously. Avolio and Waldman (1987) examined the correlations between age and cognitive functioning in workers (aged 19 to 62) defined as being exposed to different degrees of intellectual stimulation in their work. Within a single company, skilled and unskilled employees were compared on a range of tests, including verbal, numerical and mechanical reasoning. Negative correlations with age (holding constant level of education) were significantly greater for the unskilled group (exposed to less complex work environments) than for the skilled workers; for example, values were -0.28 versus -0.05 for numerical reasoning.

A related, simple, example was provided by LaRiviere and Simonson (1965). They recorded the maximum speed with which people between 40 and 69 could copy a sheet of one-digit numbers. For manual labourers and managers, speed of writing was significantly negatively associated with age, but clerical workers (who performed that task regularly in their job) showed no differences in speed associated with increasing age.

In addition to the practical importance of learning more about the influence of jobs on differential rates of ageing, this area has particular theoretical interest. Research into issues of the kind illustrated here will require more careful attention to the definition of successful ageing. It will also be necessary to specify more precisely possible pathways of influence across time, from particular long-term environmental features (including those in jobs) to aspects of physiological and psychological functioning. At present, knowledge and theory in this area are limited.

THE ACQUISITION OF NEW SKILLS

Perceptions of older workers tend to be structured around three principal components: their physical abilities (which tend to decline with age), adaptability (which also tends to decline) and general work effectiveness (which remains stable or increases with age) (Warr, 1994b). The third component covers behaviours such as thinking before action, hard work, reliability, interpersonal skills, team working, confidence and overall effectiveness (Warr and Pennington, 1993).

As jobs increasingly require cognitive (rather than physical) competence, physical ability is less salient today than it was in earlier times. In order to take advantage of the wide-ranging effectiveness that has been demonstrated in older staff (component three), it therefore becomes necessary to focus attention on the enhancement of adaptability (component two). That will often require explicit attention to the training of older people.

In general, older workers see themselves as unsuited to substantial new learning and lack confidence in training situations (e.g. Plett and Lester, 1991; Sterns, 1986). Associated with that, they do not learn as quickly as their younger colleagues (e.g. Belbin, 1965; Sterns and Doverspike, 1989). Paced instruction, where speed of information-transmission is beyond a trainee's control, is particularly problematic, as would be expected from the research into cognitive performance reviewed above; most learning situations exceed people's capacity to process and store all the material provided (activities in categories 2 and 3 in Table 13.2). However, it is clear that, given appropriate opportunities, older as well as younger employees can acquire additional job skills and perform effectively in new kinds of work.

What processes are likely to contribute to greater difficulty in learning as one becomes older? Reduced information-processing capacities and a general cognitive slowing have already been described, as have older trainees' anxiety and lower self-confidence as learners. Problems of unlearning initial errors have been stressed by E. Belbin (1964), R. M. Belbin (1965) and Belbin and Belbin (1972). They argued that older people were better able to learn if their activities were constrained so that errors were minimized early in the process. That procedure has the advantage of sustaining confidence as well as minimizing potential negative interference.

Older trainees may gain special benefit from 'guided activity (or discovery) learning'. This approach creates situations in which individuals are encouraged to learn by finding out principles and relationships for themselves; the emphasis is on learning by doing rather than through verbal or physical instruction. Discovery learning can be encouraged by asking trainees to generate and answer questions about the subject matter, rather than merely presenting them with information to be learned. Their answers to personally relevant questions will permit them to build on individual experience, and a successful process of discovery can give rise to a shift from the experience of extrinsic rewards to more intrinsic achievements (e.g. Knowles, 1984). This form of discovery learning has been demonstrated to be helpful in the training of older workers (e.g. Belbin and Downs, 1964; Sterns and Doverspike, 1989).

Older employees are often out of practice at learning itself, and they may need assistance in learning how to learn. Their potential learning ability can be much greater than the actual ability exhibited when they first enter training. Perry and Downs (1985) have considered a number of procedures to develop the skills of learning (for instance, through self-questioning, managing time and testing hypotheses), and it may be that those procedures are particularly appropriate for older people.

In most organizations, training is directed especially at younger employees, partly because of what is in effect collusion between management and older workers themselves. Since many of the latter are nervous about new learning requirements and have doubts (not necessarily justified) about their own capacity to acquire new skills, they tend to avoid new training opportunities. There is thus sometimes a self-fulfilling prophecy. Older employees in a particular company may indeed be less adaptable than younger ones, but they receive no assistance to be otherwise. As a result they remain as they are, and the negative age stereotype is reinforced. A major organizational requirement is thus to create a culture in which learning and development are given a high priority among older as well as younger employees. Companies should assist older workers to move laterally into novel and challenging jobs, and provide training which is specially tailored to their requirements (Warr, 1994c).

CONCLUDING REMARKS

In looking back on the research which has been reviewed in this chapter, two general themes may be noted. The first concerns the location of psychologists' investigations into ageing; these have most commonly been undertaken outside organizational settings. The extensive laboratory and psychometric research has undoubtedly advanced our understanding, but at the expense of a distorted picture. Studies have often focused upon maximum performance in brief, abstract information-processing tasks, and have underemphasized the importance of specialized knowledge, expertise, social relationships and personal decisions about which environments to enter or avoid. The full range of age-related topics in work settings has not yet been adequately explored.

A second theme concerns the growing need for empirical research which can support causal explanations of observed age differences. Although many early studies were restricted to bivariate associations between age and a specific variable of interest, researchers have increasingly also investigated other factors, which might be causally responsible for age-related differences in that variable. For instance, relevant job experience, activities which promote particular kinds of expertise, cardiovascular functioning and aspects of personality have all been considered as possible causal factors in explaining variations in age gradients.

Research into 'the influence of age' is thus becoming more a question of research into 'the influence in the long term of environmental factors, sustained personal behaviours, and physiological changes'. Those features, extended in time, may co-vary with age, but not always to a high degree. By investigating a range of potential causal factors, within a specific explanatory model about a given age-related variable, research is more likely to contribute to theoretical progress than has sometimes been the case in the past.

REFERENCES

Avolio, B.J. and Waldman, D.A. (1987) Personnel aptitude test scores as a function of age, education and job type. *Experimental Aging Research, 13*, 109–13.

Baddeley, A.D. (1986) *Working Memory*. Oxford: Oxford University Press.

Baltes, P.B. and Baltes, M.M. (eds) (1990a) *Successful Aging*. Cambridge: Cambridge University Press.

Baltes, P.B. and Baltes, M.M. (1990b) Psychological perspectives on successful aging: the model of selective optimization with compensation. In P.B. Baltes and M.M. Baltes (eds) *Successful Aging*. Cambridge: Cambridge University Press, pp. 1–34.

Belbin, E. (1964) *Training the Adult Worker*. London: HMSO.

Belbin, E. and Belbin, R.M. (1972) *Problems in Adult Retraining*. London: Heinemann.

Belbin, E. and Downs, S.M. (1964) Activity learning and the older worker. *Ergonomics, 4*, 429–37.

Belbin, R.M. (1965) *Training Methods for Older Workers*. Paris: Organization for Economic Co-operation and Development.

Berg, C.A. and Sternberg, R.J. (1985) A triarchic theory of intellectual development during adulthood. *Developmental Review, 5*, 334–70.

Birren, J.E. (1969) Age and decision strategies. *Interdisciplinary Topics in Gerontology, 4*, 23–36.

Bowers, W.H. (1952) An appraisal of worker characteristics as related to age. *Journal of Applied Psychology, 36*, 296–300.

Campbell, J.I.D. and Charness, N. (1990) Age-related declines in working-memory skills: evidence from a complex calculation task. *Developmental Psychology, 26*, 879–88.

Charness, N. and Bosman, E.A. (1990) Expertise and aging: life in the lab. In T.M. Hess (ed.) *Aging and Cognition: Knowledge Organization and Utilization*. Amsterdam: Elsevier, pp. 343–85.

Charness, N. and Campbell, J.I.D. (1988) Acquiring skill at mental calculation in adulthood: a task decomposition. *Journal of Experimental Psychology: General, 117*, 115–29.

Clark, A., Oswald, A. and Warr, P.B. (1994) Is job satisfaction U-shaped in age? Submitted for publication.

Dalton, G.W. and Thompson, P.H. (1971) Accelerating obsolescence of older engineers. *Harvard Business Review, 49* (5), 57–67.

Department of Employment (1992) Projected trends in the labour force 1992–2001. *Employment Gazette, 100*, 173–84.

Diener, E. (1984) Subjective well-being. *Psychological Bulletin, 95*, 1105–17.

Dixon, R.A., Kramer, D.A. and Baltes, P.B. (1985) Intelligence: a life-span developmental perspective. In B.B. Wolman (ed.) *Handbook of Intelligence*. New York: Wiley, pp. 301–50.

Doering, M., Rhodes, S.R. and Schuster, M. (1983) *The Aging Worker: Research and Recommendations*. Beverly Hills, CA: Sage.

Furnham, A. (1990a) A content, correlational, and factor analytic study of seven questionnaire measures of the Protestant work ethic. *Human Relations, 43*, 383–99.

Furnham, A. (1990b) *The Protestant Work Ethic*. London: Routledge.

Gick, M.L., Craik, F.I.M. and Morris, R.G. (1988) Task complexity and age differences in working memory. *Memory and Cognition, 16*, 353–61.

Glaser, R. (1988) Thoughts on expertise. In C. Schooler and W. Schaie (eds) *Cognitive Functioning and Social Structure over the Life Course*. Norwood, NJ: Ablex, pp. 81–94.

Glenn, N.D., Taylor, P.A. and Weaver, C.N. (1977) Age and job satisfaction among males and females: a multivariate, multisurvey study. *Journal of Applied Psychology, 62*, 189–93.

Hanlon, M.D. (1986) Age and commitment to work. *Research on Aging, 8*, 289–315.

Herzberg, F., Mausner, B., Peterson, R.O. and Capwell, D.F. (1957) *Job Attitudes: Review of Research and Opinion*. Pittsburgh, PA: Psychological Service of Pittsburgh.

Horn, J.L. (1970) Organization of data on life-span development of human abilities. In L.R. Goulet and P.B. Baltes (eds) *Life-Span Developmental Psychology: Research and Theory*. New York: Academic Press, pp. 424–66.

Kacmar, K.M. and Ferris, G.R. (1989) Theoretical and methodological considerations in the age–job satisfaction relationship. *Journal of Applied Psychology, 74*, 201–7.

Kalleberg, A.L. and Loscocco, K.A. (1983) Aging, values, and rewards: explaining age differences in job satisfaction. *American Sociological Review, 48*, 78–90.

Knowles, M. (1984) *The Adult Learner: A Neglected Species*, 3rd edition. Houston, TX: Gulf Publishing.

Kohn, M.L. and Schooler, C. (1983) *Work and Personality: An Inquiry into the Impact of Social Stratification*. Norwood, NJ: Ablex.

LaRiviere, J.E. and Simonson, E. (1965) The effect of age and occupation on speed of writing. *Journal of Gerontology, 20*, 415–16.

McEvoy, G.M. and Cascio, W.F. (1989) Cumulative evidence of the relationship between employee age and job performance. *Journal of Applied Psychology, 74*, 11–17.

Maher, H. (1955) Age and performance of two work groups. *Journal of Gerontology, 10*, 448–51.

Maslach, C. and Jackson, S.E. (1981) The measurement of experienced burnout. *Journal of Occupational Behaviour, 2*, 99–113.

Mathieu, J.E. and Zajac, D.M. (1990) A review and meta-analysis of the antecedents, correlates, and consequences of organizational commitment. *Psychological Bulletin, 108*, 171–94.

Myerson, J., Hale, S., Wagstaff, D., Poon, L. and Smith, G.A. (1990) The information-loss model: a mathematical theory of age-related cognitive slowing. *Psychological Review, 97*, 475–87.

Perlmutter, M., Kaplan, M. and Nyquist, L. (1990) Development of adaptive competence in adulthood. *Human Development, 33*, 185–97.

Perry, P. and Downs, S. (1985) Skills, strategies and ways of learning: can we help people learn how to learn? *Programmed Learning and Educational Technology*, *22*, 177–81.

Plett, P.C. and Lester, B.T. (1991) *Training for Older People: A Handbook*. Geneva: International Labour Office.

Poon, L.W. (1985) Differences in human memory with aging: nature, causes, and clinical implications. In J.E. Birren and K.W. Schaie (eds) *Handbook of the Psychology of Aging*, 2nd edition. New York: Van Nostrand Reinhold, pp. 427–62.

Rabbitt, P.M.A. (1991) Management of the working population. *Ergonomics*, *34*, 775–90.

Rabbitt, P.M.A. and Maylor, E.A. (1991) Investigating models of human performance. *British Journal of Psychology*, *82*, 259–90.

Rhodes, S.R. (1983) Age-related differences in work attitudes and behaviour: a review and conceptual analysis. *Psychological Review*, *2*, 328–67.

Ryff, C.D. (1989) In the eye of the beholder: views of psychological well-being among middle-aged and older adults. *Psychology and Aging*, *4*, 195–210.

Salthouse, T.A. (1984) Effects of age and skill in typing. *Journal of Experimental Psychology: General*, *113*, 345–71.

Salthouse, T.A. (1985a) Speed of behaviour and its implications for cognition. In J.E. Birren and K.W. Schaie (eds) *Handbook of the Psychology of Aging*, 2nd edition. New York: Van Nostrand Reinhold, pp. 400–26.

Salthouse, T.A. (1985b) *A Theory of Cognitive Aging*. Amsterdam: North-Holland.

Salthouse, T.A. (1990) Working memory as a processing resource in cognitive aging. *Development Review*, *10*, 101–24.

Salthouse, T.A. (1991) Mediation of adult age differences in cognition by reductions in working memory and speed of processing. *Psychological Science*, *2*, 179–83.

Schooler, C. (1987) Psychological effects of complex environments during the life span: a review and theory. In C. Schooler and K.W. Schaie (eds) *Cognitive Functioning and Social Structure over the Life Course*. Norwood, NJ: Ablex, pp. 24–49.

Schwab, D.P. and Heneman, H.G. (1977a) Effects of age and experience on productivity. *Industrial Gerontology*, *4*, 113–17.

Schwab, D.P. and Heneman, H.G. (1977b) Age and satisfaction with dimensions of work. *Journal of Vocational Behavior*, *10*, 212–20.

Sparrow, P.R. and Davies, D.R. (1988) Effects of age, tenure, training, and job complexity on technical performance. *Psychology and Aging*, *3*, 307–14.

Stagner, R. (1985) Aging in industry. In J.E. Birren and K.W. Schaie (eds) *Handbook of the Psychology of Aging*, 2nd edition. New York: Van Nostrand Reinhold, pp. 789–817.

Stankov, L. (1988) Aging, attention, and intelligence. *Psychology and Aging*, *3*, 59–74.

Sterns, H.L. (1986) Training and retraining adult and older adult workers. In J.E. Birren, P.K. Robinson and J.E. Livingston (eds) *Age, Health and Employment*. Englewood Cliffs, NJ: Prentice-Hall, pp. 93–113.

Sterns, H.L. and Doverspike, D. (1989) Aging and the training and learning process. In I.L. Goldstein (ed.) *Training and Development in Organizations*. San Francisco: Jossey-Bass, pp. 299–332.

Vernon, P.A., Nador, S. and Kantor, L. (1985) Reaction times and speed-of-processing: their relationship to timed and untimed measures of intelligence. *Intelligence*, *9*, 357–74.

Verrillo, R.T. and Verrillo, V. (1985) Sensory and perceptual performance. In N. Charness (ed.) *Aging and Human Performance*. Chichester: Wiley, pp. 1–46.

Waldman, D.A. and Avolio, B.J. (1986) A meta-analysis of age differences in job performance. *Journal of Applied Psychology*, *71*, 33–8.

Walker, J.F. (1964) The job performance of federal mail sorters by age. *Monthly Labor Review*, *87* (3), 296–301.

Warr, P.B. (1987) *Work, Unemployment, and Mental Health*. Oxford: Oxford University Press.

Warr, P.B. (1990) The measurement of well-being and other aspects of mental health. *Journal of Occupational Psychology*, *63*, 193–210.

Warr, P.B. (1992) Age and occupational well-being. *Psychology and Aging*, *7*, 37–45.

Warr, P.B. (1994a) Age and employment. In H.C. Triandis, M.D. Dunnette and L.M. Hough (eds) *Handbook of Industrial and Organizational Psychology*, Volume 4. Palo Alto, CA: Consulting Psychologists Press, pp. 485–550.

Warr, P.B. (1994b) Age and job performance. In J. Snel and R. Cremer (eds) *Work and Aging in Europe*. London: Taylor & Francis.

Warr, P.B. (1994c) Training for older managers. *Human Resource Management Journal*, *4*, 22–38.

Warr, P.B. and Pennington, J. (1993) Views about age discrimination and older workers. In *Age and Employment: Policies, Attitudes and Practices*. London: Institute of Personnel Management, pp. 75–106.

Wright, J.D. and Hamilton, R.F. (1978) Work satisfaction and age: some evidence for the 'job change' hypothesis. *Social Forces*, *56*, 1140–58.

Zachariah, K.C. and Vu, M.T. (1988) *World Population Projections*. Baltimore, MD: Johns Hopkins University Press.

Zelinski, E.M. and Gilewski, M.J. (1988) Memory for prose and aging: a meta-analysis. In M.L. Howe and C.J. Brainerd (eds) *Cognitive Development in Adulthood*. New York: Springer, pp. 133–58.

14 Social psychology of work
Towards 2000

Peter Robinson

Michael Argyle's *The Social Psychology of Work* (1989) is a masterly work. Comprehensive and accurate, the text is written in that clear and easily read style that his colleagues both admire and envy. Each topic or issue is first set precisely and neatly in its general social psychological framework. Then its basic and most recent ramifications in the world of work are explored. Ill-informed opinion is not allowed to substitute for empirical evidence. The target audience specified in the preface justifies the selective focus on American–British problems and studies. It would have been beyond this reasonable scope to pose more radical or dramatic questions than those considered. The title justifies the adoption of, and concentration upon, the social psychological rather than a sociological or political perspective. But is there any significance to the fact that the main topics added to this second edition are stress, ill-health, mental health at work, unemployment and retirement? None of this quintet is a plus factor in the quality of life at work or at home, except perhaps the last. And one might ask how it comes about that the optimistic *Zeitgeist* of the early 1970s, with its occasionally voiced worries about the risks of boredom arising from the expectation of full employment and added leisure, becomes realized as stress, distress and unemployment in 1989?

In *The Psychology of Happiness* (1987), Argyle was able to cite a number of occidental studies pointing to conditions of happiness and satisfaction with life in general. Are the British still that happy in 1994? Most of the statistical indicators point to factors likely to operate in the direction of increasing misery (HMSO, 1993 and earlier; see Table 14.1). In just a few years, suicides and murders are well up. So are armed robbery and rape. Car thefts are now unremarkable. The police appear to have given up investigating minor thefts and burglaries. The courts do not know what to prescribe for many young offenders. Vandalism has become endemic. Some of us now treat a year without any crime against us as a bonus year.

Neither the 'New Age' travellers nor the many homeless look as though they would tick the highest ratings on happiness scales. Official estimates

Table 14.1 Notifiable offences recorded by the police in England and Wales (thousands)

	Year		
Offences recorded	1971	1981	1991
Violence against person	47.0	100.2	190.3
Burglary	451.5	723.2	1219.5
Robbery	7.5	20.3	45.3
Theft	1003.7	1603.2	2761.1
Criminal damage	27.0	386.7	821.1

Source: HMSO *Social Trends.*

record 150,000 homeless households, which probably adds up to more than 400,000 people (Department of the Environment, 1993). If it is true that two million 'home-owners' now owe more than their homes are worth, their morale is presumably adversely affected by this state of negative equity. The three million unemployed are traditionally and demonstrably low on satisfaction and mental health indicators (e.g. Warr, 1987a). The provision of stress counselling in particular and counselling more generally are growth industries. The anxiety of both blue- and white-collar workers about their employment being secure appears to be high; between 40 per cent and 50 per cent of those in work were frightened that they will be sacked (*Financial Times*, 1993). Those working in public sector institutions in education, health, social services and welfare have been subjected to such a concatenation of imposed changes in their working practices and their conditions of employment over the last fifteen years that the as-yet-unmeasured morale of this very substantial workforce must be at a fifty-year low.

The extended implications of these conjectures are beyond the scope of both this chapter and Argyle's 1989 text, but perhaps this is a place to begin to raise issues somewhat beyond the current social psychological framework – if we are to be prepared for an uncertain future. For example, any significant and general *de facto* reduction in the purchasing power of wages and salaries of a substantial minority or majority of the workforce could shift the whole frame of reference within which jobs are experienced. A downward spiral of job insecurity, perceived efficacy and opportunities could depress and transform the society as a whole. Are current conditions such that, unless a political-sociological perspective is adopted, the social psychological now misses the major sources of variance?

Continuities

Before this issue is raised in greater detail, it may be reassuring to point to some of the likely areas of persistent concern in which it is reasonable to expect sensible rather than illusory progress to be made. The traditional problem areas covered in *The Social Psychology of Work* will remain and will no doubt continue to benefit from systematic social psychological study. At the ergonomics pole, a legion of absurdities still remain in the design and use of machines and tools, mainly perhaps because persons at the generative and design end fail to view problems from the perspectives of either typical or atypical users. These problems need to be solved. As Norman (1988) has pithily depicted, we are surrounded by artefacts whose use may be difficult to learn, whose characteristics render them difficult to operate and whose totality can mismatch human dispositions in ways that increase the probabilities of errors. The manuals or screen displays of many PCs and computers remain impenetrable, as do the instructions for assembling and operating phones, videos and TVs, all of which are becoming standard features for storing, processing, retrieving and communicating information at work stations. Just as serious is the likelihood of errors arising because designers have failed to take into account what Norman calls 'affordances', child psychologists call 'canonicality' and Aristotle might have thought of as practical reasoning. Natural iconic displays and representations are less likely to lead to errors than purely symbolic ones. These issues have become a standard inclusion in texts (e.g. Singleton, 1989) and from a user/consumer point of view the sooner machines, instruments and other artefacts are designed to match human characteristics and to be uniform in their functional features, the better. Reason's (1990) accounts of major industrial and other person-made disasters point to the simplicity and obviousness of many of the mistakes of design and operation: disasters waiting to happen. On some occasion these mistakes will co-occur and set a chain of events going whose outcome has the inevitability of a classical Greek tragedy.

Social psychologists then can expect to continue to contribute to the design of machines, jobs and systems of jobs, to studies of personal, intra- and inter-group relations at work, to personnel selection and training, particularly in impression management and social skills. These are seemingly stable fixtures in the repertoire, and there do not seem to be reasons why they should disappear. Social psychologists will also be expected to answer questions and act positively in the face of the negative features of ill-health, stress and unemployment that are the additions to current texts but, as already implied, some of these problems may well be beyond the capacities of social psychologists to handle; their solutions will require macro-structural changes at a societal level.

Discontinuities?

When Michael Argyle wrote the first edition of his *The Social Psychology of Work* (1972), he did so in a Britain that was still meandering in the direction of a mixture of public and private enterprises in which certain values appeared to be consensual, namely those associated philosophically with a Popperian social democracy (Popper, 1957) and verbally enshrined in policy reports by Beveridge (1942a, 1942b). Differentials of wealth, power and prestige were acceptable, provided that they were not too great and that access to the higher rungs of the ladders was increasingly based on merit displayed in educational and training settings. In turn these had to be designed to provide initial equalities of opportunity for all persons in the society regardless of their social category of origin. There also appeared to be a shared political concern that those least able to compete in the society should be given disproportionate provision to enable them to participate in the wider community of work, leisure and living.

Certainly there was dissent to such policies coming from both the radical left and the revisionist right, but the optimistic vision of the majority was of gradual if hesitant national progress towards a better society, one which valued social justice and consideration for others, and one where ideas of efficiency at the workplace were combined with a concern to minimize anxiety from insecurity or otherwise uncaring or unpleasant conditions of employment. Measures were being taken to enhance or retain changes which were judged to yield better results and to modify or scrap those which did not. Work was to support a welfare state, but was itself to be part of it. Hopes for higher productivity were linked to aspirations for increasing people's job satisfaction. Full employment was a national aspiration.

By the time the second edition was published in 1989, this vision had been abandoned. The notion of small evaluated changes had given way to abruptly announced revolutionary diktats to 'reform' in line with the government slogans which proclaimed the virtues of choice and competition; these were to be the mechanisms for promoting efficiency in all sectors of society. As could have been predicted by any Darwinian, the resultant 'opportunities' were seized upon most vigorously by those best placed to be predators and parasites. Mainly under the banner of demands for 'account-ability', the government imposed abrupt and radical changes to the organization and practices of the police and prisons, of the medical and social services, of primary, secondary and tertiary education. There is no evidence that this sustained onslaught of legislation has improved efficiency in any of the sectors. What we do know is that unemployment, homelessness and crime have been raised to record figures, and that educational, medical and welfare provision has had to be reduced, as income for it from the government has been eroded. Some of us now detect a gathering drift towards a society of three social strata, with the élite having its well-rewarded servants:

1 at the bottom a substantial lumpenproletariat of the chronically unem-ployed and underemployed, the unskilled, the physically, mentally or socially disabled;

2 above them, a second thick layer of small employers, private and public employees, all squeezed by threats of redundancy or bankruptcy, regardless of whether their collars are blue or white, and ranging in qualifications from the semi-skilled through to professionally qualified groups;

3 at the top a power élite (Mills, 1956), a thin layer of kings and queens acting autocratically and in concert with a somewhat fatter layer of particular professionals and bureaucrats who are pleased to be at their service, given suitable inducements.

The consequences for the social psychology of work of such political and economic changes since the first edition are not explicitly apparent in the second, but begin to be implicitly registered in the sections on unemployment, stress, physical debility and mental ill-health, as already stated.

As hinted in the opening paragraphs, social psychology in Britain has been strangely and strongly insulated from sociology, anthropology and the other social sciences, and there has always been a basis for the charge from more macroscopic social scientists that some social psychologists are prone to ignore both the socio-cultural and the historical-political contexts in which they are working. More generally, some are prone to ignore content and context altogether, attending almost entirely to process and structure. Although this was manifestly not true of either edition of *The Social Psychology of Work* and the cultural context was steady over the relevant period, for the 1990s such an apolitical perspective may be too constraining.

How significant a social psychological perspective (and any other) is varies with time, place and issues. For the workplace it may be that it was more directly significant in accounting for variability in the 1960s and 1970s than it will be in the 1990s, at least for Britain. Analogously, the tendency to transplant American experience may be presuming more similarity between Britain and the USA than is sensible. It may be necessary to work out our own solutions to our own peculiar problems.

Since the Tudors, Britain has been governed strongly from London, with, not so much a pyramidal hierarchy of political power, more a puppet show with London the HQ of the puppeteers. The people may vote occasionally in elections, but they have no training in, apparent concern with or opportunities for running their own communities. Communities are based on work groups, churches, leisure centres and social groups, not on political meetings. There is but minimal grass-roots democracy in Britain. Many of the recent changes are a devolution of responsibilities without resources, so that what may be a non-existent community is expected to run its schools, provide care for the infirm, the elderly or the homeless, but it is expected to do so without the right to raise resources to fulfil these obligations. The local councils, officially delegated with financial responsibilities for these activities, rely on central government 'handouts' and have strictly limited rights to raise taxes from households.

Why is this relevant and important to work? It is but one example of a cultural difference between the UK and the USA that one would expect to have implications for the workplace. British citizens have little or no experience of co-operative activities to bring to the workplace. What co-operation exists is probably confined to the family and friends. The workplace is not generally an organization of interdependent persons concerned to generate cake to share out with each other, but another THEM and US.

If these arguments are valid then the recently encouraged and empowered individualism of the USA, combined with devolved responsibilities and resources, might help to ensure that attitudes and behaviour of employees remain realistic and not too self-destructive in that country. Love for the company may not be great, but there should be an appreciation of inter-dependence. Alienation of the workforce might extend to a lack of personal investment in work, but the work itself will get done efficiently – in one's own interest.

The contrast with the UK would emphasize the absence of devolved resources and associated responsibilities. With local communities relying on central handouts and constrained by centrally defined limits for their budgets, learned helplessness (Seligman, 1975) and a clear external locus of control (Rotter, 1966) are realistic attitudes for most of the citizenry to adopt as citizens. Not surprisingly, such attitudes are also likely to character-ize employees, especially in large enterprises. In the last few years it has become explicit how power is distributed in British industry and commerce. Employees have been laid off and denied wage increases, while chief executives have arranged to have their salaries raised by hundreds of thousands of pounds, a differentiating trend which is continuing in spite of declines in profits. The Prime Minister expressed regrets at these massive salary rises, but his government has done nothing to control them; on the contrary, a number of ministers of earlier governments have moved on to the boards of such companies, and have become major beneficiaries of, for example, British Gas, British Telecom, Cable and Wireless, and the National Freight Consortium. Between 1979 and 1991 the income of the bottom 10 per cent of the workforce fell by 14 per cent, while that of the top 10 per cent increased by 50 per cent (HM Government, 1993). The average salary of top executives in FTSE 100 companies was £535,000 in 1992. Figure 14.1 shows how the rises relate to company profits.

In brief, many of those with the power have become well-fattened pigs at the troughs they have filled so generously for themselves. Whether the situation is embryonically revolutionary in a Marxist sense, or whether Britain will drift towards an ineffectual and vaguely unpleasant form of fascism, remains to be seen, but in either case there are likely to be dramatic changes in the social psychology of the workplace. Media commentators are fairly uniform too in their accounts of the destructive consequences of the applications of the slogans of 'choice' and 'competition', and they note that these criteria of evaluation are not applied to the subsidies, cartels and

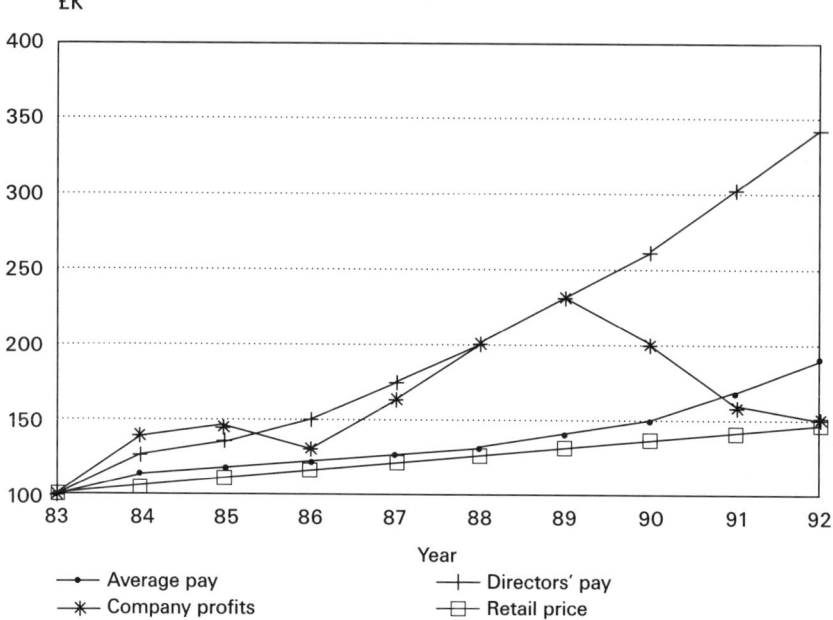

Figure 14.1 Salaries of directors of FTSE companies in relation to company profits, retail prices and national average pay

other sources of wealth of the wealthy themselves. Deregulation in industry means that those running firms are free to elevate their own wages and depress those of the workforce. The British refusal to sign the Social Chapter in Maastricht may be claimed to be a means of keeping British industry competitive and so preserve jobs, but is that for the benefit of the workers or the bosses?

That the government is guilty of at least unconscious double-think is illustrated by the Citizen's Charter (Major, 1991). This emphasizes the duties of public services; it omits the responsibilities of the state to provide resources for those services and the responsibilities of the citizens to use those services appropriately. The police are expected to be 'fair, effective and courteous'. But aren't the government expected to provide legislation and resources that enable the police to perform their duties? And aren't the general public expected to respect the police and assist them in crime prevention and detection? The police have not been given either the legislative or the material resources to cope with the requirements imposed by the Charter. The general public are probably safer if they keep their heads down and ignore their apparent rights in the Charter.

Mutatis mutandis, the same asymmetry of obligations is imposed on other state enterprises. However, no corresponding obligations or constraints are imposed on commerce or industry. They are free to form uncompetitive cartels (banking, oil) (Sampson, 1988), receive state or EC subsidies (nuclear power, farming) or demand what the market has to pay for their services (e.g. accountants, commercial lawyers, medical specialists). Top management is likewise free to dismiss staff into a pool of sufficient size to render it rational for workers in post to comply with demands made upon them; at the same time, directors are writing extravagant schemes of share options, pension rights and more than golden handshakes for themselves.

Some would argue that the various public charters of the Prime Minister merely point to the hypocrisy or naivety of the government. However honourable their writer's intentions, there are too many inconsistencies between words and actions for the rhetoric to be plausible. It is much easier to interpret the charters as policies directed to the eventual elimination of all state enterprises and the re-creation of a *de facto* totalitarian plutocracy, than to see them as being of benefit to the citizenry. There are no government watchdogs over private schools, private hospitals, private prison services, private security firms and private road transport to ensure that these provide value for money. There is no published empirical evidence and evaluation to support the presumption of their differential efficiency. If privately run enterprises had been placed either under the same obligations as publicly run enterprises or under more stringent controls, then the charters might have achieved a measure of plausibility as manifesting a genuine concern for the quality of life of the citizens rather than as serving more sinister latent functions for the new robber-barons.

This alarmist theme will be pursued in one substantive arena only – changes in organizations. The laws and rules governing the operations of organizations have been changed dramatically, and are perhaps having the most profound effect on conditions of and at work. The main analysis to be pursued here contrasts what has happened to the public sector services in the UK, both with what is known about the psychology of organizational efficiency and efficacious change and with what has been happening in private industry. The transition to a final concern with the idea of predators and parasites at work is not entirely accidental. As with social psychology generally, textbooks about work seem to make an underlying value assumption that human beings are essentially nice, with industry and commerce being benign. For most people in the world, this is simply not true, and analyses which ignore this are missing important truths. Those truths cannot all be separated from the political framework within which people work.

Changes at work: macro

While the preceding section is sprinkled but lightly with academic and not so academic references, it also contains views that cannot be found in the relevant chapters of the most recent *Annual Reviews of Psychology* (1990,

1991, 1992). Like Argyle's second edition, these are written in a very much business-as-usual manner, pointing to continuing progress on topics defined within a frame of reference that has been stable now for half a century, particularly at the micro level. O'Reilly's review (1991) refers to macro-OB (organizational behaviour) as well as to micro-OB and notes that, although these have customarily been investigated by sociologists and social psychologists respectively, the future may change this; otherwise all is normal. Since most, and in some chapters all, of the studies and ideas discussed are North American, this may be appropriate in that context. It probably is not for Britain.

In the same *Annual Review* volume, Porras and Silvers (1991) foreshadow a future where organizational transformation models may become as important as organizational development models have been. Prior to these imminent events, however, Britain has generated its own internal tensions, which require much more than social psychological analysis. For example, if the increased levels of stress in the teaching profession in the last fifteen years (Cooper and Kelly, 1993) are the consequences of governmental actions, there is very little point in social psychologists analysing the individuals within a context that may recommend an increase in counselling provision. It is not the individual teachers who cannot cope; it is their jobs which have become impossible. The same applies for other public sector employees. The psychological perspective can provide a misleading part picture – an attempt to prop up an overloaded system through individual efforts. Attempting to cure with counselling is a cynical provision, if the sensible solution is to prevent the need for counselling in the first place by rendering jobs do-able. If the public sector is not to lose or burn out its professionals (Golembiewski, Munzenrider and Stevenson, 1986; Shirom, 1989), it is job analyses not person analyses and job restructuring that will need to be the focuses of enquiries and action. Likewise, it is jobs and not counselling which are needed for the unemployed.

The academic implication of such a perspective is that there is an urgent need for psychologists to collaborate with other social scientists in their research. The resultant research reports are unlikely to remain purely academic in their significance. While the social facts need to be apprehended and analysed dispassionately, they are likely to represent a sufficiently disagreeable picture of societal ills that the ameliorative actions ought to have a strong political significance. The political implications are either that the legislators will need to educate themselves about psychology, sociology and other social sciences if they are to begin to understand how to govern a society or that they be encouraged to admit that they have already found sufficient advice in Machiavelli (1958).

One of the most pervasive phenomena of the last decade has been the privatization and decentralization of state enterprises. This avalanche of change appears to have been entirely uninformed by the work of academic experts on organizations. In many cases, expert opinion is not even needed for diagnoses of absurdity in the order of change adopted. For example, if a state wishes to devolve responsibility for the care of the mentally disturbed or disabled and close down most of its psychiatric and other long-term hospitals, it is easy to agree that any such policy needs to be enacted in the sequence: create alternative arrangements for accommodation, train staff and equip ex-patients for the transition, effect the changes. Any sane and sensibly conservative system would also try the operation out locally and learn from mistakes made before implementing the change nationally. In Britain, local authorities were required to implement 'Care in the Community' without resources against an impractical timetable. It is not surprising that the National Schizophrenia Association can record forty murders and over a hundred suicides by erstwhile inmates within two years of the enactment of the programme. It is not surprising that the population of the homeless has escalated. Many of these are expelled people who are expected to cope in today's society when coping with yester-year's was judged to be beyond their independent competence – and that was before they had been rendered less competent by institutionalization (Goffman, 1961). A disregard for the adoption of rational models of organizational change is unfortunately not exceptional, but typical of what has been required of workers in the public sector. It is difficult not to conclude that this 'irrationality' does not reflect rationality at a higher level, namely a sustained assault to destroy the quality of the public sector services and to drive out or debilitate the employees who have contributed to their success over the years.

Where what was privatized could be conceived as a business, perhaps fewer destructive organizational changes have been experienced. Water, electricity, gas, oil and road-transport industries have emerged as leaner and fitter, once they had to face quasi-market pressures to make profits. There may have been gains in efficiency under such stimuli. However, staff were shed without retraining and without anticipatory re-employment initiatives, but that has been standard British practice in both private and public sectors. Internal changes were under control of management and were not subject to direct government intervention. Some parts of privatized industry have been free, with their *de facto* monopolistic supply situation, to write up their own costs to the consumer. In spite of the projected images of greater cost effectiveness, prices to consumers for fuel and water have risen much more than inflation rates. These rises may have been subjected to government scrutiny, but they have not been prevented by the government, and one might ask in what measure efficiency has really improved and what public benefit has been achieved.

Had there been longitudinal monitoring of beliefs and attitudes in the workplace, the data might well have shown very pronounced changes in the last fifteen years, with increases in anxiety about jobs and in cynicism about the trustworthiness, competence and goodwill of employers and their political masters. The increase in anxiety would stem first from fears of redundancy and second from the nature and rate of changes in the workplace, these coming partly from technical advances, but mainly from reorganizations by management. The increase in cynicism would derive from several sources: reductions in workforces being given precedence over redeployment and retraining for the provision of new products or services; the proliferation of charters and mission statements which offer commitments to citizens, seek to impose burdens on those delivering the service, but place no responsibilities on their originators in the government. It should be noted that the public have no redress if they are denied the promises of the charters. They are words without import. The government seems to be unconcerned at the discrepancies between its words and actions.

The difficult questions, however, relate to the workforce, its organization and conditions of employment. The vertically integrated 'kaibatzu' conglomerates of Japan (e.g. Mitsui, Mitsubishi) account for less than half of the working population and their principle of employment for life cannot be guaranteed in practice in an uncertain world, but their publicized model of mutual obligation within organizations could be instituted in some measure in other countries. Ouchi (1981) illustrates how a number of consistently successful American companies have applied similar but not identical underlying principles to their cultural context. The notion of a long-term co-operative relationship between employee and company is one such principle. Another is the idea of work groups having a social component to their existence. Ouchi's examples of successful companies recognize that problem-solving groups which are entirely task-related and have no affectively based cohesion are 'artificial' in ways that are likely to be unproductive, an observation dating from the earliest studies of small group research in industrial and non-industrial settings (Cartwright and Zander, 1968). Avoidance of undue specialization of function in management is another factor, with staff making regular negotiated moves around the divisions of the company. While such companies have rejected the alternative of rapid promotion and spiralling of salaries for the presumed future élite, lower differentials between top and bottom with a high basic wage help to preclude the commitment to the company being entirely financial. Turnover and absenteeism statistics are consistent with the hypothesis that such policies create commitment on both the employee and the company side.

Whether sufficient British companies will be able to create an assumption of mutual obligation between workers and management to change the cultural norm is more doubtful. Smaller family companies have traditionally been less concerned to maximize profits, and particularly those of some longevity have reputations for a concern about their workforces, but larger public companies have no such reputations. The issues remain open, but history is not propitious. Since the beginnings of the Industrial Revolution, British ownership and management has insisted on the necessity of a low-wage economy with a permanent threat of unemployment as an inducement to worker compliance. (It is noteworthy in this context that it has not thought it desirable to train an excess of managers or professionals to create competition at these levels.) Not surprisingly, the workforce has tended to minimize its commitment to employers, preferably working within set rules. The 1950s, 1960s and 1970s witnessed the irrational consequences of these attitudes in 'restrictive practices' and 'working to rule' to an extent that led to there being less cake to share out.

Historically, however, the workers were correct. Industry and commerce has not been viewed as a co-operative enterprise where sharing of the cake is negotiated on any principled basis. Worker/management-owner conflict has been the dominant model, and not surprisingly the historical evidence has come to support the validity of this essentially self-fulfilling prophecy: owner/management beliefs about workers being the point of departure which leads to workers having instrumental attitudes towards their jobs. Unfortunately for Britain, there is no prospect of the consequences of this set of attitudes enabling British industry to compete successfully with companies in cultures whose values emphasize the importance of inter-dependence of the whole workforce of a company and the significance of each individual for the whole.

The irony is that, if analyses of the kind offered by Ouchi are sound, nobody loses in the kind of company he describes; on the contrary, everybody wins. On a Thatcher–Major model, the temporary winnings of the predators are likely to be very temporary, and entirely politico-economic; those at the top preserve their power until toppled by competitors and they make their money while they can. There is little evidence to show that the great moguls of industry and commerce are better off spiritually, morally or socially (Argyle, 1987); that is, they are not happier or more satisfied than those of us in the middle or nearer the bottom. Permitting and encouraging their existence, however, does lower the quality of life for those within their orbits of influence. A global capitalism of some 200 multinational companies will probably have even more dramatic effects. Those in the lowest stratum of all such societies will continue to be the worst-off victims, and will remain what Bernard Shaw's forked pen labelled 'the undeserving poor'.

Although social psychologists have made comparative studies of the consequences of unemployment over a fifty-year period (Fryer, 1992), we have not investigated most of the issues raised in this section. For example, while job satisfaction has been a continuing theme in occupational psychology since the Hawthorne studies (Mayo, 1949; Roethlisberger and Dickson, 1939), there appears to be a relative paucity of action research in British industry and commerce to explore job enhancement (Herzberg, 1976). This contrasts with the worker-participation ethos of Japan through which groups of workers are encouraged to generate and evaluate ideas for increasing productive efficiency and/or conditions of working. What is interesting is why British companies are not more experimental, and why they do not seek more advice from employees. Similarly, under what conditions might employees become interested to participate in such processes? Put another way, R&D in Britain is more likely to be seen as a set of technical or ergonomic problems, and not from a person/organization perspective. What percentage of organizations have an established R&D (Human Relations) Section?

The issues raised here are but a tiny fraction of those which would be likely to engage social psychologists who dared to ask questions at a more macro level than has been traditional. Standard texts on either side of the Atlantic (e.g. Miner, 1992; Huczynski and Buchanan, 1991; Warr, 1987b) do not raise these larger questions, but stay very much within a perspective of immediate problems as defined within a current ethos where economic efficiency is alleged to be paramount.

There is a sense in which the content of this section has done little more than echo the views of the liberal press, but then the press is not always adrift. Attitudes to and performance at work must be affected by the *Zeitgeist* of the culture. If the norms stress an ideal of continuing full employment, in which equitable financial rewards for appropriate productivity are dispensed, and if aspirations for efficiency are combined with a concern for work being part of living rather than a purely instrumental affair, then the wider and economic prognosis will be different from that where the gospel preached is that living is a matter of competition in which the weak are eliminated and the strong survive. Any government which promotes such an ethos must give rise to an alienated workforce. The punitive threat of unemployment is shown to be real, with a permanent pool of perhaps 10 per cent. Employers are being encouraged to minimize wages as well as conditions of employment. Employees will have no commitment but to themselves. Illegal means of obtaining resources will be either a necessary or a preferred option.

That this is the direction of change over the last fifteen years is signalled by the indicators available on employment, employees and crime and other indices of social deterioration. This has to be a movement of 'collective insanity', and for the present there is no sign of any intelligent application of social psychological evidence or theory to any of the public sector spheres of employment – or to much of the privatized sector either – and the drift continues.

There are a number of assumptions and omissions in the literature that could be relevant to a stormier future. One common assumption seems to be what might be introduced as a nice guys/*noblesse oblige* syndrome. Companies are represented as benevolent, concerned as much with employee job satisfaction, job enhancement, staff development and stress reduction, as they are with competitive edge, profits and salaries for the board of management. The extent to which the benign image corresponds to reality remains unknown, but there is scant evidence of any *noblesse oblige* when profits are at risk.

Other images might be more representative. What proportion of company staff are predators and parasites rather than herbivores? Ambition tends to be cited as a quality of public benefit, leading to more dedicated performance to the benefit of all. But uncommissioned biographies of the successful, ambitious captains of industry and commerce reveal rougher portraits, indifference to and exploitation of others, often with ruthless manipulations and occasional double-dealings. Predators succeed by outwitting and eating lesser predators and herbivores. As McClelland and Boyatzis (1982) showed, a high need for power, a low need for affiliation and a weak need for social approval predict long-term (sixteen years later) success in management. Few signs at present portend that the meek will inherit the earth. There is then an unresolved discrepancy between the images of management implied by psychologists and those portrayed by biographers.

Likewise, parasites live off herbivores. Sometimes parasites are ex-predators. Sometimes they are bureaucrats. Sometimes they are workers who minimize their productive efforts in restrictive and other more ingenious practices. The less power and status they have, the more likely the parasites are to find themselves dis-employed, although per person the lesser parasites will be the least costly to their organization.

Not many studies of corruption and criminality appear in the journals. Allegations of massive frauds and other financial illegalities are not uncommon. In Britain the Westland affair, the Guinness takeover of Distillers, the mysteries of the Blue Arrow company, the questions about Polly Peck, the plundering of pension funds by Robert Maxwell and the misappropriation of investors' funds at BCCI and Barlow Clowes are recent nine-day wonders that came to light, but with minimal consequences for those charged with offences. The possible corruption may also be organizational rather than directly personal: dangerous products, toxic waste, dangerous work conditions. Again the social psychological study of the cover-ups is precluded by their very nature. There have been both case studies and some systematic investigations of 'whistleblowing'. The results testify to the seamier side of organizations and industry rather than to their façade of *noblesse oblige*. Those who have gone public against maladministration, corruption, dangerous products or personal discrimination have typically faced a very unpleasant and unprotected future. Persecution, dismissal, 'false' accusations and an inability to find other jobs are not uncommon (Bok, 1984). The United States has a history of such cases, which extend into the industrial domain as well (Parker, 1988).

Just as events involving apprehended predators are prone to be kept hidden, so too hatreds, jealousies and vindictiveness seldom appear in studies of social relations in organizations. To what extent the functioning of organizations is sabotaged by bitter rivalries and animosities is unknown. Again, it is the biographies and newspapers rather than psychologists who offer such accounts. It could be argued that interpersonal issues are case specific and not integral to the study of organizational behaviour. That could be true under rare and improbable circumstances, but the idea that systems can function independently of the particular persons playing the significant roles is as implausible as the proposition that the system is irrelevant to the functioning of the persons.

Doubtless there are many other not so nice aspects of work situations which could be mentioned. The point of noting their existence is not to criticize colleagues for neglecting them, especially since studies of what Macmillan called the 'unacceptable face of capitalism' could be pursued only at some personal risk. They do serve as a reminder that the Pollyanna presumptions of social psychology generally seem to spill over into the study of work. However much we pretend to the contrary, there are substantial numbers of tough and ruthless characters out there, making and retaining their wealth within and beyond the law. They probably exist in all organizations and at all levels, and it is bad science to pretend that they do not.

Apologetic prognoses

The capacity to obtain a sufficient income throughout one's life is a necessary condition of survival in a non-agrarian, non-hunter-gatherer society. If everyone is to rise above the bottom layers of Maslow's (1954) pyramid of human motivation, the generation of that income will require many of us to work for much of our lives. In a capitalist society work is essential for all but that élite with inherited wealth, that 0.1 per cent who control 7 per cent of the country's wealth. How the added value of work is distributed, and against which moral principles this distribution is evaluated, has been a contentious issue from time immemorial and there will be no end to those arguments for many years to come (Jaques, 1982). Proposals and suggestions have been offered to achieve consensus for several thousand years, explicitly from the handfuls of great religious thinkers and philosophers, and implicitly from the folk-wisdom cultures and subcultures of the several thousand societies human beings have created.

While it is true that the working population of Britain of the 1950s and 1960s remained clearly divided into its social classes, with a simpler THEM vs. US split between management and labour, while its nationalized industries seemed to stress maximizing workers' rights and rewards rather than efficiency or service to the community, the general weak ideal was individualistic and co-operative, with more than a minimal quality of life being a reasonable aspiration for all.

The 1980s reasserted the value of competition, removed constraints on the (excessive) accumulation of individual wealth and incomes, and provided sufficient cheap handouts of public property to discourage enough voters from rejecting these values at further elections. Too few noticed or cared that most of the wealth they acquired was either a re-distribution of what was already held by the society as a whole or a simple writing-up of paper values through the financial markets. Both primary and secondary industrial bases shrank while the tertiary boomed and busted. And as Lord Macmillan said, you can only sell (or mortgage) the family silver once. More have now noticed that all public sectors as well as the private sector are now 'rationalizing' their workforces. Middle-aged, white-collar workers who had assumed job security have been pensioned off with the same dispatch as their blue-collar peers. Those remaining may have had their job descriptions expanded, their workloads increased to unhealthy extents. The rest of us appear to be too busy protecting our own interests to act collectively to correct these moves.

For the present, the British economic situation seems to have achieved a shaky stability, but for how long it is not at all clear. Ninety per cent of the working population is still at work. The great majority of the herd is enjoying a standard of living economically superior to anything before. Homes are easier to run than ever before. Food is easier to prepare. Transport has shrunk the country and reduced the timetable of intercontinental distances. Holidays have never been so available. Earlier physical dangers and the foulness of working conditions have been ameliorated greatly in the last fifty years. We can afford to live longer.

There has been a price to pay for such benefits. The majority of households could not enjoy their standard of living on the single income that sufficed historically. Women have joined the workforce in great numbers. Welcome as this may be from an equal rights point of view, it does mean that families now need two incomes not one.

It is also true that the average level of indebtedness of the population constitutes a degree of live-now/pay-later that has a double danger. There is a temporal limit to individual indebtedness. There are limits also to the power of lenders to recoup their loans; they can squeeze the lemons until the pips squeak, but squeaks do not repay debts. And at present individuals are still allowed, and encouraged, to build up debts way beyond their assured capacity to repay them. With the family silver mortgaged, there are limits to which families can borrow forward, especially if wage earning has been maximized by having two earners. There are now fewer buffers to cushion acute calamities in the economy.

Add to this the traditional THEM and US divisions of British industry and commerce and the history of conflict and confrontation still traceable in collective representations (Durkheim, 1895) back to the beginnings of the Industrial Revolution, and there is a possibility of the Chinese industrial dragon flapping its wings to generate some very harsh economic conditions in a future Britain.

For the present perhaps the word 'herd' is appropriate for the large majority of the population and the workforce. The general public are behaving rather like wildebeest as they try to avoid the lions and leopards. Individual mothers will initially fight to protect their offspring, but not for very long. Once the prey is being eaten, the herd resumes its grazing, paying no attention to their erstwhile member who is being devoured. This seems to be true of the unemployment situation, for example. There is no collective concern expressed in action to insist on the creation of job opportunities. There is a general indifference, just as there has been no expression of a collective will to correct the plight of the homeless or of victims of crime. The electorate has continued to return a Conservative government on four occasions now, so Britain is still choosing the kind of society it wants. The captain and crew of the ship are elected, even though it has been evident for some time that a lot of the passengers were very sea-sick – and there are plenty of icebergs.

The general move to central control appears to be happening across the country in all public-sector concerns. It is a clear move away from the social democracy of Popper's open society and towards the closed society of totalitarianism in which the will of the power élite is exercised, and debate or dissent is discouraged. The private sector, meanwhile, is becoming dominated by a combination of short-term profits and the burden of bureaucracy from London and Brussels.

Such a strong movement has profound implications for the social psychology of work. In that kind of State we can expect relaxation of safeguards for employees of blue or white collars and a more ruthless exploitation of fear and favours as incentives for compliance. The price in alienation is paid for outside in crime.

Visions of the 1960s have faded fast; there is a rapid reversal of the hesitant progress towards a social democracy which attempted to resolve the potential conflicts between *liberté, égalité* and *fraternité* in a context where both efficiency and justice were upheld as virtues. Unintentionally or not, Britain seems to be moving towards a totalitarian form of government with power heavily vested in the Prime Minister (with or without the cabinet). That the electorate chooses to vote for these changes is its right and responsibility. If the trend continues, the 1999 edition of Argyle's *The Social Psychology of Work* will be much less of a work of steady continuity and progress than the 1989 edition. Social psychologists have not noticed that 1979 may have marked the beginning of 1984.

REFERENCES

Argyle, M. (1972) *The Social Psychology of Work*. London: Allen Lane.
Argyle, M. (1987) *The Psychology of Happiness*. London: Methuen.
Argyle, M. (1989) *The Social Psychology of Work*, 2nd edition. Harmondsworth: Penguin.
Beveridge, W. (1942a) *Social Insurance and Allied Services*. London: HMSO.
Beveridge, W. (1942b) *Full Employment in a Free Society*. London: HMSO.
Bok, S. (1984) *Secrets*. Oxford: Oxford University Press.
Cartwright, D. and Zander, A.L. (1968) *Group Dynamics*, 3rd edition. New York: Harper.
Cooper, C.L. and Kelly, M. (1993) Occupational stress in head teachers: a national UK study. *British Journal of Educational Psychology*, 63, 130–43.
Department of the Environment (1993) *English House Conditions Survey*. London: HMSO.

Durkheim, E. (1938) *The Rules of Sociological Method.* Chicago: Chicago University Press (original publication, 1895).

Financial Times (1993) Sharp rise in fears among professionals and managers. 1 June.

Fryer, D. (ed.) (1992) Marienthal and beyond: 20th century research on unemployment and mental health. *Journal of Occupational and Organizational Psychology,* *65*, 4.

Goffman, E. (1961) *Asylums.* Harmondsworth: Penguin.

Golembiewski, R.T., Munzenrider, R.F. and Stevenson, J.G. (1986) *Stress in Organizations: Toward a Phase Model of Burnout.* New York: Praeger.

HM Government (1993) *Economic Trends.* April/May.

Her Majesty's Stationery Office (1993) *Social Trends, 23.* London: HMSO.

Herzberg, F. (1976) *Managerial Choice: To Be Efficient and to Be Human.* New York: Dow Jones-Irwin.

Huczynski, A. and Buchanan, D. (1991) *Organizational Behaviour.* Hemel Hempstead: Prentice-Hall.

Jaques, E. (1982) *Free Enterprise, Fair employment.* London: Heinemann.

McClelland, D.C. and Boyatzis, R.E. (1982) Leadership motive pattern and long-term success in management. *Journal of Applied Psychology, 67*, 737–43.

Machiavelli, N. (1958) *The Prince*, trans. W.K. Marriott. London: Everyman.

Machiavelli, N. (1970) *The Discourses*, trans. and ed. B. Crick. Harmondsworth: Pelican Classics.

Major, J. (1991) *The Citizen's Charter.* London: HMSO.

Maslow, A. (1954) *Motivation and Personality.* New York: Harper.

Mayo, E. (1949) *The Social Problems of an Industrial Civilization.* London: Routledge & Kegan Paul.

Mills, C.W. (1956) *The Power Elite.* Oxford: Oxford University Press.

Miner, J.B. (1992) *Industrial-Organizational Psychology.* New York: McGraw-Hill.

Norman, D. (1988) *The Psychology of Everyday Things.* New York: Basic Books.

O'Reilly III, C.A. (1991) Organizational behaviour. *Annual Review of Psychology, 42*, 427–458.

Ouchi, W. (1981) *Theory Z: How American Business Can Meet the Japanese Challenge.* Cambridge, Mass.: Addison-Wesley.

Parker, R.A. (1988) Whistleblowing legislation in the United States. *Parliamentary Affairs, 4*, 148–158.

Popper, K.R. (1957) *The Poverty of Historicism.* London: Routledge & Kegan Paul.

Porras, J.I. and Silvers, R.C. (1991) Organization development and transformation. *Annual Review of Psychology, 42*, 51–78.

Reason, J.T. (1990) *Human Error.* Cambridge: Cambridge University Press.

Roethlisberger, F.J. and Dickson, W.J. (1939) *Management and the Worker.* Cambridge, Mass.: Harvard University Press.

Rotter, J.B. (1966) Generalised expectancies for internal versus external locus of control of reinforcement. *Psychological Monographs, 80*.

Sampson, R. (1988) *The Seven Sisters.* London: Hodder & Stoughton.

Seligman, M.E.P. (1975) *On Depression, Development and Death.* San Francisco: Freeman.

Shirom, A. (1989) Burnout in work organizations. In C.L. Cooper and I. Robertson (eds) *International Review of Industrial and Occupational Psychology.* Chichester: Wiley, pp. 25–48.

Singleton, W.T. (1989) *The Mind at Work.* Cambridge: Cambridge University Press.

Warr, P.B. (1987a) *Work, Unemployment and Mental Health.* Oxford: Clarendon Press.

Warr, P.B. (1987b) *Psychology at Work*, 3rd edition. Harmondsworth: Penguin.

DATE DUE